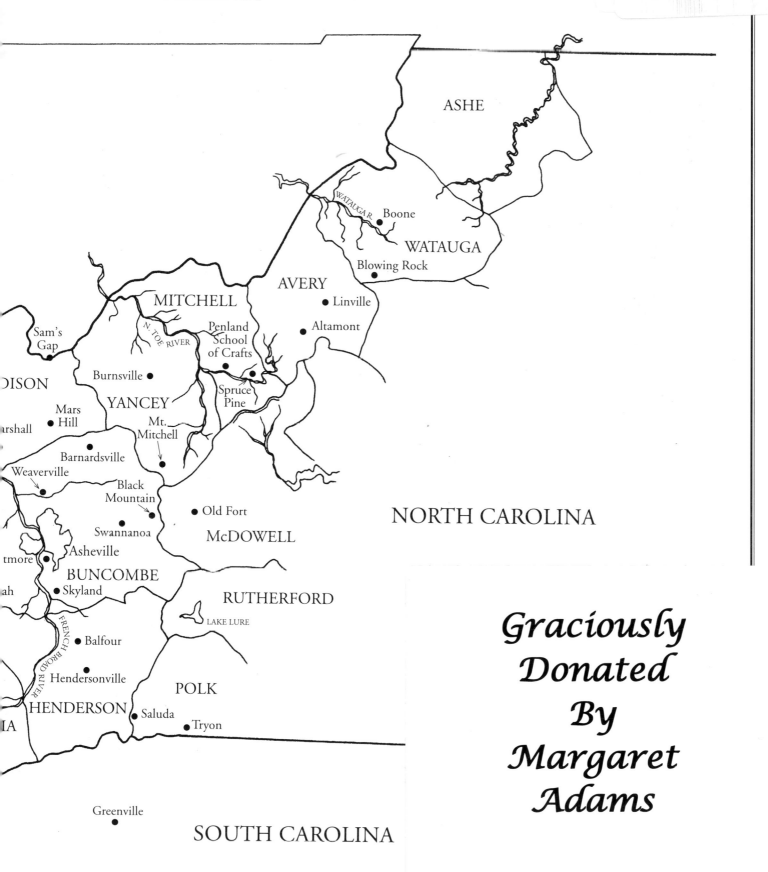

VIRGINIA

ASHE

WATAUGA R.

Boone

WATAUGA

Blowing Rock

AVERY

MITCHELL

Linville

Sam's
Gap

N. TOE RIVER

Penland
School
of Crafts

Altamont

DISON

Burnsville

YANCEY

Spruce
Pine

Mars
Hill

arshall

Mt.
Mitchell

Barnardsville

Weaverville

Black
Mountain

Old Fort

NORTH CAROLINA

Swannanoa

McDOWELL

tmore

Asheville

BUNCOMBE

ah

Skyland

RUTHERFORD

LAKE LURE

FRENCH BROAD RIVER

Balfour

Hendersonville

POLK

HENDERSON

Saluda

IA

Tryon

Greenville

SOUTH CAROLINA

*Graciously
Donated
By
Margaret
Adams*

MAY WE ALL REMEMBER WELL, VOLUME II

A Journal of the History & Cultures of Western North Carolina

EDITED BY ROBERT S. BRUNK

PUBLISHED BY
ROBERT S. BRUNK AUCTION SERVICES INC.
ASHEVILLE, NORTH CAROLINA

Editor:
Robert S. Brunk

Art Direction:
Dana Irwin

Design:
Robin Mask

Copy Editing:
Nancy Stewart, Jerry Israel,
Charlotte Brown

Book Production:
Robin Mask

Research Assistance:
Nancy Stewart, Jerry Israel

Index:
Nancy Stewart, Robin Mask,
Pat Fitzpatrick

Published by Robert S. Brunk Auction Services Inc.,
P.O. Box 2135, Asheville, NC 28802, USA
828-254-6846, Fax 828-254-6545

Copyright © 2001 Robert S. Brunk Auction Services Inc.

Printed in Hong Kong

ISBN: 0-9656461-1-4

FRONT COVER WRAP AROUND:
1943 Bayard Wootten photo, p. 281

BACK COVER (CLOCKWISE):
Rick Lockamy viewing survey maps, by Rob Amberg, p. 291; Bertha
Marler, by Tim Barnwell, p. 182; Benjamin Porter with Cirkut Camera, p.
342; 1998 view of Fontana Lake, p. 281; Tony Lord by Doris Ulmann, p. 43

INSIDE FRONT COVER:
Map of Western North Carolina, drawn by Kay Stafford

OPPOSITE TITLE PAGE (TOP TO BOTTOM):
Betsy's Gap, by Tim Barnwell, pp. 212-213; *Cabin, Apple Trees, Snow*, by Tim
Barnwell, p. 189

TITLE PAGE:
Carvers of Biltmore Estate Industries, p. 262

COPYRIGHT INFORMATION PAGES (CLOCKWISE):
View of Sunburst, North Carolina, by Herbert Pelton, p. 325; Nonconnah
pottery, p. 82; Amos Stackhouse III and unidentified passengers, p. 129; The
Smathers Band, p. 215

TABLE OF CONTENTS (LEFT PAGE TO RIGHT PAGE):
Top: detail of Karl Bitter carving, p. 357; Bottom, left to right: *Picking Up
Walnuts*, by Tim Barnwell, p. 178; Betty Jean Dozer in Stumptown, p. 141;
Right page, left to right: Lt. Col. James T. Weaver, p. 20; Douglas Ellington
house, p. 106

INTRODUCTION (LEFT PAGE TO RIGHT):
Charles D. Stackhouse after the great flood, p. 126; Stone construction by
Ektome, by Rob Amberg, p. 304

TABLE OF CONTENTS

Rodney H. Leftwich (handwritten signature)

1. To publish research and descriptive reports on the history and peoples of Western North Carolina including Native American, European, African-American and other cultures from the time of their appearance in Western North Carolina to the present.

2. To create a descriptive record which can be the basis for later comparative research and interpretation. We especially want to record information which is at some risk of being lost.

3. To encourage careful record keeping and documentation at all levels of inquiry, however fragmentary the information or informal the process.

Introduction

Many people came to me after the publication of Volume I and pointed out that we hadn't published a study of a particular event, person, or place in Western North Carolina. I always replied that there was a virtual infinity of subjects we hadn't published but what we needed were more scholars to do the work. Good research is tedious, slow, and often does not produce information worthy of publication. There were a number of studies planned for this volume which began with enthusiasm but slowly faded to a stop. Some died for lack of sound information, some dissolved because the people who were the subjects of the studies did not wish to be studied, and some ended because researchers grew weary of scant returns for their efforts.

The best studies reported in this volume are those in which the researcher did not begin with a conclusion, but rather began with an open canvas and painted

very slowly and carefully. Whatever the researcher found was what he or she was looking for. This approach is axiomatic in the context of formal research, but social research is not conducted in a void. What is chosen to be examined and the way in which questions are posed reflect a matrix of values. All the studies reported here were done by people who held beliefs about their subject matter, often with great passion. We invite readers and scholars, as we did in the introduction to Volume I, to sift and sort the information published here, to add and subtract as more work is done.

One of the themes in all these studies is cultural change. Many are illustrations of cultural memory, assimilation or invention. We understand this by watching and listening to the people—Thomas Patton and his slave Sam Cope surviving the Civil War; Luke Smathers a traditional fiddler responding to the music of the swing era; and Tony Lord, a Yale educated architect creating iron work with Daniel Boone IV. All those who speak in these pages give expression to the questions of continuity and change. What elements of material and non-material culture did they keep, or discard, or recreate? The responses to these questions are most evident in the work of architects, photographers, and craftspeople. But farmers, missionaries, merchants and residents of no particular fame also participate in this process by how and where they live, how they work and what they name their children, among many other decisions. The work and lives of all these people are sketches we examine for evidence of their choices.

We often describe research and studies of cultural history as preservation. We speak of saving information and images for those who will follow us, our descendants and perhaps other scholars. Our work may accomplish this, but I have learned that for me this work is ultimately an act of self definition. From the constellation of cultural fragments in which I live, I arrange a few in an effort to find traces of my past. Perhaps to find personal context and bearing: perhaps signs of where we are headed.

My personal thanks to all the writers and photographers who contributed to this volume. Tim Barnwell's excellent photography has been an important component of many of the studies in both Volume I and II of this Journal. I am also indebted to Charlotte Brown for editorial comments, particularly the studies of architectural history in this volume. Special thanks to Nancy Stewart for her work with the writers and for not allowing me to rush her proofreading. This volume would not have been possible without the efforts of my coworker Robin Mask whose unwavering energy and commitment to all dimensions of this project have been deeply appreciated. I am also grateful to Jerry Israel who has been my best teacher and to whom this volume is dedicated.

Robert S. Brunk, January 13, 2001

Phyllis Lang, while doing research on another subject, came upon the letters of Thomas Patton in the Southern Historical Collection. She undertook the tedious task of transcribing all 79 of his letters mostly written to his mother in Asheville while he traveled throughout the South during the Civil War. The letters create an ambiguous image of Thomas Patton. He seems steadfast and loyal in his three-year tour of duty, but many of these letters discuss his efforts to resign from the Confederate Army. Patton speaks warmly of his slave Sam Cope who was Patton's personal attendant throughout the war, but the Patton family, one of the wealthiest families in Western North Carolina, owned many slaves and bought and sold them for many years. The letters also help us understand that the Civil War was not simply violence and disruption: many of Patton's letters reflect boredom, inactivity and what he viewed as military ineptness. Thomas Patton's sustaining dedication was to his family which was changed by death, birth and Patton's own marriage in 1863. —R. B.

"My Dear Mother"

The Civil War Letters of Thomas Walton Patton

By Phyllis Martin Lang

"**M**y Dear Mother," Thomas Walton Patton wrote on July 21, 1862, "We reached here in safety on Saturday morning after a rather tiresome march. My company marched from Alexanders to the springs on friday and that was rather a forced march of twenty seven miles. On Thursday night we got shelter in Alexanders stable loft and so were sheltered from the rain." With these words, the young Patton begins a remarkable correspondence which traces his experiences during the Civil War. This first letter was written from Warm Springs (now Hot Springs), on the French Broad River just north of Asheville, North Carolina. The other 78 letters in the collection describe his war journeys from North Carolina to Tennessee, to Alabama and Mississippi and Georgia, and back to Tennessee and North Carolina.[1]

Thomas Walton Patton survived the entire Civil War. He fought in the "first serious fight of the war,"[2] Big Bethel on the Virginia Peninsula, on June 10, 1861. He was near Bennett Place, between Greensboro and Durham, North Carolina, in April 1865, when Gen. Joseph Johnston surrendered to Gen. William T. Sherman. Between June 1861 and April 1865, he fought at Murfreesboro, Chickamauga, Missionary Ridge and Atlanta. He escaped injury, capture and disease. A literate and perceptive writer, Thomas Walton Patton faithfully wrote to his mother and other members of his family back home in Asheville. He recorded perceptions of battles, frustrations with military officers and delight in simple pleasures such as fresh peaches and cool spring water. The letters chronicle the ordinary, personal side of

Figure 1. This advertisement appeared in the Asheville News *on May 15, 1862. Western North Carolina became fully involved in the Civil War under the Confederate Conscription Act of April 1862. Thomas Patton joined a group of volunteers which became Company C, part of Col. Joseph McDowell's battalion. (Courtesy, Pack Memorial Public Library, Asheville, North Carolina.)*

compelling and catastrophic events.

The Patton family arrived in the Asheville area in 1807 when James Patton (1756-1845) brought his family to the Swannanoa River, southeast of Asheville (Figure 2). In 1814 he moved into Asheville where he opened a store and a tanyard, established the Eagle Hotel and bought and sold property. When he died, he had accumulated a rich estate—land in Asheville and Buncombe County, slaves, goods in his various shops and cash.[3] Patton's first son, James Washington Patton (1803-1861), continued the family's commercial and property interests, including real estate in both Alabama and North Carolina. In 1832 he and his brother John Erwin Patton bought the drover's stand at Warm Springs, North Carolina, and began developing it as a resort hotel. In 1860, not long before his death in 1861, he was the wealthiest man in Buncombe County.[4]

James Washington Patton married twice. By his first wife Jane Clarissa Walton he had six children. Jane Clarissa died in 1837 and his third son Thomas Walton died in 1840 at age eight. In 1839 he married Henrietta Kerr from Charleston. They named their first child Thomas Walton after the son who had died shortly before the baby was born and their second child Frances Louisa (Fannie).

Around 1857, James Washington Patton built the residence, which he called "Mansion House" (later known as "The Henrietta"), at 78 South Main (now Biltmore Avenue). The extended family including Henrietta, various sisters from Charleston, daughters-in-law, grandchildren and daughter Fannie lived there during the Civil War.

Thomas Walton Patton, born in the

Civil War photographs of Western North Carolina are scarce. A copy of this photograph in the North Carolina Collection of Pack Library bears the inscription "Men enlisting for Confederacy at Pack Square." This photograph also appears as figure 2.1 on page 27 of Greg Mast's State Troops and Volunteers noting that such gatherings occurred in April and May of 1861. The view looks to the southwest across Pack Square, and one young man (in circle) to the right of the wagon may be dressed in military attire. (Private collection.)

Patton Family Tree

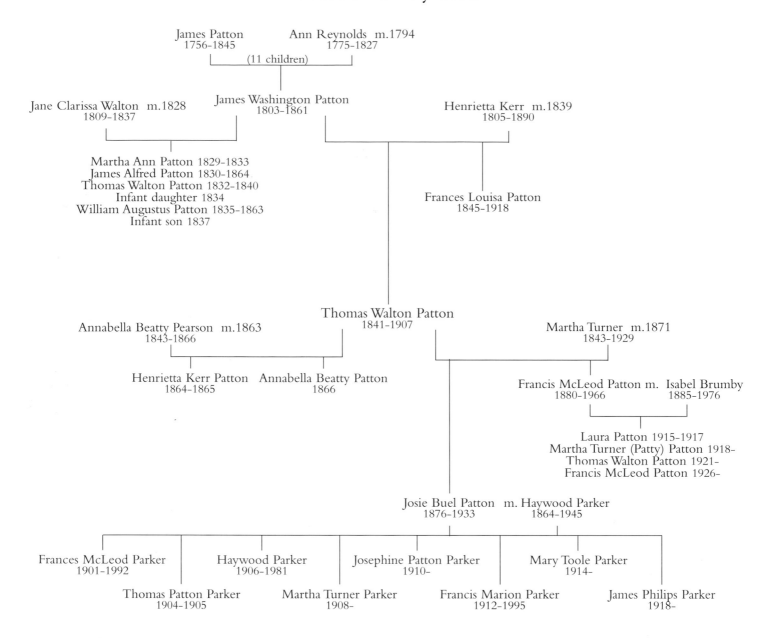

James Patton 1756-1845 — Ann Reynolds m.1794 1775-1827
(11 children)

Jane Clarissa Walton m.1828 1809-1837 — James Washington Patton 1803-1861 — Henrietta Kerr m.1839 1805-1890

Martha Ann Patton 1829-1833
James Alfred Patton 1830-1864
Thomas Walton Patton 1832-1840
Infant daughter 1834
William Augustus Patton 1835-1863
Infant son 1837

Frances Louisa Patton 1845-1918

Annabella Beatty Pearson m.1863 1843-1866 — Thomas Walton Patton 1841-1907 — Martha Turner m.1871 1843-1929

Henrietta Kerr Patton 1864-1865 — Annabella Beatty Patton 1866

Francis McLeod Patton m. Isabel Brumby 1880-1966 — 1885-1976

Laura Patton 1915-1917
Martha Turner (Patty) Patton 1918-
Thomas Walton Patton 1921-
Francis McLeod Patton 1926-

Josie Buel Patton m. Haywood Parker 1876-1933 — 1864-1945

Frances McLeod Parker 1901-1992
Thomas Patton Parker 1904-1905
Haywood Parker 1906-1981
Martha Turner Parker 1908-
Josephine Patton Parker 1910-
Francis Marion Parker 1912-1995
Mary Toole Parker 1914-
James Philips Parker 1918-

Figure 2. The Patton family of which Thomas Walton Patton was a member were descendants of James Patton who came to America from Ireland in 1783, and settled in Western North Carolina in 1807. A prominent family who owned many slaves, the Pattons began and operated several businesses and owned extensive tracts of real estate in Buncombe County. (Design, Peggy Gardner; illustration Robin Mask.)

Eagle Hotel in 1841, graduated from Colonel Stephen Lee's School in Chunns Cove, east of Asheville, in 1860. After graduation he went to Charleston to work in the office of his Uncle Thomas Kerr, a cotton broker. Patton was scheduled to enroll at Chapel Hill in the fall of 1861, following his half-brother James Alfred Patton, who had graduated from Chapel Hill in 1851. But on April 1, 1861, a few days before Ft. Sumter fell, Thomas Walton Patton, with 134 other young men from Buncombe County, enlisted in the Buncombe Rifles.[5]

In mid-April they marched to Raleigh where they joined the 1st North Carolina Regiment and traveled by rail to Virginia. On June 6 the regiment was ordered to Bethel and on June 10 they fought at Big Bethel. At the end of his six-month enlistment, Thomas Walton Patton returned to Asheville and resumed his work in the family businesses. He may have written letters during his first enlistment, but none survive.

In early 1862 war rumbled near Western North Carolina. In mid-February

Ft. Henry and Ft. Donelson, in Tennessee, surrendered to Gen. Ulysses S. Grant's forces and by February 25, Federal troops occupied Nashville. In mid-March Federal Gen. Burnside took New Bern, North Carolina. Asheville newspapers carried announcements of companies forming in Western North Carolina to protect the mountains from Federal invasion from Tennessee (Figure 1). The Conscription Act of April 1862 compelled Southern men to join the struggle.

In spring 1862, Dr. Joseph A. McDowell began to raise troops for local defense of the French Broad River valley. Thomas Patton joined a group of volunteers which eventually became Company C, part of McDowell's battalion, and later regiment.[6] The men elected Thomas Patton first lieutenant. McDowell's battalion grew to include ten companies: five from Buncombe County; one each from Madison County, Polk County, Henderson County; one from Cocke County, Tennessee, and one drawn from other larger companies.

In mid-to-late summer, Company C trained on an island in the French Broad River near Warm Springs. By mid-September Patton and his company had moved to Greeneville, Tennessee, where they guarded military stores and bridges. On October 8, McDowell's battalion officially became the 60th North Carolina and on October 9 the regiment started its journey to Murfreesboro, Tennessee, arriving there on October 15.

A total of 16 letters survive from 1862. One, written before Thomas Patton re-enlisted, reports on conditions at the plantation in Alabama and mentions Susan, Patty and Mary, three of the 36 slaves James Washington Patton had willed to his son Thomas.[7] Three letters, written during the summer training camp at Warm Springs, emphasize family concerns rather than war preparations. One mentions the sale of the Warm Springs Hotel:

I suppose you have heard that Dr McD [Col. McDowell] & Uncle John

have sold the spring property to Mr Rumbough of Greenville [Greeneville] Tenn for forty five thousand dollars. It seems sad for it to go out of the [family] connection Cousin Julia is to have four cabin rooms until fall—

On September 12, 1862, in one of two letters written from Greeneville, Tennessee, Thomas Patton wrote:

My Dear Mother

I reached here in safety with my two deserters on Wednesday evening and was rather tired too as my horse had to be left at the Springs and I had to walk over here....We are camped in a very pleasant grove and I like our present position very well, it is the general opinion that we will be ordered away from here in a few days....[8]

The 60th North Carolina arrived in Murfreesboro, Tennessee, on October 15. Nine letters were written from Murfreesboro. On November 1 Thomas Patton wrote, "On yesterday our pickets, in the neighborhood of Nashville [Nashville], captured two stage coaches tak-

Thomas Walton Patton's father, James Washington Patton, and his uncle, John Erwin Patton, bought the drover's stand in Warm Springs (now Hot Springs) in 1832 and developed the property as a resort hotel. The hotel remained in the Patton family until 1862, after James Washington Patton's death, when John Patton and his partner, Dr. Joseph McDowell, sold the hotel to James H. Rumbough of Greeneville, Tennessee for $45,000. Thomas refers to this transaction in his letter to his mother written from Warm Springs in mid-summer, 1862. The hotel burned in 1884 and was replaced by the Mountain Park Hotel. (Courtesy, North Carolina Collection, University of North Carolina Library at Chapel Hill.)

ing the passengers prisoners & seizing the mail." In a postscript Patton wrote: "Sam has been quite sick for the past two days—& his throat is still very sore but I think it is decidedly better than it was yesterday we have a fine time cooking for ourselves—" Sam Cope was Thomas Walton Patton's slave companion who accompanied him throughout the war. Patton continued on November 4, "Sam's throat is still very sore he is not yet able to cook or do anything. I hope he will get better before we are ordered away from here, for I would dislike very much to have to leave him here—"

Sam Cope is mentioned in many of the 79 letters in the collection. He had been Thomas Patton's companion since the two were toddlers, and he was one of the slaves mentioned by name as part of Thomas's inheritance in James Washington Patton's will.[9] Cope marched from campground to campground, rode the suffocating box cars, witnessed the same battles and watched men die. He looked after Thomas—foraged for food, kept track of their possessions and cooked for Thomas and his friends. The letters document Sam Cope's loyalty and a much older Thomas Patton acknowledged that loyalty, "A pure, honest, loving heart was his, What matters that his complexion was dark?"[10] In Patton's manuscript "The Sixtieth North Carolina Regiment," the aging Patton wrote:

The Law said he was my slave, but often Law makes error, In deed and in fact he was my devoted, loving friend and companion; According to the Southern custom, my Father had given Sam to me, when I was one, and he two years old, We grew up together, eat [sic] together, slept in the same room, romped over the hills of Buncombe, Got into many a boyish scrape, and received many a spanking from Mammy, all together; When I must go to the war, no one doubted that Sam must go too;...[11]

Thomas Patton's letters from

SAM COPE, THOMAS PATTON'S SLAVE

The Patton family owned many slaves. In 1860, James W. Patton, Thomas's father owned 78 slaves and was the second largest slave owner in Asheville. When James Washington Patton died in 1861, Thomas inherited 36 slaves including many on a plantation in Lowndes County, Alabama. This portion of the will mentions them by name including Sam Cope, Thomas Patton's boyhood friend and later companion during the Civil War. Little is known of Samuel Cope after the Civil War. He is listed in the Census of 1870 and in one deed dated January, 1874 for a 1½ acre lot on the south side of Old Haywood Road. He purchased the lot described as "on the side of the mountains" from W. D. Rankin and his wife E. L. Rankin. (Will of James Patton, probated October 1845, Book A, page 108, Office Superior Court, Buncombe County Courthouse.)

Murfreesboro reflect an increasing concern for military matters. On December 1, 1862, Patton wrote:

I believe we have six Lt Generals—among whom are Polk Hardee & Kirby Smith— they are in command of the three corps of this army all being under command of Bragg.... A large number of troops, composing Cheathams & Withers Divissions came here on Monday last so that I suppose there are now more than twenty thousand troops in and arround Murfreesboro ready for duty— ... I don't think I ever wrote so miserable letter as this, it is so cold that my fingers are numb ... we are living "mighty hard" on corn bread & bacon—

On December 7:

On Friday last we had a heavy snow storm almost all day—and it was in the hardest of it that Cheatham's devission was marched off. the poor fellows must have suffered considerably— ... they have good clothes and shoes but need blankets and socks terribly— Two men named Lanning from Cane Creek belonging to our company came in yesterday from home and had brought with them a considerable amount of clothing for some of our men. but when they reached the depot at this place I suppose they were "tight" and so lost them all— (Figure 3)

On December 15:

... Morgan had taken 2000 Yanky prisoners, ... Bob Coleman & I rode down to where they were about 7 miles below here. they were all huddled together in a lot surrounded by a strong guard—near a small river and every now & then the guard would cut off a drove of them of about 300 and drive them down to the river bank to drink and then drive them back & turn them into the lot again. just as if they were a drove of hogs. they were mostly Ohio <u>Dutch</u> and not a third of them could speak English—

Throughout his letters Thomas Walton Patton complained about the failures of his military superiors. He believed they frequently made decisions which endangered the soldiers and prolonged the war. Patton

Figure 3. On December 7, 1862, Thomas Patton wrote his mother from Murfreesboro, Tennessee, describing bitter cold and a heavy snow storm. He had compassion for the soldiers in Cheatham's Division who had to march off on ground "frozen hard as a rock." At that time, Cheatham's Division was part of Polk's Corps while the 60th served in Breckinridge's Division in Hardee's Corps. Cheatham's men and the men of the 60th North Carolina often fought in the same battles, including Chickamauga and Atlanta. For about a month in the summer of 1864, the 60th was part of Cheatham's command. Cheatham was also near Bennett Place when Johnston surrendered to Sherman. Pictured is Benjamin Cheatham. (Reproduced from the Collections of the Library of Congress.)

had little respect for Gen. Bragg. On December 21, 1862, Patton wrote from Murfreesboro:

A private of the 28th Alabama Regt., was shot on Friday for desertion. it was an awful sight as the men detailed to shoot him, fired on him three seperate times before they killed him. I suppose from a mistaken idea of humanity they tried not to hit him. he was buried immediately on the spot that he was shot. his coffin being ready & the grave dug by his side. Three men from this Regt. have been in jail here for several weeks, and were tried by Court Martial & sentenced to be shot, (one of them is <u>James P. Spain</u>) and I understand that one of them, named <u>Littrell</u>, is to be executed this week and the other two pardoned. I do not know if it is true. Genl Bragg is said to be very fond of such amusement.

Patton also believed Col. McDowell of the 60th North Carolina to be incompetent.

On November 3, Thomas Patton wrote:

... our Colonel is becoming more & more unpopular. he has never once attempted to drill his Regt & I think takes very little interest in it—The officers speak of getting up a petition for him to <u>resign</u>. It would be the best thing he could do for us but if I was to sign such a petition I suppose it would make all of Uncle John's family my ennemies for life—

The last sentence reflects family relationships. Col. McDowell was married to Cousin Julia Patton, his Uncle John's daughter. As a result of that connection, Thomas Patton hesitated to make public comment about his superior.

In contrast, Patton liked Gen. Leonidas Polk and sought his favor. On December 1, from Murfreesboro, Patton wrote his mother, "Fannie wrote me that Mrs Polk & her two daughters were going to Asheville. I hope you will write and ask her to stay with you for a while as by that means I might be introduced to the Genl."

Mrs. Patton did indeed befriend Mrs. Polk. In a letter from Asheville dated December 17, 1862, Mrs. Polk wrote to her daughter Kate:

> ... I had received a note from Mrs Patton of this place, inviting me to make her house my home, while making my arrangements—So I came over on the 7th coming in the RR cars as far as Green[e]ville-Tennessee—we left Green[e]ville at 2 on Monday morning, in a stage, & reached Asheville at 11 at night, it was so late I went to the Hotel, the next morning Mrs P- sent her carriage & daughter for us & has entertained us most hospitably ever since ... she & her son have actually succeeded in getting a relative to give up his house & with his family go to board & to let me have the house! there are eight furnished rooms ... The house has a garden & fruit orchard, & we have a cow included are we not fortunate—the house is in the village—& we can have an easy walk to church.[12]

Thomas Patton was invited to have Christmas dinner with Gen. Polk which he gladly accepted. "Genl Polk is a very polite old gentleman but not much like a Bishop. he did not even say grace before dinner."[13]

Gen. Polk was born in North Carolina and graduated from West Point in 1827. His classmates there included Jefferson Davis and Robert E. Lee. He chose religious service rather than military service and by 1841 had been ordained Bishop of Louisiana. Jefferson Davis urged the churchman to rejoin the military and Polk tried to resist. But in June 1861 Bishop Polk accepted commission as major general with headquarters in Memphis. He believed that his military service would be short: "I buckle the sword over the gown," he said.[14]

Gen. Polk died on June 14, 1864, on Pine Mountain, northwest of Marietta, Georgia, while reconnoitering Kennesaw Mountain with Gen. Johnston. Geoffrey C. Ward in *The Civil War, An Illustrated History* wrote: "Leonidas Polk did not make it, and was torn apart. Sherman was pleased, and wired Washington the news: 'June 14. To the Secretary of War. We killed Bishop Polk yesterday, and made good progress today.'"[15]

Thomas Walton Patton observed his first battle at Murfreesboro (Stone's River), December 31, 1862. On December 28, from Murfreesboro, he wrote to his Aunt Charlotte:

> This is a day of great excitement here. We have been hearing heavy cannonading in the direction of Nasheville [Nashville] for the two past days and it was reported that our forces were gradually falling back ... all of the forces in and around here were ordered to the <u>front</u>, and have formed line of battle, it is said extending fifteen miles across the country...—

Thomas's half-brother William Augustus (Guss), who was assistant quartermaster for the 60th North Carolina, had returned to Asheville, perhaps because of illness, and Thomas replaced him as acting quartermaster. He continued in his letter to Aunt Charlotte, "... much to my chagrin, but I suppose to your joy, I, as quartermaster, was ordered to stay in charge of the camps, which is decidedly dull work, ..." Thomas Patton assumed quartermaster's duties several times during the war. He was responsible for living quarters, food, and clothing for the troops and fuel supplies. In many cases those tasks kept him away from battle, in a position of safety.

Company C of the 60th North Carolina finally saw battle on December 31. Ordered across Stone's River, the 60th struggled up the bank. After a period of confusion the Federal troops fell back. After the battle, Thomas Patton wrote his mother a short note:

Murfreesboro Dec 31.62

My Dear Mother

I know you will all be in a great state of excitement and anxiety to hear from me, so I will try & drop you a few hasty lines to let you know that we are well—The battle commenced in earnest on yesterday & continued till dark. The Yankies getting decidedly the worst of it, our devission was not engaged. it is stationed on the Lebanon Pike near the center of the lines, and as yet the fighting has been on the left—I had to take charge of the wagon train, and broke up camp on Sunday night & moved every thing about 3 miles up the road so as to be ready for a retreat in case our army is defeated—but I don't think there is any chance of that—Ever since daylight this morning we have heard distinctly the artillery hammering away but of course cant tell what is the result. I wish Guss would hurry up for I want to rejoin my company—It is uncertain whether this will ever reach you as I don't believe we have any mail now   Wither's devission has been principally engaged. loss not very heavy—I believe we will give them a good thrashing

In haste

TWPatton

But over the next couple of days the battle pushed back and forth, troops on both sides marching and retreating through rain and mud. By January 3 both armies retreated, neither side following up on its advantage. In the first letter of the new year, dated January 10, 1863, Thomas Patton wrote his mother lamenting the Confederate retreat.

... up to last Saturday morning we were all certain that our troops had gained a great & decided victory when to our great surprise we received order to start with our wag-

"I BUCKLE THE SWORD OVER THE GOWN."

GEN. LEONIDAS POLK

ons in retreat—and had to travel through the entire night and reached Manchester about 10 o' clock Sunday morning and we have been hauled about backwards & forwards every day since until yesterday when we arrived here & encamped. Our retreat is certainly a most shamefull proceeding and I think it ought to kill Bragg—The Yankies commenced their retreat two hours before our troops commenced falling back—so that both forces were whipped—our loss in the retreat must have been considerable the road for thirty miles was lined with broken wagons & tents & cooking vessels thrown out— our loss in the battle is estimated at about 5000 killed wounded & missing while the Feds must have lost four times as many—Our Regt lost 2 killed 70 wounded & 10 missing.[16]

The Confederate troops withdrew to winter quarters at Tullahoma, Tennessee. Although Patton thought they would soon leave Tullahoma, they spent a mean winter

While in Murfreesboro, Tennessee, Thomas Patton urged his mother to befriend the family of Gen. Leonidas Polk. General Polk, an Episcopalian bishop from Louisiana, accepted a commission as a major general in the Confederate Army. In 1862 he sent his family to Asheville to find a safe home. Members of Polk's family stayed with the Patton family when they first arrived in Asheville. (Matthew Brady photo, reproduced from the Collections of the Library of Congress.)

there, struggling with snow, rain, slush and mud. In March the men of Company C elected Patton as their captain.

Thomas's half-brother Guss died on April 5, 1863. Born in 1835, Guss was only six years older then Thomas and the two of them were close companions. Several letters indicated that Guss traveled in and out of camp often, perhaps because of his illness. On March 18, 1863, from Benton, Alabama, Thomas wrote to his mother, "I hope you have heard of Augustus' safe arrival in Camp— ..." But after that letter Guss evidently became ill again and returned to Asheville. On April 4, 1863, Thomas wrote to his mother from Tullahoma:

> I had been trying to hope from your not writing by the last mail that the next letter would bring the news that Augustus was better, but from what Fannie writes, and still more from letters received by the Colonel & Major Hardy, it seems almost wrong to allow myself to hope any longer and I will try to prepare myself to receive the sad tidings to-morrow of my brothers death—Of a truth our family has been heavily afflicted and it is very hard to be away from home at a time of such trouble.[17]

After Guss's death Thomas decided he should resign his miliary position and return to Asheville to assist his mother. He first mentioned his resignation in his letter dated April 4, 1863, and in nearly every letter until July 8 when he wrote, "My resignation has this moment returned disapproved."[18] His letters reflected the young man's frustration and anger. One resignation request disappeared, another omitted essential information. The third finally made its way through the military hierarchy (Figure 4).[19] Dated May 10, 1863, it reads, in part:

> I hereby respectfully tender my unconditional resignation as Captain of Company C 60 Regiment NC Troops-to take effect immediately— The reasons which induce me to take this step are that owing to the death of my father and my brother my duty to my family most imperatively demands my presence at home— ... I have provided an able bodied substitute, forty five years of age, to take my

place after my resignation is accepted.

The substitute, John A. Patton (evidently no kin) joined the regiment in Jackson, Mississippi, in early June. In Thomas's eyes, John A. Patton played the scoundrel and took financial advantage of the situation. Thomas wrote his mother from Chattanooga, Tennessee:

> Did not my man Patton act the rascal? as long as he did not come with me I thought it best that he should be kept at home [Asheville] till I could get my resignation accepted as Capt Polk thought I might get off without having him there—please get Burgin [a friend] to get back from Murrell the stage agent the $12.00 I paid him for Pattons stage fare—[20]

Two days after his resignation was disapproved, he wrote to his mother on July 10, 1863, from Jackson:

> Old man Patton [John A. Patton] intends to start home this evening, ... I wish now that my friend Burgin had let Patton stay at home to await my orders—it would have saved a great expense. I hope you will keep an account of what things you have let his family have, and let me know what they amount to—I wrote you in my last letter to stop thier supplies as he may loiter on the road & I don't wish to support them longer—

Fifty letters and three fragments survive from 1863 and they describe the almost constant movement of Company C. On May 25, 1863, Patton wrote from Chattanooga (Figure 5):

> ... it is very hot to-day, travelling very disagreeable in freight cars—we have been nearly thirty six hours coming this far & unless we do better hereafter the reinforcements will not be in time to do much good—

From Jackson, Mississippi, on June 15:

> The 60th was out on picket duty all day yesterday and last night, we do not mind it all however as it is one of the pleasantest & coolest places about here. and we always take the opportunity of foraging while we are out.

Ordered to Vicksburg on July 1, they were too late to relieve the city, and returned to Jackson. From here, he wrote to

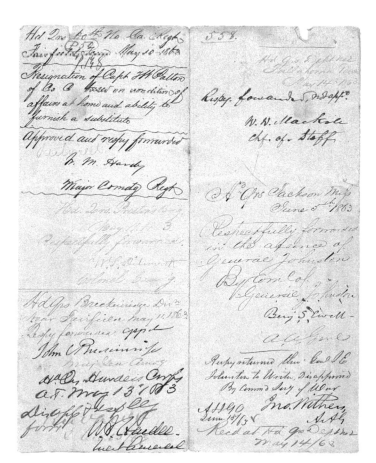

Figure 4. Many of Thomas Patton's letters mention his efforts to resign from the Confederate Army. Top, left. On May 10, 1863 after the death of his father and half-brother, William Augustus, Patton wrote Gen. Cooper, tendering his "unconditional resignation as Captain of Company C" stating that "my health, after two years service, has so failed that I am unfit to fill the position I now occupy." Patton had arranged to provide a substitute to take his position "after my resignation is accepted." Bottom, left and right. The request worked its way through the military hierarchy, but was disapproved. (Letters, courtesy, Southern Historical Collection, University of North Carolina Library at Chapel Hill.) Gen. Joseph E. Johnston, pictured above, was one of three generals who rejected Thomas Patton's letter of resignation.(Reproduced from the Collections of the Library of Congress.)

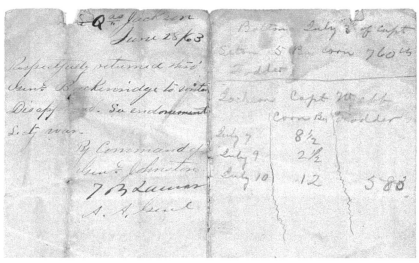

Figure 5. These scenes would have been familiar to Thomas Patton in his travels with Sam Cope. They sometimes traveled in boxcars, and many troop movements and battles were related to railroads. Both of these views (above and opposite page) are of the depot in Chattanooga, Tennessee. On May 25, 1863, Patton wrote from Chattanooga and described traveling 36 "very disagreeable" hours by boxcar. Above. Confederate Prisoners at Railroad Depot.(Photo reproduced from the Collections of the Library of Congress.)

Thousands of men in Western North Carolina participated in the Civil War. Pictured right is Lt. Col. James T. Weaver who served first as captain of Company A of the 60th North Carolina. He took command of the 60th at Chickamauga after Col. James Ray was wounded. Weaver died at Murfreesboro, Tennessee, on December 7, 1864. (Reproduced from the Collections of the Library of Congress.)

his mother on July 8, 1863:

Vicksburg is fallen! this is the terrible thought that I cannot get rid of—and it is assuredly the heaviest blow that has been struck us yet—in my opinion far worse than would have been the fall of Richmond or Charleston, or both. I had almost made up my mind that if we lost Vicksburg our cause was lost—but then I had no idea that such a catastrophe was in store for us, and now I force myself to change my mind as to the final result—and still hope for the best—for surely if we should be subjugated complete & entire ruin awaits each & every man in the South—

After Vicksburg surrendered, they returned to Jackson, then to a camp halfway between Meridian and Jackson. On July 15 he wrote from Jackson:

We captured four Beautifull stands of colors & a hundred & fifty prisoners on Sunday— our loss very small, two artillery men killed the only casualties in our Brigade—I still think we will eventually be obliged to evacuate this place and I expect quite soon at that—There were some beautiful buildings, burnt up by our men on Sunday morning. I went into one of them just before it was set fire

to—the furniture had all been left— it contained a handsome library—I brought away as many books as I could carry.

On July 24, 1863, from a place Patton called Camp No Where at All (probably near Morton, Mississippi) he wrote to his mother:

We evacuated Jackson the night after I wrote to you: ... at dark all the other troops were withdrawn and we [were] left until the very last to watch the Yankies—The evacuation was managed very well—fires were kept burning and bands of music playing till late at night after all the troops except us had gone; we remained on the field until two o'clock and then quietly withdrew. the ennemy knew nothing of it until after day-light.... Well after being in the war for two years I have at last got one shot at a live Yanky—but fear I did not hurt him as he was a long way off in the woods and I could only guess at his wherabouts by the report and smoke of his gun—I secured a fine Enfield rifle off the battle field—which I fired at him. I am sorry to say that I have lost my sword, and it is now in the hands of the ennemy—

In late August the 60th began moving

Boxcars and Depot with Federal Calvary. (Photo reproduced from the Collections of the Library of Congress.)

Travels of McDowell's Battalion and the 60th North Carolina Regi

1862 ——————————
1863 ....
1864 ....
1865 — — — — — — —
Return Home ——————

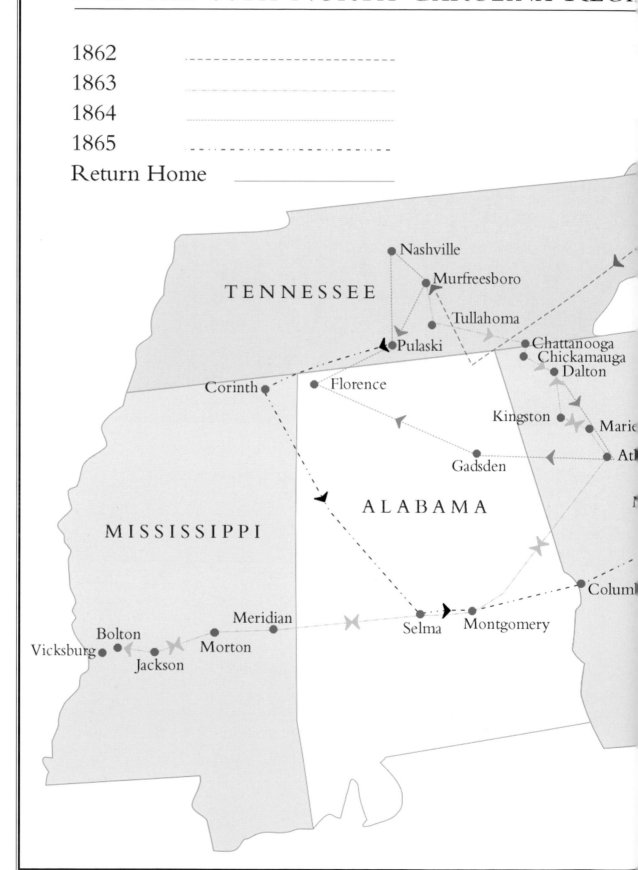

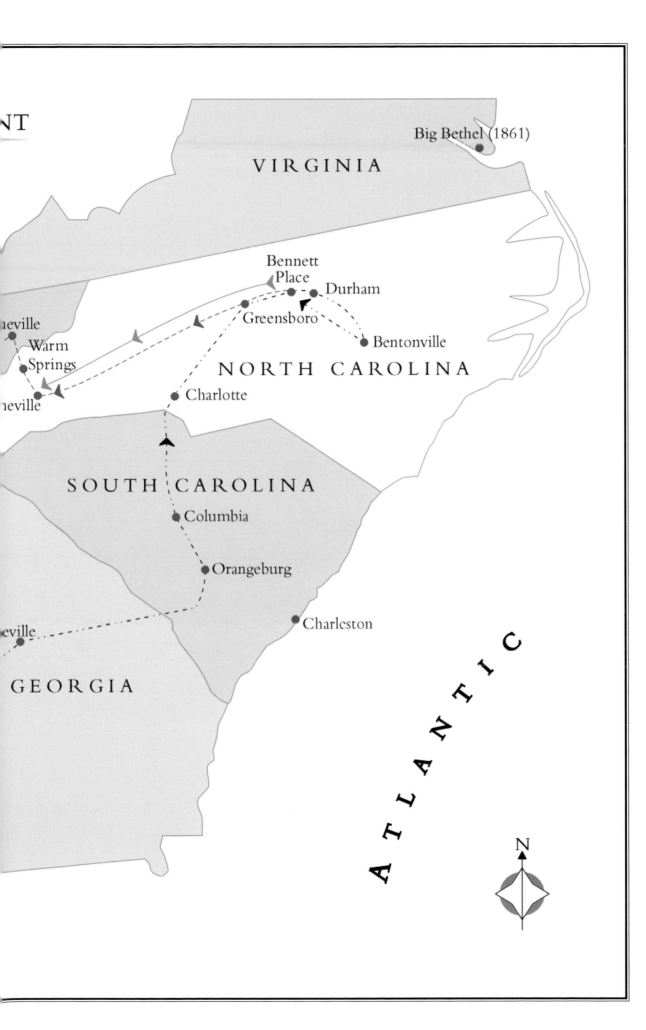

NT

Big Bethel (1861)

VIRGINIA

Bennett
Place
Durham

heville
Warm
Springs
Greensboro

Bentonville

heville

NORTH CAROLINA

Charlotte

SOUTH CAROLINA

Columbia

Orangeburg

Charleston

eville

GEORGIA

ATLANTIC

N

McDowell's battalion became the 60th North Carolina Regiment on October 8, 1862. Between 1862 and 1865 Thomas Walton Patton, accompanied by his slave, Sam Cope, traveled throughout the South with the 60th North Carolina. Some of this travel was on foot or horseback, but sometimes they traveled by train. After Gen. Johnston surrendered to Gen. Sherman at Bennett Place near Durham, North Carolina, Thomas Patton, Sam Cope and a broken-down horse began their journey back to Asheville (green line). (Illustration Keith Leonard, Design Peggy Gardner.)

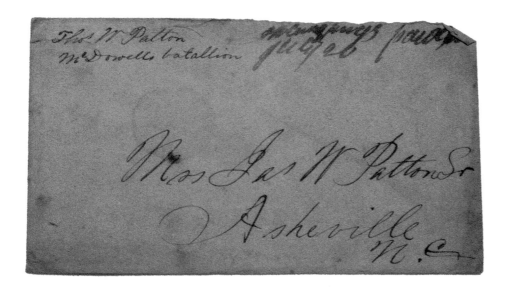

It is not known how many letters written by Thomas Patton did not survive. He was a regular correspondent and there are several large gaps in the collection. Most of the letters are written on heavy paper and in clear penmanship, as evidenced by these three envelopes. (Photos, Robin Mask.)

towards Chickamauga, Georgia, where they would fight in one of the bloodiest battles of the war. From the depot in Kingston, Georgia, Patton wrote:

> Knoxville has been evacuated by our troops—falling back to Louden [Loudon]—if the Yankies get into East Tenn—a raid will be very likely to visit you—& so my advice is that you have Mr Ray to take immediate steps to conceal all of your silver—& let not a soul know where it is except <u>him</u> and <u>you</u>—I always thought Buncombe was safe but do not think so any longer—[21]

A day later he continued:

> The ennemy are in sight on the opposite side of the river but seem very quiet & have not done any thing in the way of shelling since Saturday last. Genl Bragg seems to be making every endeavor to be ready to meet them in a great battle which will probably come off soon—and I have great hopes that he will be successful. if we are defeated here it will be almost as heavy a blow as the fall of Vicksburg.[22]

From LaFayette, Georgia, he wrote on September 10:

> There is a good deal of deserting in our Regiment—we have lost over fifty men in the last week—I can hardly blame the poor fellows—for a great many of them are bare-footed and the marching is terrible on them—although this is a bad excuse for them to <u>walk</u> home—our Brigade QM is so trifling that he does not keep us supplied with shoes, or any thing—he has been gone after them now for more than a month and I hear he is frolicking in Montgomery—

The Battle of Chickamauga lasted two days, September 19-20. Company C was part of the charge which penetrated the Federal lines on the second day. On September 21, 1863, Thomas Patton wrote his mother:

> I have been in a hotly contested battle—and thanks to our Heavenly Father have escaped unhurt—... our Brigade made two noble charges on yesterday, in the first we were repulsed by superior numbers we rested a while and just at dark

charged again and drove the ennemy from their position and held the field—the old 60th acted bravely—loss heavy in wounded, not many killed, ... [I] am sure that the same kind providence, which watched over me yesterday will do so again—...The Yankies, as far as I can judge are getting decidedly the worse of it, we now hold the main Chattanooga road which has been the point of contention for two days past— ... Genl Helm of our Devission killed—Gen Adams of the same, wounded & a prisoner— ... Lieut Davidson is only slightly wounded in the leg—Lt White had a leg amputated. Lt Reynolds' right hand amputated— ...

Much later in his life Patton recalled that "my company, at first consisting of forty-five men, had been reduced to one, my-self, all others killed or wounded...."[23] After the battle of Chickamauga, Company C spent October and November on Missionary Ridge and participated in the Battle of Missionary Ridge in late November. Afterwards, the Confederate forces retreated into winter quarters, this time to Dalton, Georgia.

In many of his letters, Thomas Patton refers to news about other battles. On May 12, 1863, after the Battle of Chancellorsville, he wrote to his mother:

What a glorious achievement that was of Gen Forest— and how thankful we should be for the victory in Virginia, although it was dearly bought by the death of Gen Jackson & to think that he should be killed by his own men—

After Gettysburg, Patton wrote to his sister Fannie: "What very sad news we have from the 11th Regiment; I have never known a company suffer as much in one battle as Jim Young's has—"[24] Many of the 11th Regiment had originally enlisted in 1861 as part of the 1st North Carolina. Jim Young's men in Company K were from Buncombe County. The 11th Regiment, under command of Brig. Gen. Pettigrew, joined Maj. Gen. George Pickett's men in the charge on the third day at Gettysburg.

Throughout the letters Thomas Walton Patton provides detailed descriptions of

camp conditions. On May 28, 1863, he wrote from Montgomery, Alabama:

I reached here in safety this morning, but after one of the most disagreable journeys I ever made—in freight cars all the way—crowded to suffocation. all of yesterday and last night I had to ride on top of one of the cars, most of the time in a pouring rain. Sam came in a train just ahead of mine—I was detained by an accident, and on reaching here found that he had gone on with most of the Regiment and taken my valise with him so I am in a nice fix without a stitch of clothes or a blanket!

On June 4, 1863, he wrote:

... there is a bold spring not more than a hundred yards off which affords us plenty of excellent water, and then we are just on the banks of Pearl River and so have an excellent place for swimming and batheing so it will be our own fault if we do not

keep our bodies clean—which of course will go a great way in preserving our health— ... Company B (Frank Pattons Co) has a regularly enlisted laundress: a Mrs Prater, wife of one of the men. she does all the washing for the officers and does it very well charging fifteen cents a piece—I expect she is making a fortune... . she sleeps on the ground in the woods just like the other soldiers—she is a great convenience as she washes much better than Sam—[25]

On June 9 he wrote to his sister Fannie from Jackson, Mississippi:

we all go without coats and a good many minus thier nether garments—the citizens here say that the hot weather has not commenced yet. I dont see how it can get much hotter ... I can lay under our shade and have Sam to bring plenty of cool water and so manage to keep from melting away....There are a great many fish in the river near here. some fine large cats have been caught in baskets—

A few days later, he wrote, "[T]he bed is made out of small poles covered with green brush and leaves—it is fully as comfortable as a spring mattress and much

The battle at Chickamauga, Georgia, near Chattanooga, Tennessee, was one of the bloodiest of the Civil War and lasted for two days in September 1863. The North Carolina 60th was engaged in the battle and 46 men were killed or wounded including Lt. Samuel Davidson, Sgt. Francis Bailey, Lt. John Reynolds and Col. James Ray. This marble monument was erected in 1905, primarily due to the efforts of Col. Ray, to honor Buncombe County soldiers who fought in the Civil War. One side of the obelisk lists the activities of the 60th for three years and follows the same chronology as Thomas Patton's letters. His name is seen with the list of captains from the battle of Chickamauga. The monument was moved to its present site on the north side of the Buncombe County Courthouse in 1928 when the new courthouse was constructed. (Photo, the Editor.)

cooler—"[26] Later in the month he wrote:

> ... we take advantage of being out on pickett every fourth day, to forage on our own accounts—day before yesterday we got a fine lot of vegetables—beans, squashes, beats [sic], irish and sweet potatoes, chickens, eggs, butter, and <u>ripe peaches</u>. only think of eating peaches in June.[27]

Prices of goods were always of interest, especially to the son and grandson of merchants. He wrote on June 9, 1863:

> ... [flour] is selling in town [Jackson, Mississippi] at $175.00 pr barrell which is 87 1/2 cents pr pound—did you ever hear of anything to equal that? ... Bacon 50 cents pr pound—sugar 50 cents. Beef 20 cts. Molasses we have to buy in town at <u>five dollars pr gallon</u>. Coffee $5-pr pound—it will cost our mess $160.00—that is $40 a piece per month to live even as we do here—at Murfreesboro we used to live on ten dollars each and splendidly at that—[28]

A couple of months later he wrote, "... a decent uniform, coat & pants, cannot be bought there [Mobile, Alabama] for less than <u>five hundred dollars</u>, did you ever in your life hear of such a thing."[29]

He responded often to news from home. His mother evidently sought advice from him on many matters. On June 23, 1863, he wrote to her from Jackson:

> I was very sorry to hear that you were so much troubled with everything—I think Brother James ought to stay more at home and thereby relieving you of the trouble of attending to the Estate business— ... I think the $3000 you wrote about and also any other ready money you can command ought to be paid at once on the bank debt while confederate money will be received in payment of it. it is as good as so much gold or silver—& I fear it will soon cease to pay debts—

On August 16, 1863, he wrote to his mother, "What glorious accounts we receive from all quarters of the crops in Buncombe! there seems to be no prospect of starving there—"[30]

In late October 1863 he wrote to his mother about rumors:

> Capt Roberts came in a day or two ago and reports the Yankies at the Warm Springs— Rumbough being taken prisoner and Old Mr Garrett killed—I hope you will get safely home before they pay Asheville a visit... [31]

Then a few days later he wrote, "We hear that the people of Asheville are panic stricken, and moving out into the county— this is certainly very silly—for no place can be safer than Asheville."[32]

In 1863 Thomas Patton moved from Tennessee to Mississippi, back to Tennessee and then into winter quarters at Dalton, Georgia. After his half-brother Guss died, he felt compelling responsibility to his mother and her concerns with his father's large estate. He entered battle and saw his companions die.

But there were happier moments, too, in his courtship of Annabella (Nannie) Beatty Pearson and their marriage in late 1863. The niece of North Carolina's Chief Justice Pearson, she lived on a plantation near Greensboro, Alabama.

Evidently Nannie and Thomas planned to be married after the war was over. But in

Phyllis Martin Lang ■ THE CIVIL WAR LETTERS OF THOMAS WALTON PATTON

1863 Thomas worried that the war was coming close to Nannie. On August 25, 1863, he wrote to his mother from Morton, Mississippi:

> "... there seems to me to be a great chance of Alabama being over-run by the ennemy—or at all events to be made the battle ground. I almost think it would be best ... to be married at once and take Nannie to Asheville—which will surely be safe if any place in the Confederacy is safe ...."

Nannie and Thomas married on November 29, 1863. After a brief honey-moon on the steamer St. Charles at Selma, Alabama, he took Nannie to Asheville to join his mother's household.[33] Arrested shortly after the marriage, perhaps because he was late returning from Asheville, Thomas wrote to his mother on December 31, 1863, from Dalton, "I was kept under arrest longer than I anticipated, but was released on yesterday by the unanimous appeal of the company officers...." His release paper reads:

Dec 29 1863

> In obedience to the written request forwarded to there [sic] Head Qrs, signed by the Company Officers of the 60th NoCa Reg to the effect that Capt- Thos. W. Patton Co. C 60th NoCa — "should be released from arrest, and charges should not be preferred," that officer is released from arrest and will return to his Company for duty—In this yielding to the expressed wishes of the Officers of this Command the Col. Com. desires it distinctly understood that hereafter similar derelictions of duty will not be lightly passed over, but will be visited with severe pun-ishment.

By order of Col Hardy
R. M. Clayton Lt. and A. Adjut[34]

Twelve letters survive from 1864: nine from Dalton, Georgia, two from Atlanta, and one from Gadsden, Alabama. Now, Thomas Patton's letter writing duties include his wife, Nannie. Four of these sur-viving letters are addressed "My Dear Wife," one is addressed to his sister, "My Dear Fannie," and the remaining seven

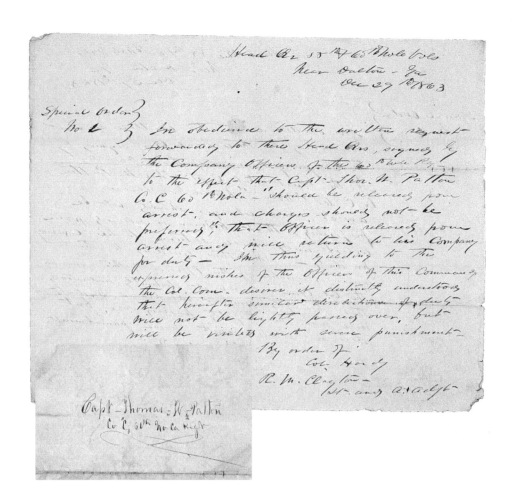

begin "My Dear Mother."

The scant number of letters creates difficulty in determining Thomas Patton's travels during 1864. James Taylor in his work on the 60th North Carolina does comment, however, that the 60th North Carolina was involved in nearly every battle and movement around Dalton, Resaca, Kennesaw Mountain and Atlanta, Georgia. They then moved across Tennessee to Murfreesboro, to the same battleground where they fought in December 1862. The troops again retreated to temporary winter quarters, this time in Mississippi.[35] Patton's letters verify only a few of those move-ments.

Thomas Patton continues his critique of the military superiors. In the first letter of 1864, January 23 from Dalton, he wrote to his mother:

> I believe I wrote you that Genl Hardee had gone off to be married, he has not yet returned, but has the handsomest house in Dalton fixed up in elegant style for the reception of his bride and his daughters, so much for being a General.

He continued:

I do not like Genl Johnstons course much thus far, he has issued a very ridiculous order trying to make every things [sic] very strict and in accordance with Army Regulations— he even goes so far as to appoint the hours for eating breakfast, dinner and supper—which seems rather farsical, when you reflect, that the foot soldiers do not get more rations for all day than are sufficient for one good meal—[36]

In late February, 1864, the 60th was engaged in a skirmish at Rocky Face Ridge, north and west of Dalton, and suffered casualties.[37] On March 2, 1864, from Dalton, Thomas Walton Patton wrote his mother:

I suppose you have receved news before now, of the little disturbance we had here last week— ... The action could hardly be called a battle but was decidedly a brisk skirmish where our Brigade was engaged—For a few minutes our Regiment was exposed to the hottest & most accurate shelling that I ever experienced, but fortunately for some reason this only lasted a very short time—resulting however in wounding twenty four & killing three among the latter of whom I regret to say is My Second Lieutenant Thos H Riddle— he was struck on the right side by a shell ....

On August 22, 1864, he wrote from Atlanta to Nannie:

Every thing has been going on as usual in our front .... The Yankees keep up an almost constant shelling of the town, doing a great-deal damage to the houses on this side of it— especially on Marietta & Peach tree Streets ... not a single house has escaped without being struck, and many of them torn all to pieces. It is wonderfull how little loss of life has occurred. I have heard of only very few casualties.

In 1864 Patton lost another half-brother James Alfred Patton on March 3, less than a year after Guss died.[38] James Alfred served with the Buncombe Rifles but did not rejoin active service after his first term of enlistment. He took care of the Patton businesses and served on

Thomas Patton's first wife was Annabella (Nannie) Beatty Pearson, whom he married in 1863 while he was a soldier. They had two daughters, Henrietta and Annabella, but both daughters and Nannie had died by 1866. All three are buried in Riverside Cemetery in Asheville (right). Patton's second wife, Martha Turner, whom he married in 1871, is buried with him (left), also in Riverside Cemetery. Seen to the right behind Thomas Patton's grave are the graves of his father, James Washington Patton (obelisk with urn), and his grandfather, James Patton (short obelisk). (Photos, the Editor.)

Phyllis Martin Lang ■ THE CIVIL WAR LETTERS OF THOMAS WALTON PATTON

Governor Zeb Vance's Council of State.

Like Guss, James Alfred also had continuing health problems. In the earliest 1862 letter Thomas wrote, "I hope Brother James' health is improving ..."[39] On February 10, 1864 from Dalton, Georgia, Thomas wrote to his mother, "I was very sorry to hear that Brother James had been so sick—" Five days after James's death, Thomas wrote to his mother from Dalton on March 8, 1864:

> I received both your's and Aunt Charlotte's letters on last Sunday they gave me the first reliable information about brother James' critical condition—from them I could not doubt what would be the termination and was therefore not surprised when the news of his death reached me this morning by a letter from Mr Aston to Capt Gilliland— Although we had long known that his health was very bad I never anticipated the end being so near at hand, and accordingly his death was a great shock to me—

A little over two months after their marriage, Nannie came to Dalton, Georgia, in early February, 1864 to visit Thomas. Nannie and Mrs. Roberts, wife of Capt.

Roberts, traveled together without escort and Thomas was both proud and dismayed, "You will all agree with me now that I have a smart wife—I had no idea that the two ladies would undertake to come entirely alone without any gentleman to accompany them."[40] In a later letter to Fannie, Thomas wrote:

> I am glad to give the folks in Asheville something to talk about— In fact I never before thought it right for ladies to visit the army to see thier husbands, but "circumstances alter cases" you know— and it is only to be expected that marrying would cause me to change my opinions on some points—[41]

On November 8, 1864, their first daughter, Henrietta Kerr, was born. Fannie Patton in her diary wrote on November 9, 1864, "I have just finished a long letter to Brother telling him of the birth of his daughter—It seems so ridiculous for Brother & Nannie to have a child—It is a large fat child but <u>ugly</u>—weighs 10 pounds."[42] But Nannie in a letter to an unidentified aunt wrote:

> How I wish you could see the

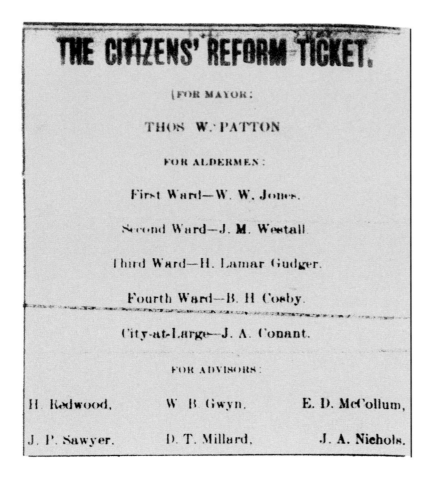

THE CITIZENS' REFORM TICKET.

(FOR MAYOR:

THOS. W. PATTON

FOR ALDERMEN:

First Ward—W. W. Jones.

Second Ward—J. M. Westall.

Third Ward—H. Lamar Gudger.

Fourth Ward—B. H. Cosby.

City-at-Large—J. A. Conant.

FOR ADVISORS:

| H. Redwood, | W. B. Gwyn, | E. D. McCollum, |
| J. P. Sawyer. | D. T. Millard, | J. A. Nichols. |

Figure 6. Following the Civil War, Thomas Patton became an active leader in projects to improve the city of Asheville. He helped found the Public Library and the Buncombe County Children's Home, and in the spring of 1893 was elected Mayor of Asheville. This advertisement for the Reform Ticket appeared in the Asheville Daily Citizen *April 29, 1893. An article in the* Asheville Weekly Citizen *on May 4, 1893 stated that Thomas Patton "at the age of 52...is almost the oldest resident born within the corporate limits." (Photo courtesy, Pack Memorial Public Library.)*

baby, ... I thought at first she was all Pearson, but now she is growing more like the Pattons she has beautiful eyes, but a <u>tremendous</u> mouth, everyone says she is remarkably bright, and as for goodness she cannot be surpassed, never cries all night-long just wakes up to nurse and then goes to sleep again, ... I thought of naming her Eliza Pearson, but we had agreed if it was a daughter Mr P should name her, and if a son I should: he of course wanted her called for his Mother, so she is named "Henrietta Kerr" none of us think it a pretty name, but Mother has been so kind to me and has done and does do so much for the baby, I think it but right she should have her name.[43]

Baby Henrietta was christened February 19, 1865, and Fannie in her diary indicated that Thomas was home for the christening.[44] The baby died on July 21, 1865.

Their second child, also a daughter, named Annabella Beatty Patton, was born on September 5, 1866, after the war was over and Thomas had taken his family to Alabama. Nannie died a few days later on September 12, 1866, and Annabella died on

September 23, 1866.[45]

Between December 1861 and September 23, 1866, Thomas Patton mourned six deaths in his immediate family: his father, his two half-brothers, his two daughters and his wife.

Only one letter survives from 1865, written to his mother on January 6, 1865, from Lowndes County, Alabama. The letter discusses several of the slaves and Patton's views of slavery:

I promised Susan [mentioned in the letter dated February 12, 1862] to write to you particularly for her giving her best love etc—& beging that you will try and communicate with her folks at Mr Robertson's & let them know that "she is well & doing well" she has a fine baby a girl—all of the negroes here seem to be better contented than I ever found them before—they make no complaints at all to me. they are all all [sic] well shod from shoes made by one of them the leather being tanned on the place.... It is the general opinion out here that our "peculiar institution" is forever dead—and I am inclined to that opinion myself. If such is the case I am sure the negroes are most to be pitied—Mr Fagg offers to take a hundred dollars in gold for every one he has—so certain is he that they are lost to us forever as slaves—

No other letters remain. Thomas Walton Patton was a dedicated correspondent and he surely must have continued to write to his mother and his wife until the last days of the war. There are two possible explanations for the missing letters. During the last months of the war, communications in the South grew more difficult. His letters home may have not arrived at his mother's house on South Main Street. Or perhaps the letters disappeared. During the last days of the war, Fannie reported in her diary that the Federal troops ransacked and occupied Henrietta's house. The letters could easily have been lost or destroyed during those final weeks of turmoil.[46]

In mid-January 1865 the 60th North Carolina moved across Alabama and Georgia to Columbia, South Carolina. They then proceeded into North Carolina to

Phyllis Martin Lang ■ The Civil War Letters of Thomas Walton Patton

Charlotte and Salisbury and finally to Bentonville and Smithfield. At that point the 58th and 60th were consolidated and assigned to guard government stores in Greensboro.[47] On April 17, 1865, Gen. Johnston and Gen. Sherman met at Bennett Place, between Greensboro and Durham, to discuss surrender, but terms were not complete until April 26. On May 1 the men received their paroles. Patton in "The Sixtieth North Carolina Regiment," remembers that "Only about Seventy five of our Regiment is left; Only Three men of my Company are to be surrendered; ..."[48]

Patton himself decided not to surrender but started his journey home without parole or authorization, accompanied by his servant, Sam Cope, and an old broken down horse. Northern troops, led by Col. Palmer, one of Stoneman's raiders, captured them near Rutherfordton. Palmer paroled Patton and eventually Thomas arrived at Alexander Robertson's house near Arden, and finally home.[49] Fannie's diary indicates he arrived home on April 29, 1865.[50]

Thomas Patton returned to Asheville to find his family struggling with debts, a town suffering from disorder, and a region facing long years of rebuilding. Devastation haunted Asheville for the remainder of the decade. Broken families mourned the loss of fathers and brothers. Refugees, returning soldiers and freed blacks trudged through the struggling town on their way to some place else.[51]

Thomas Patton vowed to pay off the debts associated with his father's estate and decided to go to Alabama to Nannie's cotton plantation. His granddaughter, Mary Parker, said they packed up everything in wagons but the wagons never arrived in Alabama.[52] Nannie died there, as did his second daughter.

After his futile attempt to manage lands in Alabama, Thomas Walton Patton returned to Asheville. He built a house, a smaller version of "Mansion House," on Charlotte Street on land long-owned by the Patton family, where soldiers had once drilled at Camp Patton. In 1871 Patton

married Martha Turner and they had two children. His mother, his Aunt Charlotte and his sister spent the rest of their lives in that house; his granddaughters still live in the residence.

In the 1870s and 1880s Thomas Patton accepted increased responsibility for civic improvements and other projects which benefited the Asheville community. He worked to establish the electric streetcar and the water systems. He was president of the Asheville Cemetery Association, which established Riverside Cemetery. He served two terms as county commissioner. Then, campaigning on a reform platform, Thomas Walton Patton won election as mayor of Asheville in 1893 and 1894 (Figure 6). During his tenure he reduced expenses, cleaned up city streets, and prepared a new city charter.[53] His leadership helped in the creation of the public library, the YMCA and YWCA, Mission Hospital and the Buncombe County Children's Home. He believed that responsibility accompanied privilege and that belief motivated the last decades of his life.[54]

Thomas Patton wrote faithfully to his family during the Civil War. Seventy-nine letters and four fragments survive and are part of the James W. Patton Papers in the Southern Historical Collection, University of North Carolina at Chapel Hill. This photo of Patton dates from 1893 when Patton was 52 years old and the newly elected Mayor of Asheville. (Courtesy, North Carolina Collection, Pack Memorial Public Library, Asheville, North Carolina.)

Thomas Patton's mother and other family members lived in the "Henrietta" on South Main Street (now Biltmore Avenue) during the Civil War. The Greek revival mansion had been built by Thomas Patton's father in the 1850s, and was demolished in 1949. In the late 1860s, Thomas built a new and smaller residence on Charlotte Street, seen here, where descendants of Thomas Patton still reside. (Photo, the Editor.)

At age 57, Thomas Patton left Asheville on May 1, 1898 to serve in the Spanish-American War. He enlisted in the Asheville Light Infantry as a private. Because of his age and experience, however, North Carolina Governor Daniel L. Russell commissioned him as an adjutant. On December 12 Patton arrived in Havana where he was associated with the 7th Army Corps at Marianso. He knew he was too old to move into battle lines but he wanted to serve as a counselor and example for the young soldiers. He returned to Asheville to a hero's welcome in late April, 1899. His political supporters urged him to run for mayor once again, but he refused.

Thomas Walton Patton lived seven years into the new century. Suffering from poor health the last few years of his life, he sought medical treatment in Philadelphia in autumn 1907. He died there on November 6, 1907.

In many respects, Thomas Walton Patton was not an ordinary soldier during the Civil War. Although his family was in debt following his father's death, he still had the advantages of wealth. He was well educated, he could purchase boots and clothes, and Sam Cope, his personal servant, accompanied him throughout the war. Relatives

in Tennessee and Alabama fed and sheltered him, and his responsibilities as an officer, first as a lieutenant and then as a captain, also provided privileges. He traveled away from the battlefield with some regularity, to see Nannie in Alabama or to visit Asheville. Early in the war his duties as acting quartermaster kept him back from the lines and in a position of safety.

Even though Thomas Patton may have had advantages over other less wealthy and less educated soldiers, he still faced the dangers of war. He endured cold nights and poor food and the rigors of prolonged marches. He was close enough to the front lines so that bullets zipped around him, missing him while striking companions. He acted bravely, led his men well and carried out all his duties. He watched his friends suffer injuries and die in battle. He mourned the deaths in his immediate family. He saw war devastate the towns and countryside and knew the struggle had changed his life forever. Apparently, he never surrendered hope, at least not in these letters. He had faith that he would return to Asheville, whole and energetic. He would resume his roles as son, husband and father.

The last letter in the collection, written after the fall of Atlanta in mid-1864 but before the final catastrophes of the war in spring 1865, reflects that optimism. Near the end of his letter written from Lowndes County, Alabama, on January 6, 1865, he says:

> There seems to be a good deal of despondency felt among the people out here about the final issue of the war—many of them have given up all hope—I am not by any means among this number but still feel confident that all will yet be well.... I still have strong hopes of seeing you all this winter—so keep in good spirits at home.

> I remain yr affec son
> Thos W. Patton

Acknowledgements:
Thanks to Nathan Mann, research assistant; the North Carolina Collection, Pack Library, Asheville, North Carolina; the Southern Historical Collection, Wilson Library, University of North Carolina at Chapel Hill; and Special Collections, Ramsey Library, University of North Carolina at Asheville.

Notes

1. All of these letters are part of the James W. Patton Papers 1798-1907(#1739) in the Southern Historical Collection (SHC), University of North Carolina at Chapel Hill. All letters are addressed to his mother, unless otherwise noted. Original spelling and punctuation have been retained throughout.
2. Daniel Harvey Hill, *A History of North Carolina in the War between the States, Bethel to Sharpsburg* (Raleigh: Edwards and Broughton Company, 1926), vol. 1, p. 47, gives a detailed account of the Bethel Battle.
3. See James Patton's will, probated October 1845, Book A, page 108, Office Superior Court, Buncombe County Courthouse.
4. John C. Inscoe, *Mountain Masters, Slavery, and the Sectional Crisis in Western North Carolina* (Knoxville: University of Tennessee Press, 1989), p. 265.
5. See "The Old 'Buncombe Riflemen,' Original Muster Roll of the Company," a clipping from the *Asheville Daily Citizen*, September 12, 1895, North Carolina Collection, Pack Memorial Library, Asheville.
6. A company usually consisted of 100 men, a battalion consisted of 2-9 companies; a regiment consisted of 10 companies.
7. To his mother, February 12, 1862, from Lowndes County, Alabama.
8. Desertion would prove to be a continuing problem for the 60th. Many of the men volunteered in order to escape conscription. They were older than Thomas Patton, with family responsibilities. Furthermore, they believed they would be assigned duty in the mountains of Western North Carolina. Instead, by the end of the war, they had traveled thousands of miles.
9. See James Washington Patton's will, probated January 1862, Book 1, page 213B, Office Superior Court, Buncombe County Courthouse.
10. "The Sixtieth North Carolina Regiment: Infantry," typed manuscript, signed by TW Patton, Southern Historical Collection, University of North Carolina at Chapel Hill, p. 17.
11. Ibid. Sam Cope returned from the war with Thomas Patton. His name is found in the 1870 census where he is listed as laborer. But his name does not appear in any later census rolls or in any Asheville city directories. His brother Mat Cope, however, continues to appear in both census and city directory records through 1907. Furthermore, Sam Cope's name does not appear in any cemetery rolls. No members of the Cope family appear to be known in the contemporary African-American community in Asheville.
12. Gale and Polk Family Papers, 1815-1940 (#226), Southern Historical Collection, University of North Carolina at Chapel Hill.
13. To Aunt C. (Miss Charlotte Kerr, Henrietta Kerr Patton's sister), December 28, 1862, from Murfreesboro, Tennessee.
14. William M. Polk, *Leonidas Polk, Bishop and General*, 2 vols. (New York: Longmans, Green, and Co., 1915), vol. 1, p. 362.
15. Geoffrey C. Ward with Ric Burns and Ken Burns, *The Civil War, An Illustrated History* (New York: Alfred A. Knopf, 1990), p. 323.
16. To his mother, from Tullahoma, Tennessee.
17. Weymouth T. Jordan Jr. in *N.C. Troops, 1861-1865 A Roster* (Raleigh: Division of Archives and History, 1998) Vol XIV, p. 502 reports that Augustus resigned on February 24, 1863, because of "hypertrophy of the heart." His resignation was accepted on April 5, the day he died. He is buried in Riverside Cemetery alongside his three children, Willie, Allie, and Augustus. All the children died between 1863-1865. The footstones on their graves read, "Our first born," "Our second," and "Our last."
18. To his mother, from Jackson, Mississippi.
19. This third request survives in the James W. Patton Papers, SHC.
20. Probably written on May 25, 1863 from Chattanooga, Tennessee. This letter indicates Thomas Walton Patton had been in Asheville recently, perhaps shortly after Guss's death.
21. To his mother, September 1, 1863.
22. September 2, 1863, from Chattanooga, Tennessee.
23. "The Sixtieth North Carolina Regiment," p. 11.
24. August 4, 1863, from Morton, Mississippi.
25. June 4, 1863, from Jackson, Mississippi.
26. June 12, 1863, from Jackson, Mississippi.
27. June 28, 1863, from Jackson, Mississippi.
28. To Fannie Patton, from Jackson, Mississippi.
29. August 2, 1863, from Camp Hurricane (near Morton, Mississippi).
30. From Morton, Mississippi.
31. October 24, 1863, from Camp 60 NC (probably on Missionary Ridge, Tennessee).
32. October 30, 1863, from Camp (probably on Missionary Ridge).
33. January, 30, 1864 from Dalton, Georgia.
34. James W. Patton Papers, SHC.
35. James Taylor, *The 60th North Carolina Regiment: A Case Study of Enlistment and Desertion in Western North Carolina During the Civil War.* Unpublished master's thesis, Western Carolina University, 1996, pp. 32-49.

Camp Smith July 21 1862

My Dear Mother

We reached here in safety on Saturday morning. after a rather tiresome march. My company marched from Alexanders to the springs on friday. and that was rather a forced march. of twenty seven miles. On Thursday night we got shelter in Alexanders stable loft and so were sheltered

Portion of Thomas Patton letter written to his mother, July 21, 1862. (Courtesy, Southern Historical Collection, University of North Carolina Library at Chapel Hill.)

36. January 23, 1864, from Dalton, Georgia.
37. Taylor, p. 32.
38. James Alfred Patton is also buried in Riverside Cemetery, next to his brother William Augustus.
39. February 12, 1862, from Lowndes County, Alabama.
40. February 10, 1864, from Dalton.
41. February 14, 1864, from Dalton.
42. Fannie Patton's unpublished diary, private collection.
43. January 11, 1865, from Asheville. Letter found in James W. Patton Papers, SHC.
44. Fannie Patton's unpublished diary, entry dated April 9, 1865.
45. Nannie and the two babies are also buried in Riverside Cemetery, not far from the graves of James Alfred and William Augustus.
46. Fannie Patton's unpublished diary, entry dated May 11, 1865.
47. Taylor, pp. 49-57.
48. Page 16. Jordan in *N.C. Troops* reports that 1,212 men joined the 60th and 114 men were part of Company C. During the war years men from the 60th were injured and subsequently discharged or killed. Some were taken prisoner. Some resigned and were allowed to return home. Others deserted. Some, like Patton, served their time and then walked away in the last few days of the war.
49. "Thomas Walton Patton: A Biographical Sketch," (No publisher, no date), North Carolina Collection, Pack Memorial Public Library, Asheville, pp. 13-14. The sketch was probably written by his sister Fannie Patton.
50. Entry dated May 11, 1865.
51. Fannie Patton's unpublished diary, entry dated May 11, 1865.
52. Interview with Mary Parker, June 9, 1995.
53. "Thomas Walton Patton: A Biographical Sketch," pp. 19-23.
54. Much of his commitment to responsibility grew from his strong religious faith. A member of Trinity Episcopal Church, he evidenced his concern for others through programs for the less-advantaged: orphans, paupers and prisoners.

Bibliography
Published Materials:
Clark, Walter, ed. *Histories of the Several Regiments and Battalions from North Carolina in the Great War 1861-'65.* 5 vols. Goldsboro, N.C.: Nash Brothers Book and Printers, 1901.
Hill, Daniel Harvey. *A History of North Carolina in the War between the States.* 2 vols. Raleigh: Edwards and Broughton Company, 1926.
Inscoe, John C. *Mountain Masters, Slavery, and the Sectional Crisis in Western North Carolina.* Knoxville: University of Tennessee Press, 1989.
Jordan, Weymouth T. Jr., ed. *North Carolina Troops, 1861-1865: A Roster.* Vol. XIV: 57th-58th, 60th-61st Regiments. Raleigh: Division of Archives and History, 1998.
Mast, Greg. *State Troops and Volunteers: A Photographic Record of North Carolina's Civil War Soldiers Vol. I.* Raleigh: North Carolina Department of Cultural Resources Division of Archives and History, 1995.
Polk, William M. *Leonidas Polk, Bishop and General.* 2 vols. New York: Longmans, Green, and Co., 1915.
"The Old 'Buncombe Riflemen,' Original Muster Roll of the Company." The *Asheville Daily Citizen.* September 12, 1895. North Carolina Collection, Pack Memorial Public Library, Asheville, North Carolina.
"Thomas Walton Patton: A Biographical Sketch." N.p, n. d. North Carolina Collection, Pack Memorial Public Library, Asheville, North Carolina
Ward, Geoffrey C. with Ric Burns and Ken Burns. *The Civil War, An Illustrated History.* New York: Alfred A. Knopf, 1990.

Unpublished Materials:
Gale and Polk Family Papers, 1815-1940. Collection Number 226. Southern Historical Collection, University of North Carolina at Chapel Hill.
James W. Patton Papers, 1798-1907. Collection Number 1739. Southern Historical Collection, University of North Carolina at Chapel Hill.
Parker, Mary. Interviews June 9, 1995 and June 23, 1997.
Patton, Fannie. Unpublished diary, entries dated October 26, 1864, to May 30, 1865. Private collection.
Taylor, James. *The 60th North Carolina Regiment: A Case Study of Enlistment and Desertion in Western North Carolina During the Civil War.* Master's thesis, Western Carolina University 1996.
"The Sixtieth North Carolina Regiment: Infantry." Typed manuscript, signed by TW Patton. Southern Historical Collection, University of North Carolina at Chapel Hill.
"Thomas Walton Patton." Typed biographical manuscript. Includes typed version of a clipping giving details of departure of Buncombe Rifles. James W. Patton Papers, Southern Historical Collection, University of North Carolina at Chapel Hill.
Will of James Patton, probated October 1845, Book A, page 108, Office Superior Court, Buncombe County Courthouse.
Will of James Washington Patton, probated January 1862, Book 1, page 213B, Office Superior Court, Buncombe County Courthouse.

When Tony Lord died in 1993, those close to him had the challenging task of sorting and sifting the objects and collections he left. These friends and companions knew him to be a self-effacing but remarkable man; an engineer, architect, artist and horticulturist. But they found evidence of an even more supple and creative mind than they had known. Scores of watercolors, meticulous drawings, finely made tools, plans and projects; evidence of curiosity, intent and technique. His life and work seemed always to be grounded, substantive and gently self-conscious. He was deeply committed to the quality of life in his community.

Through Myron Gauger, Peter Austin was given Tony Lord's drawings and photographs of Lord's ironwork executed in the early 1930s when there was little work for a recently graduated architect. This study examines that work and how Tony Lord created a viable business during the Great Depression. It also poses some intriguing encounters. What did the photographer Doris Ulmann say to Tony Lord as he stood with his tools and work? And he to her? What did Daniel Boone VI make in Lord's shop? How did they work together: Boone the fourth generation Yancey County, North Carolina blacksmith and Lord the self-taught blacksmith educated at Yale as an architect? One imagines fertile collaboration and humor. Men pounding iron with heavy hammers. —R.B.

INTRODUCTION

The Ironwork of Tony Lord

By Peter Austin

Anthony (Tony) Lord, who died in 1993, was well known in Asheville, North Carolina as an architect and community leader. Six Associates, the architectural firm he helped found on the eve of World War II is still an active firm in the region and many of the buildings he designed in Asheville such as the Citizen-Times Building in downtown Asheville (Figure 1) and the Dillingham Presbyterian Church in Reems Creek are still prominent landmarks.1 The room at Pack Memorial Library used for public meetings is named for him, an honor

A young Tony Lord, probably in his teens, operating a simple forge in the backyard of the Lord home on Flint Street in Asheville. Lord (second from right) is turning a pulley which is attached to a blower and tubing which delivers the forced air to the forge. Other people pictured and date of photo are unknown. (Courtesy, Myron Gauger.)

Figure 1. Anthony (Tony) Lord is well known for his architectural work in Western North Carolina. In 1938-39 he designed the Citizen-Times Building on O. Henry Avenue in a distinctly art moderne style. (Courtesy, North Carolina Collection, Pack Memorial Public Library, Asheville, North Carolina.)

reflecting his service on the library board for nearly 40 years. Trees that he fought to have planted along the streets of Asheville during the decades when it seemed that his interest was largely a personal eccentricity are grown now, and provide the shade and coolness he promised. In 1995, an account of Tony Lord's 1927 journey to Europe and North Africa with several friends from Yale was published and illustrated with many of his watercolors (Figure 2).2 One aspect of Tony Lord's life and work is less well known however, his work as a blacksmith during the Great Depression. Between 1929 and 1937 "Lord" (as he was called by many who knew him) owned and managed a blacksmith shop on Flint Street in Asheville. He designed and executed ironwork for buildings at Yale University and the Washington National Cathedral (the Cathedral Church of St. Peter and St. Paul) in Washington, D.C., among others, and for some of the few houses being constructed in the Asheville area during the Depression. He also mended broken hand tools, and produced fireplace tools and other functional objects for the local craft market.

Anthony Lord was born in Asheville in 1900, and spent nearly all of his life in the

area, leaving only for education and travel. He grew up on Flint Street in the Montford section, in a house designed by his father, the architect William H. Lord. William Lord and his wife, Helen Anthony Lord, were from New York state and had moved to Asheville in the 1890s. William Lord was a respected architect who held office in professional associations at the state and national level, and designed many buildings in the Asheville area including the David Millard and Biltmore School Buildings. Prior to her marriage, Helen Anthony Lord had worked with Jane Addams at Hull House in Chicago.

In 1918 Lord graduated from Asheville High School and in 1922 he received a B.S. in mechanical engineering from the Georgia School of Technology. After working in Asheville, and studying drawing for a year at the Art Student's League in New York City, he went to Yale in 1925 to study architecture and graduated with a Bachelor of Fine Arts in architecture in 1927. His training at Yale was beaux-arts based and would have included the study of drawings, composition, watercolor, and courses in the history of architecture, art and landscape design. Lord's travels abroad were an appropriate extension of his formal education. When Lord returned from his tour of Europe and North Africa in early 1928, he joined his father's architectural practice in Asheville, then renamed Lord & Lord, but there was little work for the firm that year, and even less in the Depression years that followed.

Asheville was hit particularly hard by the stock market crash because the economy of the city and region had already been weakened by the collapse of land speculation in the late 1920s. In 1926 the largest bank in Western North Carolina, the Central Bank and Trust Company of Asheville was virtually insolvent. When the national economy collapsed in 1929, not only did the bank close, but the $6 million that the city and county governments had deposited in the bank was gone. The local economy ground to a virtual stop.[3] Lord

Figure 2. After graduating from Yale with a degree in architecture in 1927, Tony Lord and a group of friends traveled to Europe to study architecture and art history. Among his many talents, Lord was an accomplished watercolorist. This view of the village of Saint-Paul-de-Var was painted in the fall of 1927 (13x10" [sight]). (Courtesy, Miegan Gordon; photo, Tim Barnwell.)

describes it as a time in which there was "no architecture work to be done whatsoever, nothing in that line."[4] So he turned to blacksmithing.

When Lord began his ironworking business, he could not have known that the Great Depression was just beginning. He did not have a clear notion of how long it would engage him, how he could make it work, what he would make and to whom he would sell his work. Perhaps he didn't even regard it as a business at first, but simply as a hobby that would engage him during a period of slow business.

Lord had an early interest in smithing, describing himself as "a wide-eyed young man of string bean configuration during the summer of 1917...(who) went to work for the W.S. Whiting Manufacturing Company as a helper in the blacksmith shop."[5] The Whiting Manufacturing Company operated a lumber mill and logging railroad in Watauga County, North Carolina. That summer Lord learned to

Figure 3. The first ironwork made by Tony Lord was probably a pair of door pulls made for an orphanage designed by Lord and his father, William H. Lord. (One pull shown, above left.) Their firm was known as Lord & Lord and was formed when Tony Lord returned to Asheville in 1928. The location and date of the orphanage is not known, although it was probably built in Western North Carolina in the late 1920s. The remaining two photos are of other hardware used in the same project. (Courtesy, Anthony Lord Photographic Files, author's collection.)

repair the equipment used to cut and handle logs and lumber including peavys, cant hooks and heavy metal tongs. Later, while traveling in France in the summer of 1927, smithing again caught his interest. In a small village market in Brittany, he noticed that "in one booth they had an anvil—a good, sizable anvil weighing perhaps a hundred pounds...which seemed very strange to be hauling around the county to street markets."[6]

THE IRONWORK

The first known ironwork made by Tony Lord were door pulls installed on an orphanage designed by Lord and his father in the late 1920s. Lord felt that some "fancy door pulls"[7] might add to the building's charm, but couldn't find a smith to do the work, so he made them himself (Figure 3). He was soon providing ironwork for buildings designed by others, making, as Lord described it, "certain items of ornamental ironwork, decorative wrought iron, hardware for doors and hinges and handles and such things."[8]

Lord eventually named his business Flint Architectural Forgings. This name does not appear in the city directories until the mid 1930s, although it is found on drawings done in late 1931 for work at Yale University. The transition from being an architect to an ironworker was a gradual one, and the name of Lord & Lord still appeared in the Asheville city directory in 1932. Perhaps Lord considered himself an architect for the entire period that he was engaged in the iron business, and was simply "otherwise engaged." The architecture business also changed when William H. Lord, Tony's father, died in 1933.

Lord's two largest and best documented ironwork projects were for buildings on the campus of Yale University, and work for All Saints Episcopal Church in Worcester, Massachusetts. He also made hardware for Washington National Cathedral in Washington, D.C., but little documentation exists for this project.[9]

Tony Lord's work at Yale University was for James Gamble Rogers and this relationship led to other work for Lord. Rogers, a prominent and well connected architect with offices in Chicago and New York, had a long and successful career as a designer of large university and medical buildings, including the Columbia Presbyterian Medical Center, buildings on the campuses of New York University and Tulane University, the Yale University Memorial Quadrangle and several buildings donated to Yale by John W. Sterling.[10] Rogers' long time patron, Edward Harkness, was an heir to the Standard Oil fortune and an influential Yale supporter who was willing to give vast portions of his private fortune for the construction of educational buildings.

Rogers therefore was in an unusually strong position for an architect. Although he officially worked for the Yale Corporation when he designed for that campus, this did not prevent him from going directly to Harkness in the event of a dispute.[11] In the early 1920s Yale embarked on a building program to accommodate a growing student body following World War I. Bertram

Goodhue designed some of the major buildings, although Rogers was by then the university's consulting architect. Goodhue's untimely death in 1924 left a void that was rapidly filled by Rogers.[12] Lord and all other Yale graduates in architecture had a particular friend in James Gamble Rogers. It was Rogers' belief that design work on the Yale campus should be carried out by Yale trained architects, and he gave preference to them when choosing staff for building projects there.[13] Presumably this bias extended to Yale graduates working as blacksmiths.

Although it is not clear how Lord first got involved in the construction at Yale, by the early 1930s, Lord was fashioning ironwork designed in Rogers' office for the doors and windows of the Gothic buildings

Figure 4. Lord's work at the Yale Colleges was primarily designing and making door hardware. This handle for a door (left) at Branford College may have been executed in the mid-1930s as Tony Lord's card (below) on back of the photo refers to Flint Architectural Forgings as an earlier business name. (Photo, Anthony Lord Files.)

Far left. Pair of wrought iron door pulls, Trumbull College, Yale University. (Courtesy, Anthony Lord Files.)

Hardware, Branford College,
Yale University,   (Handle)

From
ANTHONY LORD
Maker of HAND FORGED IRON
at ASHEVILLE, NORTH CAROLINA
FORMERLY FLINT ARCHITECTURAL FORGINGS

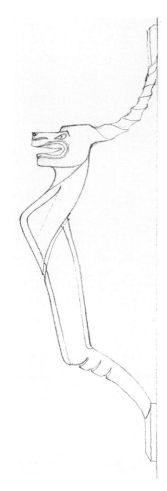

Below. This architectural tracing from Flint Architectural Forgings, dated November 4, 1931, shows interior and exterior views of the hardware for double doors to the courtyard at Jonathan Edwards College of Yale University. The office on Church Street was used for design work by Lord and his father while the forge was located on Flint Street. (Courtesy, Anthony Lord Files.)

Figure 5. Above, left. Two pairs of animal form handles are on the outside of the double doors leading from the courtyard to the mail room of Jonathan Edwards College. (Photo, the author.) Although they do not show Lord's mark, they can be clearly linked to him through his drawings (top right). This photo (top center) was probably taken by Lord shortly after installation. (Photo, Anthony Lord Files.) After 68 years of daily use, the handles show little wear.

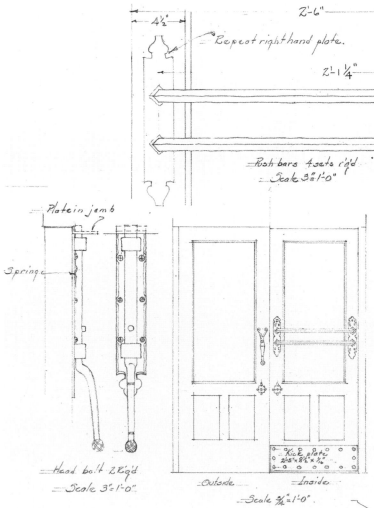

Figure 6. These drawings (below) for Jonathan Edwards College indicate many of the forms Tony Lord used on the door hardware he designed for James Gamble Rogers, the primary architect for the construction at Yale in the 1930s. (Drawings, Anthony Lord Files.) This door (left) appears today much as it did in the original drawings. (Photos, Ezra Rosser.)

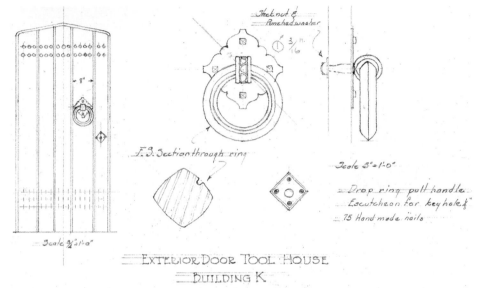

that were rising on campus. Lord's iron work at Yale is found on a series of residential college buildings that were completed in the 1930s. These include Jonathan Edwards College, built 1924-32; Trumbull College, 1932-33; and two colleges formed out of Harkness Memorial Quadrangle, Branford College and Saybrook College, built 1930-33.

As with most major ironwork projects, more than one maker was involved and it is not always possible to determine which firm executed which pieces at Yale. Some of the work is unmarked, or the mark is placed where it cannot be seen. Some of the work on a building's exterior has deteriorated from weathering, and the paint has bubbled from rust, which may also conceal some identifying marks. Some nearby ironwork is known to be by other smiths, among them Samuel Yellin (1885-1940)

regarded by many as one of the foremost ironworkers in the country. Yellin's work at Yale included one ornate gate in the Harkness Memorial Quadrangle and another at the nearby Sterling Memorial Library.

The Tony Lord and Samuel Yellin firms also had work at Washington National Cathedral, and at All Saints Episcopal Church in Worcester, Massachusetts. Both firms supplied ironwork that was appropriate for structures designed by revivalist architects including Rogers, Adam Cram and others who specialized in Romanesque and Gothic revival design. These revival buildings "bore the sign of the struggle between historicism and utilitarianism.... (They) employed the most advanced steel skeletons and mechanical equipment...yet externally they were clothed in elaborate and carefully detailed historicisms."[14] These buildings, designed to look as if they were from a much older time, needed Lord's and Yellin's work which was derived from Gothic and Renaissance sources. Following World War II this style of work was no longer popular. At Yale, Tony Lord, a relatively unknown blacksmith from North Carolina, would get the bid for the utilitarian hardware on the doors and windows, with a few artistic flourishes on some door pulls, and Samuel Yellin would display his skill on grand college gates.

Lord's work at Yale can be identified from his labeled photographs and drawings, however, these documents were not meant to indicate the extent or placement of the work on the building. At Yale, for example, the information on the photographs generally places the work in a particular college, labeled "Branford College," without indicating where the work was placed (Figure 4). The drawings are sometimes even less exact than the photographs in placing the work. Some tracings by Lord for ironwork in Jonathan Edwards College are simply marked "High & Library Quad" for the location, with High being a bordering street. However, these tracings do provide exact date information (Figure 5).

An inspection of the buildings in Jonathan Edwards College revealed a number of examples of ironwork bearing Lord's mark, and a larger number that are almost certainly his, because they are distinctive works which match work shown in Lord's drawings (Figure 6). Much of this work is hardware on wooden exterior doors opening onto the central court at ground level,

Figure 7. Drawing for hardware for an exterior wooden gate at Jonathan Edwards College, Yale University, and Lord's photograph of the completed work. (Drawing and photo, Anthony Lord Files.)

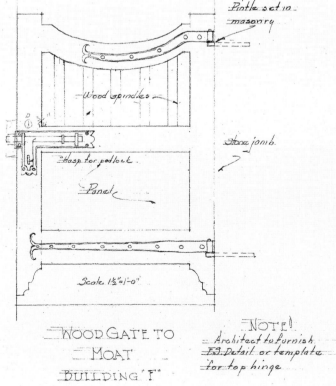

Figure 8. On one of her tours across the Southern Appalachians in the early 1930s, the noted photographer Doris Ulmann took these photos of Tony Lord in his shop. Ulmann traveled throughout the South, accompanied by her assistant John Jacob Niles, taking large format photographs of craftsmen, mountain people and black agricultural workers. Many of the craftspeople Ulmann photographed were not formally trained, and Tony Lord, while a Yale-educated architect, had no formal training as a blacksmith. (Used with the special permission of Berea College and the Doris Ulmann Foundation.)

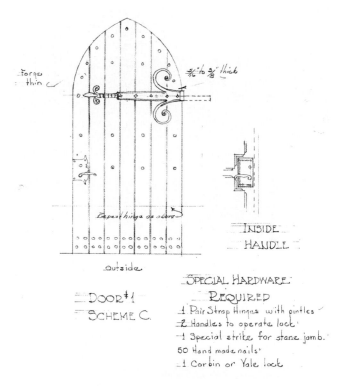

Figure 9. Lord's ironwork on Washington National Cathedral was done for the firm of Frohman, Robb & Little. There is little record of his designs for Washington National Cathedral, but several labeled photos and drawings make it possible to document and identify his door hardware. All the hardware pictured derives from one architectural tracing with a revised date of August 1, 1932. Shown are ornate strap hinges, handles, strike plate, and nails for an exterior door at the East Cloister Walk. The mark for Flint Architectural Forgings can be seen faintly near the end of the hinges in the detail photo. (Courtesy, Anthony Lord Files.)

and interior doors between the common rooms. Door pulls, hooks, stops, straps and dozens of large headed rustic nails were produced as well as hardware for a wooden gate adjacent to a building at Jonathan Edwards College (Figure 7). This work is further documented in the notes for the photographs of Lord taken by Doris Ulmann on one of her tours of the Southern Appalachian Mountains. John Jacob Niles, Ulmann's assistant, wrote that "Mr. Lord is credited with having designed and executed all the metal door fixtures, window fixtures...etc., hasps, hooks, locks, metal eyes, window snaps and hinges in Harkness Hall, Yale University, New Haven, Conn." (Figure 8).[15]

In 1932 Tony Lord was involved with ironwork for Washington National Cathedral. This project was supervised by the architectural firm of Frohman, Robb & Little of Boston which specialized in Neo-Gothic church design, in much the same way as James Gamble Rogers was known for "Collegiate Gothic." [16] The senior partner, Philip H. Frohman, had been the principal architect of the Washington National Cathedral since 1921, and would remain in that position until his death in 1972, eighteen years before the building was completed in 1990.[17] The two other partners, E. Donald Robb and Harry B. Little were also well known for their church architecture. As at Yale, it is not clear when Lord began this work or how he made contact with the firm. Lord's

Peter Austin ■ THE IRONWORK OF TONY LORD

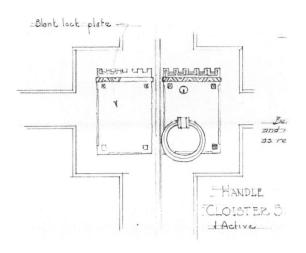

Drawings for the ironwork on Washington National Cathedral indicate at least three designs for lock plates and handles for doors. (Photos and drawing, Anthony Lord Files.)

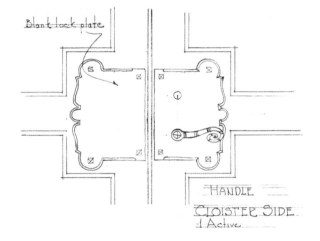

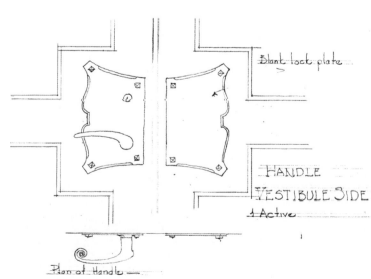

Cost   January 3, 1934
Estimate on gated chapel All Saints
Church, Worcester Mass. —

"A"   75 hrs B.S. $81.00 on
                                              81 — ✓
overtime basis. —

"B"   do above —   81 — ✓

"C"   19½ hrs B.S.   21.06
                forging
Total cost top work   188.44
            1 piece
Finishing 30 hrs helper   21 —
Material, estimated 60#   6.60

                                      216.04

The ironwork produced in Lord's shop required considerable skilled labor. These figures show that almost 170 hours of a smith's labor at $1.08 per hour was required for a portion of a chapel gate for All Saints Episcopal Church, Worcester, Massachusetts. (Courtesy, Anthony Lord Files.)

commissions were limited to door hardware, although some of it was elaborate and was labeled "special hardware" on the drawings. All the drawings date from August and September of 1932 and place the work in the East Cloister Walk, but the dates of production and installation are not known. The installation may post date the drawings by several years (Figures 9).[18]

By 1933 Lord was involved in the rebuilding of All Saints Episcopal Church in Worcester, Massachusetts which had been destroyed by fire in the previous year. This project was also supervised by the firm of Frohman, Robb & Little who were impressed with Lord's work and wanted him involved on the job. In a letter from Harry B. Little to Lord in September, 1933, Mr. Little wrote:

> ...I sincerely wish we were doing a lot of business together, and I hope the time may come when such will

be the case....We have an interesting problem in lighting fixtures for All Saints Church in Worcester, Mass., that will be coming along when, as, and if the parish can raise any money.[19]

Little's two-page, single spaced letter gives a detailed description of the problem of lighting the church and he asks Lord if it:

> ...would...interest you as a pure speculation at this time to work up a design for these four wrought iron fixtures. If they were ordered, and your design accepted, there will eventually be at least ten more like them down the nave.[20]

Lord promptly replied:

> Your lighting problem sounds very interesting to me...and I would like to have a go at these fixtures and I shall be very glad to submit scale sketches....[21]

Before the year ended Lord and Little would exchange over 20 letters concerning the details of the fixtures, but Lord would never make any lighting fixtures for All Saints Episcopal Church. In a letter dated December 21, 1933 E. Donald Robb informed Lord that the job had been given to the Pettingell- Andrews Company of Boston. Robb did inform Lord that he was to proceed with the production of hardware for a memorial door for the church, and he asked Lord to bid on "a wrought iron grille with gates to go to the entrance to the Chapel."[22] A third job involving hardware for another door was also mentioned although a donor had not yet been found to pay for it.

The memorial chancel door had been mentioned in a letter to Lord from Little in October:

> We have some doors and their accompanying hardware to do in the same church. One is a memorial door...(which we will) want to be pretty nice....Could you do something nice for [$]200 or less on these doors?[23]

Lord answered with a two-page letter on October 26, devoting two-thirds of the letter to the lighting fixture question, but at the close stating that "we could certainly do two very nice handles and a latch for each door but there would not be very much left over for hinges" (Figure 10).[24] This was the first of at least four doors at All Saints Episcopal Church for which Lord would make hardware. On April 10, 1934 he submitted individual bills for each door as each was to be paid for by an individual donor. The hardware ranged from $75 to $200 for each door.[25]

Lord was then invited to bid on several other pieces for the church including three hymn boards. That job went to another firm, the W.C. Vaughn Company of Boston who put in "a ridiculously low estimate."[26] Lord hoped to get the nod to do the fancy "wrought iron grille with gates" for the chapel, but this work did not come to him either. It was awarded to Samuel Yellin. Writing to Lord in January of 1934, Harry B. Little announced that:

> The grille and gates for the chapel are being made by Yellin, who is doing the work for the niggardly sum of $1,000—but you and I and Yellin all know very well that it will cost him a great deal more than that; but that was all we could finally jimmy out of the building committee; and Yellin is doing it merely to keep busy regar less [regardless] of the cost. We

Figure 10. Tony Lord worked again with the firm of Frohman, Robb & Little to make door hardware at All Saints Episcopal Church in Worcester, Massachusetts. This project gave Lord an opportunity to design and execute hardware which was more elaborate than some of his earlier work. This door pull with an ornate ring and plate (left, detail below left) was created for the chancel door and incorporates Gothic elements to match the carving on the door. The ring handle for the sacristy passage door (below, right) features a shield decorated with a harp mounted on three interlocking rings descending from a cube. (All photos, drawings Anthony Lord Files.)

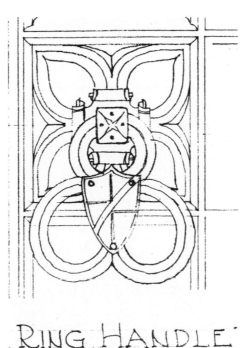

RING HANDLE

Despite the fact that he began his ironworking business during the Great Depression, Tony Lord spared no detail to promote his fledgling enterprise. He used his drawing and designing skills in the creation of his business files and stationary. The files he circulated to prospective clients (above left) included the mark of the stamp he used on his finished pieces of iron, a stylized F-A-F for Flint Architectural Forgings, and a drawing of a large lantern made by Lord for a residence designed by Asheville architect Henry Irven (above right). Lord had his business stationary watermarked with a hanging sign with the business name and logo. He often carried with him a heavy sample of his work to show prospective clients (right). (Lantern photo, Anthony Lord Files.) (Sample 28-1/2x16x1", Author's collection; photo, Tim Barnwell.)

all think it is wrong, but in these days churches seem to be getting the benefit of the unfortunate state of affairs.[27]

Lord may have executed other projects for the church but they are not mentioned in drawings and letters that survive.

In August of 1935 Lord wrote Little to ask, "Nearly a year again, I find, since I have written to you people.... What ever happened in the matter of the hardware for All Saints Church doors? I never happened to hear."[28] Lord was referring to the main doors for the front of the church which he had been requested to bid on.

There are also undated drawings in Lord's records for a street lamp for a Mrs. Battle in Asheville, a mailbox, and a large silhouette sketch of a golfer about to tee off, but the work at the forge on Flint Street was winding down by 1937. Late in his life Lord reflected that he "ran a smith shop until about 1937, when things picked up a bit architecturally and then after that I didn't do any more iron work."[29]

The project that pulled him away from ironwork, or allowed him to leave it, was the design of the Asheville *Citizen-Times* Building in downtown Asheville. Built between 1936 and 1938, it was his first big architectural commission and did receive some national attention. In 1938, he was elected Vice-President of the North Carolina Chapter of the American Institute of Architects, and in 1940 he was elected president. World War II brought several government projects to Lord and the five other designers who collaborated to form Six Associates. Lord never worked with iron again.

FLINT ARCHITECTURAL FORGINGS

Although it is not possible to fully document Lord's business practices at Flint Architectural Forgings, it is possible to reconstruct not only how he promoted the shop's work, but also how he carried out the commissions. His promotional ideas were thoroughly modern while the patterns he used were as old as smithing itself.

Lord was a skillful painter, sketcher and photographer, all of which helped him promote his work to architects and other clients. He made the most use of photography, taking photographs of his ironwork both in the shop and after it was in place on the job. These photos were then printed in bulk and handed or mailed out to potential customers, stamped on the back with either Lord's name or the firm name. It is clear that they were effective; the early letters between Lord and Harry B. Little contain at least four references to Lord's photographs. On September 15, 1933, Little wrote, "I was very interested in the photographs of the hardware you are making for Mr. Rogers at Yale. Your stuff has a genuine feeling about it that is very pleasant." He closed the letter with another reference, noting that his partner, Mr. Robb, was out of the country, "...but I would like to keep these photographs of the Yale hardware for him to see, unless you would like to have me return them at once, which I will do if I so hear from you."[30]

Lord also entered his ironwork in architectural shows. In 1934 he sent two large photographs of a pair of wrought iron gates he made for a house in Biltmore Forest, North Carolina to the annual exhibition of the Architectural League of New York (Figure 11). He also had at least two portfolios of photographs of his work to show to clients. If these portfolios didn't convey the quality of the work being offered, Lord had a sample of his work to carry with him as he made his rounds, so potential clients could see a portion, at

---

...HE RECEIVED CONSIDERABLE HELP FROM THE BOONE BROTHERS, LAWRENCE, WADE AND DANIEL, OF BURNSVILLE, NORTH CAROLINA....

least, of the real thing. This sample seems to duplicate a small section of the Biltmore Forest gate that Lord had photographed and submitted to the exhibition of the Architectural League of New York.

Lord could also write a good letter. Between 1933 and 1935 Lord exchanged over 80 letters and telegrams with either Mr. Robb or Mr. Little. While most of the writing was given over to technical discussions of the details of the design or cost of the work, a type of banter crept in between Lord and Mr. Little, with whom he most often corresponded. Some of the jesting concerned the differences between Swedes and Norwegians, with Lord taking the role of the Swede. Little writes on January 31, 1934:

> We have your letter of January 29th with the weather reports of Asheville, N.C. You say that the cold north wind may perhaps be good for Norwegians but not for you, but you cannot really make me believe that you have Swedish blood in your veins as I know you too well. To me you will always be one of the Norwegians just the same.[31]

No complete list of the workers who helped Lord with the ironwork in the shop on Flint Street exists, but it is clear that he received considerable help from the Boone brothers, Lawrence, Wade and Daniel, of Burnsville, North Carolina. All three worked as blacksmiths in Asheville during

Figure 11. Much of Lord's early architectural ironwork was made for large houses in and around Asheville. These gates at the entrance of a house built for an unknown client in Biltmore Forest, North Carolina are some of Lord's most detailed ironwork. Photographs of these and other projects were circulated to architects and other potential clients to attract future business. (All photos, Anthony Lord Files.)

the 1930s. Wade and Lawrence are listed in the Asheville city directory as working together at various locations in Asheville throughout the 1930s. The city directory for 1937 lists Lawrence Boone working at Flint Architectural Forgings, and letters from 1934 also place Daniel there.[32]

Daniel Boone VI of Burnsville, North Carolina was one of the best known blacksmiths in North Carolina in the 20th century. He came from a long line of smiths, and was said to be a direct descendent of Boone the frontiersman. He learned blacksmithing from his father, Kelse Boone, starting as a helper at the age of eight. By the age of 14 he was working as a smith for a logging company, shoeing horses and repairing gear. But he also showed an early interest in decorative ironwork, preferring "to sketch intricate designs and produce ornamental iron instead of horseshoes."[33] He made andirons, toasting forks, mailboxes, railings, door hardware, and a working model of a steam powered locomotive, complete with cars large enough to carry adults. The train ran on an eighth mile loop of track around a museum Boone opened in Burnsville in the mid-1960s. In the late 1930s he taught ironwork to students at Lees-McRae College in Banner Elk, North Carolina. He also helped produce reproductions of wrought ironwork for the restoration of Williamsburg, Virginia.

> ...I supervised a lot of ironsmiths on that job - all the Boones in the territory. I had my father, my brother Wade, and an uncle working. Had my forge at Spruce Pine then. We had four fires going at one time.[34]

That project lasted for over two years.

In addition to having the benefit of Daniel Boone's considerable skill in his shop, Lord seems to have spun some good stories out of the association with Boone. The members of the firm of Frohman, Robb & Little seemed fascinated with the fact that Daniel Boone was wielding a hammer in Lord's shop. Lord introduced Boone in a letter to Little early in 1934. "The original Coon Skin Boone of Burnsville is

Details, Figure 11.

Top. The interior door handles were modified scrolls with quatrefoil back plates.

Center. Detail, upper door panel.

Bottom. The exterior of the doors included heavy round pulls with geometric sunburst-style decoration.

now holding forth in my shop with great effect and the hardware for the memorial door will shortly be done."[35] Little replied on February 16, "...I wish we could come down and watch the Original Coon Skin Boone of Burnsville knocking out this hardware."[36] A few days later while pointing out that a door in question must be ready for the Easter Service, Little wrote "Give Dan Boone a drink of Texas Fire Chief Gasolene (sic) for pep. I am assured over the radio that this assures quick starting."[37]

Elmo Brown also joined Lord in the shop during this period. Brown was a local resident who was also idled by the lack of business. Lord described Brown in later years as a partner who had fashioned a power hammer for the shop out of a Model T transmission. In a list of his personal effects, Lord also mentions "the old trademark punch which Brownie made,"

which was the stamp used to mark work executed at Flint Architectural Forgings.[38]

Although Lord does refer to Brown as a partner, and acknowledges his skill in the shop, he is not mentioned in any of the business correspondence, and does not seem to have remained connected to Lord's business. This view is supported by his daughter, Miss Eleanore Brown of Asheville.[39]

How extensive was Lord's work at the forge? Or asked another way, who made what? No records exist indicating which smiths made which pieces, but it is clear that as the business grew, and particularly when large projects were involved, the Boones and perhaps other skilled workers did the forging while Lord ran the business, directing the work of the forge and dealing with architects and clients. In a letter to Little in November of 1933, Lord asks "Will there be any hurry about delivery of the door hardware? If there is not, I can do the work myself in odd moments, or rather, odd days, which would be (better)."[40] The following year with several projects going in the shop, Lord comments "...the gang is now at work on the rest of the Huntington Hall Door Hardware...."[41] Clearly the Boones were capable of producing the designs agreed upon by Lord and the church architects.

Lord's sense of design and knowledge of the history of architecture further shaped the collaboration. He had several standards which influenced the ironwork made in his shop. For example, Lord believed that Swedish iron was the best material for wrought ironwork although he would sometimes agree to use "good grade American iron (not steel)"[42] to reduce costs. All of Lord's work was hand wrought and joined with forge welds. Hand wrought meant that it was worked by hand, by men wielding hammers, although Lord did use a power hammer for shaping large pieces. In forge welding, all parts forming a larger piece were welded together by being placed in the forge, heated until they were malleable, then hammered into one piece. This is in contrast to a weld formed with an acetylene torch, which was available during the time that Lord was working, but did not require that the iron pieces be hammered together. Lord would point out to clients that he worked in this way, stating in a letter to an architect that "The hinges etc. would be made as were the hinges of the period—no torch welding—and as well as we know how to make them."[43] This method required the expenditure of considerable human labor and a great deal of coal. One bid for a large gate estimated that four tons of coal would be needed, along with nearly 600 hours of labor. This method and pace of work gave the pieces produced in Lord's shop the appearance mentioned by Harry Little, the "genuine feeling...that is very honest."

What were the design sources for Lord's work? When Lord died he left all his blacksmith tools and books on ironwork to Daniel Miller, a metal worker near Waynesville, North Carolina. Miller who felt Lord was "an excellent smith" observed that Lord never claimed to have done any original design work in the iron he produced, but to have freely conceded the influence of source books on ironwork, and the ironwork he had examined while traveling in Europe.[44] Lord favored in particular English, Italian and Eastern European work.

What Lord especially brought to the work was [the] incredible sense of design that he just soaked up from his travels in Europe and from books...[he] didn't bring anything new technically to the work, what was exceptional was its aesthetic quality.[45]

Miller also notes that judging by the quality of the shop tools that Lord left to him, Lord was a skilled tool maker, with a good understanding of tool tempering and design. He estimates that about two-thirds of the tools in the collection were made in the shop. In a list directing the disposal of his personal effects written shortly before he died in 1993, Lord spoke of his tools:

Many of the old blacksmith shop tools are in the wing off the garage

part of the shop. A lot of the anvil tools are there; hardies, fullers, swages, flatters, cleavers, and such, probably the old trademark punch which Brownie made, my what skill! The anvil is in the living quarters and down in the gardening shed is the punch on a wooden stand, a sledge block and a cone all wonderful and useful tools. Also, a partially finished bolt heading device which we worked on at intervals and decided to make look good looking as well as useful. At the time, we were making many ornamental nails or studs and needed a device in which they could be quickly clamped, upset and headed. There are several small blowers around the place used as forge

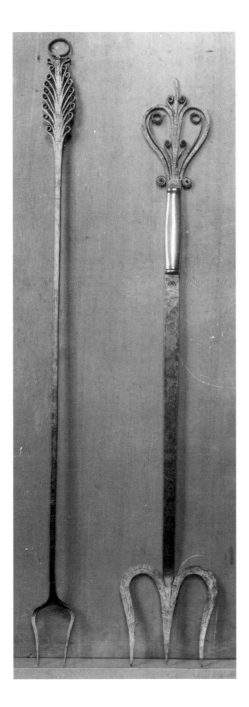

There is little record of Lord's ironwork made for the craft market. These toasting forks, photographed in Lord's shop, may have been marketed through the Southern Highland Handicraft Guild of which Lord was a member. Note his mark on the shorter fork, at the top of the shaft. (Courtesy, Anthony Lord Files.)

These ornate lanterns (above and next page) flanked the entrance drive to In the Oaks in Black Mountain, North Carolina, the summer home of Mr. and Mrs. Franklin S. Terry. Mr. Terry had been a vice-president of General Electric Corporation and in 1913 built In the Oaks, at the time one of the largest private homes in Buncombe County. The property was later given to the Episcopal Diocese of Western North Carolina which uses part of the property as Camp Henry, a summer camp for children. The current location of the lanterns is not known. These undated drawings by Lord (right) show similar lanterns including one still in use at Yale University (below). (Photos, Anthony Lord files; Yale photo, the author.)

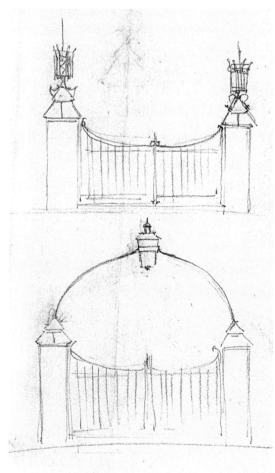

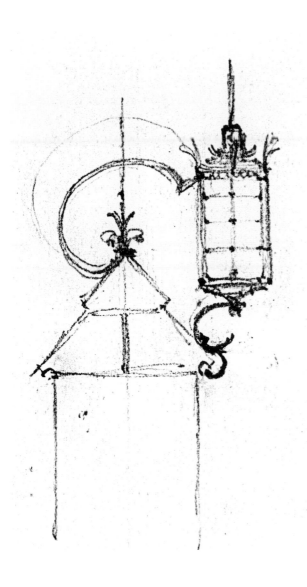

blowers. They were originally parts of oil burners....Smith's tools are simple and generally the smith makes his own for special purposes. I forgot to mention an excellent heavy blacksmiths's vice which is in the cellar at 267. Somebody stole a 300 pound anvil out of Meigan's shed years ago. What a man! Maybe the best bet here would be to turn the stuff over to Dan Miller, formerly the resident artist at Haywood Tech. He is an excellent smith and if he is going to do anything beyond teaching, he might make good use of it. It is absurd to suppose that this stuff can be sold. It has no commercial value.[46]

But the tools once had great commercial value. The tools, like Flint Architectural Forgings, provided a viable livelihood for Lord and his colleagues during the Great Depression. The evidence of

their work is visible at several sites.

Lord possessed experiences, talents and training that contributed to his success. He held degrees both as an engineer and architect, and had been educated in the South and North. He had studied drawing at the Art Student's League in New York City and had worked at a sawmill in the mountains of North Carolina. This range of experience helped him communicate with a wide range of people. Daniel Boone and Lord had both worked in sawmill blacksmith shops, and Lord had traveled for months in France, where James Gamble Rogers and Harry B. Little had studied architecture. Lord had an uncommon set of skills that he used to design and execute his works in iron, and social skills and shared experiences which helped him work with a wide range of co-workers and clients.

Following the Lindbergh kidnaping in 1932 some families increased security around their homes, to the benefit of local ironworkers. Lord installed an iron grille around this porch on a house in Biltmore Forest, just south of Asheville, North Carolina. In a letter to architect Harry B. Little on August 3, 1935, Lord wrote: "The shop has been busy for a couple of months now with some grilles and gates...[which] I rather like the looks of, and [they] should be good protection against human and insect prowlers....This little spurt of business is due, I believe to the kidnaping scare as there are both money and a baby in the family." (Photo, Anthony Lord Files.)

Notes

1. Six Associates is now known as ENG/GA.
2. Anthony Lord and Elizabeth Kostova, *1927 The Good-Natured Chronicle of a Journey* (Asheville, North Carolina: the Captain's Bookshelf, 1995).
3. John L. Bell Jr., *Beginnings of the Great Depression in North Carolina* (Raleigh: North Carolina Division of Archives and History, 1982), pp.14-21.
4. Bruce Johnson, interview conducted with Tony Lord, May 17, 1993, published in "Pebbledash" January 1994, (monthly newsletter of the Preservation Society of Asheville and Buncombe County Inc.).
5. Anthony Lord, "Sawdust Reminiscence," unpublished and undated text of speech delivered to the Pen and Plate Club, Asheville, North Carolina.
6. Lord and Kostova, p. 22.
7. Maggie Lauterer, "Age Has Not Dulled Architect's Mental Vision," Asheville *Citizen-Times*, August 19, 1988.
8. Johnson, p. 4.
9. Almost all of the records, drawings and photographs of Lord's ironwork were left at Lord's death to Myron Gauger who then gave them to the author. Documentation of the ironwork projects varies considerably. Some of the projects are documented with drawings, letters, correspondence and photographs, while others have only a few drawings or photos. There is likely some work for which there is no documentation. The work at All Saints Episcopal Church in Worcester, Massachusetts is represented with blueprints, tracings, photographs and over 75 pieces of correspondence. There are few records relating to local projects, and none relating to the mending of tools since that was likely a walk-in business which did not involve photography or drawings. It is only known because Lord mentioned this in later years.
10. "James G. Rogers, Architect, Is Dead," obituary, *The New York Times*, October 2, 1947, p.27.
11. Aaron Betsky, *James Gamble Rogers and the Architecture of Pragmatism*, (New York: Architectural History Foundation, 1994), pp. 56-58.
12. See Betsky pp.116-119 for a discussion of Rogers' role as consulting architect to the Yale Corporation and his activities following the death of Goodhue. Lord might have competed for the ironwork for later Goodhue buildings had Goodhue lived. Tony Lord could have reminded Goodhue that Lord's father, William Lord, had been the supervising architect for the construction of Trinity Episcopal Church in Asheville, North Carolina which Goodhue had designed.
13. Betsky, pp. 119-120.
14. Leland M. Roth, *A Concise History of American Architecture* (New York: Harper and Row, 1979), p. 250.
15. Robert Boyce, Art Department, Berea College, Berea, Kentucky in a letter to the author January 13, 1999 describes Niles' comments as coming from a "loose leaf note book that is signed by both J. J. Niles and his wife Rena which discusses photos 79, 152, and 153." These numbers refer to Doris Ulmann photos.
16. Betsky, pp. 56-58.
17. "Philip Hubert Frohman Dies; Designed Washington National Cathedral," *The New York Times*, October 31, 1972, p. 48.
18. It is not clear from Harry B. Little's letters when he became aware of Lord's work or if the Washington National Cathedral work was installed before or after the work at All Saints Episcopal Church.
19. Harry B. Little to Tony Lord, September 15, 1933.
20. Ibid.
21. Tony Lord to Harry B. Little, September 22, 1933.
22. E. Donald Robb to Tony Lord, December 21, 1933.
23. Harry B. Little to Tony Lord, October 10, 1933.
24. Tony Lord to Harry B. Little, October 26, 1933.
25. Four bills dated April 10, 1934 were sent with a letter from Tony Lord to Miss McLean of Frohman, Robb & Little.
26. Harry B. Little to Tony Lord, March 20, 1934.
27. Harry B. Little to Tony Lord, January 31, 1934, pp. 1-2.
28. Tony Lord to Harry B. Little, August 3, 1935.
29. Johnson, p. 4.

30. Harry B. Little to Tony Lord, September 15, 1933.
31. Harry B. Little to Tony Lord, January 31, 1934.
32. Lawrence Boone is listed in *Miller's Asheville, North Carolina City Directory Vol. XXXIV* (Asheville, N.C.: Piedmont Directory Co., 1937), p.84; Lawrence and Wade Boone are listed in the 1936 Directory (p.156); and Lawrence is listed in two locations in the 1939 Directory (p.75). Several letters mention Daniel Boone in Lord's shop: Harry B. Little to Tony Lord on February 16,19 and 23, 1934, and Tony Lord to Harry B. Little on February 27, 1934.
33. John Parris, "Daniel Hammered A Legend On The Anvil," Asheville *Citizen*, November 8, 1970.
34. Articles on Boone include Jean Ritchie, "Dan'l Boone VI", *Collier's*, May 10, 1952, pp. 56-57; Frances B. Floore, "Daniel Boone VI a Burnsville Smithy," *News and Observer*, Raleigh, North Carolina, July 3, 1966, p. III-9, " Daniel Boone VI," *American Magazine*, February 1953, p. 48; Edward Dupuy and Emma Weaver, *Artisans of the Appalachians*, (Asheville N.C.: Miller Printing Company, 1967), pp. 110-111.
35. Tony Lord to Harry B. Little, February 13, 1934.
36. Harry B. Little to Tony Lord, February 16, 1934.
37. Harry B. Little to Tony Lord, February 19, 1934.
38. The Model T is mentioned in *Anthony Lord, A Retrospective*, (Asheville, North Carolina: Asheville Art Museum, 1984), p.12.
39. Interview with Miss Eleanore Brown, March 9, 1999.
40. Tony Lord to Harry B. Little, November 7, 1933, p.2.
41. Tony Lord to Harry B. Little, March 28, 1934.
42. Tony Lord to the firm of Frohman, Robb & Little, January 4, 1934.
43. Tony Lord to E. Donald Robb, June 14, 1934, p.2.
44. Two publications in Tony Lord's library which may have provided design sources, Ulrico Hoepli, editor, *Il Ferro Battuto, Sbalzato E Cesellato* (New York: E. Weyhe, 1929); *Forged Iron Hardware, Catalog No. 6* (Pittsburgh: McKinney Manufacturing Company, 1929).
45. Interview with Daniel Miller, April 24, 1999.
46. Anthony Lord, "List for Executor, Personal Effects," unpublished, December 2, 1993, p. 6.

Tony Lord donated this adjustable bridge lamp to the Asheville Art Museum in 1981. It incorporated a wide range of decorative elements and is felt by many to be one of his best pieces of ironwork. (Courtesy Asheville Art Museum; photo, Frank Thompson.)

Western North Carolina is in the midst of very rapid social change. Rural communities once based on the rhythms of agriculture are now home to light industry and residential developments. Economies once based on local goods and services are increasingly based on international markets and global communication. To older people, some of whom grew up in an essentially pre-industrial culture, it must feel as though the very ground is shifting beneath their feet. People mark these changes in very different ways, some collect old photographs, some work on family genealogies and some write and sing of the old times and ways. Bill Hart has an unusual way of noting change and hedging against the cultural losses he senses. For many years he has read the obituary pages of the local newspaper and recorded names he felt may be passing into extinction. —R. B.

Emalucy, Hooney, Twitchell, Eranious and Golden Meldonia:
An Informal Study of Western North Carolina Names

By William A. Hart Jr.

I feared that the names would be forgotten. It was this simple concern that resulted in collecting old Christian names of persons born in Western North Carolina. The thought of saving these names developed gradually as I read the obituary pages and noticed the deaths of older Western North Carolinians with interesting first names. The names that appealed to me most were those which differed from the norm, names with a certain charm and uniqueness. These names are remnants of earlier naming practices when the region was primarily rural and less under the influence of mass communications.

At first, I simply read and enjoyed the names, but in time I realized that many of these names were unlikely to be used again, and with their disappearance a small part of the region's history would be forgotten.[1] I have recorded over 1500 names since I began keeping records in 1985. I wanted to preserve and honor names used primarily in the first 30 years of this century in the hope that others may choose to select them in the future.

My interest in unusual names began with members of my own family. My maternal great-grandfather was John Anthony Reeves from the Little Sandy Mush section of Madison County, North Carolina. He married Rachel Clementine Ferguson from Haywood County. They raised 11 children and gave several of them interesting names: Farady, Mallie Boyd, Etta Angie, William Ebed, Lura Mae, Plato Vance, Bertha Mary, Amanda (Maud), Riley Jefferson, Otto Atkins, and Jerome Lyda.[2] (Figure 1). Mallie Reeves, my grandfather, married Cora Della Brown. They named my mother Mabel Savannah. Names from preceding Reeves generations included Malachi, Jincy Jane, William Zachariah, and Claracy Avie.[3]

I have followed a few guidelines in selecting names. Generally, I recorded the names of people who were in their 70s, 80s and 90s when they died. I recorded gender, age and the date of the obituary notice. I have collected primarily first names and have not included nicknames or names expressed as initials. In some cases, it was not possible to determine gender. These names are recorded at the end of the alphabetized listing. No effort has been made to record race or ethnicity.

Most of the collected names were for persons born in the 14 counties of Western North Carolina; Cherokee, Clay, Graham, Macon, Swain, Jackson, Haywood, Transylvania, Buncombe, Henderson, Madison, Yancey, Mitchell and Avery. In rare instances, I selected names from the Western Piedmont counties of Polk, Rutherford and McDowell when the charm of a name was too compelling to omit it from my collection. The *Asheville Citizen-Times* obituary pages are the source of most of the names.

If all people are created equal, it might

be argued that all people have the right to value their names equally and view them with the same esteem as royalty. This was impressed upon me 40 years ago by a story told by Orpha Shuford, a man who was born and lived in the Barnardsville section of Buncombe County. He was called "Orph" by his friends.

When a lad, Mr. Shuford was hoeing corn on a hot summer day at his family's farm when an automobile drove up the road and stopped by the field where he was working. A man got out and addressed him, "Young man, I bet you don't know who I am." Mr. Shuford replied, "No, sir, I don't," to which the man responded, "I'm Henry Ford." Mr. Shuford's unhesitating response was, "And I bet you don't know who I am either, I'm Orph Shuford."[4]

Many names come with a story. My mother's name, Mabel Savannah, was the result of a compromise. My grandmother's sister, Savannah, told my grandmother, "If you'll name the baby after me, I'll make her a white serge coat."[5] My grandmother was reluctant to use Savannah as a first name

and used it as a middle name instead. Presumably, this arrangement satisfied her sister and resulted in a new coat for Mabel Savannah.

In other cases, names are uniquely creative as illustrated by a story told by the late Nancy Brown, former owner of the Book Mart in Biltmore, North Carolina. During World War II, Miss Nancy Brown lived in Erwin, Tennessee, and worked as a public health nurse in Eastern Tennessee. Her job entailed registering new babies, giving them inoculations and providing child care instructions to new mothers. She gave this account of one of her visits. "One day I visited a good-natured woman…who had recently had a baby. When I asked her the name of the baby, she responded, 'Hit's Ragus.' I told her that was an interesting name and inquired how she chose it, to which the woman replied, 'Hit's sugar spelled backwards.'"[6]

Several patterns are evident in the origins and sources of names. Some names such as Glenella, Luegene and Jo-Benard may be the result of combining a portion of

Figure 1. The children of John and Rachel Clementine Ferguson Reeves pose for this photograph in the South Turkey Creek section of Buncombe County, ca. 1902. Left to right. Front row, Plato, Etta, Mallie (author's maternal grandfather), Lura, Jerome and Farady; back row, Bertha, Otto, Riley, Will and Maud. (Courtesy, Evelyn Reeves Taylor.)

one or both of the parents' first names to create a new name. Some unusual names may be the result of uncertain or phonetic spelling: "Eyner" for Ina, "Irl" for Earl and "Niner" for Nina. Other patterns include the following:

Geographic Names:
  Kansas, Indiana, Manila, Miami, Iowa, Vienna
Famous People and Titles:
  Commodore Perry, Christopher Columbus, Cicero, Woodrow Wilson, Plato, Taft, Lafayette, Judge, General
Biblical Names:
  Ezekiel, Obidiah, Ishmael
Mythological Names:
  Atlas, Ulysses, Romulus, Aurora
Character Traits:
  Charity, Love, Meek
Names of Birds and Flowers:
  Narcissis, Arbutus, Swan, Dovie, Ibis
Girls' Names Ending in "ie":
  Fleecie, Allie, Jencie, Dessie

This study addresses names popular in the early 20th century, but what names will be favored in the early 21st century? One writer predicts the top five girls' names in 2008 will be Alexis, Madeline, Emma, Sydney and Gabriel, and that the most popular boys' names will be William, Michael, Zachery, Austin and Noah.[7] It will be interesting for a later scholar to reflect upon which names seem close to extinction in Western North Carolina in the late 21st century.

FEMALE NAMES

Abalean	Arnessa
Ablene	Arnetter
Addie	Arrie
Adgie	Arsie
Affie Mae	Arthia
Aggie	Arthie
Aglestia	Artie
Aileen	Arvenia
Alaf	Arvilla
Alberta	Arwilder
Albif	Athleen
Alcovia	Atlas
Aletha	Attawa
Alfa	Attlas
Alga	Aubree
Algeria	Aurelia
Algie	Aurora
Alice	Austrella
Allie	Aver
Alma Mary Janie	Averyl
Alonzie	Avie
Alpha	Azalea
Alphamae	Azalia
Alsie	Azelia
Alta	Azoline
Althelnar	Barthemia
Altunia	Baye
Alura	Bedell
Alwayne	Belah
Alyce	Belle
Alza	Belvia
Amarintha	Belzora
America Jolina	Bergie
Amie	Berlyn
Anetha	Bernita
Annice	Bertsie
Anzora	Bervilee
Arbutus	Beryl
Ardell Bone	Beta
Arey	Bethie
Argana	Bettystein
Argylle	Beulon
Arie	Beuna
Arietta	Bevie
Arleasie	Bexie
Arlecia	Bida
Armildia	Biddie
Arminta	Biddie Beth Anna
	Bird
	Birdella

Birdie
Bitha
Bleka
Blossie
Blye
Bonada
Bonetta
Britty Mae
Bueton
Bulena
Burdell
Burla
Burlie
Burr
Byra
Callie
Camilla
Candus
Canty
Carene
Carma
Carmon
Carra
Carta
Cartha
Cartie
Cashie
Cassie
Celestial
Cena
Cesareen
Charity
Charlesina
Chassie
Cherrie
Chetta Mae
Chetty
China
China Bea
Chinara
Chineary
Chloe
Christabell
Christell
Cilla
Cippie
Clairine
Claranette
Clarcie
Clarine

Cleethel
Clema
Clemis
Clemmie
Clestelle
Cleva
Cloa
Clota Lee
Clyda
Clyde
Colena
Cora Lee
Cordia
Cordie
Corona
Coza
Cremo
Creola
Cubie
Cumi
Cumy
Daffina
Dahlia
Daintey
Dallie Louise
Dallise
Daphnic
Darris
Data
Datha
Debranda
Decie
DeEtta
Deffie
Delcie
Delda
Delee
Delia
Delie Lee
Delight
Delitha
Della
Dellma
Delova
Delovia
Delphia
Delsie
Delta
Delza
Delzie

Dema
Demia
Derosette
Derotha
Desma Mae
Dess
Dessie
Desta
Destrula
Detossie
Diord
Dissie
Divola
Doch
Docia
Dolether
Dollie Mae
Dona
Donia
Donie
Doras
Dorial
Dosha
Doshey
Doshia
Dosie
Doskie
Douschkia
Dova
Dovenia
Dovie Mae
Dovil
Drama
Drucilla
Duga
Dullie Kate
Dupre
E. LeVenia
Early
Earshlie
Easter
Ebbie
Eddith
Edra
Edrie
Edris
Effa
Effie Ella
Elfleda
Elia

Eliza
Ellarmae
Eller Belle
Elna
Elva
Elwynne
Elynora
Elzie
Elzora
Ema Elizabeth
Emaline
Emalucy
Ena
Enis
Enna
Era
Erah
Ercie
Eria
Ersie
Ertha Elizabeth
Escue
Essie
Esta
Estalee
Estey
Estie
Estoy
Estrel
Etha
Etrulia
Ettress
Eugenie
Eula
Eulala
Eunay

The family of Samuel Blakely and Lavina Johnson Lovin in Graham County, ca. 1886. The back row includes (left to right) nephew Osco Sneed, Sara Lovin Sneed, Samuel Blakely Lovin, Lavina (holding Ripp), and Dallas. Osco's brothers and sisters included Peco, Viola, Manco and Iowa. (Courtesy, Don Mills, Graham County Heritage Vol. I, Walsworth Publishing Co., Don Mills, Inc., 1992, p. 147.)

The Vista and Columbus Robinson family of the Burnsville area of Yancey County. Their four children were Welzy (front row, far left) and Mack, Missouri and Melvin (back row, left to right). Other relations, included Zilphia, Vandalia, Zenas and Perida. (Courtesy, Lloyd Bailey, The Heritage of the Toe River Valley, Volume II 1997, Walsworth Publishing Co., p. 357; photo possibly by Jack Ramseur.)

Eupha	Fleedie	Gennetie	Ilean
Euphia	Fleeta	Gerlie	Ilene
Eura	Fleeto	Gesna	Imogene
Eurie	Flemmie	Gillie	Indiana
Eursley	Fleta	Ginus	Iness
Evalyn	Flo	Girthia	Intha
Everlena	Floiree	Glee	Iona
Evlet	Flora Mitty	Glene	Iowa
Evylene	Florabell	Glennella	Iowa Lecie
Exie	Florrie	Glennie	Irie
Exum	Flossie	Glennis	Ironee
Eyner	Flota	Glera	Isabella
Fairie Ellen	Floy Laura	Gliftie	Islean
Fairlee	Floya	Gliftylee	Iva Lera
Falicia	Fora	Glyde	Ivarae
Fanella	Fourtha	Golden Meldonia	Ivory
Fannie Mae	Freeda	Goldia	Izola
Farmie	French	Gomery	Jacksie
Farra	Fronie	Gordie	James Albun
Felicia	Fuchia	Gradie	Jamie
Femie	Fuchsia	Guilna	Jamima
Femmie	Fusha	Gursie	Jaundree
Fern	Garda	Gussie	Jencie
Fernie	Gartha	Gypsy	Jennedie
Fidelia	Gazzie	Hallie	Jennive
Finey	Gearene	Hannie Rachel	Jenova
Flara	Gearl	Hariette Manerva	Jensey
Flaude	Gela	Hassie Mae	Jensie
Fleecie	Gencie	Hattie Mae	Jervey
Fleeda	Genncie	Hela	Jessie Luna
		Hellen	Jettie
		Helma Mae	Jincie
		Helyn	Jo-Ben
		Hermie	JoBesse
		Hessie Belle	Johnsie
		Hester	Jometa
		Hettie	Jonella
		Hezzie	Joretta
		Hicks	Jossie Marie
		Hilma	Judia
		Honorine	Jund
		Hope	Junie
		Hulda	Kansas
		Ibbie	Katherleen
		Ibeuria	Kayte
		Ibis	Kella
		Icia	Keren
		Idella	Kettie
		Idola	Kitter
		Ila	Kitty

Kodell	Loduska	Malissie	Minta
Lacie	Logner	Mallie	Mintalou
Lacy	Loice	Mallye	Mintha
Ladelia	Lola Iola	Malva	Mintie
Lakey	Loma	Mamie	Missouri
Lala	Lona	Mammie	Mittie
Lali	Lona Belle	Mana	Modean
Lanelle	Lonia	Manila	Monnie Lou
LaRue	Lonora	Maphrie	Monta
Lasca	Loree	Marcella	Mora
Lassie·	Lossie	Mardecia	Murphy Ann
Lattie	Lota	Mardell	Mutie
Laurunetta	Lottie	Marilla	Mynota
Lavada	Loudella	Marvie	Myrene
Laveita	Lovata	Marylene	Myrth
Lavenia	Love	Marywill	Nada
Lear	Lovey	Masie	Nadge
Leatha	Lovicia	Matilda Elee	Nannie
Lecie	Lovie	Mattie	Naphra
Leeila	Lowee	Maude	Narcissus
Legia	Lucretia	Maudie	Narmie
Leilla	Lucy Lou	Mauveline	Neaner
Lella	Luegene	Maxie	Nebraska
Leneta	Luise	Maymee	Neley
Lennie Lee	Lula	Maymie	Nemola
Leola	Luna	Maythorne	Nepel
Lephar	Lura	Mayzola	Nepul
Lesa	Lurline	Mazaline	Nessmith
Lessell	Luthena	Mazel	Nettie
Lessie	Lutlelia	Mazeline	Nevada Missouri
Leta	Luzene	Mazie	Nezbit
Leucittia	Mabee	Meanie	Nicie
Leva	Mabel Savannah	Media	Nimmo
Levornia	Mabry	Medie	Niner
Lexie	Mabyn	Meed	Nishia
Lexine	Macy	Meldona	Noba
Lida	Madel	Meldonia	Nola
Liddia	Madeth	Mellie	Nonive
Liddie	Madie	Melverna	Nonnie
Lilpah Rebecca	Madora	Melvina	Nonnieve
Linchie	Maeburr	Merfule	Noriene
Linnie Dell	Maedine	Mettie	Nota
Lissie	Mafra	Miami	Notre
Lithia	Mafria	Milda	Nova
Lizzette	Maggie Ozella	Mildia Burnetta	Novile
Lizzie Dee	Magnetta	Milla	Nyder
Loada	Mailishia	Milon	Nyles
Loammia	Maleta	Milton	Oakla
Lockey	Malissa	Minda	Obera
Lockie	Malissia	Minnie Loe	Oberia

Ocie Rosella	Oshia	Poshie	Starr
Octa	Ossie	Prince Ola	Stellar
Octavia	Ota	Princie	Sudie
Octia	Ouida	Queen	Swan
Odee	Oveda	Queenie	Sybrinnie
Odema	Ovilla	Rayford Stella	Tassie Mae
Oif	Owa Lola	Reatha	Teanie Mae
Oley	Ozetta	Reeva	Tebbie
Olive	Pallie	Relda	Telka
Ollie	Palma	Rell	Tempie
Olsie	Pantha	Rellie Lee	Tempy
Oma	Para Lee	Renzie	Teney
Omah	Paralee	Ressie	Tennie Mae
Omega	Parlee	Reta	Tessie
Omie	Parrah	Retta	Texa
Ona	Patra	Rettie	Texanna
Onabea	Patrae	Revena	Texie Anne
Oneva	Pearl Savannah	Rhee	Tharon
Oney	Pearle	Rhuemna	Theophia
Onie	Pearleen	Riddie	Theora
Onnie Ethel	Pearlie	Rissie	Thora
Onolee	Perchie	Robena Iona	Thosa
Opha	Pereda	Roby	Tiela
Opie	Pettrenella	Roma	Tilda
Opievee	Phame DeVenny	Rosey	Tincie
Ora	Pherne	Rosha	Tincy
Orah	Phronie	Rossie	Tishue
Orie	Phylona	Roxanna	Tokie
Origanna	Pluma	Roxie	Toy
Orita	Pocohontas	Rozalia	Trannie
Orla Mae	Polley	Rubenia	Trivola
Orpha	Porshie	Ruie	Trynnie
Orphia Mae	Posey	Rushell	Tula
		Rushia	Tulen
		Russie	Tulon
		Rutha	Una
		Sali	Unavee
		Salinda	Ura
		Sarah Glee	Urie
		Seivwers	Utha Mae
		Selelia	Uva Maude
		Selenia	Vacie
		Sena	Vadie
		Sibbie	Vaeria
		Signa	Valare
		Siscley	Valeree
		Slate	Vallie
		Snoe	Vanarah
		Sophronia	Vashti
		Starlie	Vashtie

The family of G.W. Tomberlin, Yancey County, North Carolina, ca.1901. Left to right. Front row, beginning third from left, Auron, G.W. Tomberlin and Mary Elzie Tomberlin; back row, Nola, Lollie, Texanna and Gazarine. (Courtesy, Lloyd Bailey, The Heritage of the Toe River Valley, *Volume II, 1997, Walsworth Publishing Co., p. 392.)*

Vastie
Vauchanta
Vaughtie
Vauldie
Veanah
Velcey
Velvia
Vendetta
Venia
Vennie
Venora
Verda
Verdie Mae
Verlan
Verlee
Verneena
Vernie
Versa
Versie
Vertie
Vervena
Vessie
Vesta
Vester
Veva
Vever
Vicie
Vienna
Villa
Vina
Vinetta
Vinia
Vinnie
Viola
Viona
Virgie
Vista Eula
Vistie
Viva
Vonnie
Vyola
Wanatha
Waneta
Watha
Waudie
Wavie
Wilfa
Wilhelminia
Willadean
Willo

Willodean
Willoree
Wilsie Mae
Winnie Mae
Winona
Wylma
Zadah
Zadie
Zagie
Zannie
Zara
Zeffra
Zelda
Zelia
Zell
Zella
Zelma
Zelpha Mae
Zelphia
Zenna
Zennie
Zenobia
Zenolva
Zenovia
Zeomia
Zera
Zerilda
Zeta
Zetta
Zettie
Zilla Bell
Zilpha
Zinnie
Zoe

Zoie Bell
Zola
Zola Lee
Zollie
Zona Mae
Zonia
Zula Mae
Zura

MALE NAMES

Abrahart
Adger
Alga
Almer
Alvah
Alver
Alvin Tighe
Alvish
Alvoid
Ambers
Amble
Angus
Annis
Anon
Ansel
Anzlee
Arbeth
Arcemus
Ardis
Arlett Columbus
Arney
Arseamus
Arson
Arthar

Artis
Arvelyn
Arvid
Arvis
Asa
Asbury
Astor
Atmon Clura
Atticus
Aud
Audie
Aughyer
Augustus
Auttie
Ayard
Ayscue
Azrie
Azure
Baccus
Back
Baile
Bam
Baxter
Bayard Elijah
Bealer
Beeler
Beler
Berdell
Berry
Beuford
Bevily
Bickett
Birdir
Bis

Will and Depina Blanton pose with their 13 children in the Ochre Hill section of Jackson County in 1900. Many nicknames are as interesting as given names. Left to right. Front row, Berry (Christian Berry), Hute (Houston); second row, Will, Piney (Depina), Monroe (James Monroe), Alice (Mary Jane Alice), Ham (William Hamilton); third row, Mariah (Lucretia Mariah), Charlie, Hester, Cumi (Talitha Cumi); fourth row, Erastus, Rob (Robert Lee), Mann (George Manuel) and John. Will Blanton's nickname was "Sheriff" in memory of the time he ran for the Sheriff of Jackson County and received one vote. (Courtesy, Rick Frizzell, Jackson County Heritage North Carolina *Vol. II 1992, Jackson County Genealogical Society, Walsworth Publishing Co., 1992, p.81.)*

Most families used names from a variety of sources including biblical and historical references, some familiar and some not. Here the family of Washington Lafayette Curtis (known as "Wash") and Nancy Saunders Curtis pose with some of their children. Left to right. Front row, Julius Hightower, "Wash," Ernest Howard and Nancy; back row, Mary Timoxenia, Anna and Margarette. (Courtesy, The Heritage of Macon County North Carolina *1987, Jessie Sutton, Editor, Hunter Publishing Company, Winston-Salem, North Carolina, p.206.)*

		Commodore	Earsie
		Cona	Echerd
		Coralie	Eckle
		Cos Napolean	Edley
		Coye	Edwion
		Coze	Elba
		Crait	Ellard
		Cread	Elles
		Creed	Elmo
		Cress Well	Elmon
		Crom	Elroy
		Cullie	Elsberry
		Cullis	Eltis
		Culver	Elwin
		Cyrus	Elzie
		Daitus	Emmot
		Dalma	Enoch
		Daphfney	Enzy
		Darcus	Eranious
		Dawes	Erastus
Biss	Carll	Deaston	Erca
Blannie	Carnal	Decard	Erdnal
Bluford	Carsie	Dee	Ernest Rethual
Bluphard	Carthie Malachia	Deelee	Errold
Blythal	Cash	Deff	Ersie
Boice	Casone Faungo	Delious	Eslie
Bon	Cassius	Delmar	Essmond
Bonner	Cennis	Delmer	Estes
Boydston	Chalmus	Delos	Estom
Bragg	Champ	Delzie	Eston
Branchville	Chaunley	Demus	Estoy
Bristo	Chivous	Denvis	Eular
Brodes	Cicero	Dercie	Eurschel Ubert
Bron	Clay	Derieux	Evert
Brown	Clee	Derry	Exer
Brownlow	Clellan	Derwerd	Ezekiel
Bulen	Cleofus	Desford	Fairl
Bulo	Cleon	DeVoe	Fairlight
Bunyan	Cleophus	Deward	Faraday
Burder	Cletus	Docer	Farlan
Burger	Cleve	Dock	Fate
Burgon	Clindon	Donford	Fatie
Burla	Cline	Dorsie	Fayne
Burm	Clingman	Doss	Feltz
Burnis	Clint	Dosser	Ferrell
Burzell	Clyne	Dowers	Fessie
Byard	Coby	Dowzell	Filete
Bynum Herbert	Coley	Durgin	Flavel
Caesar	Columbus	Eamus	Flaville
Came	Coman	Earshel	Flavius

William A. Hart Jr. ■ AN INFORMAL STUDY OF WESTERN NORTH CAROLINA NAMES

Flay	Herv	Joby	Latt
Fleet	Hesey	Johnsie	Lattie
Fleetwood	Heston	Jonie	Lawson
Flint	Hiawatha	Jude	Laxton
Fondly	Hilery	Judge	Leamon
Fonslow	Hobson Hirman	Jule	Leanes
Foy	Homer	Julius	Leeland
Fralow	Hooney	Junard	Leen
Frend	Hooper	Juney	Lehmon
Friel	Hoy	Junius	Lemie
Fuce Henry	Hulan	Junnius	Lemmie
Gaither	Hulet	Jurea	Lemuel
Ganes	Iler	Kettern	Lensey
Garlan	Irl	Kiah	Letch
Garmon	Isaac	Kidder	Letcher
Garnett	Ishmael	Kimsie	Levister
Garney	Isie	Klinworth	Lewie
Garvis	Ismel	Knowles	Lexter
Gay	Jace	Kye	Lige
Gedwin	Jadie	Kynzer	Ligie
General	James Von	Lafayette	Litton
Geter	Jasper	Lairl	Locke
Gilleard	Jennings	Landie	Loly
Gladstone	Jep	Landry	Lonas
Glenwood	Jeter	Larch	Loner
Gline	Jirden	Larens	Lono Bill
Gola	Jirden John	Lark	Loomis
Gomery	Jobie	Larkin	Loranzie
Goran			
Gordie			
Gornie			
Gracian			
Granville			
Green			
Greenberry			
Groce			
Guston			
Halford Agusta			
Hall			
Hallet			
Halmond			
Hardoman			
Harl			
Harla			
Harlie Gollette			
Harve			
Haven			
Hayne			
Haze			
Henri			

John Douglas McConnell, blacksmith, (far right) and his second wife Martary Vernitta (second from right with child on her lap) are pictured in front of their home in the Bethel Community of Macon County in 1898 with several McConnell children. Left to right, Anna Arizona, Dolly Clarinda, Statira, Ida, William and John. (Courtesy, The Heritage of Macon County North Carolina 1987, *Jessie Sutton, Editor, Hunter Publishing Company, Winston-Salem, North Carolina, p. 344.)*

Lovel Delmas
Lovey
Lovin
Loy
Loye
Luches Vaudney
Ludie
Ludy
Lum
Lummie
Lunnie
Lusco
Lush
Luster
Macole
Mailon
Mainous
Major
Malgram
Mallie
Manassie
Mannie Lee
Manson
Manson Dock
Manus
Marba
Mays
McFee
McQuide
Mead
Medus

Meek
Meldrun
Melzo
Memary
Memory
Memphis
Milas
Milo
Mont
Mose
Murhl
Murt
Namon
Nane
Narl
Nave
Nealie
Need
Nehemiah
Ney
Noal
Noble
Noe
Nural
Oakie
Obed
Obidiah
Obie
Obray
Ocol
Odd
Ode Fred
Odies
Odis
Odus
Ogreater
Okal
Oke
Ollen
Olus Roy
Oren
Orse Theodore
Orval
Orves
Ottaway
Ottis
Otus
Ova
Ovie Zeno
Oviet

Owren
Ozville
Paden
Padey
Page
Parley
Paru
Paunee
Pelvin
Percival
Philetus Victor
Philo
Plato
Plez
Plumer
Plummer
Pralo
Quay
Quinton
R. Sezar
Radney
Rafe
Raleigh
Rankin
Rannell
Ransom
Rant
Raphael
Rasho
Rass
Raymus
Raynous
Recy
Rhuben
Rial
Rixie
Robie
Roby
Rogers
Rom
Rombo
Romulus
Roosevelt
Rotha
Rothy
Ruben
Rufe
Rufus
Rumbo
Ruport

Samie
Sankey
Savoy
Seamen
Selph
Selwyn
Shearod
Sherlie
Shifley
Shufford
Sink
Slite
Solan
Solon
Speedy
Squire
Starling
Sterling
Stokes
Stonewall Jackson
Swan
Sydenham
Taft
Tallus
Tarp
Tascol
Ted Cling
Tench
Theadore
Theodore
Thonnie
Tice
Tillery
Tolliver
Tomhall
Tonie
Toy
Trilby
Tubie
Tull
Turner
Tux
Twitchell
Ulas
Ulus Vascom
Ulyses
Ulysses
Vader
Vaxter
Velt

The John B. and Ibby Robinson family, Yancey County, North Carolina. Left to right. Front row, Fred, Manassa ("Nass"); second row, Ibby Dulcenia, John B., Millard Filmore; back row, Mary Adocia, William and Suel. (Courtesy, Lloyd Bailey, The Heritage of the Toe River Valley, *Volume II, 1997, Walsworth Publishing Co., p. 360.)*

Venis	Whit
Vennear	Wig
Vennoy	Wilder
Venus	Will
Veodus	Willie
Verdra	Wilse
Verge	Wintfred
Vester	Wirron
Vestie	Wix
Virgus	Woodfin
Voaid	Woodford
Vollie	Woodrow Wilson
Vonno	Woolsey
Vorrest	Worthen
Vynoy	Wres
Wadsworth	Wroe
Waie	Wyitt
Waits	Wylie
Waitsel	Wymer
Waitsul	Yoder Pinkey
Wanzel	Yuit
Waverly	Zack
Way	Zade
Waye	Zeatees
Weaver	Zebulon
Welzie	Zell
Welzy	Zemery
Wentford	Zeno
Western	Ziska

This undated photograph of the George Barton family in the Cathey's Creek section of Transylvania County includes Rufus, Harkles, (front row, 3rd and 5th from left) Mildred and Seldon (back row, 6th and 7th from left). Daughter Beulah is not pictured. Several of their ancestors were named Latha, Dameris, Elihu and Millington known as "Mint." (Courtesy, Don Mills, Transylvania County Heritage *1995, Walsworth Publishing Co., Don Mills Inc., 1996, p.79.)*

NAMES OF UNDETERMINED GENDER

Alcie	Kessie
Alverta	Lafus Sid
Arlevia	Landie
Belvie	Lannau
Birdie Mae	Larkin
Cester	Lawt
Dezey	Lelloween
Dimple	Loccie
Esper	Lona
Eunie	Namer
Fadie	Nebraska
Fronnie	Olivan
Garthain	Phlenia
Greenberry	Tecora
Haskit	Thurl
Jeruska	Trula
Juandree	Welzie
Judson	Zettie

Notes

1. The top 10 girls' names nationally in 1990 were Brittany, Ashley, Jessica, Amanda, Sarah, Megan, Caitlin, Samantha, Stephanie and Katherine. The most popular boys' names were Michael, Christopher, Matthew, Joshua, Andrew, Nicholas, Ryan, Justin, David and Daniel. Hollis L. Engley, "How and Why We Choose the Names That We Do," *Asheville Citizen-Times*, May 19, 1996. Ed. note: Out of the top 10 list of girls' names in 1990, only the names Amanda and Sarah were common in the early 20th century.
2. William A. Hart Jr., *Rachel Clementine Ferguson and John Anthony Reeves: A Brief Family History* (Asheville, North Carolina: privately printed, 1995), p.8.
3. Ibid, p.4.
4. Henry Ford was a visitor to the Grove Park Inn in Asheville shortly after it opened. See: Bruce Johnson, *Built for the Ages, A History of the Grove Park Inn* (Dallas: Taylor Publishing Company, 1991), p.37.
5. Evelyn Reeves Taylor, interview, December 12, 1998.
6. Nancy Brown, interview, December 12, 1998.
7. Deborah Solomon, "1899: The Names Have Changed But the Worries Remain," *Newsweek*, January 11, 1999.

North Carolina enjoys rich and multi-layered traditions of pottery making. Western North Carolina shares this history which includes decorated Pisgah Phase Native American earthenware (1200-1450 A.D.), utilitarian alkaline glazed stoneware produced by potters of European ancestry from the mid-19th century to the mid-20th century, and a wide range of stoneware and porcelain art pottery produced throughout the 20th century. This study examines one of the earliest efforts to make pottery which was to be sold for its decorative and aesthetic value, not just its utilitarian qualities. Nonconnah Pottery was made in the early years of the 20th century near Memphis, Tennessee by Nellie Randall Stephen and her son Walter. After his parents died, Walter Stephen moved to Skyland, North Carolina, just south of Asheville, and from 1913-1916, with the aid of several individuals, produced "Nonconnah Art Pottery." This was the first of several periods of Stephen's work which, after 1926, was called Pisgah Forest Pottery. After Stephen's death in 1961 the pottery was continued to the present by Thomas Case, Stephen's step-grandson. —R.B.

The Nonconnah Pottery of Tennessee and Western North Carolina: 1904–1918

By Rodney Henderson Leftwich

TENNESSEE NONCONNAH

Near Memphis, Tennessee, shortly after the turn of the 20th century, Nonconnah Pottery was founded by Nellie Randall Stephen and her son, Walter. Nonconnah typified small studio potteries established in the wake of the American Arts & Crafts movement. Wares produced in this pottery indicate that although the Stephens' started from humble beginnings, they eventually produced a slip-decorated, high-fired art pottery of some merit. Pottery making began with Walter Stephen's chance discovery of clay on the family farm near Capleville, in Shelby County, Southwest Tennessee. Stephen described his discovery: "In a ditch, I saw a layer of clay[;] pink, white, and yellow in stripes and spots. I took some home out of curiosity."[1] Shortly afterward, clay was also discovered in a deserted old well in their back yard.[2] Filled with enthusiasm, but lacking prior experience in pottery, Stephen and his mother investigated the possibilities of this clay.

There is some disagreement as to the year when the Stephens began their experiments and several writers have given dates as early as 1897, 1900 and 1901.[3] However, Stephen's writings indicate a later beginning. He wrote, "I was not raised in a pot shop, being about twenty seven years old when I first tried the clay."[4] Since Stephen was born in 1876, this would place his initial attempts with clay no earlier than 1903. In another memo he describes his first attempts at pottery making in connection with the 1904 St. Louis World's Fair.[5]

This 1904 fair, known as the Louisiana Purchase Exposition, was important to the Stephens for another reason. Many of the Stephens' neighbors in Capleville and nearby Memphis, Tennessee, visited the fair, including Miss Maud Jackson. Miss Jackson's stories of the man who demonstrated pottery, turning large fine shapes on the potter's wheel, captivated Mrs. Stephen.[6] This potter was probably the eccentric George E. Ohr of Biloxi (Mississippi) Art Pottery, who demonstrated his pottery making skills during the fair.[7] Inspired by stories of the potter at the fair and their newly discovered clay, Mrs. Stephen reasoned that she

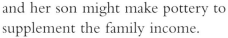

Figure 1. Molded ovoid vase. 4 x 6-3/4 in. Flat slip-painted cotton blossoms and leaves of white, pink, gray and green on green mat. Incised NS (for Nellie Stephen) on side and "Stephen & Son / Capleville Ten" on base. This piece of Tennessee Nonconnah Pottery may be the first decorated piece sold by Nellie Randall Stephen and her son Walter Stephen, probably around 1904. It is the only known piece signed in this manner. (Courtesy, Ronnie Pevahouse. All photography by Tim Barnwell unless otherwise noted.)

and her son might make pottery to supplement the family income.

In an undated personal memo, Walter Stephen described the beginnings of the Tennessee Nonconnah work:

Between the years 1897 and 1910 I lived with my Father & Mother in Shelby Co West Tennessee. Memphis was the nearest town of any size about 16 miles from the place where we lived. In that period occurred the St. Louis World's Fair. Some of the people of Capleville, a small town nearby went to the Fair. A lady Miss Maud Jackson who saw the Fair told us about the potter who used the wheel at that time. He was turning large fine shapes with the greatest of ease, like the man on the flying trapeze. My Mother who was very artistic seemed to be greatly interested. Shortly after we found some beautiful clay of mixed color & we found later several deposits of clay that later proved to be of excellent quality, and now West Tennessee clay is used the nation over and I still believe that is better than English, French or any foreign product.

My mother thought we might make some small articles from the mixed color clay for sale. It was a fine idea, only we had not the remotest idea of the difficulties & work it would lead to.

We made a start whittling ash trays & other small articles with a pen knife. I built a small kiln, smaller than a cook stove to bake them in firing coal. The sudden heat made some of them pop open. First lesson of experience, but the streaked clay burned very pretty colors & led us on. Then we thought some glaze would help them but we didn't know what glaze was made of. Father stopped at the Stone Ware plant in Memphis & got acquainted with the Boss. He asked the man what do they make glaze of. The man said Feldspar. A very elusive answer about one of the most complex arts known to man.[8]

Stephen continues his description of their early work in another undated memo:

We started with <u>enthusiasm</u> I built a kiln about a foot square inside and 16 inches high. Dad had been to see a pottery where they made Stoneware in So. Memphis.... He brought home a few pounds of spar. I had rigged up a foot wheel out of an old sewing machine. It makes me smile now to think of it. I managed with much work to turn a vase

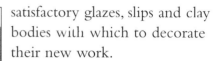

Figure 2. Top left. Ink sketch of frost daisies from Nellie Stephen's sketchbook. Mrs. Stephen called their pottery Nonconnah after a Native American name for a stream near Memphis, Tennessee and the word was usually applied to the bases of pieces with white or black slip. (Private collection.)

Top right. Molded sugar bowl with handles and lid. 3-1/8 x 7 in. Molded cream pitcher. 3-1/2 x 7 in. Both with white and green slip-painted frost daisies on mat blue. Light gray-green interior. (Courtesy, Ed Provine.)

NONCONNAH *lettered with black slip on base of pitcher.*

about 9 inches high. A neighbor happened along and saw it She gave us an order for it. Mother the artist made a relief decoration of Cotton blooms on it. Well I fired it in the tiny kiln, with coal. It came out a good green color half way up, but the top part was dry and dead looking. We decided that a little ignorance went a long way and I was blue enough. but the little Mother told me not to try be defeated but to [try] it again. That was one of the best lessons I ever got from her or anyone else. I took the vase, turned it upside down an fired it again. And it was green all over, and most of all the lady was pleased and paid for it. I found that Felspar was a good start but it took a terrific heat to fuse it. So the Felspar put me on a high fire basis. High Fire glazes have a soft beauty unmistakable that is what made the old chinese ware what it is. [9]

Only one piece of Tennessee Nonconnah Pottery decorated with cotton blooms was found in the course of this study, and it may be the piece Walter Stephen was describing. It is also the only known piece signed "Stephen & Son / Capleville Ten" (Figure 1).

Prior to the turned vase Stephen described, the Stephens' work consisted of trays, figurines, boxes, ashtrays and other small articles. The construction of the wheel was an effort to increase their pottery production. By experimenting, reading books and taking a very thorough course in chemistry, Stephen eventually developed

satisfactory glazes, slips and clay bodies with which to decorate their new work.

The Stephens' persistence paid off, and the pottery was well received by the community. Mrs. Stephen wrote:

Our neighbors and acquaintances have been true art patrons, taking our work for their homes and encouraging by kindly interest and suggestions. So, here's to the kind-hearted people of Memphis and hereabouts; long may they prosper. [10]

Stephen had tried several jobs, but by 1905, the pottery production had reached a level that allowed him to work at it full-time. Like his father and grandfather, Stephen had learned the trade of masonry and stone cutting. Stephen had also studied law under C. E. Woods, a county attorney in Rushville, Nebraska, the year before the family moved to Tennessee. [11] Despite these other trade skills, Stephen chose pottery making to be his occupation for the greater part of his life.

Nellie Stephen selected the name "Nonconnah" for the pottery. As she explained: "It was one of the dear old Indian names we could not resist. We searched long and diligently for the meaning of the name and at last thought of the oldest inhabitant, Dr. Leon Richmond, who remembered the Indians and their language." [12] He informed the Stephens that "Nonconnah" meant "long stream," the

name the Native Americans had given a sluggish stream that meanders around Memphis. This word in capital letters, applied to the bases of their pottery with white porcelain or black slip, became the mark for Tennessee Nonconnah Pottery (Figures 2,3).

The Tennessee Nonconnah Pottery works operated for approximately six years. In 1910, both of Walter Stephen's parents died within three months of each other, and were buried in a small cemetery on the north side of Holmes Road, a few miles south of Capleville. Following the death of his parents, Stephen traveled widely throughout the United States for two years. He sold their home and the approximately 100 acres of land to Ed Crump, a friend of the family, who was to become one of Tennessee's most powerful politicians.[13] When the site was visited during the 1950s, the only evidence of the Stephens' occupation and the Nonconnah Pottery was "a well in a turnip patch on the back of the lot."[14] Today the pottery site is covered by a crowded housing development and few local people recall the Stephens and their Tennessee art pottery.

Several techniques were employed to

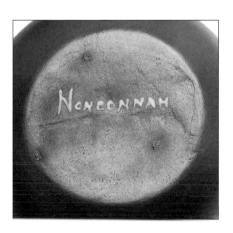

shape the Nonconnah wares. Initially, small objects were whittled or carved from the native clays with a penknife; however, as the Stephens gained experience, hand building from rolled-out slabs or coils was found to be more practical. The walls of a 12-inch tall, straight-sided pitcher were formed from two curved slabs (see Figure 20).

To develop more efficient means of production, the Stephens used a potter's wheel and molds. Working at the wheel, Stephen turned cups, teapots, plates, vases and jardinières, but molds were the primary method of manufacture. It is unclear who designed the Nonconnah molds: Stephen may have created them from pieces he formed on the wheel, or they may have

Figure 3. Top left. Ink sketches of rose petals and leaves from Nellie Stephen's sketchbook. (Private collection.)

Top right. Molded bulbous vase. 4-3/4 x 6-1/2 in. Slip-painted high-relief decoration of roses in white and green on dark-green mat. Caramel-brown speckled interior. (Private collection.)

NONCONNAH mark on base with white slip.

*Figure 4. Large ovoid vase.
11 x 6-1/2 in. White, light green,
gray, yellow and brown slip-painted
landscape with road, bridge and trees.
Signed "morning" and "N.
Stephen." Cypress branch on each
side of landscape and
NONCONNAH worded below
scene—all on mat green. (Courtesy,
Tony McCormack.)*

*Above. Ink sketch of dewberry blossoms and leaves from Nellie Stephen's
sketchbook. (Private collection.)*

*Above right. Molded teapot. 5 x 7-1/2 in. White, green and brown slip-painted
alder berry blossoms on mat blue-gray glaze. White glaze interior.
NONCONNAH lettered in brown slip on base. (Author's collection.)*

*Right. Molded bulbous jar with domed lid. 5-1/2 x 7 in. Cotton bolls and
leaves slip-painted in white, green and brown with a wavy blue band on mat
green. Interior mat green. NONCONNAH lettered on base with white slip.
(Private collection.)*

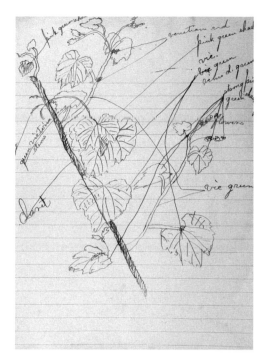

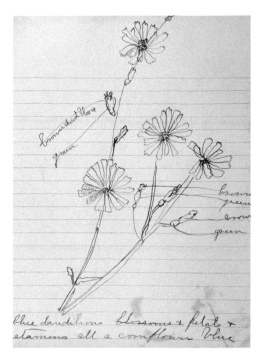

been purchased. Molded vases 8-5/8 in., 6-1/2 in., 6 in., 5-3/4 in., and 4 in. in height have been found. The 5-3/4 in. mold was also used to make lipped or spouted pitchers with separately applied handles.

Designed first on paper and then on the wheel,[15] shapes were kept simple and had smooth exteriors. Following an interior glazing, usually of brown or white, the exterior, including the base, was coated with mat-to-semi-mat colored slip. Occasionally light blue, but more frequently light or dark green, the slip coated the exterior surfaces and created an appropriate background for Mrs. Stephen's decoration. Using an approach that evolved naturally from her interest and training in painting, Mrs. Stephen created designs from successive layers of brushed-on, translucent, porcelain slip. These layers became so thick that designs often rose above the pottery surface in multicolored combinations of white, brown, pink, black, green or yellow (Figure 4).

Mrs. Stephen chose the native flora of the area for most of her designs; however, a few non-plant designs have been discovered. She kept a sketchbook with detailed pen and ink sketches of many local plants including chestnut burrs, roses, morning glories, sycamore leaves, narcissi, violets, grape leaves, dewberries, tulip poplars, wild

Figure 5. Nellie Randall Stephen decorated many of the Tennessee Nonconnah pieces with native flora. Her sketchbook indicates her efforts to record both the shapes and the colors of each species accurately. She apparently planned the decoration of each pot carefully before applying the slip to the clay body. (Private collection.)

phlox, dandelions, black-eyed Susans, May apples, frost daises and many others (Figure 5). She labeled her sketches with detailed color descriptions to aid her depictions on the pottery. A few non-plant sketches including moths, men smoking pipes and a lady's head in profile were utilized and have been found on Nonconnah Pottery (Figure 6). Other non-plant subject matter found on objects but not recorded in

Figure 6. Right. Molded spouted pitcher. 5-3/4 in. Slip-decorated profile of woman, mat green glaze, interior speckled brown. (Private collection, author's photograph.)

Far right. Ink sketch of portrait profile from Nellie Stephen's sketchbook. (Private collection.)

Right. Ink sketches of men smoking pipes from Nellie Stephen's sketchbook. (Private collection.)

Far right. Cylindrical tobacco jar or humidor with domed lid. 5 x 4-1/2 in. Four slip-painted heads of men smoking pipes in dark brown on band of white on low-gloss green. Lettered below heads in white slip "HALE FELLOWS WELL MET." NONCONNAH lettered in white slip on the base. (Courtesy, Asheville Art Museum, Tom and Dorothy Case collection.)

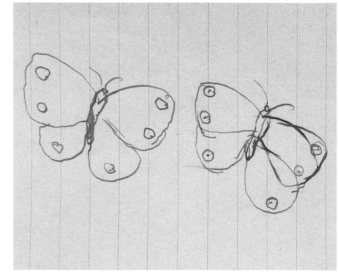

Right. Match holder with domed lid. 5 x 4-7/8 in. Slip-painted candlestick, matches and moths. NONCONNAH in slip on base. (Private collection, author's photograph.)

Far right. Ink sketch of moths from Nellie Stephen's sketchbook. (Private collection.)

her sketchbook included sailing ships, an old man telling stories to children and cathedral street scenes. These images were used on a plate, plaque and vases respectively (Figure 7).

The earliest example of slip decoration attributable to Walter Stephen is a mat green vase decorated with a white cameo-like branch of leaves and a flower. The base is hand-incised "Adelaide," under which is "W. Stephens" [sic] and below, "1912." Since Stephen did not move to North Carolina until 1913, and he had traveled for two years after his parents death in 1910, it is not known where this vase was made or who "Adelaide" might have been (Figure 8). [16]

Thus, with much enthusiasm and persistence, Nellie Stephen and her son Walter had produced a line of hand-built, wheel-turned and cast pottery that was well received by the local community, and was sufficiently successful to support Walter Stephen as a full-time potter. Walter Stephen, most interested in the chemical and technical aspects of the business, constructed kilns and potter's wheels; and, using native clays and porcelains, developed clay bodies, slips and glazes. Following an application of glaze and decoration with colored slips, the pottery was fired by Stephen in their homemade kiln. Nellie Randall Stephen decorated the forms her son produced with porcelain slip, often using floral motifs based on her detailed drawings. She combined the two most popular art pottery trends of her time—mat green glazes and slip-painted scenes of native flora (Figure 9). Her careful attention to each piece created unique, high quality art pottery. After her death in 1910, her son carried this tradition to Western North Carolina.

North Carolina Nonconnah Pottery

North Carolina Nonconnah was Walter Stephen's second pottery operation, which he established in 1913, following his move from Tennessee to North Carolina.

Unpublished Letter By Nellie R. Stephen

A letter written by Stephen's mother to a Mrs. Maples provides insight into her art training and involvement in the Tennessee Nonconnah Pottery. The letter was evidently in response to a request for information about Mrs. Stephen and her work. The letter probably dates c. 1907. The letter is recorded as written with spelling and markouts unchanged.

Nonconnah Place

Sep. 23 - Oct [no date]

Dear Mrs. Maples

I have written out a little sketch of our work which I hope will help you. I have quite decided not to send my picture: it is the work and not the women. If you wish to say something about me just say I am small & plain with grey hair & grey eyes. I enclose an ink sketch of our place.

Mr. Stephen will deliver your jardiniere after the fair. Yours Sincerely

Mrs. A. Stephen

(Enclosed)

The equipment for the Nonconnah pottery work is very simple. Plenty of patience and dogged persistence brought over from Scotland. The Chemist and potter Walter Stephen took up clay modeling and form study at school and later a very thorough course in chemistry.

Our glazes porcelains & have all been dug out of the chemistry and are our own [sic].

Our models are the work of both the artist & potter, designed first on paper and then on the wheel.

We have used the native clays as much as possible; ~~and~~ The name Nonconnah is one of the dear old Indian names we could not resist.

We searched long and diligently for the meaning of the name and at last thought of the oldest inhabitant: Dr Leon Richmond, who remembered the Indians and their language.

Dr. Richmond, who is over eighty years old, says the name Nonconnah means long stream.

Our motto has been "Art is the interpretation of nature."

Our teachers have been Nature, John Ruskin and the Chemistry.

Our neighbors and acquaintances have been true art patrons; taking our work for their homes and encouraging by kindly interest and suggestions. So, here's to the kind-hearted people of Memphis and hereabout; long may they prosper.

Mrs. A. Stephen began her art studies at fourteen years of age. Ten years we[re] given to portrait work in water color and pen drawing. Ten years were given to sketching and painting the Sioux Indians in the Black Hills, and teaching pen drawing and blackboard work at the teachers institutes.

While in the Black Hills country Mrs. Stephen wrote out west stories & rhymes illustrating them with pen drawings for the Children's Page of the Youth's Companion.

She also wrote of western woman's work for the Chicago Inter-Ocean, The Woman's Kingdom department.

Ten years have been spent in shelby Co Ten. painting water color landscape & sending them north & west. The first landscape painting was sent to the Centennial at Nashville and won a prize. The painting was of Pigeon Roost Road between Capleville & Mineral ~~Springs~~ Wells.

Figure 7. Above, front and back. Two vases. 6 in. and 6-1/2 in. Unsigned but attributed to Nellie Stephen by her descendants. Each combine views of churches with leaf and vine decoration. (Private collection, author's photographs.)

Right. Slab-built tile. 6-5/8 x 9-3/8 in. Slip-painted relief of two seated boys listening to man on a wagon. Possibly a copy of a Dutch painting. Blue, brown, white, yellow and black slip on white stoneware body. Unsigned–attributed by family to Nellie Stephen. (Courtesy, Asheville Art Museum, Tom and Dorothy Case collection.)

Left. Footed plate. 11-1/2 in. Sailing ship at sea with NONCONNAH lettered on back. (Courtesy, Asheville Art Museum, Tom and Dorothy Case collection.)

Figure 8. Right. Thrown bulbous rose bowl. 5-1/4 x 4-7/8 in. White slip-painted rose with stem and leaves on mat green. Unglazed interior. Incised on base "Adelaide / W. Stephens [sic]/1912." Probably one of the last pieces made and decorated by W.B. Stephen at his Tennessee pottery. (Courtesy, Norman and Barbara Haas collection.)

Figure 9. Above. Molded pitcher with squared handle. 6-5/8 x 3-1/2 in. Slip-painted relief decoration of dewberry in white, green and brown on mat brown. Light gray-green interior. NONCONNAH lettered on base with dark red-brown slip. Most pieces of Tennessee Nonconnah pottery were slip-decorated over green mat glazes, but several pieces with brown and blue glazes have been found. Thrown rose bowl. 3 x 3-3/8 in. White slip-painted grapevine and butterflies on mat blue background. Mat white interior glaze. NONCONNAH lettered on base with dark-brown slip. Probably made and decorated by W.B. Stephen at the North Carolina pottery. (Courtesy, Ed Provine collection.)

Above right. Ink sketch of dewberry from Nellie Randall Stephen's sketchbook. (Private collection.)

Above left. Tumbler, probably thrown. 3 x 3-1/4 in. White, green and black slip-painted relief of morning glories on mat green. Mat blue interior. NONCONNAH lettered on base with black slip. (Courtesy, Asheville Art Museum, Tom and Dorothy Case collection.)

Above center. Ink sketch of morning glories from Nellie Stephen's sketchbook. (Private collection.)

Above right. Molded pitcher with applied handle. 6-7/8 x 8-1/4 in. White, green and black slip-painted relief of morning glories on mat green. Mat blue interior. NONCONNAH lettered on base with black slip. (Courtesy, Asheville Art Museum, Tom and Dorothy Case collection.)

Left. Molded bud vase. 5 x 7-1/4 in. High-relief lily of the valley slip-painted in white, brown and green on dark mat green. Caramel-brown interior. NONCONNAH lettered on base with white slip. (Courtesy, Ed Provine collection.)

Figure 10. Mr. and Mrs. C.P. Ryman, partners of W.B. Stephen at the Skyland, North Carolina Nonconnah Pottery. Mrs. Ryman decorated wares with ivy and grapevines. (Courtesy, Virginia Morrison.)

Figure 11. North Carolina Nonconnah Pottery began production in 1913 in Skyland, North Carolina with the construction of these two buildings. Pottery was made here for about five years after which the buildings, probably newly constructed in these photos, became rental cottages. (Courtesy, Virginia Morrison.)

While some of the wares he produced in North Carolina resembled those made in Tennessee, new co-workers and other design influences led to the development of several distinctly different shapes, glazes, and methods of decoration. Most importantly, Stephen developed as a creative artist, taking on more of the responsibilities for decoration of the pottery he produced.

In May 1913, Walter Stephen settled in the Skyland community, located a few miles south of Asheville, in Buncombe County, North Carolina.[17] Here, he met a socially prominent couple, Mr. and Mrs. C. P. Ryman. Impressed by examples of Stephen's Tennessee Nonconnah wares, Mr. Ryman proposed a partnership with Stephen.[18]

Ryman agreed to finance a pottery if Stephen would supply the knowledge and skill to operate it (Figure 10).

Ryman leased land on the east side of Highway 25 in Skyland from two sisters, Ella and Pink Case.[19] Marion Case Havener, a cousin of the sisters, recalled that the triangularly shaped lot was bordered on the back or east by the railroad, on the south by a stream and hill, and on the northwest by the highway. The new pottery consisted of two buildings, one with an inside kiln. The building parallel to the railroad, faced west, while the second, placed at a 90 degree angle to the first, faced north (Figure 11). Constructed of rough sawn lumber with weather boarding strips, the two buildings were unpainted except for white trim on the doors, windows and outside corners. A long sign along the crest of one building's tar-papered roof read, "NONCONNAH ART POTTERY."

By late 1913 or early 1914, the pottery was in operation. Mr. Ryman hoped the regional tourist trade would provide a healthy profit for the venture, as the cool, beautiful mountains of Western North Carolina had long attracted seasonal visitors. A number of local markets were found for the wares. Mrs. Ryman's mother, Mrs. Coe, offered Nonconnah Pottery for sale at her Bonnie Crest Inn in Skyland.[20] Stephen also sold pottery to the Grove Park Inn and gift shops in Asheville. Markets outside the area could conveniently be reached through

use of the nearby railroad and Skyland station.

Although Stephen had learned much at his Tennessee Nonconnah Pottery, sources of information on pottery making were few, and no easy solutions were available for the problems of beginning a full scale art pottery operation. Stephen conducted many experiments to develop clay bodies and a suitable line of glazes for the new venture. Mrs. Ryman remembered him having many books on pottery,[21] and while these certainly must have helped, materials had to be assembled and formulas tested and retested.

Stephen's responsibilities for all stages of the pottery production kept him busy. Artus Moser, an artistically gifted high school student who lived nearby, was employed by Stephen and Ryman. He observed that "Stephen was always at the potter's wheel. He was a man of a quiet, calm disposition, never letting anything

Figure 12. Interior main building, Nonconnah Pottery, Skyland, North Carolina. Standing left to right. Artus Moser, unidentified worker and Walter Stephen. (Courtesy, Virginia Morrison.)

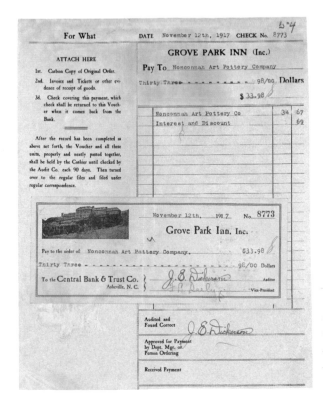

Figure 13 This bill of sale is dated November 12, 1917 for an unspecified amount of pottery sold to the Grove Park Inn, Asheville's largest resort at the time. (Courtesy, Bruce Johnson.)

bother him much...even though a whole kiln of pottery might turn out badly. 'Keep your shirt on,' he would say."[22]

Mrs. Jacques Busbee, who was to become famous for establishing the Jugtown Pottery in Moore County, North Carolina, was also impressed with Stephen's efforts. In 1916, as chairperson of art for the North Carolina Federation of Womens' Clubs, she wrote about the Nonconnah Pottery:

> The kiln of Skyland is very inter-
> esting...doing work that resembles
> Wedgewood [sic]. He [Stephen] is
> experimenting with more intelligence
> than anyone in the State. He is study-
> ing and working constantly. His work
> is known as Nonconnah Pottery and
> will soon be in the class with the best
> work done in any of the States
> (Figure 12).[23]

The pottery venture was not the finan-

cial success Stephen and Ryman had hoped. There were a few cars and tourists traveling Highway 25, but the majority of visitors still entered Asheville by train. What little automobile and buggy traffic there was on the road, was slowed even further in 1916 when construction began to change the macadam surface in front of the pottery to pavement.[24]

In 1916, Stephen left the partnership. He worked for a time in an aluminum plant in Badin, North Carolina, then returned to Asheville and worked as a mason before opening Pisgah Forest Pottery south of Asheville in 1926. After Stephen left, Nonconnah Pottery continued under Ryman's direction. A bill of sale for pottery delivered to the Grove Park Inn newsstand indicates that Nonconnah was still in operation on November 12, 1917

(Figure 13). However, with the uncertainties and economic changes brought on by America's entry into World War I, the pottery ceased operation by 1918. Control of the leased property was returned to the Case sisters who converted the pottery buildings into rental cottages. During the 1980s the buildings were torn down and the property was developed to make room for the current South Park office complex.

North Carolina Nonconnah consisted primarily of souvenir items–tobacco jars, vases, bowls, mugs, candlesticks, teapots and match or cigarette holders. Produced both on the potter's wheel and in molds, each piece of pottery was signed "NONCONNAH" or "TRADE / NONCONNAH / MARK" on the base (Figure 14). Sometimes the mark was neatly incised or scratched in. On other examples, it was brushed on in block letters with black, brown, blue or blue-green glaze, and often included the mold, or more likely reorder numbers. No existing examples of

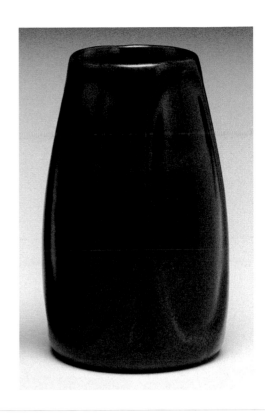

Figure 15. Left. Molded eight-sided vase. 5-1/4 x 1-3/4 in. Decoration of incised art nouveau style lines. Cinnamon brown. Cream interior. NONCONNAH lettered on base in green slip. (Author's collection.)

Right. Molded vase with indented panels. 5-1/4 x 3 in. Dark-gray semi-mat with buff interior glaze. NONCONNAH and 157 lettered on base in blue glaze. (Author's collection.)

Figure 16. This photograph of North Carolina Nonconnah Pottery taken about 1916, is the only known photo of a group of Nonconnah pottery on exhibit in the shop where it was made. A wide range of wares are shown including baluster, square and hexagonal forms, vine and leaf decoration, geometric decoration and one piece showing part of a fence and tree. (Courtesy, Virginia Morrison.)

North Carolina Nonconnah Pottery have been found with the artist's name or pottery location.

Apparently, Stephen sold or left his Tennessee Nonconnah molds behind because he developed new ones in North Carolina. When an especially pleasing or successful design was turned, he made a mold. Due to the nature of wheel work, the molds Stephen created from wheel prototypes were some variant of a cylindrical form. Seven different molded North Carolina Nonconnah vases, including two with handles, one molded pitcher and one molded, lidded jar have also been found.

Two of the most interesting pieces examined were a five-inch molded vase with evenly spaced indented geometric panels, and a flat-sided tapering vase with incised line decoration (Figure 15). A circa 1916 photograph of a display of Nonconnah art pottery shows a wide range of shapes and decoration with many molded shapes, and several square, rectangular and hexagonal vases (Figure 16). Few of these geometric forms seem to have survived. While some of these may have been hand built from slabs, it is likely they were molded.

North Carolina Nonconnah's simple well-designed shapes were glazed with semi-mat, or less frequently, dry-mat glazes. On January 6, 1915, Stephen listed 28 formulas he wanted to test, including a variety of chrome green and cobalt blue glazes, and a fawn brown glaze. Barium added to many of his formulas, produced a soft mat surface popular with many Arts & Crafts potters.

Figure 17. Left to right. Thrown, flaring cylindrical vase, heavily potted. 7 x 4 in. Unglazed red and brown and buff swirl exterior. Dark blue-gray interior. NONCONNAH and 263 incised on base. Thrown bowl. 3 x 5 in. Unglazed red, brown and buff swirl exterior. Dark blue-gray interior. NONCONNAH incised on base. Thrown bowl with short collared rim. 5 x 5 in. Unglazed red, brown and buff swirl exterior. Dark blue-gray interior. NONCONNAH incised in base. (Private collection.)

Base of left vase.

A penciled note in Nellie Stephen's sketchbook dated 1916 indicates Walter Stephen did a series of glaze tests, and added black, yellow, gray and white to his palette.

North Carolina Nonconnah Pottery was usually glazed with one exterior glaze and a contrasting interior glaze. The most commonly used interior glazes were gray-white, red-brown, tan and blue-green. Only occasionally was an interior left unglazed. Stephen also produced a line of pottery he called "Terra Cotta" with unglazed exteriors. These unglazed wares were usually characterized by decorative stripes and swirls of different-colored clays. Stephen created these pieces by spinning together clays of mixed colors at his wheel including combinations of cream and red-brown, and gray and orange (Figure 17). A 6-1/2 in. lidded tobacco jar of this swirl construction is pictured in the 1978 catalogue of the Mint Museum of Art (Charlotte, North Carolina) exhibit of the pottery of Walter Stephen.

Stephen continued his mother's decorative technique of applying porcelain slip with a brush to create raised designs. Unlike his mother's colored designs however, all North Carolina Nonconnah Pottery decorated with raised slip designs, appears to have been made using only white porcelain slip. The sharp contrast

between the all-white designs and their solid brown, green or charcoal gray background, created a classical look that customers compared to the white cameo decorations on English Wedgwood Pottery. Later, at Stephen's Pisgah Forest Pottery, these all-white decorations came to be called "American Cameo" or "American Wedgwood."

The most commonly used North Carolina Nonconnah design patterns were of naturalistic ivy or grapevines and leaves. While Walter Stephen, Artus Moser and Mrs. Ryman are known to have decorated North Carolina Nonconnah, examples attributed to Mrs. Ryman with delicate leaf and vine decoration are most frequently encountered (Figure 18). Stylized geometric lines and shapes, designed to fit square, hexagonal and circular forms were also used, and this style of decoration was probably done by Walter Stephen. These design elements are related to Native American themes: triangular shapes have been called "arrowheads" and zig-zag lines compared to Indian blanket or basket designs of the American West (Figure 19).

Following Stephen's departure from Nonconnah in 1916, Ryman continued the pottery another year, narrowing the selection of forms and glazes. The Rymans, Moser and another unidentified worker made molded and slab-built forms either

Figure 18. Left to right. Molded tapered mug. 5-1/4 x 5-1/4 in. White slip-painted grapevine on semi-mat green. White glaze interior. NONCONNAH incised on base. (Private collection.)

Molded cylindrical jar with short raised rim. 3-1/2 x 5-3/4 in. Slip-painted grapevine on semi-mat green. White glaze interior. NONCONNAH, 1914 and S incised on base. This is one of the few known dated pieces of Nonconnah Pottery. See detail, left. (Private collection.)

Molded flaring tumbler. 5 x 3-1/8 in. White slip-painted high-relief of grapevine on mat green. White glaze interior. NONCONNAH incised on base. (Private collection.)

Molded pitcher with squared handle. 5-1/2 x 6 in. White slip-painted ivy on mat green. Unglazed interior. TRADE / NONCONNAH / MARK incised on base. (Private collection.)

Figure 19. Thrown vase. 6 x 4-1/2 in. Greek key-style white slip on dark gray-brown mat glaze, pale yellow mat interior, incised NONCONNAH and dated 1915. (Private collection.)

Molded footed bowl. 3-1/2 x 6-1/4 in. Dark green mat exterior, white glossy interior, signed on base NONCONNAH in green slip. (Private collection.)

Thrown vase with collared rim. 6-1/2 x 4-3/4 in. White slip arrowhead decoration. Dark brown mat exterior, gray glossy interior. Base incised NONCONNAH. (Private collection.)

unglazed, or with brown or blue exterior glazes. Moser, and occasionally Mrs. Ryman, applied the cameo decorations. A 1917 bill of sale indicates that Nonconnah was paid $33.98 for 31 pieces of pottery, after a 33-1/3 percent discount was given to the buyer.[25] By 1918 the North Carolina Nonconnah Pottery had closed.

Thus, Nonconnah Pottery was produced in Arden, North Carolina for a short period of time, roughly 1913 to 1917. Stephen's venture at the new Nonconnah Pottery produced pieces decorated with only white porcelain slip, and it was during this period of time that Stephen began experimenting with his own decorating skills. This work anticipated Stephen's later decorative work at Pisgah Forest Pottery which was to become his hallmark: pate-sur-pate slip decoration called "American Cameo."

Pisgah Forest Pottery was the last of three pottery businesses established by Walter B. Stephen. From 1926 until his death in 1961, Stephen operated the Pisgah Forest Pottery in Arden, North Carolina, approximately six miles from the Nonconnah site. This pottery's wares show marked changes in form and glaze from Stephen's earlier production. While he continued to decorate his pottery with his unique cameo decoration of bas-relief scenes in hand-painted porcelain, he

replaced the ivy and neoclassic designs of Nonconnah, with scenes of American folklore. Based on his childhood experiences, these scenes included the covered wagon, buffalo hunt, fiddler and cabin, and square-dancers. He also achieved much success with crystalline and crackle glazes. Walter Stephen continued his experimental approach to the work and produced a wide range of forms and decoration for which he became well known as a major figure in the American art pottery movement.

NONCONNAH POTTERY AND THE ARTS & CRAFTS MOVEMENT

The production of Nonconnah Pottery occurred during a period of great interest in handcrafted objects, including pottery, and reflected the national interest in the Arts & Crafts movement. In her younger years, Mrs. Stephen had taught school and read avidly. She was apparently familiar with the English Arts & Crafts philosophy, for in her correspondence to Mrs. Maples, she commented, "Our teachers have been nature, John Ruskin, and the Chemistry."[26]

Although the Arts & Crafts movement was English in origin, the American Arts & Crafts movement focused attention on Native Americans as the country's original artists and craftsmen. As the 20th century commenced, many craft workers felt it desirable to cultivate a craft style that would be characteristically American, and adopted Native American names and motifs.[27] The Stephens chose to use a Native American word, "Nonconnah," as did other art potteries of the period. Thus, we see "Ouachita," "Arequipa," "Pewabic" and "Shawsheen" Pottery produced. Clifton Art Pottery of Newark, New Jersey, introduced Clifton Indian ware in 1906. Rookwood and other potteries decorated surfaces of their vases with portraits of Native Americans, noble people in feathered head-dresses.[28]

The Stephens were not immune to the influences of Rookwood, Grueby and other art potteries of their time. Stephen's description of his first fired piece of pottery indicates their attempts to produce wares in the latest Arts & Crafts styles. He described this first vase as "Glazed with feldspar which was tinted green with chrome oxide, over which Mrs. Stephen applied a relief decoration of cotton blooms."[29] The two major decorative techniques of the Arts & Crafts movement were used on this vase, mat green glaze and slip-painted decoration. Nearly all observed examples of

pottery produced at the Tennessee Nonconnah operation have these two qualities.

Many art potteries exhibited mat green glazes at the St. Louis Fair, and Tennessee Nonconnah wares were also glazed on their exteriors with the popular mat green. Nonconnah's green varied from light to dark and was dry and flat, more closely resembling Merrimac Potteries' glaze than Grueby's rich pooled and feathered green glaze. Most examples of Tennessee Nonconnah observed during this study had green glazes, the exceptions being a teapot, sugar and creamer glazed in shades of blue-gray, and a green-brown vase.

Another characteristic of the Arts & Crafts movement evident in the production of Tennessee Nonconnah Pottery was the use of female decorators. During the 19th century, women were considered frail and artistic, not suited to the heavy, dirty production processes of pottery work. In many cases, the role of men and women was clearly divided with women as decorators and men as chemists and potters: the work arrangement at Nonconnah Pottery was no exception. Mrs. Stephen wrote, "Our

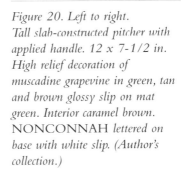

Figure 20. Left to right.
Tall slab-constructed pitcher with applied handle. 12 x 7-1/2 in. High relief decoration of muscadine grapevine in green, tan and brown glossy slip on mat green. Interior caramel brown. NONCONNAH lettered on base with white slip. (Author's collection.)

Concave, slab-constructed tall vase. 11-7/8 x 4-1/2 in. White slip grapevine on mat green. Interior mat white. Base incised TRADE / NONCONNAH / MARK. (Author's collection.)

Molded cylindrical vase with inward carved lip. 12-1/8 x 4-1/2 in. White, green and brown slip-painted relief of roses on mat green. Speckled caramel-brown glaze interior. NONCONNAH lettered on base with black slip. (Courtesy, Bill Lane collection.)

These pieces demonstrate the general differences between the decoration of Tennessee Nonconnah (left and right), and North Carolina Nonconnah (center). The center piece was probably made and decorated after Walter Stephen left the pottery in 1916.

Figure 21. Left to right.
Thrown pear-shaped vase.
7-3/4 x 4-1/4 in. Semi-mat
blue-gray with tiny dark specks.
Interior with same glaze.
NONCONNAH incised on
base. Buff body. (Author's
collection.)

Molded, collared vase with
squared handles. 5-3/4 x 8-1/2
in. Semi-mat dark blue-gray.
Cream glaze interior.
NONCONNAH and 412
lettered on base in mat green slip.
Buff clay body. (Private
collection.)

Molded, collared vase with
squared handles. 4 x 6-1/2 in.
Cinnamon-brown semi-mat.
Light-gray interior.
NONCONNAH and 411
lettered on base in dark olive slip.
(Author's collection.)

Thrown pear-shaped vase.
5-3/4 x 7-1/4 in. Semi-mat
caramel brown. Red-brown
interior. NONCONNAH
incised in small block letters on
base. (Author's collection.)

models are the work of both the artist and potter, designed first on paper and then on the wheel."[30] While she decorated their wares, her son experimented with clay, created forms, formulated glazes and attended to the firings.

Other trends in the art pottery movement including the use of molds, simple well-designed shapes, and naturalistic slip-painted decoration were evident at the Tennessee Nonconnah Pottery. Following their introduction to the American public through the many expositions held in the late 19th century, Oriental wares and decorative styles gained great popularity. Their graceful forms with asymmetrically placed decoration offered welcome relief from the cluttered extravagance of Victorian ceramics. The Stephen's use of simple forms and asymmetric decoration reflected the influence of the Oriental aesthetic.

The most common slip-painted decoration on American art pottery during the Arts & Crafts movement was naturalistic flowers and plants, and Nellie Stephen adopted these contemporary tastes. By using native flora, such as cotton blooms and wild grapes, Mrs. Stephen's decorated wares represented a regional influence and

style. Nonconnah's motto was, "Art is the interpretation of nature," and their designs were mostly of native flora.[31]

Mrs. Stephen's slip-painting was slightly different from the typical slip-painted underglaze wares of most Arts & Crafts potters. Whereas most art potters sealed their slip designs under a clear glaze, Nellie Stephen did not. Following a coating of background slip over the entire surface, including the base, successive layers of white and colored porcelain slip were painted on to create the design. Tennessee Nonconnah examples are decorated with white, brown, pink, black, green or yellow multicolored slips. Some designs were flat, thin, and reminiscent of Mrs. Stephen's watercolor painting background while others have low relief built up in selected areas. Those examples with flat decoration most closely resembled the slip-painted art wares of Rookwood, Weller and Owens (Figure 20).

Tennessee Nonconnah forms were simple and included vases, cups, plates, teapots and jardinières. Some examples were identical to the molded and wheel-thrown Oriental forms made at Rookwood Pottery. Puffy-looking domed lids on

Nonconnah jars and teapots closely resemble the lid on a Rookwood chocolate pot pictured in a 1904 mail order catalog. Similar lids were also used on tobacco humidors produced by Rookwood Pottery around 1900.[32] Other Nonconnah forms resemble those produced by Fulper Pottery of New Jersey and may have come from an illustrated 1915 Fulper mail order catalog found among Stephen's papers.

While some of the wares produced at the North Carolina Nonconnah Pottery resembled the Tennessee product, others emulated the latest art pottery trends. All pottery made at the Skyland Nonconnah Pottery shows the unmistakable influence of the Arts & Crafts movement and maintained the principle of individually made and decorated objects. While forms remained simple, and green to brown mat glazed wares with slip decoration continued to be made, Stephen also created stylized geometric lines and shapes in white slip to fit circular, square and hexagonal forms. Several American art potters, including Artus Van Briggle, had begun to experiment with similar styles of decoration.[33] The geometric slip decoration of triangular shapes resembling arrowheads may have a parallel in Roseville Pottery's Mostique line introduced in 1915. Marblehead Pottery in Massachusetts also offered wares with geometrically composed patterns of incised lines, although none appear identical to Stephen's designs. The cameo ivy designs created at Nonconnah Pottery may reflect the general Art Nouveau emphasis on stylized plant forms and rhythmically repeating curves, but this specific form of slip decoration appears to be unique in American art pottery.

Many art wares made at Nonconnah Pottery were not slip decorated, having instead one monochrome exterior glaze with a contrasting interior glaze. Ornamental glazes had gained popularity since the early 1900s introduction of mat glazes by art potters such as Grueby, Merrimac, Wheatley, Rookwood and numerous other art potteries. Stephen experimented with a variety of formulas in 1915 and 1916, developing a series of glazes in browns, yellows, blues, dark grays and whites. Stephen's most successful glazes had satin-like mat textures closely resembling the fine glazes produced by Marblehead Pottery in Massachusetts (Figure 21). Stephen's familiarity with Marblehead Pottery is also evident in the similarity in forms he created for his ornamental glazes.

Nonconnah "Terra Cotta" ware with swirled clay bodies was glazed only on the interior, and related to several other art potteries. As early as 1909, the Niloak Pottery of Benton, Arkansas, manufactured swirled art ware on a large scale.[34] Originally designated as "Niloak's Mission" Pottery, it was selling well in all parts of the country by 1912. Similar wares were produced concurrently by White Pottery of Denver, Colorado and later in the 1930s by Probst, Rhinehart and North State Potteries in North Carolina.[35]

Though their wares shared similar characteristics with other American art pottery of the same period, Nellie Randall Stephen and Walter Stephen seldom receive the attention of the better known Arts & Crafts potters. Mrs. Stephen, who had demonstrated skill as a versatile artist, might have become an important figure in the American art pottery movement with the financial support, publicity and urban exposure of her contemporaries. Her work consisted primarily of slip decoration, and was all created at the Tennessee Nonconnah Pottery. Walter Stephen worked at both the Tennessee and North Carolina Nonconnah Potteries and his work consisted of building kilns, mixing clay bodies, creating pottery forms and developing glazes along with some decoration of pottery. The early years from 1904 to 1916 were Walter Stephen's formative ones and much that he learned and discovered as a self-trained potter anticipated his later work at the Pisgah Forest Pottery. In 1926 he resumed pottery making and founded Pisgah Forest Pottery where he worked until his death in 1961.

Figure 22. Left to right.
Small molded vase.
4-1/2 x 3-1/2 in. Burnished
unglazed exterior. Dark-brown
glaze interior.
NONCONNAH and 22
lettered on base in blue slip.
Initials DWB in ink probably
added later. (Author's collection.)

Thrown low bowl.
3-1/8 x 5-1/4 in. Unglazed
exterior with swirled orange and
gray clays. Dark blue-green
interior. NONCONNAH and
209 incised on base. (Author's
collection.)

Small thrown vase with shaped
neck. 4-1/4 x 3-1/4 in. Dark
blue-green semi-mat with light-
gray interior. NONCONNAH
on base in green slip. (Author's
collection.)

Thrown, flaring vase with collared
rim. 5 x 3-1/8 in. Blue-gray
semi-mat with yellow-tan
interior. NONCONNAH on
base in green slip. (Private
collection.)

Acknowledgments:
The author wishes to thank the many individuals who generously shared their personal knowledge and experiences for this study. Of major importance were interviews with Mr. and Mrs. Thomas Case, the current owners of Pisgah Forest Pottery, and Grady Ledbetter, a potter who has been employed at the pottery since 1929. Interviews with Mrs. Sara Austin, who worked with Stephen at his pottery in 1951 and 1952, and Mrs. Marion Case Havener, a local historian whose family rented property for the North Carolina Nonconnah Pottery, were also beneficial.

Notes
1. Walter B. Stephen, Undated, unpublished memo No. 4. This memo and other personal memos and papers were recovered from his library building at the Pisgah Forest Pottery in 1992. Stephen's library had flooded in 1977 and several memos may be incomplete for this reason. Each memo used in this text is recorded as written including errors in grammar and spelling.
2. V. Terrell, "Pisgah Forest Pottery is Unique Industry," *The Sunday Citizen*, Section B, June 19, 1927, pp. 1-2
3. L. Henzke, *American Art Pottery* (New York: Thomas Nelson, 1970), pp. 24, 132, 296. M. Ray, *Collectible Ceramics* (New York: Crown Publishers, 1947). W.B. Stephen, "Pottery Handicraft in the Western North Carolina Mountains," *Saluda Magazine*, Vol. 1, No. 4, Winter 1936-37, pp. 23, 74.
4. Walter B. Stephen, Undated, unpublished memo No. 4.
5. Ibid, No. 1.
6. Ibid.
7. G. Clark, R. Ellison Jr, and E. Hecht, *The Mad Potter of Biloxi: The Art & Life of George E. Ohr* (New York: Cross River Press, Ltd., 1989) p.34.
8. Walter B. Stephen, Undated, unpublished memo No. 1.
9. Ibid, No. 5.
10. Nellie R. Stephen, Unpublished letter c. 1907.
11. C.E. Woods, Letter of reference addressed to "Whom it may concern," September 14, 1896, on file at Pisgah Forest Pottery.
12. Nellie R. Stephen.
13. B. Lindau, "Walter Stephen's Pottery is in White House, Museums," *Asheville Citizen*, July 5, 1953.
14. J.F. Conger, Personal communication, February 16, 1992.
15. Nellie R. Stephen.
16. N. Haas, Personal communications, June 24, 1993.
17. P.H. Johnston, "Pisgah Forest and Nonconnah Pottery," *The Antiques Journal*, 32, Vol.5, May 29, 1977, pp. 8-13.
18. Ibid.
19. M. C. Havener, Personal communication, April 23, 1992.
20. Ibid.
21. Johnston.
22. Ibid, p. 10.
23. Ibid, pp. 8-13.
24. M. C. Havener.
25. B. E. Johnson, Personal communication, February 17, 1993.
26. Nellie R. Stephen.
27. J. Kardon, Ed., *The Ideal Home 1900-1920: The History of Twentieth Century American Craft* (New York: H. N. Abrams in Association with the American Craft, 1993).
28. H. Peck, *The Book of Rookwood Pottery* (New York: Bonanza Books, 1968).
29. Walter B. Stephen, Undated, unpublished memo No. 5.
30. Nellie R. Stephen.
31. Ibid.
32. K. R. Trapp, *Towards the Modern Style: Rookwood Pottery, The Later Years 1915-1950* (New York: Jordan-Volpe Gallery, 1983).
33. R. Kovel and T. Kovel, *Kovel's American Art Pottery: The Collector's Guide to Makers, Marks, and Factory Histories* (New York: Crown Publishers, 1993), pp. 2-274.
34. P. Evans, "An Encyclopedia of Producers and Their Marks," in *Art Pottery of the United States*, 2nd Ed. (New York: Feingold & Lewis Publishing, 1987), pp.1-404.
35. D. Bridges & K. Preyer, Eds., *The Pottery of Walter Stephen: Journal of Studies of the Ceramic Circle of Charlotte, North Carolina*, Vol. 3 (Charlotte: The Mint Museum, 1978) pp. 8- 9.

Additional References and Sources:
Anscombe, I., and Gere, C., *Arts and Crafts in Britain and America*. (rev. ed.) New York: Rizzoli International, 1983.
Bachelder, O. L., Letter from Bachelder, O. L. to Stevens[sic], W. B., September 10, 1918. On file at Pisgah Forest Pottery.
Boris, E., *Art and Labor: Ruskin, Morris, and the Craftsmen Ideal in America*. Philadelphia: Temple University Press, 1986.
Callen, A., *Women Artists of the Arts and Crafts Movement 1870-1914*. New York: Pantheon Books, 1979, pp. 78-86.
Clark, G., *American Ceramics 1876 to the Present*. (rev. ed.). New York: Abbeville Press, 1987, pp. 13-62.
Clark, G. & Hughto, M., *A Century of Ceramics in the United States: 1878-1978*. New York: E. P. Dutton, 1979, p. 9.
Clark, R. J., Ed., *The Arts and Crafts Movement in America: 1876-1916*. Princeton, NJ: Princeton University Press, 1972.
Cumming, E., "Sources and Early Ideals," in E. Cumming and W. Kaplan, *The Arts and Crafts Movement*. New York: Thames & Hudson, 1991, pp. 6-28.
Eidelburg, M., "Art Pottery," in R. J. Clark, Ed., *The Arts and Crafts Movement in America: 1876-1916*. Princeton, NJ: Princeton University Press, 1972, pp. 119-127.
Purdy, R. C., "The Craft Potters of North Carolina: Busbee, Hilton, and Stephen; The Influence of Oscar Louis Bachelder," *American Ceramic Society Bulletin*, 21(6), June 15, 1942, pp. 84-87.
Triggs, O. L., *Chapters in the History of the Arts and Crafts Movement*. New York: B. Blom., 1971, (Reprint of 1902 ed.), p. 3, 110-111.
"Walter Stephen, 85, Pisgah Forest Founder, Is Taken By Death," *Asheville Citizen*, January 1, 1962.

Western North Carolina is a region with rich opportunities for studies of architectural history. One can study pole structures of Native Americans prior to European settlement, joinery techniques used in early log structures, the rustic lodges and hotels of the early 20th century, or even the great variety of stone walls, chimneys and bridges scattered throughout the region. This study examines the work of one formally trained architect who was responsible for many of the most familiar public buildings in the Asheville area. Architects often leave signatures in their work, details which invite students to trace the repeating patterns in the work of designers and builders. Henry Henderson who in 1901 built the Dock Fox farmhouse at the head of Sugar Creek in Buncombe County, used rows of nails on the battens of his doors to create geometric patterns, often incorporating his initials. Douglas Ellington's signature on many of his buildings include the use of octagons, winged floor plans and a warm vocabulary of surface and color. —R. B.

An Inventory of Douglas Ellington's Architectural Work in Western North Carolina

By Clay Griffith

Born in 1886 in rural Clayton, North Carolina, Douglas Dobell Ellington was the oldest of three sons born to Jesse and Sallie Ellington. Jesse Ellington was a farmer, sheriff, Baptist preacher and veteran of the Confederate army. Ellington was an imaginative child and showed signs of being a dreamer. He preferred drawing and creative activities to athletics and exhibited a quiet, gentle disposition. He grew up close to his younger brothers, Kenneth and Eric, and following Eric's death in an airplane accident in 1913, Douglas and Kenneth became even closer.[1]

Ellington attended Randolph-Macon College in Virginia and received his architectural training at Drexel Institute and the University of Pennsylvania. In 1911 Ellington won the Paris Prize from the Society of Beaux-Arts Architects in New York City, an award that provided for study at the Ecole des Beaux-Arts in Paris. In 1913 Ellington won the Prix de Rougevin, the top honor for decorative competitions at the Ecole, and was the first American ever to do so. With the outbreak of World War I, Ellington returned to the United States and utilized his artistic skills serving in the Navy's newly formed camouflage unit. Following military service, Ellington assumed teaching posts in architecture at Drexel, Columbia University, and Carnegie Institute of Technology in Pittsburgh, all programs affiliated with the Beaux-Art tradition which underlies much of Ellington's work.

Ellington began his architectural practice in Pittsburgh in 1920 and maintained an office for five years while teaching at Carnegie. Ellington established his practice with his brother Kenneth, a lawyer, as office manager. Sallie Middleton, Ellington's niece, suggests that Kenneth served "to keep Uncle Douglas out of trouble, professional and otherwise."[2] His work during these years shows a relatively rapid evolution from the classical vocabulary of the Beaux-Arts to the modern aesthetic of Art Deco.

With the commission for the First Baptist Church, Ellington relocated to Asheville in 1926 with his brother and his brother's family. In Asheville he found a growing city with a co-mingling of architectural styles, and as a well-traveled and well-educated architect, Ellington was able to create a practice based on his own individualistic style. "He was able to fly free."[3] A perfectionist in his work, Ellington often joined workmen on site to demonstrate exactly how he wanted to place a stone or other element in a building. In his private life Ellington maintained European manners and bohemian dress.

Ellington's designs executed in the late 1920s, including the Asheville City Building (1927), Asheville High School (1929) and the S&W Cafeteria (1929) are among the finest Art Deco buildings in North Carolina. The energy and excitement of Asheville in the 1920s ended suddenly with

the economic depression of 1930, and as real estate speculators went bankrupt and the city's projects ground to a halt, architects in Asheville were left without work. Ellington, like other designers, turned to the federal government for employment in the 1930s. Ellington sold his Chunns Cove house to his brother's wife, Margaret R. Ellington in 1932, and moved to Washington, D.C., although he would frequently return to Asheville during the summer months.[4] He teamed with Reginald Wadsworth to design the structures for the new town of Greenbelt, Maryland, sponsored under a federal program begun in 1932 by President Roosevelt.[5] Ellington remained in Washington for several years for the design and construction of Greenbelt, but returned to Western North Carolina to work on at

least one private commission near Asheville during the 1930s, the entrance to Chimney Rock Park.

In 1937 after Greenbelt was completed, Ellington moved to Charleston, South Carolina, to direct the reconstruction of the historic Dock Street Theater. Ellington decided to re-establish his office in Charleston and worked there almost exclusively during the years of the second World War. He designed numerous churches, residences, government housing projects and facilities associated with the Charleston Naval Base. Though he never lived in Asheville again, Ellington returned to the mountains regularly during the summers, and in the late 1940s and early 1950s, he worked on a number of residential projects in the Asheville area. Through his social contacts and business connections, Ellington maintained a steady clientele in Asheville while working from his office at 5 Exchange Street in Charleston. Ellington grew ill from cancer in the last years of his life and died quietly in 1960 at his former home in Chunns Cove. He was buried on the property beneath a simple, carved stone of his own design.[6]

Douglas Ellington was one of the most important architects to practice in the state of North Carolina in the mid-twentieth century. Though most of his clients came from Asheville, he designed buildings across the state including two fraternity houses on the University of North Carolina campus in Chapel Hill and several residences in Wilmington. This study describes all of Ellington's known architectural projects in Western North Carolina, including those that were never constructed and those that were built and have since been torn down or altered. The full range of his work has been eclipsed by the few well known buildings constructed in the late 1920s. Ellington introduced a unique synthesis of Beaux-Arts classicism, modern functionalism and fashionable Art Deco styling on several highly-visible civic projects in downtown Asheville, but these buildings do not present the full spectrum of Ellington's talent.

First Baptist Church, 5 Oak Street, Asheville, 1925-27

The First Baptist Church commission marked the beginning of Ellington's career in Asheville and Western North Carolina. The first of Ellington's large and highly visible projects, the church plan combined Beaux-Arts planning and Art Deco ornament and introduced many elements of design and decoration that appear in his later work.

The church complex is an assemblage of five buildings that pyramid into a single structure capped by a copper cupola. A slightly bellcast dome sits atop the octagonal main auditorium and a large hectastyle portico greets visitors from the entrance. The main sanctuary is flanked by an educational plant consisting of four smaller structures, two of which are two stories in height and two that are three stories high. The whole ensemble is load-bearing brick construction.[7]

Although the outward form of the church appears to be neoclassical, the deco-

rative patterns and surface ornament reflect the fashionably modern Art Deco style of the 1920s. Ellington composed the primary exterior materials, marble and brick, in a variety of low relief planes and patterns that enrich the wall surfaces with variations of texture and color. Exterior terra cotta moldings display alternating bands of chevrons and nail head designs, while geometric star patterns set in low relief panels accentuate the exterior doors. Interior details include geometric stars, stylized floral and feather motifs, diamond-shaped panels and abstract diagonal fretwork.

The pastor's home, which stood detached from the church to the east, was constructed of the same heather brown brick in an adapted Georgian style. A projecting entrance vestibule with a peaked parapet and single terra-cotta medallion enlivened the otherwise plain two-story, double-pile structure with one-story wings.[8] Construction of the cross-town

Ellington's first project in Asheville has become a familiar downtown landmark. The First Baptist Church was completed in 1927 and introduced the Beaux-Art and Art Deco design elements Ellington used in many public buildings. The variations in surface textures and colors seen in the friezes above the windows of the church also characterized much of Ellington's work. (Photo, Nick Lanier.)

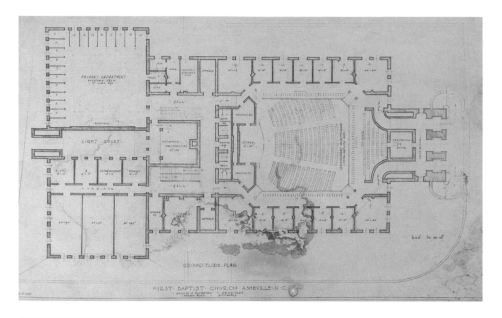

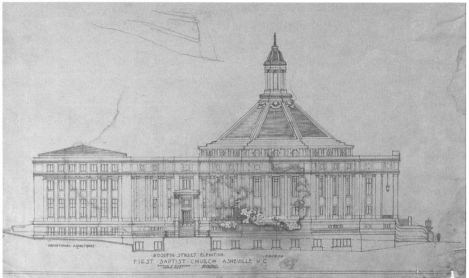

expressway (I-240) and the extension of Charlotte Street to the south destroyed the pastor's house in the 1970s.

Ellington's building was the fifth house of worship for First Baptist Church since its organization in 1829. Church membership grew from 37 in 1874 to approximately 1,500 members in the early 1920s. The new complex provided seating for 2,000 in the main auditorium and space for 3,000 in the educational buildings, and contained one million cubic feet of space within its 101 rooms. When dedicated, some church members reportedly expressed doubts that the main auditorium would ever be filled, but by the early 1950s church membership had grown to 2,720. Miller Engineering Corporation constructed the new church complex at a cost of $635,000 for the site, buildings and equipment.[9] The Reverend Robert J. Bateman, pastor of First Baptist Church during the building campaign, expressed his pleasure with the new facility, which he described as "a magnificent church of rare architecture, and one in which the denomination as a whole may feel a pardonable pride."[10]

Above. Although damaged, many of Ellington's drawings survive in the collection of the Asheville Art Museum. This drawing of the proposed church as seen from Woodfin Street bears only a general resemblance to the finished structure. (Drawings, courtesy, Asheville Art Museum.)

Left. Detail of exterior.

Right. Ellington's interiors used variations of feather, star and diamond motifs as seen in this photograph of the interior of the sanctuary taken in August of 1930. (Courtesy, North Carolina Division of Archives and History, Western Office; published in Architectural Record, *August, 1930, p.117.)*

CITY-COUNTY PLAZA (PROPOSED), PACK SQUARE AND PROPOSED EXTENSION TO THE EAST, ASHEVILLE, 1926

PACK·SQUARE·TERRACE·DEVELOPMENT·OF·THE·OLD·CITY·HALL·SITE

With explosive population growth and development through land speculation in the 1920s, the City of Asheville and Buncombe County lagged behind in both services and infrastructure. Under the administration of John H. Cathey, who served as mayor 1923-27, the city initiated an ambitious civic building campaign called the "Program of Progress" with 94 objectives to improve municipal facilities. Ellington was selected to design several of the major projects, and the modern architectural style he introduced set the stage for other architects to explore modern architecture in Asheville.

Ellington's plan for the City-County Plaza presented a dramatic conception of Asheville's civic identity. His design included a complementary city building and county courthouse, rendered in a visionary modernistic style intended to reflect the prosperous, cosmopolitan atmosphere of the time. His master plan for the City-County Plaza recognized the formation of Asheville at the intersection of Cherokee trading paths, which evolved into the major streets of downtown. The plan maintained these two major axes while expanding the scale of the square to serve the city's future needs. Ellington submitted conceptual designs to the mayor and county commissioners proposing two similarly treated, yet distinct, buildings for the city and the county government offices joined by an arcade. The scheme placed the buildings on a new site, several blocks east of Pack Square, and accommodated the grade change of the expanded site through an axial system of monumental stairs and terraces. Fellow architect Henry Gaines summarized Ellington's City-County Plaza as "a valiant effort to bring some symmetry out of the racing hodgepodge...."[11]

A perspective rendering showing Ellington's design for the paired buildings appeared in the Asheville *Citizen* newspaper on September 26, 1926. Unfortunately, a local political squabble ensued and the full scheme was never realized. Regarding Ellington's design, one of the county commissioners reportedly remarked: "Who the hell ever heard of a courthouse without columns?"[12] The city used Ellington's plan for the city building, while the county officials commissioned the Washington, D.C., firm of Milburn, Heister & Company to produce designs for the Buncombe County Courthouse. In his response to the county commissioners Ellington wrote:

> The general scheme as originally contemplated was the only logical solution of the problem possible under the circumstances; and with the buildings and grounds not treated in accordance therewith, then the result will inevitably be nothing more than two separate structures unrelated, inharmonious, misplaced... [the commissioners'] final action was a very thorough repudiation of me and my work.[13]

Ellington's proposed plan for the City-County Plaza presented a dramatic conception of Asheville's civic identity. (Courtesy, Asheville Art Museum.) For more detail on the courthouse, see "Public Architecture, Civic Aspirations and the Price of 'Progress': A History of the Buncombe County Courthouse" by Daniel J. Vivian, this volume, p.154)

Although Douglas Ellington's plans for an architecturally integrated City-County Plaza and city and county buildings did not materialize, Ellington's bold design for the Asheville City Building is one of his finest works. Ellington used a stepped octagonal roof, stylized feather designs, and an emphasis on verticality to relate the building to the mountain skyline of the region. (Photos, Nick Lanier.)

A landmark of civic architecture, the Asheville City Building is one of Ellington's finest designs. The structure rises from a fortress-like base and emphasizes its verticality through setbacks, embellished central fenestration and a stepped octagonal roof. While the base is classical in its treatment, Ellington enriched the upper stories of the building with innovative Art Deco details. In each unit of the upper-story windows, the tapering stem of the stylized feather separates the two windows and then continues beyond the cornice line. The peaked window shapes and lintels, along with the jagged cornice, suggest upward motion. The repetition of terra cotta diagonals against the brick background multiplies the effect of vertical movement. The brightly colored tile roof, which is the dominant decorative element, steps back from its octagonal base to a raised cupola. According to Ellington the roof form came about "as an evolution of the desire that the contours of the building reflect the mountain background and that the building be equally presentable from all points of view."[14] Ellington claimed that he was "privileged to entertain a fresh point of view

Clay Griffith ■ AN INVENTORY OF DOUGLAS ELLINGTON'S ARCHITECTURAL WORK IN WESTERN NORTH CAROLINA because of the freedom of the surroundings and because of the broad outlook of the officials who had the project in charge."[15] At the time of dedication in 1928, an article in the local newspaper assured the citizens that the city building was in "the style of architecture now being used by the Metropolitan architects in the new school of building which are refashioning the whole face of the large cities of the land."[16]

Miller Engineering, who had also worked on the First Baptist Church, constructed the city building for $750,000.[17] Local architect William East later reported that the Buncombe County Courthouse, generally considered to be the lesser of the two structures architecturally, cost twice as much per cubic foot as the city building.[18] Speaking at the dedication of the new city building, former Mayor Cathey stated, "Time alone can tell us whether we spent wisely or foolishly. We are willing to submit what we have done to time."[19]

The city building, with 59,000 square feet of office space, has had a variety of tenants and uses. From 1928 to 1941, the city leased the upper floors of the building. Many of the tenants were physicians and dentists, and the building was well used by local residents. In 1943, the U.S. Army Air Corps' Flight Control Command moved into the building, "from basement to belfry," and relocated city officials and employees, medical offices, the Sondley Library, the Office of Price Administration, two city draft boards, the War Production and Rationing Board, the War Manpower Commission, the U.S. Employment Service and the North Carolina Unemployment Commission. The Flight Control Command returned the building to the city in 1946 when city officials and employees, along with physicians and dentists, moved back into the building. By 1956, the city offices expanded and for the first time filled the building.[20] The Ellington-designed structure continues to serve as the center of civic government.

Ellington used design elements from a wide range of historic sources. These classically derived portals set off the three second floor windows above the west entrance to the building.

The set back corner lights on the sides of the entrance to the city building have similar contours to the entire structure.

An entrance to the city building with the Seal for the city carved above in marble.

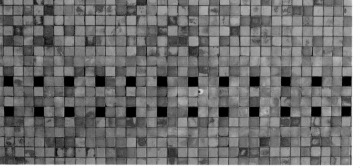

Ellington's color vocabulary for the building incorporated many shades of pink as seen in these rows of mosaic tile on the exterior of the first floor.

Not all of Douglas Ellington's projects came to fruition. These drawings for a 15-story tower on the north side of Pack Square, (bottom) and for the "Alcaza" recreational center (top) are for structures which were never built, probably due to the economic collapse in Asheville in 1930. The recreational center appears to be very similar to the Grove Arcade, designed by Charles N. Parker in 1926. (Courtesy, Asheville Art Museum.)

Two drawings suggest that Ellington's vision for downtown Asheville extended beyond his City-County Plaza design. The first of these drawings depicts a tower approximately 15 stories in height intended for the north side of Pack Square, where I. M. Pei's Akzona Building (currently the Biltmore Building) sits. The proposed tower, commissioned by an unknown investor, included a thoroughly designed exterior brick skin punctuated by ornament over the central entrance and rising to a steeply-pitched pyramidal roof. The level of detail in the proposal suggests every intention of completion.

The second drawing for the Alcaza, "recreational center and bowling alleys of Asheville," does not indicate a specific site although presumably slated for downtown. The proposed building bears a striking resemblance in mass and form to the Grove Arcade, designed by Charles N. Parker in 1926, though the detail in Ellington's rendering favors the Exotic Revival Style to Parker's Tudor Gothic Revival. Again, the level of detail in the drawing suggests that Ellington had a client committed to the completed project. The crash of 1930 likely doomed both projects.

Merrimon Avenue Fire Station, 300 Merrimon Avenue, Asheville, 1926–1927

Above. Detail, brick window, alcove on south wall. (Photos, Nick Lanier.)

The Merrimon Avenue Fire Station is perhaps the most modest of Ellington's civic designs, but it demonstrates his ability to respond to varying functions and context. Designed in 1926 and built in 1927, the building is a highly articulated, symmetrical arrangement of rectangular masses with flat roofs behind parapet walls. The load-bearing masonry structure is veneered with rose-colored brick. The front portion of the building consists of a tall two-story central mass flanked by shorter two-story blocks. Another rectangular mass of three stories with a basement level, revealed by the slope of the site, extends across the rear. A six-story training tower also used for hanging and drying hoses stands at the southwest corner of the building. The front center section of the building has two semi-circular arched door openings for fire trucks. Centered above and between the arched openings is a small wrought-iron balcony with a paneled nine-pane door, transom and a decorative brick lintel design, reminiscent of Ellington's feather motif.

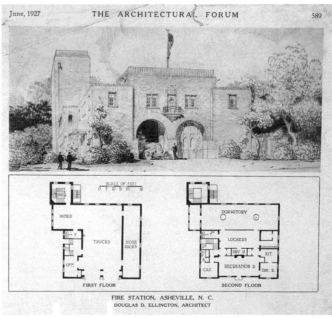

Ellington's least flamboyant civic project was probably the Merrimon Avenue Fire Station completed in 1927. The two-story brick structure featured two arched entries for fire trucks, and a training tower at the southwest corner also used for drying hoses. (Courtesy, Asheville Art Museum. Drawing originally published in Architectural Forum, *vol. 46, no. 6, June 1927, p.587.)*

While the geometric qualities of this building are in keeping with Ellington's other civic buildings, the Merrimon Avenue Fire Station lacks the detailing and flourishes that characterize some of Ellington's other work in this period. The Fire Station reads as a modern, functional design and is further evidence of the architectural aspirations of Asheville in the 1920s.

ASHEVILLE HIGH SCHOOL, 419 McDOWELL STREET, ASHEVILLE, 1927-29

Ellington's design for Asheville High School, completed in 1929, may be his most familiar to many Asheville residents as thousands of high school students have walked its halls for over 70 years. The new high school cost $1,362,301 and was originally part of the "Program for Progress" plan for civic architecture in Asheville. (Photos, Nick Lanier.)

The entry tower (middle) to the high school resembles many of Ellington's other domes and roofs. The rows of inset stones relate to similar work on the exterior of the First Baptist Church. Right. Ellington's buildings used a wide variety of materials: in this case the cut stone adds to the fortress-like quality of the structure.

In designing the new senior high school just south of downtown, Ellington faced a wooded, rolling site with two natural rises joined by a wide ravine. The high school and a municipal college were to occupy the site, sharing a stadium and athletic field located in the natural depression that separated the two campuses. Ellington selected the northern point of the site for the high school and approached the design "in such a way as to secure symmetry and coordination of requirements and location without disturbing the natural earth slopes any more than was necessary."[21] The building radiates from the central entry tower into three equal wings, two for classrooms and the third for the auditorium. A gymnasium and vocational laboratory join at the southern ends. The classroom wings and attached structures nestle into the sloping contours, allowing Ellington to establish a hierarchy of building masses without sacrificing the simplicity and order of the plan. The crescendo of functional blocks, like

Clay Griffith ■ AN INVENTORY OF DOUGLAS ELLINGTON'S ARCHITECTURAL WORK IN WESTERN NORTH CAROLINA

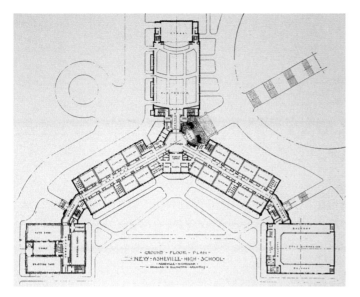

those of the First Baptist Church, refers to both the site and the distant mountains.

Another landmark among Ellington's civic buildings, Asheville High School exhibits the full spectrum of his architectural talent. The Palmer-Spivey Construction Company constructed the building for $1,362,301. The high school was originally part of the "Program of Progress," initiated in the 1920s. It was known for a time as Lee Edwards High School, named in 1935 in honor of Principal Lee H. Edwards following his unexpected death. The name was changed back to Asheville High School in 1969, when the city schools were racially integrated.

The structure was tripartite with equal wings surrounding an entrance hall and rotunda, with the primary entrance on the east side. (Courtesy, North Carolina Division Archives and History, Western Office. This drawing and photograph were originally published September, 1929 in Architectural Record, *66, pp. 196-197.)*

PARK AVENUE SCHOOL ADDITIONS, 30 PARK AVENUE, ASHEVILLE, 1927, (DEMOLISHED)

Ellington designed additions to the Park Avenue School as part of the "Program of Progress." Opened in 1902, the school sat on the crest of a hill in the West End section of Asheville overlooking the French Broad River. Architect Frank Elwood Brown designed the original eight-room school, and in 1910, prominent local architects Richard Sharp Smith and Albert Carrier provided plans for the first of several additions to the school building. Ellington designed an auditorium and two additional classrooms for the building. Miss Queen Carson supervised the neighborhood school from the time it opened until her retirement in 1945. In 1935, the city school board renamed the school in her honor. The buildings were razed in the 1960s by the city for a bus maintenance facility.

In 1927, Douglas Ellington designed an auditorium and two classrooms for the Park Avenue School which stood on Park Avenue overlooking the French Broad River to the west. The eight-room school was originally built in 1902 and had subsequent additions designed by Richard Sharp Smith and Albert Carrier. In 1935 the school was renamed in honor of Queen Carson who supervised the school from 1902 to 1945. The building was torn down in the 1960s when the site became a city bus maintenance facility. (Courtesy, North Carolina Collection, Pack Memorial Public Library, Asheville, North Carolina.)

Lewis Memorial Park, 415 Beaverdam Road, Asheville, 1927

In 1927, Robert Jackson Lewis, a successful funeral director, commissioned Ellington to design the office for a new cemetery, Lewis Memorial Park, he had established just north of Asheville on Beaverdam Road. Lewis became acquainted with Ellington's work when Lewis was chairman of the building committee of the First Baptist Church that oversaw the construction of the new sanctuary. Though small in scale, the building exhibits a similar vocabulary of forms, materials and motifs to that employed by Ellington in the city building, Asheville High School and the First Baptist Church.

The office is composed of a monument-like central structure capped by an octagonal roof and flanked by arched gateways. It is constructed of both smooth and rough-faced masonry of several textures and colors punctuated with stylized lettering and floral images.

Robert Jackson Lewis, chairman of the building committee for the First Baptist Church, commissioned Ellington to design the office at the entrance of a new cemetery, Lewis Memorial Park located on Beaverdam Road. The monument-like structure incorporated many of Ellington's favorite forms: octagonal roof, arched gateways and textured stone to achieve a restrained design appropriate for a cemetery. (Photo, Nick Lanier.)

Sylvan Theater, Main Street, Sylva, 1927

The Sylvan Theater opened July 1, 1927, on Main Street in Sylva, North Carolina, and may have been Ellington's first commission in Western North Carolina outside of Asheville. The project appears on building lists he submitted to the Federal government in the 1930s. Ellington had designed a theater in Pennsylvania in the early 1920s, which may have been known by his Asheville client. J. S. Higdon built the Sylvan for Theodore "Bo" Stevenson, who also owned theaters in Waynesville and Asheville. E. B. Drake of Pittsburgh was the residential manager of the new theater, which had a seating capacity of 500 with 300 on the first floor and 200 in the balcony. The Sylvan closed in the 1930s, and the building was extensively remodeled for offices.

The Sylvan Theater was one of Douglas Ellington's few commissions in Western North Carolina outside of Asheville. The building apparently incorporated minimal architectural detail. The theater closed in the 1930s and was remodeled for offices. (Photo, Nick Lanier.)

S&W Cafeteria, 56 Patton Avenue, Asheville, 1929

The S&W Cafeteria is Ellington's most refined and urbane example of the Art Deco style. Whereas his other Art Deco designs are tempered with a response to the natural setting, the S&W building incorporates finely detailed ornament suited to a man-made environment. The sophistication of the building reflects its setting in the heart of downtown Asheville. Another civic landmark, Ellington's cafeteria design captured the modern aspirations of its time.

Asheville's S&W was the third in a chain of cafeterias started by Frank O. Sherrill and Fred R. Webber whose other restaurants were in Charlotte and Winston-Salem. The first S&W opened in 1920 in Charlotte and was the first cafeteria in the Carolinas. In 1922, Asheville's S&W opened in a leased building on Patton Avenue that was once the Asheville Opera House. The cafeteria was an immediate success and within eight months of opening, the operations were expanded with additional dining space in the basement and mezzanine. In 1929, Frank Sherrill, who had bought out Webber's interest in the business in 1926, authorized construction of a new building to be designed by Ellington exclusively for use as a cafeteria.

Built adjacent to the 1895 Drhumor Building, the facade of the S&W building continues the street wall along Patton Avenue. Ellington addressed the development of downtown by subordinating the symmetry of the facade to the axis along Haywood Street immediately in front of the building. Two monumental round-arched windows flanking the entrance comprise the primary section of the facade while a secondary portion is similar, although restrained, in its detail. The crenellated parapet of blue and green tiles unifies the whole facade. Glazed terra cotta panels, slate, glass and wrought iron serve as the principal materials. Colors include black, gold, cream, blue and green. Large stylized fountain designs of wrought iron

Douglas Ellington's design for the S&W Cafeteria on Patton Avenue in downtown Asheville is perhaps the most refined and urbane of Ellington's work in the Art Deco style. Ellington sought a festive mood in both the interior and exterior of the building. The large arched windows are similar to the double-arched entrances of the Merrimon Avenue Fire House. (Photos, Nick Lanier.)

The S&W Cafeteria in Asheville was the third in a group of cafeterias opened in North Carolina in the 1920s by Frank O. Sherrill. The Asheville cafeteria opened in 1922 in leased space which had once been the Asheville Opera House. In 1929 Sherrill authorized construction of a new building designed by Ellington. This photograph (damaged) shows the front facade under construction. (Courtesy, Asheville Art Museum.)

The entrance on the left side of the facade of the building is framed with borders of blue chevrons with canted corners at the top and gilt muntins delineating the glass panes.

The carved marble sign over the principle front entrance rests above stylized scrolls and under a frieze of gilt and cobalt terra cotta panels and a central painted relief panel of grapes and other fruit.

were once located in the monumental round-arched windows.

The brightly colored facade and richly decorated interior dining rooms provided a modern venue for the cafeteria. Ellington enjoyed the opportunity to apply "unhampered architecture to an individual commercial need," and stated that the building had been "custom built," in both its utilitarian and aesthetic aspects. He claimed that:

> The note of gaiety which has been struck in both the facade and in the interior has been deliberate, this cheerful or semi-festive quality being regarded as fitting to the purpose of the establishment and in keeping with the life of a community where recreation is an important activity.[22]

The John M. Geary Company constructed the building. The Asheville S&W remained in the Ellington-designed building until 1974, and served as many as 5,000 customers a day, six days a week.[23] From 1974 into the 1980s the building housed Dale's Cafeteria. After being closed for a number of years, the facility reopened in 1994 as a multipurpose space and currently is occupied by a bar and music club.

The paired windows on the second floor are separated by large panels of stylized plants with gilt surfaces.

ELLINGTON HOUSE, 583 CHUNNS COVE ROAD, ASHEVILLE, 1926–1930

Ellington purchased a three-acre tract on Ross Creek at the head of Chunns Cove in 1926 from an area farmer, W. M. Taylor, and set about building a home for himself.[24] Ellington arranged his house around an old log cabin on the site and continued to develop and expand his residence for the next several years, often incorporating building materials salvaged from his other civic projects. Ellington refused to draw any plans for the house, preferring to craft the place as he went along. Ellington chose to rely on local craftsmen for the construction of the house, although he did employ an Italian stonemason to lay up the massive stone fireplace that dominates the main living space.[25]

At first impression, the house strikes the viewer as stylistically different from Ellington's civic work. Romantic and irregular, in contrast to the classical formality and modern treatment of his public buildings, the stylistic vocabulary of Ellington's house is drawn from European vernacular

sources rather than high-style precedents. While residential design has always lent itself to greater informality than would be expected in public architecture, the rustic Welsh Cottage style of the Ellington House veils a highly ordered design.

Much like Ellington's civic work, the house derives in part from its topographical setting. Ellington divided the house into small component parts arranged along the contours of the hill. The spaces within the house are enhanced by their placement at varying levels along the hill, and with their integration with outdoor terraces and yards. The building appears as an outgrowth of the hill, and the same sensitivity to site can be seen in the more formal, radial organization of the wings of Asheville High School.[26]

The plan of the house, as it negotiates the hillside, also allows for the development of a variety of interior spaces. The house progresses from intimate rooms such as the library contained in the old log cabin, to the grandly scaled hall with its large stone

In 1926 Ellington purchased three acres of land in Chunns Cove and began construction of his own home. Though based on a vernacular Welsh Cottage style with many romantic and irregular features, the building is a highly ordered design. Ellington drew no plans for the house and built the structure using many local craftsmen, often with salvaged materials. (Photos, above and top next page, Doug Swaim, January 1985; courtesy, North Carolina Division of Archives and History, Western Office.)

fireplace as the focal point. Small rooms and circulation corridors link the main spaces of the house and contribute to the eclectic, almost Medieval, feel of the place. The narrow stone stairs and dark hallways contrast with the more open living spaces and add a sense of mystery and discovery when moving through the house. Likewise, Ellington emphasized the vernacular character by giving each section of the house a different architectural treatment on the exterior, whether it was brick, stone or log.

Ellington lived in the house with his brother and brother's family until he moved to Washington D. C. in 1932. He sold the property to his brother's wife, Margaret R. Ellington and lived there when he visited Asheville in the 1940s and 1950s. The house remains a private residence.

Biltmore Hospital Extension, 14 All Souls Crescent, Asheville, 1929–30

In 1930 Ellington designed a 65-room addition to the Biltmore Hospital in Biltmore Village. The original 20-room frame structure had been designed by Richard Sharp Smith and remodeled by William Lord. This commission did not afford Ellington much opportunity for flamboyant details, but the first floor and ends of the building are faced in cut stone similar to other Ellington designs. The arched and offset stone entrances relate to similar examples at Asheville High School and Lewis Memorial Park. (Photo, Nick Lanier.)

In 1930, Ellington was commissioned to design an addition to the Biltmore Hospital in Biltmore Village. Founded in 1899 by George Vanderbilt and two cousins, the hospital, originally named in honor of Clarence Barker, began as a small community facility. Richard Sharp Smith, the resident architect for Biltmore Estate, designed the original hospital building, and Asheville architect William H. Lord remodeled and designed additions to the rambling 20-room frame structure. Ellington's addition, known as the Battle Wing, contained 65 rooms in a new four-story brick and stone fireproof building. Although lacking the exuberance of his earlier works, the hospital building was thoroughly modern in appearance, especially compared to the original structure, and was touted as "an innovation in its particular type of structure."[27] The John M. Geary Company constructed the Biltmore Hospital Extension at a cost of $125,000. Memorial Mission Hospital eventually acquired the Biltmore Hospital, but sold the buildings to the Imperial Life Insurance Company in 1952. The building has been used subsequently as a nursing facility.

ROYES–SMATHERS SHOP, 15 HAYWOOD STREET, ASHEVILLE, 1930 (DEMOLISHED)

Although cited by Ellington on resumes and building lists, the Royes–Smathers Shop remains something of a mystery and may have entailed only an interior remodeling. In 1921, Roy E. Swartzberg (hence "Royes") opened a store at the corner of Haywood and College Streets at the rear of the Central Bank and Trust Building. The store offered "exclusive toggery and sports apparel for gentlemen" and prospered during the 1920s.[28] In 1929-30, Swartzberg teamed with W. M. Smathers to open Royes–Smathers, Inc., at 15 Haywood on the northern corner of College Street. Swartzberg, previously employed by the Asheville *Citizen* newspaper, was later president of the Asheville Merchants Association. Smathers became aware of the architect when he was a member of the Asheville City School Board building during the erection of the new high school. The Swartzberg-Smathers business association apparently failed rather quickly since Smathers had returned to farming by 1935.[29] The store operated until 1938 as Royes Inc.— "haberdashery, clothing and shoes."

CHIMNEY ROCK PARK GATES, CHIMNEY ROCK PARK, US 74, CHIMNEY ROCK, 1934

Douglas Ellington moved to Washington D.C. in 1932 to work on the design and construction of the town of Greenbelt, Maryland, but he returned to Asheville often in the ensuing years. In 1934 he was commissioned to design and supervise construction of new entrance walls, gates, offices and related facilities at Chimney Rock Park, in Chimney Rock, North Carolina. Ellington often used cut and faced stone in his projects, and the Chimney Rock project featured it almost exclusively. Chimney Rock can be seen in the distance in this photo. (Photo, Nick Lanier.) Even in this rustic setting, however, the familiar curved line of the Art Deco vocabulary can be seen on the sides of the entry. These entries are articulated with large, wedge-shaped stones which form arches similar to those above the fireplace in Ellington's home (right). (Detail of fireplace, Douglas Ellington House, Doug Swaim, January 1985; courtesy, North Carolina Division of Archives and History, Western Office.)

Ellington conceived a design for a new inn on the Chimney Rock property, which survives only in a painted photograph (top). Ellington's proposal was a fantastic castle-like stone structure that emerged from a towering eminence as an extension of the forest and mountain on which it was to be built. Ellington's proposed inn called to mind the alpine castles of Bavaria and the Greek monasteries of Meteora. Sadly, this wildly romantic project never progressed beyond Ellington's initial concept. Ellington's gates still stand, but the offices have been moved into new buildings within the park. (Photo, Paul Jeremais; courtesy, Asheville Art Museum.)

Inset. The original photograph on which Ellington painted his castle was taken by George Masa, a Japanese photographer known for his photographs of mountain scenes. (Private collection.)

After surviving the lean years of the Great Depression, Chimney Rock Park began to undertake a series of improvements in 1934, including a stone entrance wall and gate, ticket office, visitor restrooms, administrative offices, reflecting pool and upgraded parking area. The park hired Ellington to oversee these projects and ensure that their design complemented the natural beauty of the property. Ellington frequently accompanied workmen around the park to select stone for the new structures. He insisted that the moss and lichens be left on the rock so that the new buildings would blend in with their natural setting.[30]

REYNOLDS/OERTLING HOUSE, REYNOLDS MOUNTAIN ROAD, ASHEVILLE, 1946

In the late 1940s and early 1950s, Ellington visited Asheville regularly and worked on a number of residential projects in and around Asheville. Frances Reynolds Oertling, daughter of Senator Robert Rice Reynolds from his first marriage, commissioned Ellington to design a house on Reynolds Mountain with expansive views of Asheville and the surrounding countryside to the south. Reynolds ("Our Bob") was a colorful and controversial United States senator from Buncombe County, and he retired to this house with his daughter, following the death of his fifth wife.[31] The Reynolds House is a rambling one-story log and stone dwelling with a front porch terrace and picture windows to provide 270-degree exposure. Like some of Ellington's other house plans, the wings of the house attach to the center block at a slight angle to capture the panoramic vistas. The house remains a private residence.

In 1937, after completion of the Greenbelt Project, Ellington moved to Charleston, South Carolina to direct reconstruction of the Dock Street Theater. In the late 1940s and early 1950s he returned regularly to Asheville and worked on a number of residential projects. In 1946 Ellington completed at least 19 drawings for the Reynolds/Oertling house on Reynolds Mountain. The rambling one-story log and stone dwelling featured two side wings and a 270-degree view from the central room. (Photo, Nick Lanier; drawing, courtesy, Asheville Art Museum.)

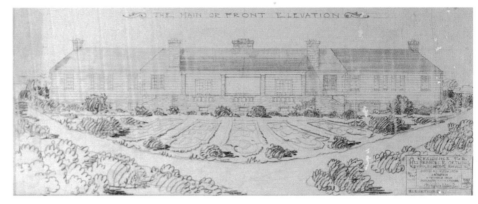

PEEK HOUSE, 128 WINDSOR ROAD, ASHEVILLE, 1948

In 1949, Coleman C. and Helen Peek moved to their new house at 128 Windsor Road in the Beaver Lake Development, which was redesigned by Ellington. With its stone and wood siding, this modest one-story dwelling closely follows popular house styles during the mid-20th century. Ellington's contributions appear to be minimal. Peek, who was a member of First Baptist Church, owned and operated Peek's Service Center, an auto repair shop, until 1972.[32] The house remains a private residence.

Bottom, right. This drawing is titled "Supplement Drawing to the Enlow Design For Mr. & Mrs. C.C. Peek, Beaver Lake Asheville N.C." Ellington's contributions to this modest home are not clear, but they probably consisted of remodeling. (Photo, Nick Lanier; drawing, courtesy, Asheville Art Museum.)

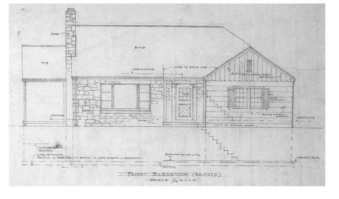

BROWN HOUSE ("KELLS CASTLE"), 24 KIMBERLY AVENUE, ASHEVILLE, 1949-50

Ellington designed this extraordinary home for Sanford and Rose Brown. Rose Brown, an accomplished painter and designer, took the inspiration for the residence from the *Book of Kells*, which Ellington had loaned to her, and from the architecture of medieval Irish monasteries. She reportedly challenged Ellington that he could not build her a house of cinder block that she would like. Inspired by the challenge issued to him, Ellington constructed the house of exposed cinder block with brick accents and banding and covered with a red tile roof. He succeeded in providing the Brown's with one of the most distinctive houses in Asheville and one that reflected their tastes and personality.

Similar to the design of his own home in Chunns Cove, Ellington arranged the Brown House in a series of distinct volumes organized on a sloping site, with open terraces extending the living space into the outdoors. Two arched doorways provide access to the house—one to the main residence and one to Rose Brown's light-saturated studio. The interior includes a formal great room with heavy timber roof framing and a large north-facing window. A hallway separates the kitchen and bedrooms east of the great hall. The bedroom wing and main block of the house form an ell at the rear of the house surrounding the rear porch and terrace areas. Mrs. Brown also executed wall murals throughout the house drawing upon the *Book of Kells* for inspiration.[33]

Rose Brown's artistic temperament complemented that of Ellington, and the house was a collaborative effort between the two creative individuals. In addition to painting, Mrs. Brown designed jewelry, ceramics, hats, book jackets and perfume bottles. In the early 1950s she traveled with her husband, a prominent local attorney, to France, where they met and became acquainted with Picasso, Matisse and Chagall.[34] Substantially rehabilitated in 1995, the house remains a private residence.

DRAKE HOUSE, CHUNNS COVE ROAD, ASHEVILLE, 1948

In June 1946, Ellington began designing a house for John R. Jr., and Georgiana Drake on Chunns Cove Road on Beaucatcher ridge just east of Asheville. Drake, who had served in the Navy, was the first of several clients with military careers to commission Ellington for their homes. Ellington's designs show a simple one-story frame dwelling dominated by a projecting porch with off-center entrance. The Drake House was also one of several in this vicinity which were lost during the cutting of Beaucatcher Mountain for the construction of I-240 in the mid-1970s.

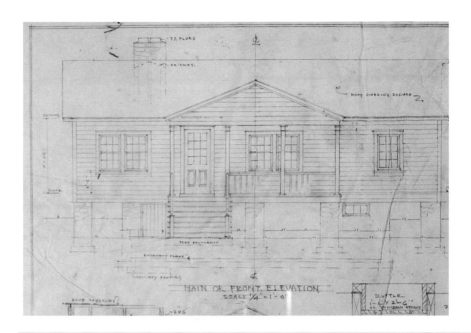

Ellington designed several homes in the Chunns Cove, Beaucatcher ridge area. One of these, the Drake House, was torn down for the construction of the I-240 expressway in the mid-1970s. Designs for the house show a simple one-story frame dwelling dominated by a projecting porch with off-center entrance. (Courtesy, Asheville Art Museum.)

CARRINGTON HOUSE, CHUNNS COVE ROAD, ASHEVILLE, 1948

Beginning in 1948, Ellington designed several houses in Chunns Cove and on Beaucatcher Mountain to the west. Ellington designed a house for Walter S. and Irma H. Carrington on the south side of Chunns Cove Road. Mr. Carrington was a sales manager for Automatic Kitchen Equipment in 1950, the only time they are listed in city directories.

Ellington conceived of the Carrington House as a rambling one-story dwelling built along modern lines, but softened by the use of exterior stone and wood. A large picture window dominates the long front wall of the main section which is capped by a side gable roof and prominent end chimney. The arched entrance to the house is located adjacent to the chimney in the end wall from a stone terrace. A smaller one-story wing joins the house at this end and is connected by a terrace. Extending beyond the wing is a stone two-car garage with a front gable roof. The house no longer stands.

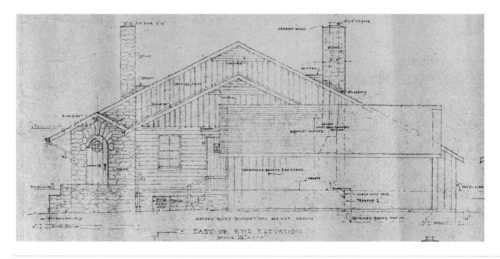

Two drawings exist for a home designed by Ellington for Walter and Irma Carrington in 1948. This story-and-a-half traditional brick residence featured a curved porch and ornate iron posts and brackets. This home no longer stands. (Courtesy, Asheville Art Museum.)

Skypark Housing Project, Poplar Street and Tunnel Road, Asheville, 1949 (Never built)

Ellington worked with Sanford and Rose Brown on a housing project near the west entrance to Beaucatcher Tunnel. This project for black residents was to be built with federal funds and included four apartment buildings and a supermarket beside the entrance to the tunnel. The drawing of the supermarket was superimposed on a photograph of the tunnel and the Esso service station which stood at that time. The project was designed in 1949, but was not built. (Drawings, courtesy, Ewart M. Ball Collection, Ramsey Library Special Collections, University of North Carolina at Asheville.)

Ellington proposed designs for an African-American housing project to be built with federal funds and promoted by Sanford and Rose Brown. The project, at a cost of $300,000 included plans for a housing development and a supermarket to be located at the west end of Beaucatcher Tunnel. Drawings show four proposed apartment buildings constructed of fireproof materials. The buildings were long, two-story structures containing approximately six units each. The relatively undistinguished exteriors featured shed-roof entry porches and one-story end bays. The most remarkable element of the project was Ellington's design for a new supermarket rendered in the streamline modern style popular in the mid-20th century.

COGGINS HOUSE, BEAUCATCHER MOUNTAIN, ASHEVILLE, 1950

In September 1950, Ellington prepared designs for a house for Mr. and Mrs. George Coggins on the east side of Beaucatcher Mountain. The plans show a one-story modern brick house under a flat, projecting roof with a garage located below grade. The U-shaped plans focused on a flagstone patio with interior galleries providing circulation throughout the house. The interior rooms center on a sunken living room lit by a picture window. Large, single-pane windows provide light throughout the house.

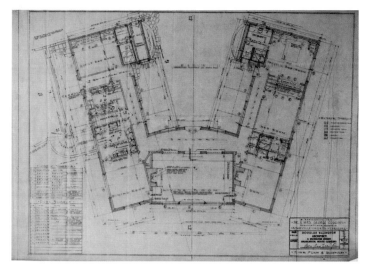

Several drawings exist for residences which were constructed but not according to Ellington's plans. The George Coggins home, proposed in this detailed drawing completed in 1950, was built using different plans. (Courtesy, Asheville Art Museum.)

Coggins was a member of numerous public and private organizations and committees, and he worked with Senator Reynolds to secure a federal grant for Asheville's civic auditorium in 1938. Coggins was president of Bee Tree Vermiculite Mines, manager of Chemclad Sales Division, and later developed and sold real estate, including Westgate Shopping Center in 1956. The house was built but not according to Ellington's plans.

MALLETT HOUSE, 4 BOXWOOD LANE, ASHEVILLE, 1950

Ellington designed a house in 1950 for Colonel and Mrs. Pierre Mallett on Beaucatcher Mountain. Two one-story wings, extending at a slight angle to the rear, flank a central two-story block capped by a tall hip roof. Three sets of French doors across the main facade open onto a loggia connecting the principal interior spaces. One wing contained the living room and kitchen while the master bedroom and study occupied the other wing. Additional bedrooms were located on the second level. A projecting dining room bay at the rear of the house provided a focus for the plan. With rough cut wood siding and stone foundation, Ellington's design for the house blends fairly traditional forms with several features typical of his residential projects, especially those located on sloping sites with sweeping views.

Col. Mallett had fought in both world wars before retiring to Asheville. Later, Ellington prepared plans for a guesthouse on Mallett's property. The Mallett House was destroyed in 1976 during the cutting of Beaucatcher Mountain for the construction of I-240. Timber from the house was salvaged and reused in the construction of a chapel on the family estate, Bryn Avon, in Henderson County.[35]

Ellington designed several residences on sloping land often with views of the surrounding landscape. In 1950 he designed a home for Col. and Mrs. Pierre Mallett on Beaucatcher Mountain with sweeping views of Asheville. The design incorporated Ellington's often used device of a central area with wings angled to the sides much as he designed Asheville High School many years earlier. The Mallett House was torn down for the construction of I-240 in 1976. (Courtesy, Asheville Art Museum.)

SLUDER HOUSE, 472 CHUNNS COVE ROAD, ASHEVILLE, 1951

The Sluder House, constructed in 1951, featured a sunken living room and two 45-degree bays. This structure was one of several residences Ellington designed in the Chunns Cove area, near the home he constructed for himself more than 20 years earlier. (Photos, Nick Lanier; drawing, courtesy, North Carolina Division of Archives and History, Western Office.)

In 1951, Dr. and Mrs. Fletcher Sluder commissioned Ellington to design their house, which evolved as a collaboration between the architect and owners. Dr. Sluder recounts that Ellington met with them on several occasions, at least once staying for dinner, to get a feel for their needs and tastes. Ellington maintained a desire to give his clients what they wanted, and the Sluders requested a variation of the modern ranch style house with some unique design features. In plan, Ellington turned the two rooms on either side of the central, sunken living room 45-degrees to form sharply projecting bays on the exterior. A main hall running the length of the house at the rear connects the multiple public and private living spaces. Built low along the western side of Chunns Cove, the Sluder House incorporates a variety of natural materials and interior finishes to provide a thoroughly modern living space in harmony with its surroundings.[36] It remains a private residence.

Detail of front entrance. Note the relief panels above the doors with oak leaf and shield motifs.

Pettigrew House, 602 Chunns Cove Road, Asheville, 1951

Mr. and Mrs. James Pettigrew, Ellington's niece and her husband wanted Ellington to design a good quality, inexpensive house. As a result, Ellington designed a relatively simple, square-plan, one-story house covered with board-and-batten siding and capped by a pyramidal roof. A large living room dominates the interior of the one-bedroom house. With a stone fireplace, wood floors, and chestnut paneling, the living room is enlarged by a bank of large single-pane windows along two walls overlooking a flagstone terrace. In the interest of economy, the house lacks much of Ellington's typical decorative touch, with the exception of the scalloped fascia boards and heavy wooden doors with iron strap hinges. The house remains a private residence.

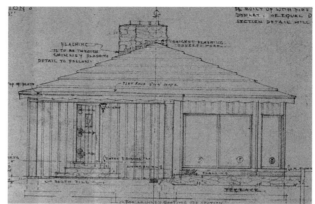

The Pettigrew House is the only known residence designed by Ellington which called for board-and-batten exterior construction. This small one-story building has a pyramidal roof and large stone fireplace. (Photo, Nick Lanier; drawing, courtesy, Asheville Art Museum, Asheville, North Carolina, Gift of Dr. W.E. Ogilvie III.)

Moritz House, Beaucatcher Mountain, Asheville, 1951 (Never built)

Ellington also designed a house in 1951 for Mr. and Mrs. L. A. Moritz. One of his most unusual designs, Ellington conceived the house as a sprawling one-story ranch-style dwelling with a modified H-plan. Each wing extended at an angle from the center section. Two large wings housed the living room and the playroom with a stone terrace filling the space in between. Two smaller wings contained the master bedroom suite in one and the children's bedrooms in the other. A large foyer overlooking the terrace occupied the center section with the kitchen and dining room behind. The low horizontal structure was covered with wood siding on a brick foundation. This house was not constructed.

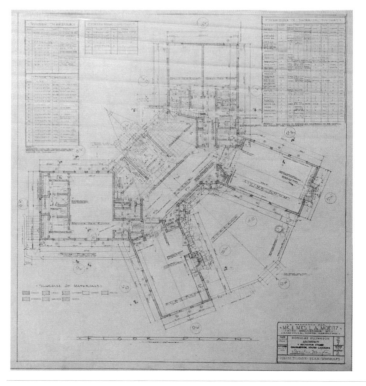

Drawing for the proposed Moritz House, 1951. Not constructed. (Courtesy, Asheville Art Museum.)

STRIBLING HOUSE, 500 ELK MOUNTAIN SCENIC HIGHWAY, ASHEVILLE, 1952–54

Between 1952-54 Ellington completed at least eight drawings for the Stribling House which was constructed on Elk Mountain Scenic Highway. The plan called for a large round living room with 270-degree views and for landscaped areas based on oval and circular designs. Ellington intended for the house to be faced with pink granite, but the owners chose other less expensive materials. (Courtesy, Asheville Art Museum.)

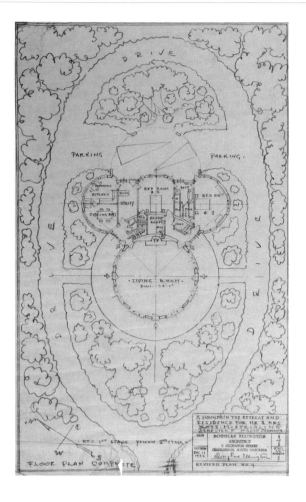

In March 1954, Ellington completed designs for a residence for Mr. and Mrs. Ross M. Stribling atop Elk Mountain, north of Asheville. Ellington had begun developing plans for the Stribling's house in 1952. With a bold, geometric plan, Ellington's design centers on a circular living room with 270-degree views. Indeed, the whole arrangement of the property including the driveway and landscaping radiates from the cross axis of the living room. The dining room, kitchen and bedroom spaces are also contained in rooms formed by overlapping circles in plan. Ellington intended the house to be faced with Salisbury pink granite, which the owners elected not to use. The main fireplace, however, was constructed of the pink granite, and the interior finished with pine paneling. The Striblings occupied the house periodically as a mountain retreat. Now extensively remodeled, it remains a private residence.[37]

STARNES HOUSE, 2 CLARENDON ROAD, WEST ASHEVILLE, 1952–53

In 1952-53 Ellington designed the Starnes House in West Asheville. The residence was based on a T-plan with nine-over-nine windows and Colonial Revival details. The home has been remodeled and bears only a faint resemblance to the original drawing. (Photo, Nick Lanier; drawing, courtesy, Asheville Art Museum.)

Ellington designed a house for Mr. and Mrs. Hal Starnes at 2 Clarendon Road in West Asheville in 1953. Ellington's drawings show a one-story T-plan design capped by a high hip roof. The house is finished with rough-cut wood siding, numerous nine-over-nine double-hung windows, and simple Colonial Revival details. The house still stands in the Malvern Hills area, but has been altered with the addition of brick veneer or possibly rebuilt. It remains a private residence.

Starnes was a loan officer with the Imperial Life Insurance Company. The year before the Starnes House was completed, the company moved its headquarters into the Biltmore Hospital Extension, which Ellington may have redesigned partially in the 1950s to accommodate the building's new tenant.

Cazel House, 131 Shelburne Road, West Asheville, early 1950s

Ellington prepared designs for a remodeling of the F. A. Cazel House, which still stands at 131 Shelburne Road in West Asheville. Renovations to the Cazel's one-story dwelling included rough-cut exterior wood siding, exterior stone chimneys and replacement of the original windows with steel-sash casements. Cazel owned Cazel's Auto Service, a repair shop, on Coxe Avenue from 1919 to 1954. The house remains a private residence.

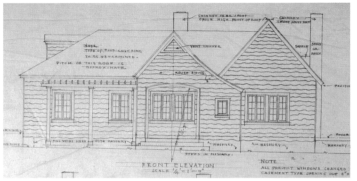

One of Ellington's last architectural projects was the remodeling of the F.A. Cazel House in West Asheville. Ellington's plans included rough-cut exterior siding and stone chimneys. (Photo, Nick Lanier; drawing, courtesy, Asheville Art Museum.)

Dalton House, 103 Wembley Road, Asheville, 1954

In 1954, Ellington prepared designs for additions and remodeling of the home of James N. and Evelyn L. Dalton on Wembley Road in the Beaver Lake development. The Daltons had resided in the house since 1947. Former president and treasurer of Piedmont Paper Company, Dalton is buried in Lewis Memorial Park.[38] Like the nearby Peek House, Ellington's contributions to the remodeling of this house appear to be minimal. The most significant change Ellington made to this two-story brick, Georgian-style dwelling was the construction of a detached two-car garage with an apartment. The decorative detailing shown on the plans—including ironwork railings and hinges—apparently was never constructed or has been changed. The house remains a private residence.

Several drawings exist for the remodeling of the Dalton House, located near the Peek House, in the Beaver Lake development. Ellington's plans added a detached two-car garage and apartment to the Georgian-style brick house. (Photo, Nick Lanier; drawing, courtesy, Asheville Art Museum.)

QUARTERMAN HOUSE, 15 BOXWOOD LANE, ASHEVILLE, 1953-54

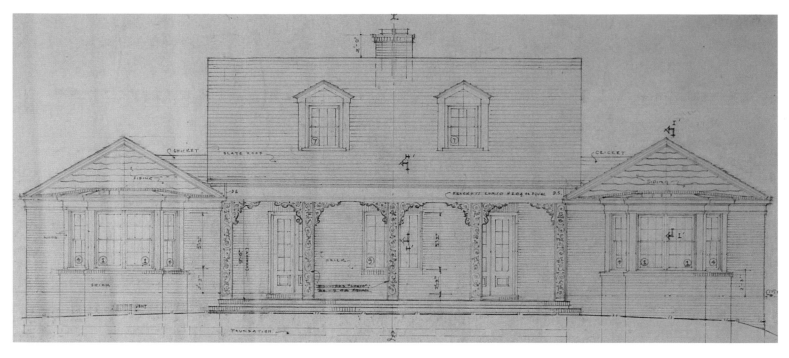

The Quarterman House is a traditional story-and-a-half brick structure with two front gabled wings. It features a large curving porch and large picture window. The house stands near the top of the I-240 highway cut. (Courtesy, Asheville Art Museum.)

Perhaps with the reference of a mutual military acquaintance, Colonel Mallett, Ellington designed a house for Mr. and Mrs. W. H. Quarterman at 15 Boxwood Lane on Beaucatcher Mountain. W. H. Quarterman retired from the Army in 1953, moved to Asheville and taught at Asheville-Biltmore College.

One of Ellington's more traditional designs, the Quarterman House is a one-and-one-half story brick structure with a prominent side gable roof and two gabled dormers. A deep curving porch supported by fanciful iron posts and scrolling brackets shelters the main facade which includes two sets of French doors on either side of a central picture window. One-story front gable wings flank the main section of the house and projecting bay windows punctuate the end walls. An inset rear porch is supported by Tuscan columns. The house still stands near the top of the I-240 highway cut and remains a private residence.

GIBSON HOUSE, WEST ASHEVILLE, EARLY 1950S (DEMOLISHED)

The house Ellington designed for Mr. and Mrs. James Edward Gibson ranks as the most traditional of his residential projects. Built in the Malvern Hills section of West Asheville, the Gibson House was a two-story, wood-sided dwelling with a tall side gable roof and a simple pedimented entrance. A second gabled porch canopy sheltered the side entrance to the house.

Ellington's first designs for the house depicted an elaborate two-story brick residence with a two-story rear ell and arcaded side porch. As was typical of many of his projects, Ellington started with the consummate design and gave up ground from there in order to meet his client's needs and tastes. The house no longer stands.

Notes

1. Sallie Middleton Parker, "Douglas Ellington: Profile of a Gentle Man," unpublished manuscript in the possession of the Asheville Art Museum, p. 2.

2. Sallie Middleton, interview with the author, February 5, 1993. Also see Charlotte V. Brown, "Douglas D. Ellington," North Carolina Preservation (Summer 1987), p. 3.

3. Middleton interview.

4. Buncombe County Deed Book 438, p. 99.

5. Leland M. Roth, A Concise History of American Architecture (New York: Harper & Row, Publishers, 1979), pp. 268-69.

6. "Ellington, Architect and Artist, Dies Here," Asheville Citizen-Times, August 28, 1960, and Parker, op. cit.

7. "The First Baptist Church of Asheville, N.C.," Architectural Record, v.68, no. 1, August 1930, pp. 107-18.

8. Elma Towe, "Dedication of the First Baptist Church, Asheville, NC," church pamphlet, March 6, 1927, pp. 2-3.

9. Ibid., p. 3. Also see Gertrude Ramsey, "First Baptist Church to Hold Three-Day Victory Celebration," Asheville Citizen-Times, December 31, 1950, p. 10A; and First Baptist Church National Register Nomination, April 5, 1976.

10. Robert J. Bateman, "Baptists Are Building Notable Church in Asheville," The Southern Tourist, September 1926, p. 55.

11. Henry I. Gaines, King's Maelum (New York: Vantage Press, 1972), p. 28.

12. Ibid., p. 28.

13. Douglas D. Ellington, letter to commissioners of Buncombe County, January 18, 1927.

14. Douglas D. Ellington, "The Architecture of the City Building, Asheville, North Carolina," Architectural Record, v. 64, no. 2, August 1928, p. 89.

15. Ibid., p. 89.

16. "Simplicity and Utility Combine with Fine Cameo Beauty in New City Hall," Asheville Citizen, March 18, 1928.

17. John H. Cathey, Four Years in Review and recommendations upon Asheville's civic development of the future, City of Asheville, May 24, 1927, n p

18. "Tremendous Cost of New Courthouse is Shown in Report by Architect East," Asheville Advocate, March 19, 1929.

19. "Throng Sees Dedication Ceremonies at City Hall," Asheville Citizen, March 29, 1928, p. 3A.

20. Bill Moore, "Asheville City Hall is 50 Years Old Today," Asheville Citizen-Times, March 19, 1978.

21. Douglas D. Ellington, "The New Senior High School of Asheville, North Carolina," Architectural Record, v.66, September 1929, p. 193.

22. "Architect Says New S&W Cafeteria Embraces Many Innovations in Plan, Arrangement; Cites Conveniences," Asheville Citizen, July 15, 1929.

23. "People ate a little bit slower Friday at the S&W Cafeteria," Asheville Citizen-Times, May 23, 1974.

24. Buncombe County Deed Book 359, p. 444.

25. Douglas Ellington House National Register Nomination, April 10, 1976.

26. Harry Weiss, "The Douglas Ellington House" pamphlet for the Preservation Society of Asheville and Buncombe County, December 13, 1992. Author's files.

27. "New Biltmore Hospital to Open Thursday," Asheville Citizen-Times, July 16, 1930.

28. Ernest H. Miller, ed., Asheville, North Carolina City Directory 1923, Vol. XXII (Asheville, N.C.: The Miller Press, 1923), p. 430.

29. "Rites Today for Smathers, Business, Civic Leader," Asheville Citizen, July 13, 1926, p. 1A; and Baldwin's and Advocate's Asheville, North Carolina City Directory 1935 (Asheville, N.C.: Baldwin Directory Company and The Asheville Advocate), p. 407.

30. "The Story of Chimney Rock Park," Chimney Rock Park, n.d., n.p. Promotional brochure in the possession of the author.

31. Doris Cline Ward, ed., The Heritage of Old Buncombe County, North Carolina, vol. 2 (Asheville: The Old Buncombe County Genealogical Society, 1986), pp. 309-10.

32. Peek obituary, Asheville Citizen, May 26, 1985.

33. Nelson Warner, "Ancient Designs Used in Modern Home," Asheville Citizen, October 15, 1950.

34. Agnes McCarthy "Mrs. Rose Brown Captivates Atlanta with Ceramics" Asheville, News, May 7, 1954.

35. "Gen. Mallett Dies, Fought in 2 Wars," Asheville Citizen, April 3, 1969, p. 1A, and Bryn Avon National Register Nomination, December 1998.

36. Dr. Fletcher Sluder, interview with author, May 10, 1999.

37. Ross M. Stribling, interview with author, November 22, 1999.

38. Dalton obituary, Asheville Citizen, December 5, 1975.

Douglas Ellington died of cancer at age 74 leaving an extensive array of buildings he designed in Western North Carolina. He is buried near his former home in Chunns Cove, his grave marked by a carved stone of his design. (Photo, Nick Lanier.)

The French Broad River lies west of the Continental Divide and flows through Western North Carolina into Tennessee in a generally northward direction from its headwaters in Henderson and Transylvania counties. The waters of the French Broad River have over time created a valley with terrain suitable for some of the Buncombe Turnpike created in the 1820s, and for the railroad which was laid through the valley in the 1880s. The creation of the railroad began an era of great extraction of two of the region's natural resources, timber and minerals. Prior to the railroads, the Buncombe Turnpike was the artery through which hundreds of thousands of animals were driven to markets in South Carolina. The bawling of cattle was replaced by the sound of steam whistles, band mills and the creaking of railroad cars as millions of board feet of lumber and thousands of tons of minerals left the region.

In this study, Jacqueline Painter examines three villages which prospered briefly on the French Broad River as the railroad, timber and mining companies sought their fortunes. Stackhouse, Putnam and Runion were typical of hundreds of similar villages which sprang to life as new jobs were created. Jacqueline Painter was born in Madison County and writes from the viewpoint of a neighbor. The railroad remains, but there are now very few traces of the three villages. —R. B.

Stackhouse, Putnam, and Runion:
Villages on the French Broad River

By Jacqueline B. Painter

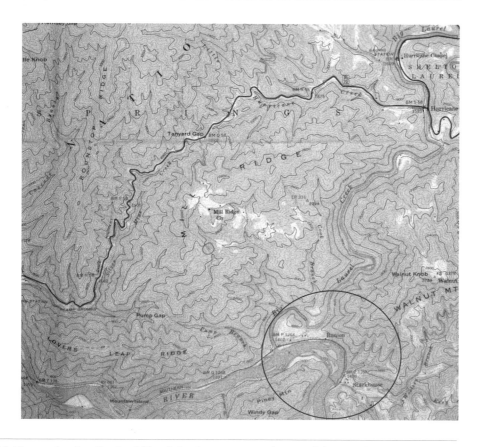

1940 map showing Runion hill and the three remaining houses of the Laurel River Logging Company town (circle). Flagged symbol of Stackhouse school marked near Woolsey Branch is seen at lower right. Map by U.S. Geological Survey and Tennessee Valley Authority, Hot Springs, North Carolina Quadrangle. (Originally produced by TVA Maps & Survey Department.)

First-time rafters on the French Broad River, four miles above Hot Springs, often look up from the white water in wonder at the mansion on the eastern bank. The structure on the steep mountainside has across its front a large one-word sign "STACKHOUSE". "Is it a school, or a hotel?" they often ask. River guides also warn boaters about the line of bent, rusty, reinforcing rods protruding from rocks in the water. "Remnants of a power dam," the boaters are told. To the right, briar-enshrouded concrete foundations pose other queries. Three-quarters of a mile down river, hikers are similarly puzzled when they stumble over the remains of Runion, first called Putnam. Grown-up roads, moss-covered piers, rebar stems, crumbling chimneys, even a concrete strong house are all that remain of this ghost town. These hidden and once-bustling railroad villages lie almost in the center of Madison County, and have long presented a mystery to area visitors.

Both Stackhouse and Runion came into being as a result of the migration to Western North Carolina of one Pennsylvania Quaker, Amos Stackhouse. His ancestors—teachers and ministers as a rule—had come from Yorkshire, England, in 1682 with the William Penn party, settling in what is now Bucks County, Pennsylvania.[1] Born in Philadelphia, Amos was educated at the Society of Friends' School, and, afterward was partner in his family's foundry business.[2] He moved in 1850 to Richmond, Indiana, where there were already relatives and a community of

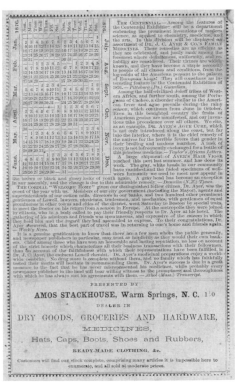

Figure 1. Top. Stereoscopic view card of the Warm Springs Hotel located across the river from Amos Stackhouse's turnpike store. At the time, the Warm Springs resort consisted of little more than the hotel, Amos' store and a few dwellings. This view of the back of the hotel dates from the 1880s, after the building of the railroad. (Courtesy, the author.)

Lower left. Shown here is a page from an 1879 charge account at Amos Stackhouse's Warm Springs store. The customer, Henry Oettinger, owned a large farm, ferry and drover's inn two miles down the turnpike on the river's west bank. Amos apparently marked through each charge when it was paid. Other customers walked the long distances from the surrounding creeks and coves, paying cash, or more often, bartering for the items they could not grow. A Stackhouse ad appears as late as 1883 in the Ayer's American Almanac. (Private collection.)

Lower right. Back cover from 1876 Ayer's American Almanac advertising Amos Stackhouse's store on the Buncombe Turnpike. The almanac included many references to the American centennial celebration of 1876. (Private collection.)

Letterhead from the lumber company operated by the Stackhouse brothers, Amos Jr. and Charles D. about 1904. When in his 80s Amos Stackhouse Sr. rented his small sawmill to his two sons. (Private collection.)

Right. Photo portrait of Amos Stackhouse, 1903, founder of Stackhouse, North Carolina. (Private collection.)

Quakers. In the next seventeen years, Stackhouse lived in Chester, Indiana; Fort Recovery, Ohio; and Piqua, Ohio, working as postmaster, farmer and merchant.[3] Amid the unrest following the Civil War, Amos bought a farm near Jacksonville, Florida, and grew oranges for four years.[4] In 1871 he married Anna Myers, the daughter of a former Ohio neighbor who had also migrated to Florida.[5]

After a few months, Stackhouse took his young bride to Warm Springs, North Carolina "because of the mineral water and mountain air," states family tradition.[6] If Anna were indeed unhealthy, she quickly recovered to become a strong helpmate in this new place.

Directly across the river from the famous Warm Springs Hotel, Amos and Anna opened a general store and stock

stand on the Buncombe Turnpike, the well-used stagecoach and drovers' route connecting eastern Tennessee and western North Carolina to coastal South Carolina and Georgia (Figure 1).[7] Since Turnpike travelers had to cross the French Broad River to reach the warm springs and hotel on the west bank, having a bridge in place was important. Flooding frequently washed out the wooden structures. In March, 1879, Amos Stackhouse, James Rumbough and other associates formed the Warm Springs Toll Bridge Company "for the purpose of acquiring or erecting and keeping in repair a bridge across the French Broad River at or near the Warm Springs in Madison County." The bridge crossed at Amos' east-bank store where the toll collection likely took place. Toll for a six-horse wagon was 75 cents, while a loose mule was 5 cents, with sheep, cattle and hogs crossing at 2-1/2 cents each.[8]

In 1878 Amos Stackhouse, now 59 years of age, purchased 600 acres of river front farm and timberland, formerly the Thomas Woolsey place, four miles upriver on the turnpike.[9] Amos cleared land, built fences, barns, stock pens and a small store. Attached to the store were three side rooms to which Stackhouse moved his wife and two small sons in late 1879.[10] About a year later, on a lofty hillside overlooking the scenic French Broad River, 200 yards behind his store, Amos built a large home, ending his travels at last. With its two full stories, tall bay window, twin front porches, fancy moldings, painted white siding and green shutters, Amos' house looked like a castle to his cabin-dwelling neighbors. Stagecoaches, drovers and others stopped at the new "Stackhouse's place," just as they had in Warm Springs.[11] This was the birth of the village of Stackhouse, home to several generations of the Stackhouse family.

Using most of the old Turnpike as a bed for the new tracks, the Western North Carolina Railway finally completed its route through Madison County to Paint Rock and Morristown, Tennessee in 1882.

When railroad officials began buying rights-of-way along the French Broad, Amos Stackhouse gave them what they needed in exchange for his own private siding.[12] One of four stations on the route between Asheville and Warm Springs, the settlement appeared as "Stackhouse" in tariff books (Figure 2).[13] A year later Stackhouse, North Carolina, could boast a post office, with Amos as the first postmaster.[14]

For his two growing children, Amos Stackhouse built a long narrow building near the north side of his home called "a ten-pin alley " where the family and visitors enjoyed bowling. To the south on a small rock bluff, a summer house (gazebo) was added to the mountain estate. Across Woolsey Branch, farther south, another knoll afforded enough level land for a tennis court. Amos' children were brought up with books and toys and clothing purchased on trips north, plus oranges and imported nuts at Christmastime. They also had bows and arrows, snow sleds and even ice skates. Amos Jr. skated all the way to Hot Springs one especially cold winter when the French Broad ice was "thick enough to support a team."[15] When old enough, Amos Jr. was sent to a boarding school in Parrotsville, Tennessee, but his brother Charles attended school in Buncombe County and was tutored at home, he being a sickly child, prone to pneumonia.[16]

Besides food, clothing, medicine and tools, Amos and his store provided for a variety of other needs. Local mountain people bought spellers and slates, violin strings and harmonicas, indigo and lace, pistols and horseshoes, coffin nails and burial clothes. When Amos visited his family in Philadelphia and New York, he carried a list of special orders to fill for his customers at home. Stackhouse also served as pharmacist, veterinarian, banker and consignment agent—accepting herbs, beeswax, and skins of fox, 'coon, bear and muskrat to sell. Near his rail siding on the riverbank, Amos built an undershot waterwheel to power a

Distance.	STATIONS.	1st Class.	2d Class.	
177	Salisbury......... ...	7 90	6 90	80
164	Third Creek	7 35	6 45	80
159	Elmwood..............	7 15	6 25	80.
152	Statesville ....:	6 80	5 90	70
139	Catawba...............	6 25	5 45	70
126	Newton..............	5 65	4 90	60
123	Conover.................	5 50	4 80	60
116	Hickory......	5 25	4 55	50
106	Icard........	4 75	4 20	50
96	Morganton..	4 35	3 75	40
90	Glen Alpine	4 00	3 55	40
86	Bridgewater	3 85	3 40	40
75	Marion......	3 40	2 95	30
63	Old Fort..	2 85	2 50	30
60	Henry's.........	2 70	2 40	30
48	Black Mount...	2 25	1 90	30
45	Cooper's.........	2 00	1 80	20
37	Asheville Junction.......	1 70	1 50	20
32	Asheville.................	1 50	1 30	20
22	Alexander's.........	1 00	85	10
12	Marshall......	60	50	10
5	Barnard's Stand...........	35	35	10
0	Stack House	00	00	
5	Warm Springs.............	35	35	10
12	Paint Rock.........	60	50	10
	DUCKTOWN LINE.			
42	Hominy...........	1 90	1 65	20
52	Pigeon River........	2 40	2 00	30

Figure 2. 1882 Western North Carolina Railroad agent's book showing cost and distances from Stackhouse to neighboring towns. (Photo, John Newman; private collection.)

sawmill. In addition, he constructed small rental houses for workers. As he cleared, planted, sawed and built, he hired local people, providing much-needed jobs (Figure 3).

Soon Amos was raising the new cash crop tobacco. He also furnished seeds, fertilizer and other supplies for neighboring farmers, often holding mortgages until harvest time when he received his cash portion. Barns were built and equipped with stone furnaces from which ran flue pipes across the interior, drying the tiers of hanging tobacco leaves. Both day and night workers kept fires in the furnaces for the prescribed curing period. The venture resulted in profit, reaffirming that Madison County had a propensity for fine tobacco production.

Figure 3. Right. Unidentified villagers gathered on porch of Stackhouse store, the hub of the community. Background hillsides were cleared for grain planting by Amos Sr. "He had three pens for feeding drovers' stock," related Nancy Stackhouse Aumiller, Amos Sr's. great-granddaughter, in a 1997 interview. (Private collection.)

Above left. Train No. 12 ready to catch the mail (between white bars) at Stackhouse. Date unknown. (Private collection.)

Center right. Stackhouse School, grades one through eight, ca. 1914. Front row, second from left is Gilbert Stackhouse, wearing shoes. The large one-room school had a small stage at the back, with a cloakroom at the front entry. The inside walls were plaster, the floor was heart pine and a pot-bellied stove provided heat. "It was a very nice school, as the early schools went," remembered Mrs. Juanita Stackhouse in 1998. About 1942 Stackhouse School merged with Walnut School and the building reverted to the Stackhouse family. For awhile the local Church of God congregation used it, then it was converted to a four-room rental house. (Private collection.)

Right. On the porch of the old Stackhouse home in 1903. Left to right. Top, Amos Stackhouse Sr., his wife Anna, his daughter-in-law Hester; front row, unidentified woman (probably housekeeper Tenny Thomas), Ernest Stackhouse, Amos Stackhouse III. (Private collection.)

The 1878 deed to Amos' farm included an 1846 lease agreement in which one half of all mineral rights was granted to Thomas Lanier Clingman for whom the Smoky Mountains' highest peak is named.[17] In 1884, Clingman, who had studied the geology of Western North Carolina, turned to his old mine lease when he was in financial straights.[18] Owning the other half of the interest, Amos Stackhouse joined Clingman in a modest barite enterprise, creating additional employment in the community. "Barite" is the mineralogical name for barium sulfate and is known commercially as "heavy spar" or "barytes." Commonly white, the mineral was used at that time in the manufacture of paint, paper, rubber and pottery glazes. Clingman wrote to Stackhouse on September 13, 1884:

> Dear Sir, I have engaged Richard Bostick to go down with another man Monday morning. I have given him three dollars to pay their passage down and they are willing to work for one dollar per day and find themselves. I think it probable they may be satisfied with less, if you keep them sometime employed. I paid eighty cents for the picks which they carry down. I will probably come down in a few days. Yours truly, T.L. Clingman.

On September 29th Clingman again wrote Amos Stackhouse:

> I wish the men to blast at least six feet from the bottom across the vein in the direction of the river or towards west. I have advanced as follows

To you	$10.00
For drill & fuse	2.45
For picks	.80
To Bostick	3.00
To Conner	1.80
	$18.05

> T.L. Clingman

The results of Clingman's efforts are not known, but in 1890 and 1891 James Turner Morehead (son of Governor John Motley Morehead) also mined barite on Amos Stackhouse's property.[19] Morehead might have secured Clingman's half-interest or initiated a new lease on his own. He had likely met Amos Stackhouse a decade earlier when involved with the Western North Carolina Railroad promotion.[20] During the summer of 1890 Mrs. Morehead boarded with Anna and Amos Stackhouse, then later rented one of Amos' houses at $4.00 per month, no doubt enjoying a respite from the heat of her Leaksville home. Furthermore, Morehead rented four other houses at $1.50 each, probably for mine workers.[21]

Amos sold the Morehead project picks, mattocks, wheelbarrows, rope, singletrees, axle grease, wagon wheels, buckets, hay,

Amos Stackhouse Sr. Family Tree

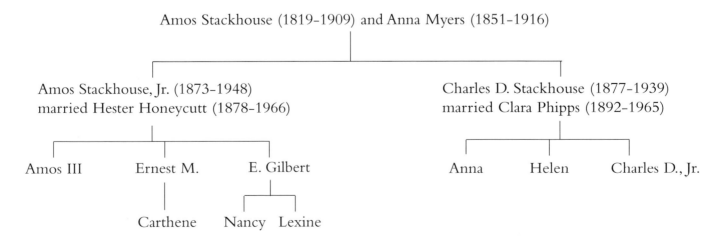

Amos Stackhouse (1819-1909) and Anna Myers (1851-1916)

Amos Stackhouse, Jr. (1873-1948) married Hester Honeycutt (1878-1966)

Charles D. Stackhouse (1877-1939) married Clara Phipps (1892-1965)

Amos III   Ernest M.   E. Gilbert

Anna   Helen   Charles D., Jr.

Carthene   Nancy   Lexine

Above. After the great flood in July of 1916, Charles D. Stackhouse stands amid debris from the Stackhouse log dam. The Carolina Barytes Corporation seen in the background to the left did not reopen. (Private collection.)

Figure 4. Below. The Carolina Barytes Corporation's crushing plant at Stackhouse, ca. 1912. The white dust was annoying, but tolerated, since the plant furnished jobs. (Private collection.)

lumber, nails and numerous other items. He also paid hands 10 cents an hour to repair the road and to load ore into cars of the Richmond & Danville Railroad—Morehead's railroad of which WNC Railway was a division. Although Turner Morehead's operation proved longer-lived than Clingman's, Morehead, too, had his financial difficulties, going bankrupt in 1893.[22] By August of 1894 Southern Railway System had bought WNC Railway at the auction block and Amos was dealing with a new freight line.[23]

During the next few years Amos Stackhouse shipped car after car to a barytes processor in Lynchburg, Virginia, known as Dingee & Weineman, who may have taken over the Morehead interest. Amos also sent at least one car a month to flour milling companies in East Tennessee where the supposedly harmless material was added to their product to increase its weight.[24]

It is not known exactly when or why Stackhouse discontinued efforts at the Morehead mine, but in 1903 he secured a larger barytes operation and new employment for the community.[25] A broad vein named the Klondyke was discovered on a 56 acre tract Amos had purchased in 1883 adjoining his original farm, and across Woolsey Branch from the Morehead mine.[26] Now, two decades later, Henry Moore of the Carolina Barytes Corporation leased the tract and developed the Klondyke, paying the Stackhouse family an annual royalty. Moore also leased from Amos Jr. one and a quarter acres next to the rail siding, erecting a crushing plant, large waterwheel, wheelhouse, and wooden dam across the French Broad for generating electricity (Figure 4).[27] The power output was 165 to 250 horsepower, depending on the season and flow of water.[28] It was enough power to light the mine and the homes of Amos Stackhouse Sr. and Amos Jr.

Tramways were built from the mine on the mountain down to the plant at riverside. For light in the tunnels, workers had only smoky "coon-shine" lamps that burned a thick grease. In the beginning, having no air drill, the drilling was done by hand-hammering. After the miners had dug the white rocks, they loaded it onto tram cars and sent it to the mill which consisted of a crusher, jig, grinders, dryer, screens and bleaching vats. First the barite was crushed to the size of corn kernels. Next, it was

Looking north, Woolsey Branch (at right) meets the French Broad River at the railroad in the great flood of July, 1916. The Stackhouse store and barn are in the background. The flood changed the economy of the Stackhouse community, destroying the undershot wheel of the Stackhouse brothers' sawmill and the large wheel of the barytes plant. (Private collection.)

steam-cleaned with water and a little sul-phuric acid, rinsed with more water, dried, and finely ground in a series of three burr-stone mills. The barite powder was packed into barrels made on the premises in the cooper shop from low-grade oak, then loaded onto freight cars.[29] In addition to local ore, barite from several Tennessee mines was shipped to the Stackhouse mill, necessitating hiring a night shift. In later years, it was estimated by mine officials that over 200,000 tons of the high-grade prod-uct came from the Klondyke.[30]

The lure of employment brought peo-ple to Stackhouse from other communities, prompting Amos Jr. and his brother Charles to build more rental houses. Family tradi-tion says that each owned about 20. Nealie Price was one worker who walked from his Doe Branch home everyday, then took his handmade wooden boat across the French

Broad to Stackhouse. "Everybody along the river had rowboats back then," recollected Nealie. "That barytes mill was a good job, too—paid $1.25 a day," he added.[31]

In 1912, the barytes mill burned completely and was never as successful after rebuilding. To meet growing demand for finer meshes, the burrstones were replaced by a steel ball mill. This mill reduced the ore to the required fineness but contaminated the ground material with iron. Finally, the owners replaced it with a Raymond roller type mill, only to meet a fresh problem. Although the vein continued to be thick, and was worked to a depth of nearly 400 feet, galena (lead) was encountered in the barite ore. The mill had no separation process and there was no market for their mixed product. When the great flood of 1916 washed out the power dam, the barytes company did not rebuild, reverting both Stackhouse homes to lamplight for years to come.

Charles E. Hunter of Tennessee Valley Authorities' Division of Chemical Engineering reported in 1936 on "Barite in the Vicinity of Stackhouse, North Carolina," stating: "The Stackhouse area, as a whole, no doubt still contains large reserves of barite." Since then others have periodically analyzed the mines and reopened the adits that dot the Stackhouse hillsides, but no

operation has lasted very long.

Timber and lumber speculation also form a large portion of Stackhouse history. In 1885 Amos Stackhouse purchased an adjoining tract of 100 acres which he called "the Big Laurel farm."[32] The property was located on a high bluff about three-quarters of a mile down the railroad track from Stackhouse, at the confluence of the Laurel and French Broad Rivers. It included 40 or more arable acres, plus timber, and access to Shelton Laurel and Tennessee by way of a crude, winding road along the Laurel River.

Later, in 1897 Stackhouse leased these 100 acres to Charles W. Putnam of the North Carolina Land and Timber

mill at Runion *mill at Runion*

Company.[33] The corporation built a sawmill, dams, trestles, blacksmith shop, dwellings and a church-school building for workers' families. The village was named Putnam, and appears on an 1898-1899 map of the area.[34] North Carolina Land and Timber also purchased 40,000 acres of land north along the Laurel River to the Tennessee line and including some land in Tennessee. By 1905, unfortunately, bankruptcy had closed their operations and Putnam lay await of future direction.[35]

Meanwhile, Amos Stackhouse—grown old and deaf—had turned over his sawmill and other business to his sons, Charles and Amos Jr., reserving a life estate for himself and Anna.[36] Married, with a family of his own, Amos Jr. began building, about 50 yards down the hill from his father, a ten-room home with panoramic view of river and mountains (Figure 5). He paid workers a dollar a day to dig, using hand pick and shovel, then by small flat-bed wheelbarrows, to haul dirt and rocks down to the railroad for dumping. Hiring Asheville contractor J.C. Campbell, Amos Jr. spent $4000 and four years completing his house. With its three porches, four bay windows and circular tower, the cream-colored Queen Anne

style dwelling was even fancier than the home of his parents. On her trips North to visit in-laws, Hester Stackhouse, wife of Amos Jr., selected crystal chandeliers, mirrored mantles, Swiss lace curtains, Oriental rugs and other furnishings to make her home a showplace in Madison County.[37]

Moving from his father's house into his own, Amos Jr. also began assuming more responsibility in the community. He served on the county school committee, became an officer in the Walnut Methodist Church, and functioned as vice president and director for the new French Broad Bank at Marshall. Amos Jr. was appointed postmaster of Stackhouse, and his brother, Charles, assistant postmaster. In partnership with Charles, Amos Jr. operated his father's store, sawmill and farm. They even sold large quantities of tobacco and flour wholesale to small store owners in Marshall and up on Laurel. These products were delivered to Stackhouse in carload lots, taking the local trains as much as two hours just to unload.[38]

Amos Stackhouse Sr., spent his last years pursuing his limited, but favorite, pastimes of reading, writing poetry, enjoying his grandchildren, corresponding with his

Above left. Southern Railway depot and siding at Runion, ca. 1920. Stackhouse children looked forward to Friday afternoons in the summer when the train from Newport brought ice cream to a little store next to the depot. According to a 1997 interview with Anna Stackhouse Meek, loaves of light bread could also be delivered from Asheville if the order were placed at Runion the prior week. (Private collection.)

Above right. Scrip was issued to company employees for commissary spending between paychecks. It conserved cash for the mill by extending the payroll period, while providing the workers with food and other needs during the wait. In a June, 1999 interview, Clyde Dockery of Weaverville remembered playing with company tokens and paper coupons as a child living at Runion in the 1930s. "The tokens were made of aluminum and called 'lightweights'," said Dockery. "We did not keep any—don't know what happened to them." (Courtesy, Ralph Morgan. Examples of scrip and tokens similar to those used at LRLC are illustrated by Terry N. Trantow in his Catalogue of Lumber Store Tokens *privately published in Ellensburg, Washington, 1978. Used by permission of Terry N. Trantow.)*

Left. Laurel River Logging Commissary at Runion, ca.1918. Jeter Edward Wardrep, manager, at the telephone. (Private collection.)

many cousins and friends and smoking Cuban cigars. The founder of Stackhouse, North Carolina, died in February, 1909, at age 90 and was buried within 30 yards of his home in his prescribed gravesite on "summer house point." Earlier, a Pennsylvania publication had stated: "Throughout his long and useful life, Mr. Stackhouse has been upright and honorable in all his transactions, zealous in advancing the welfare and material growth of his community...and a firm adherent of the doctrines of the Society of Friends."[39]

The Stackhouse torch then passed completely to Amos Jr. and his brother Charles, who further benefited the commu-

---

...THE NAME OF THE NEW STATION WAS CALLED RUNION, FOR MARION "PADDLEFOOT" RUNION WHO CARRIED THE MAIL ON HIS BACK TWICE DAILY FROM AMOS STACKHOUSE'S POST OFFICE ABOUT A HALF-MILE UP RIVER.

---

nity three months later through the sale of the "Big Laurel farm," site of Putnam, to the Betts family of Troy, New York. Betts had also purchased the 40,000 acres north of Putnam toward Tennessee from the bankrupt North Carolina Land and Timber Company. In October, 1909, the Laurel River Logging Company (LRLC) was chartered with Anson G. Betts as president, and office address of Stackhouse, North Carolina.[40] Beginning capital was $10,000, increased two years later to $350,000. In 1911, two hundred men were employed for construction of a standard gauge railroad along the Laurel River to the Tennessee line. The completed system—Madison County Railway—would serve Betts' two sawmills at Putnam and at Pounding Mill, located several miles north on the Laurel River, where it was expected to cut 75,000,000 feet of white pine and 45,000,000 feet of poplar, hemlock and other timbers.[41] The large bandsaw mill at Putnam, with its twin dynamos, two dry kilns, planing mill, two blacksmith shops (one for rail and train repair), updated trestles and other facilities, became Madison

County's largest employer.[42] When the Southern Railway added a depot and siding, the name of the new station was called Runion, for Marion "Paddlefoot" Runion who carried the mail on his back twice daily from Amos Stackhouse's post office about a half-mile down river. More than likely the name was changed from Putnam to Runion because there was already a North Carolina town named Putnam in Moore County.

Trees were felled by crosscut saw and axe. The logs were dragged by horse or mule teams down to the railroad along the Laurel River and loaded onto flat cars for Runion. Before the railroad was built, and sometimes afterwards, the rough terrain and lack of roads required other solutions to the log-transporting problem. "Splashing" was a means of forcing logs down the mountain creeks to the sawmill locations. By constructing temporary dams on the creeks a "splash" could be triggered, sending the logs miles downstream. For months ahead, logs would be piled on the stream banks waiting on rain to swell the streams. Timing was critical. As the water rose, dynamiting of several dams would be synchronized—the planned hour relayed from "holler to holler," warning the crews. They would dot the creek banks with peaveys and other prodding equipment, ready to re-position stuck logs. It was not always smooth work. The logs could hit rocks, or create log jams requiring more blasting. Sometimes a few men in hobnail boots, carrying spike poles, walked the logs in the rushing water to clear the jam—a treacherous job.[43] "Splashing" often inundated creek side farms, or deposited logs and rocks onto fields, blocking the plowing and planting, and causing hostility towards the loggers. Many aspects of lumbering were dangerous, and the railroad was also used to carry injured workers to Runion to meet the train to Asheville, though most of these workers died before getting to the hospital.[44]

After the logs reached the railroad, they were loaded by a steam-powered loader with tongs which were clamped over

Chimneys still standing from Runion homes, 1997. (Left photograph, the author; right photograph, Dan Slagle.)

the logs by the "tong-hooker" man, then swung to the rail car. The steam loader was transported each day from Runion and back, to load and unload the logs. Carrie Landers Johnson recalled how her father, James Landers, worked as "loaderman" at Runion in the early 1920s. Her father also had a fireman responsible for keeping up the steam on the loader. "The train made one trip a day up into Laurel and back to Runion, the loader being the last piece to go on the train," said Carrie. The night shift rolled the logs into the millpond, serviced the engine and made up the train ready to go to Laurel the next morning.[45] From the water, cleaned of dirt and debris, the logs went to the sawing carriage in the mill-house. Waste wood slabs were ground into chips by a machine called a "hog," and fed into the steam boilers that powered the bandsaw and planer.[46] A bandsaw capacity was several times that of the circular saw such as the one operated by Amos at his mill. Twenty to thirty thousand feet of lumber were cut daily, sometimes more.[47] Inclines moved the fresh-cut boards to the dry kilns and stacking yards, ready for grading, sizing, planing and shipping. Some lumber was sold "in the rough," and some was picked up by local customers.[48]

For shipping, the LRLC train ran almost to the French Broad, stopping at a loading platform on the Southern Railway spur. "It was called 'shipping and receiving'," remembered Clyde Dockery, Runion native. Loads of lumber were brought to the dock and left until enough accumulated to fill a particular order, whereupon it was loaded onto railroad cars for distant points. Equipment and commissary supplies also arrived by freight train. "The old concrete piers are still there, down near the Southern trestle," added Dockery.

Although there were logging camps and sawmills all around Western North Carolina, each place offered certain varieties of wood. Laurel River Logging Company cut wild cherry, poplar, oak, basswood, walnut and large amounts of white pine. "Some was virgin timber—poplars four to five feet across," recollected former 1920s worker Nealie Price. "It was cut into seventeen inch wide boards and called 'paneling'."

The Runion lumber plant was constructed on the steep hillsides of the ravine in order to use the Laurel River and the

The villages of Stackhouse and Runion grew up on a broad bend in the French Broad River. In this 1923 view the French Broad River and the Western North Carolina Railroad are seen on the left. The ribbon-like plank road between the river and the railroad was built from Stackhouse to the Runion depot to keep vehicles above the mud and ruts. The large house with a pointed tower was built by Amos Stackhouse Jr. in 1904. Far right in the photo and only partially visible is the home of Charles Stackhouse built ca. 1881 by his father Amos Stackhouse Sr. (Private collection.)

Southern Railroad. On the north side, however, the hill flattened somewhat where LRLC laid out its small village for workers. There were two rows of houses, numbering between 25 and 50, with four rooms each. "The rooms were large," said Nealie Price, "And the rent was $3.00 a month in the '20s." Surface-mounted electric wires ran along the ceilings, providing a light for each room. "Every house had a water spigot packed in sawdust to prevent freezing," remembered John Herbert Waldrup, former lumber grader at Runion. The water came from the top of Runion Mountain which had been dug out to make a large reservoir. Old-timers said that nearby Pump Gap and Pump Branch received their names because the water was pumped to Runion at night to fill the reservoir. A few nicer, larger homes for company officials had indoor plumbing, but the mill homes had privies. Wooden sidewalks connected the dwellings to the church and school building, commis-

sary, livery stable, club house for Southern Railway officials and boarding houses for those who lived too far to walk. The mill whistle blew loud and shrill three times a day—at six in the morning, at noon and at six in the evening. (Figure 6)[49] The average worker made a $1.50 per ten-hour day. Even a volunteer fire department and a Laurel River Logging Company baseball team were organized.[50] Games were played across the French Broad River on more level terrain.

"Everything pointed to a care for the people on the part of the owners, and it will mean income to many persons for years to come," wrote W.E. Finley, editor of the Marshall *News-Record* on June 21st, 1912, after a trip to Runion. Two weeks later, Finley reported on a disease that was killing chestnut trees in Madison County. He announced that LRLC had sent a man to Pennsylvania to study this blight. "The company desires to save the chestnut trees

and stands ready to help others save theirs," wrote Finley. He advised people to examine their trees and destroy the affected ones.

The Laurel River Logging Company operation, the Carolina Barytes Corporation mining venture, and the Stackhouse's store and farm were the basis for an era of prosperity from 1910-12. In 1911 the Southern Railway's fast new "Carolina Special" began two daily trips through Stackhouse, as numbers 27 and 28, making a total of six passenger trains per day. The four locals—numbers 11, 12, 101 and 102—always stopped at Runion and Stackhouse, but the two "Specials" stopped only if flagged. The combined population of Runion and Stackhouse was reported to be 500 by Southern Railway Company in 1912.[51] However, community tradition doubles that figure to include workers who walked in from adjoining areas.

To accommodate employees from Mill Ridge, Walnut Creek and other sections to the north, LRLC constructed a swinging bridge across the Laurel River 20 feet or more high above the mill dam. Mounted on thick steel cables the walkway was about four feet wide and 100 feet long and floored with boards, according to Clyde Dockery who lived at Runion in the late 1920s and '30s. Amos Jr. and Charles Stackhouse also walked to Runion to work periodically, grading lumber for Betts and selling farm produce to the villagers and the commissary.

Laurel River Logging Company's labor supply diminished somewhat as Western North Carolina's young men joined World War I or were drafted. Amos Stackhouse III, left his Duke University studies to become a soldier. Moreover, during the unusually cold winter of 1918, the LRLC was forced to suspend work due to ice and flooding which washed away several trestles. "The company had not been able to run its band mill at Runion lately on account of the impossibility of carrying on logging operations during the severe weather," announced the *Asheville Times*.[52] Next came the Spanish influenza pandemic, affecting employment worldwide. It seemed that every household in Stackhouse was stricken by at least one case. Mrs. Ada Wardrep, whose husband operated the commissary, took pots full of her chicken soup to the doorsteps of Runion friends, daring not to go inside. The entire Stackhouse family came down with the disease. Gilbert Stackhouse, son of Amos Jr., would tell his children years later, how he had as a teenager recovered from the flu, then helped to bury the corpses in the Stackhouse community. When persons succumbed, the other sick family members could only drag the dead outside to the porch or dooryard.[53]

In May of 1920, The Laurel River Logging Company sold to Asheville entrepreneur E.W. Grove nearly 24,000 acres of its Laurel holdings in northern

Madison County between Runion and the Tennessee line.[54] On July 16th, Grove placed a full-page advertisement in the *News-Record* declaring his purchase of the Betts land and offering tracts for sale with financing at six percent and no commission. Soon, Griffith Lumber Company of Huntington, West Virginia, took over the Runion logging operation giving steady employment again to the surrounding communities.

Carrie Landers Johnson lived in Runion as a child in the early 1920s. She remembers about 35 families occupying the mill village at that time. She went to school there and to Sunday church services when there was a minister available. "We had Prayer Meeting on Wednesday nights, too," related Carrie. Her family rented one of the few painted houses in Runion, formerly the home of an LRLC official. "We had the nicest place up there," she added. Carrie also remembered the Club House as a plain, unpainted, rough-built place with tables and chairs and a cook woman. Mill workers or visitors could buy a hot meal, but Carrie was not allowed to go there, especially on weekends. "The men gathered to play cards and drink, usually ending with fights," she said.[55]

After a few years, Griffith, too, reduced its operations, closing completely in 1925, and marking the end of Runion's life as a thriving mill village. The depletion of timber, chestnut blight, ravages of weather, aging of equipment, employment problems and shortage of investor funds have all been advanced as reasons for the shutdown. Three or four families lived on at Runion, recalled Carrie Johnson, whose father helped with the cleanup operation. The school closed, the mill pond was drained and the whistle ceased to blow. "We sure missed that whistle, too," said Carrie. She and her siblings walked to Stackhouse to school and to church. The commissary's closing meant that her family had to buy groceries in Marshall or Stackhouse. Her mother boarded a few workers, mostly relatives.

In their typical country store, the Stackhouse brothers sold many items straight from large wooden barrels. Flour, meal, sugar, salt, crackers, and even lard, were dipped out into brown paper sacks and weighed for the customer—the lard soaking through by arrival home. "We used those bags to start fires in the stove," Carrie Johnson recollected. Candy, chewing gum and tobacco products were kept in a large glass case at the front of the store. At the back, on the floor, stood a tree slice, over two feet across and table-high. "It was level, and nice and smooth on top," recalled Carrie. On this wooden block was cut the cured pork middlings (bacon), another mountain staple. "They kept the block covered with a cloth between customers," added Mrs. Johnson.[56]

Nealie Price was another worker who stayed at Runion after the mill closed. "We had to take care of the million feet already cut and ready to ship," Price recalled years afterward. "We all knew about it ahead of time, but still the closing depressed the people. They had nowhere to go, to live, to work. It had been there a long time and made jobs for a lot of folks," Price concluded.[57]

Pine Creek, Sandy Bottom and other adjoining communities lost population rapidly. Randy Fowler of Doe Branch recalled that a number of his uncles and cousins had worked at the sawmill since its opening—"It affected whole families."[58] Several of those former employees, including Price, as well as Amos Jr. and Charles Stackhouse, went to work for Biltmore Lumber Company in Buncombe County. Others found jobs at Black Mountain, Woodfin and Azalea. Many remained on their steep rocky farms waiting for fresh, albeit smaller, logging operations to arrive in Madison County, set up, saw out, and move on, leaving the unsightly, bare mountainsides exposed to erosion.

A Greensboro firm purchased most of the LRLC machinery, renting Amos' old barytes plant to store it, and hiring Amos' son Gilbert to sell it, piece by piece, during the next decade. "An old train engine was

Figure 8. In the late 1970s several structures were still standing in the Stackhouse and Runion communities.

Top. Unidentified person stands on porch of former Stackhouse school house, ca. 1975. The building burned a few years later. (Private collection.)

Center left. One of three dwellings remaining at Runion in 1978. This house was thought by community residents to have been a mill superintendent's home. (Photo, Dan Slagle.)

Below left. The old Runion school building in 1978. "Through the years, the school just rotted down," stated Nancy Stackhouse Aumiller in a 1997 interview. Her father, Gilbert Stackhouse, had attended the school at times, as did his cousin Anna Stackhouse. Anna recalled going to both Stackhouse and Runion schools in the early 1920s, since their three-month sessions were not simultaneous. Miss Jean Garrett, graduate of Dorland-Bell and Asheville Normal Presbyterian schools, was the teacher in 1912. (The Marshall News-Record, June 21, 1912, Marshall, N.C.; author interviews, 1997.) (Private collection.)

Top right. Remains of the foundation of the band mill at Runion, 1997. (Photo, John Newman.)

Bottom right. Concrete strong house of the Laurel River Logging Company commissary at Runion, November 1997. (Photo, author.)

still sitting at Runion in World War II until salvagers from Asheville came with a torch and took it out in pieces," remembered Runion native Clyde Dockery in 1999.

Besides the industry at Runion, other losses were endured by the shrinking Stackhouse community in the coming years. The home built by Amos Sr. in the early 1880s, a Stackhouse landmark, was destroyed by fire in 1925. The owner, Charles Stackhouse, and his family were living in the house, but escaped unharmed. Neighbors rallied with buckets but saved only a few furnishings. Charles moved back into his childhood home—the store side-rooms—for a few weeks until leaving for Biltmore. Amos Jr. boarded in Biltmore, too, riding the train home on weekends. While both brothers were working in Buncombe, the Stackhouse store was leased outside the family, first to one, then another.[59] The post office remained in the back of the store, with Hester Stackhouse serving as postmistress in her husband's absence. "Daddy Amos did the official reports when he came home on Saturdays," related Juanita Stackhouse, daughter-in-law, in 1999.

The Great Depression simply worsened the economic situation at Stackhouse. When the nation's banks failed, Amos suffered heavy losses. With the closing of Biltmore Lumber Company, he returned to Stackhouse, eking out a ghost of his former living. Since she was fortunate enough to retain her good cow, Hester Stackhouse sold milk and butter to the few who could buy it or barter with labor about the farm. Amos had difficulty turning down the pleas of credit from his neighbors who had large families and no employment. He co-signed notes for them, then had to pay. Years later he told his grandchildren, "You cannot begin to imagine the awful poverty here during the Depression."[60] Charles Stackhouse, too, was financially devastated, losing his half of the original 600 Stackhouse acres.[61]

Around 1932 Amos Stackhouse Jr. tore down the old Stackhouse store at the railroad and moved its stock and the post office up to the large brick building behind his home. Here he reopened the store, operating the post office as before. Shortly, Southern Railway built a "waiting room" shelter with benches for passengers flagging trains at Stackhouse. In the summertime, people of the community gathered at the little building, sitting inside visiting or playing horseshoes in front.[62]

Up at Runion some of the mill houses and buildings were sold for the lumber, others were used for stovewood, and quite a few more rotted down. Only two or three

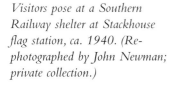

Visitors pose at a Southern Railway shelter at Stackhouse flag station, ca. 1940. (Re-photographed by John Newman; private collection.)

houses remained habitable, being rented to Stackhouse natives who farmed the fields on shares with the owners—first, Edgar Betts, until 1935, then, Ellsworth Vandervort, brother-in-law of Ernest Stackhouse. The cabled foot bridge across Laurel River at the Runion dam was demolished "when the boards began to break, making it dangerous," stated Clyde Dockery who lived there at the time. The dam, too, was removed in the late 1940s by wildlife officers who blasted the center so fish could swim upstream.[63]

As part of its program for phasing out its one-teacher schools, the Madison County Board of Education closed Stackhouse school in 1946.[64] The grand-children of Amos Stackhouse and their dozen or so neighbors enrolled in Walnut School a few miles away. During these postwar years, the county had few buses, so a taxicab was sent from Walnut to pick up the Stackhouse pupils. "We were packed tight in that little car," recalled Lexyne Stackhouse Norris, years later. Soon, how-ever, a "school bus" was devised from a pickup truck outfitted with benches and a chicken wire "cage" for safety, topped with a tarpaulin to protect from the weather. "The next year or so, there was a *real* school bus, though," added Lexyne. Thus, the Stackhouse school building reverted to the Stackhouse family and served at differ-ent times as a community church, tobacco barn and rental house until it accidentally burned.[65]

At age 70, in 1943, Amos Stackhouse Jr. was required to retire from the U.S. Postal Service but his wife Hester was appointed postmistress. Hence, Amos Jr. continued hoisting the flag and "working the mails," as he called his daily tasks.

Two episodes created a brief respite from the decline of Stackhouse. Amos Jr. and his son Gilbert, in 1942, built another small sawmill at "lumber yard bottom," adjoining the Stackhouse rail siding. They worked three or four men, cut some timber for themselves, and a few house patterns for others. This mill operated about two years.

In 1944, another lumberman, C.N. Garland from Jonesborough, Tennessee, began sawmilling in the Laurel area and doing business in Stackhouse.[66] While he did not reopen Runion, he did buy local timber and offer employment. Amos Jr. was in charge of grading and loading at his Stackhouse rail siding. "There are so many grades of white pine, that no one else knew

them like Amos Stackhouse," recalled for-mer Runion worker Nealie Price, years later. Amos Jr. worked until three months before his death from leukemia in October, 1948.

Alas, two months before this, the U.S. Postal Service had terminated Stackhouse Post Office, routing the mail to Marshall, and ending another era in Stackhouse his-tory (Figure 7).[67] The little Stackhouse store closed, too. Although for the first time in 70 years there was no outgoing mail bag or general store, trains continued to stop for Amos Jr.'s widow or any of the other vil-lagers needing a ticket, until 1968 when all passenger services ended between Asheville and Knoxville, Tennessee. Since the small railway waiting shelter was no longer needed, the green and white "Stackhouse" sign was given to Gilbert Stackhouse who lived in his father's large home. He mounted the sign on the porch fascia where it is still visible from river and railroad.

Gilbert's mother, Hester, had died in 1966, her will further dividing the property among her three sons, two of whom lived at a distance. Many of these acres, too, would eventually be sold out of the family. She left to Gilbert, not only the responsibil-ity of home, but also of heritage. In addition to his work as a commercial builder and procurer of sawmills, he farmed his grand-father's remaining acres, took a leading part in the Methodist Church, and raised his children to respect their birthright. Eventu-ally, Gilbert Stackhouse had his own health problems, prompting the return home of his daughter and her family. In 1989 he died in the same house as his birth.

Two years later the 100-acre tract purchased by Amos Stackhouse in 1885, site of Putnam and Runion milltowns, became part of the Pisgah National Forest.[68] A portion of the old Laurel River Logging Company railroad bed is now shown on Forest Service hiking maps as the "Laurel River Trail," open to the public.[69] Southern Railway System has become the Norfolk & Southern, carrying only freight trains through Stackhouse, except for excursion charters. And while there is no depot or store, no post office or school, sawmill or tramway, there is a boat launch where busloads of rafters and canoers come to ride the French Broad rapids—phrasing their questions about the deserted river bend settings that once teemed with people, noise, dust and activity (Figure 8).

The descendants of Amos Sr. continue his legacy in the Stackhouse home and community, tending their acres, helping their neighbors, preserving the traditions and maintaining their privacy. Among the several dwellings remaining in the community, the centerpiece is the lovely 1904 Stackhouse home, still a venerable, albeit mysterious, presence on the Western North Carolina landscape.

Notes

1. For information of the history of the Stackhouse family see William R. Stackhouse and Walter F. Stackhouse, *The Stackhouse Family*, second edition. (Morehead City, N.C.: The Stackhouse Foundation, 1993), and Eugene G. Stackhouse, *Stackhouse, An Original Pennsylvania Family*, (Baltimore: Gateway Press, 1988).
2. *History of Chester and Delaware Counties* (Pennsylvania, 1903), author and publisher, unknown, p.16.
3. A. W. Young, *History of Wayne County, Indiana* (Cincinnati: Robt. Clarke & Co., 1872) p.141.
4. Amos Stackhouse family private papers.
5. Register of Deeds, Duval County, Florida, Book 2, p.821.
6. In 1886 the town's name was changed to Hot Springs.
7. Elizabeth Rumbough Baker Dotterer, interview, 1989. Ed. Note: A stock stand was an overnight stopping place for drovers and their stock. It offered shelter for the drovers and pens and feed for the animals.
8. *Public Laws of North Carolina* (Raleigh: Observer, State Printer and Binder, 1879), Chapter 49, p.632.
9. Madison County, North Carolina, Register of Deeds, Book 8, p.11.
10. Amos Stackhouse family private papers.
11. James R. Gilmore, "On the French Broad," *Lippincotts Magazine*, November 1884, p.431.
12. Nancy Stackhouse Aumiller, interview, 1998.
13. Western North Carolina Railway agent's book, published 1883.
14. Vernon Stroupe, *Postoffices and Postmasters of N.C., Vol. II* (Charlotte, N.C.: Postal History Society, 1996) p.2-273.
15. Kenneth Burgin, interview, 1973; Aumiller, interview, 1997.
16. Anna Stackhouse Meek, interview, 1999.
17. Madison County Register of Deeds, Book G, p.164.
18. Wm. S. Powell, *Dictionary of N.C. Biography, Vol. I* (Chapel Hill: U.N.C. Press, 1979). Lewis S. Brumfield, *Thomas L. Clingman and the Shallowford Families* (Yadkinville, North Carolina: self- published, 1990).
19. Amos Stackhouse family private papers.
20. Wm. S. Powell, *Dictionary of N.C. Biography, Vol. IV* (Chapel Hill: U.N.C. Press, 1991) p. 320.
21. Amos Stackhouse family private papers.
22. Powell, *Vol. IV*, p. 321.
23. *Asheville Weekly Citizen*, August 23, 1894, p.1.
24. Aumiller, 1998.
25. Madison County Register of Deeds, Book 17, p.144.
26. Ibid., Book 3, p.548.
27. Ibid., Book 29, p.56.
28. Charles E. Hunter, (Asheville: Report to TVA, February 10, 1936). Courtesy of N. C. Geological Survey, Asheville office.
29. Private papers, author's collection.
30. Hunter.
31. Nealie Price, interview, 1997.
32. Madison County Register of Deeds, Book 9, p.565.
33. Ibid., Book 9, p.558.
34. *National Geographic*, Vol.1, pp. 291-300, surveyed 1898-1899, August, 1901; reprinted, 1921.
35. Madison County Register of Deeds, Book 19, p.530.
36. Ibid., Book 13, pp. 58-59.
37. Amos Stackhouse family private papers.
38. Juanita Caldwell Stackhouse, interview, 1998.
39. *History of Chester and Delaware Counties*, p. 16.
40. Madison County Register Of Deeds, Corporation Records, p.46.
41. *Manufacturer's Record*, Vol. LIX, No.5 (Baltimore: 1911), p.55.
42. *News-Record*, Marshall, July 21, 1912.
43. Dan Slagle, 1998; Phillip Franklin, 1999; Clyde Dockery, 1999, interviews; and from Ronald Eller, *Miners, Millhands and Mountaineers* (Knoxville: U.T. Press, 1982), p.90.
44. *Madison County Heritage, Vol. I* (Marshall: Madison County Heritage Book Committee, 1994), p.16.
45. Dockery, 1999.
46. Jinsie Underwood, *This is Madison County* (American Revolution Bicentennial Committee of Madison County, 1974), pp. 44, 45.
47. Price, 1997; Waldrup, 1991.
48. Carrie Landers Johnson, interview, 1999.
49. Ibid.
50. The *News-Record*, Marshall, July 5, 1912.
51. *The Western North Carolina Section at a Glance* (Washington, D.C.: Southern Railway Company, 1912), p.32.
52. *Asheville Times*, January 30, 1918.
53. Aumiller and Meek, interview, 1997.
54. Madison County Register Of Deeds, Book 41, p.6.
55. Johnson, 1999.
56. Ibid.
57. Price, 1997.
58. Randy Fowler, interview, 1998.
59. Price, 1997; Johnson, 1999; and Meek, 1998.
60. Aumiller, 1997.
61. Madison County Register Of Deeds, Book 56, p.63.
62. Lexyne Stackhouse Norris, interview, 1999.
63. Raymond Ramsey, interview, July 1999; and Dockery, August 1999.
64. Norris, 1999.
65. Aumiller, 1999.
66. Amos Stackhouse family private papers.
67. Stroupe, p.2-273.
68. Madison County Register Of Deeds, Book 115, p.511.
69. *Appalachian Ranger District, French Broad Station, Hiking Trails for the Hot Springs Area* (U.S. Forest Service, 1997).

Sociologists are fond of studying social cohesion, especially the values and behaviors which bind people together in the midst of economic hardship. This study examines the lives of families who lived in Stumptown, a small neighborhood of black people who lived adjacent to Pearson Drive in Asheville from the 1880s to about 1970. In the last half of the 20th century, the lives of many poor black people in Asheville revolved around Federal programs and agencies; Public Housing, Urban Renewal, Public Welfare, Public Health, and Model Cities. Urban renewal changed the physical landscape of Stumptown in the late 1960s. The leaning houses, dirt yards, and streets without sidewalks and curbs were replaced with tennis and basketball courts, a baseball field and a community center. This study, based on interviews conducted by the author, documents the vibrant social structure of this community which now exists only in the memories of a few individuals. —R.B.

Growing Up In Stumptown

By Pat Fitzpatrick

On fewer than 30 acres of sloping ground where the Montford Community Center now stands in Asheville, North Carolina, there was formerly a community known as "Stumptown." This strong church-oriented community, nestled in a jog in the boundaries of Riverside Cemetery, was home for as many as 250 families and created a legacy still felt in the larger community today.

The area was given the name "Stumptown" for the tree stumps that remained after the land was first cleared. This area, bounded by the cemetery to the west and the woods between the homes and Pearson Drive to the east, housed black residents from the 1880s to the 1970s. The children and grandchildren of early residents now gather each month in the community center, a portion of which stands on property where once there were houses and apartment buildings, gardens and chickens, and children playing games in the unpaved streets. When former residents stand in front of the community center today and look across the parking lot and tennis courts, they recall a neighborhood from a special time and place that exists only in their memories.

Top. This view taken in March, 2000 from the rear of the community center shows the ball field in the center and Riverside Cemetery in the distance. The lights are in "the hollow," "Red Hill" and the former coal yard rose between the ball park and the cross street. The cross street through the center of the photo is old Morrow Street. (Photo, the author.)

Bottom. Betty Jean Dozer poses on Morrow Street in 1958. The house in the upper left is approximately the site of the new community center, and the house in the upper right is located near the site of the new tennis courts. (Courtesy, Phyllis Sherrill.)

The Stumptown community existed in a small area, about 30 acres. These two early maps indicate the relation of the small black neighborhood to the city of Asheville. The Montford area to the east of Stumptown developed as a suburb of Asheville in 1890-1910. Many Stumptown residents worked at the Battery Park Hotel (slightly to the southeast) and other nearby hotels, in affluent homes in the Montford area, and at the Riverside Cemetery to the west. The boundaries of Stumptown (shown in red) were Pearson Drive to the east, Courtland Drive to the south, Birch Street to the north and Riverside Cemetery to the west. Above. This "Birdseye View of Asheville 1891" shows several rows of homes in the south area of Stumptown. (Private collection).

Right. This later 1916 "Map of the City of Asheville, North Carolina," indicates a more developed neighborhood, but several streets and their names are omitted. (Courtesy, North Carolina Collection, Pack Memorial Public Library, Asheville, North Carolina.)

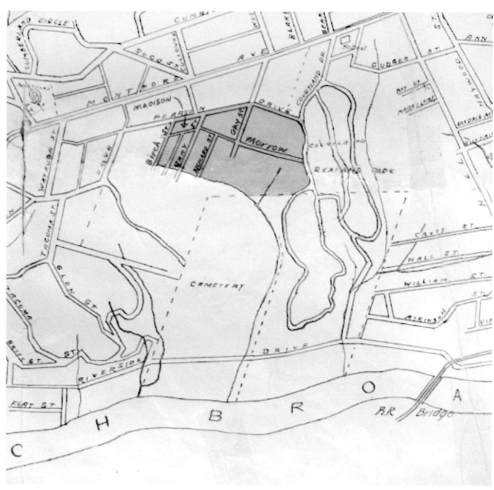

We were happy. There was no fear, no enemies. We were all like one family. If you did something bad, another mother might give you a spanking and you knew you would get another one when you got home. You had to be on the porch when the street light went on or be yelling, "I'm coming, Mama."…There were 200 to 250 families. Many had big families and most had two parents. Many lived in "shotgun" apartment buildings with four units to a building. You could see the back door when you entered the front door. We had a three-room house. If anybody needed help, neighbors just pitched in. Nobody needed to ask them. They all got together and worked things out, whatever happened. First, we were working together to get our streets paved…. My grandfather was head deacon of the church and my grandmother, the mother of the church. There was always a hubbub of activity around the church—food on the grounds, singing. We would go to church two or three times on Sunday and also go during the week. Church is a whole other subject. Church played a big part in our lives as well as the children's recreation. Everything revolved around church, school and family. My grand-daddy would sponsor a trip for us every year to Charlotte to what's now Carowinds. That's where we could take our boyfriends and get to sit with them on the bus. And we'd have quartet singing, and we had dinner on the grounds some Sundays. Everybody would bring something and we ate downstairs. Those were the good wholesome fun things.

— *Phyllis Sherrill*
(1998), former Stumptown Resident

Although there may have been blacks in Eastern North Carolina in the late 17th century, there were few blacks in Western North Carolina until the late 18th century and early 19th century. Many large farms and businesses in Western North Carolina had slaves during the early and mid 19th century. James Alexander who built a hotel, tanyard, wagon factory and ferry on the Buncombe Turnpike in the 1830s had many slaves he housed in his "Negro Quarters."[1] The Patton family, one of the largest slave-owning families in Asheville owned 78 slaves in 1860.[2] The coming of the railroad in the 1880s and the growing tourist

industry also prompted black people to move to the mountains in the late 19th century.[3]

Discrimination against blacks by legal sanction and traditional mores persisted throughout the 19th and 20th centuries until the Civil Rights Legislation of the 1960s. Discrimination in Asheville was similar to restrictions in other North Carolina communities including segregated schools and public buildings with separate drinking and bathroom facilities. Asheville's many restaurants and hotels served only white or black patrons. In train stations black passengers had separate waiting rooms.[4]

"WE WERE HAPPY. THERE WAS NO FEAR, NO ENEMIES. WE WERE ALL LIKE ONE FAMILY."

By 1910, the city's population was over 18,000 of which over 5,000 were black.[5] Blacks lived in segregated neighborhoods just southeast of downtown (Eagle Street), south of downtown (South French Broad), West Asheville (Burton Street) and just west of Montford Avenue (Stumptown). Substandard and inexpensive housing prevailed in these black neighborhoods.[6]

The death rate for blacks in North Carolina in the late 1880s was more than double the rate for whites. The poor living conditions of the majority of blacks in Asheville, insufficient food and clothing, lack of firewood, inadequate health care, and very cold winters account for the high death rate. Acute bronchitis, pneumonia, and measles were the main causes of death among the blacks in Asheville during the late 1880s.[7]

Many black residents worked for Asheville's wealthier home and business owners who were mostly white. Although there were some black businesses and offices, most were "crowded into dilapidated buildings in the Eagle Street area." And a few black residents "owned a small percentage of the properties within their neighborhoods."[8] In 1896, there were nine black churches in the downtown area and a black newspaper, the *Colored Enterprise,*

located on S. Court Square.[9]

The majority of employed blacks in the 1880s worked in the fields of domestic and personal service, and fell into six general categories of occupation "...barbers and hairdressers, laborers, laundresses, nurses and midwives, restaurant and saloon keepers and servants."[10] Early Asheville city directories listed the black population separate from the white population and indicate specific jobs blacks held at the turn of the century. They provided services in hotels and restaurants, schools, hospitals and churches, dairies, nurseries and grocers, the tannery and the coal yard, the Vanderbilt estate, the railroad, the cemetery and the newspaper. Men listed their skills as laborer, gravedigger, office boy, hosteler, elevator boy, driver, stonecutter, musician, teacher, barber, blacksmith, janitor, grocer, yard man, coachman, harness maker, woodworker, carpenter,

brick mason, pastor, waiter, butcher, bellboy/man, teamster, drayman, fireman for a specific business or inn, shoemaker, undertaker, painter, plasterer, furniture repairman, horse trader, chiropodist, brakeman, railroad station hand, newspaper pressman and bootblack. Although a few black women worked as nurses and teachers, and in businesses as cooks, waitresses, chambermaids or housekeepers, laundress or seamstress, most worked in the homes of white families and listed their occupation as house girl, servant, waiting maid or cook.[11]

My mother did domestic work. A lot of it was right up here on Montford. She worked for those people for years. They died out, she worked for their sister, and she worked for a lady right across from the police place out here. And then she worked at Highland Hospital. At that time, I remember rent being about $4 a month for one of those apartments. Besides 10 [Morrow] where we lived, we also lived at 4 Morrow. I went to work at Highlands. I also worked for Dr. Carroll. He was one of the founders of Highland Hospital and I worked in their home. They lived out on Midland Drive. So I worked out there as a downstairs maid and as a waitress. I went to school in the morning and then came back home and went back in the afternoon. I would serve dinner and that sort of stuff. And I worked at Highland Hospital and the department store, but I'd always go back to Ms. Carroll. After I came out of the service, I went back to her. I quit that because I hated to iron.

— Geraldine Hill
(1999), former Stumptown resident

My grandmother worked as a maid up on Lakeshore Drive, for a doctor. She worked for them for years as a cook. I haven't seen anybody make homemade cakes like she did. Oh, it was the most delicious thing you ever put in your mouth. She cooked. That was all she did. Wasn't a housekeeper worth 15 cents.... My grandfather worked for the City of Asheville. But he worked building Biltmore Forest, Biltmore House out there. He dug the roads and stuff for 25 cents a week. A week! He found out that wasn't what he wanted to do and then he applied for a city job as a maintenance person, a garbage person, or whatever. And he started out in the maintenance department and then he moved up to elevator operator. So he retired from the city as an elevator operator, but in the meantime he was perhaps among the first minority entrepreneurs in the city starting with his own little sweet shop in a room next to his house in Stumptown. And he told me he didn't go any further than the fourth grade, but if you would talk to him you would think he was a college graduate....My father applied for the service. He didn't pass, they said his heart was funny or something. At that time, if you didn't pass the physical, then you had to do something here to help the war effort. And he was assigned to a defense plant in New Haven, Connecticut. So he went there, he was up there maybe eight or nine months. I still have letters that he wrote to my mom. It was just amazing. And letters she wrote to him. So he was up there and sent for us. We stayed maybe two or three years. When we came back here to live he worked at a flower shop,

Whitehead's Flower Shop in the Flatiron Building, right there at Wall Street, right there where it's a jewelry store now. He worked there for about 16 or 18 years, and then he worked for Southern Railway for years. Then when they discontinued the railroad service here, they wanted him to move to Greensboro, Washington, or Nashville, Tennessee, I believe. He didn't want to go anyplace.

— Phyllis Sherrill

Mr. and Mrs. Wells and their daughter Audrey planting in their garden in the "flats" where the community center now stands. Photo dates from the early 1940s. (Courtesy, Phyllis Sherrill.)

"THE OLD STOMPING GROUND — STUMPTOWN"

20's, 30's, and 40's

Born, reared here in northwest Asheville, maybe considered centrally located; bordered by Pearson Drive, Birch Street, Riverside Cemetery, and Courtland Avenue.

Memorable landmarks at the time were "The Red Hill" between Madison Street and Morrow Street and "The Hollow" at the end of the neighborhood bordered by Riverside Cemetery where caucasian neighbors pastured their cows and where the kids played ball. Also, "Campbell Woods" across Courtland Avenue where we took a shortcut to school (old Hill Street) in good weather. Otherwise, we had to pass the nearest school all white Randolph (formerly Montford School) to reach our school.

There were the neighborhood grocery stores – Pack on Pearson Drive; Jack Pack Book Store on Gray Street; Morrow Street Corner Store; Mr. Howard's Store on Gay Street; and don't forget Shigley's Drug Store and the grocery store next door on Montford Avenue.

Neighborhood churches – Welfare on Madison Street; Rev. Mason's church on Gray Street; and Elder Perkins church on Morrow Street. Other Ministers – Rev. Mills and Rev. Beasley went out of the neighborhood to their churches and some neighbors went out of the neighborhood to church.

Gray Street was the first to be paved (we skated there on the hill). All others were unpaved. Few people had telephones; very few refrigerators (most families had ice boxes); not all families had electricity anyway. Coal or wood stoves to heat and cook; tin tubs for baths; flat irons to iron; almost no cars – we depended on the old square styled buses with $.06 fares for transportation (always sitting in the back).

We made it regardless – men and some women worked; all children went to school when time came (all black schools). Everyone (children) could read, write, and do arithmetic. Teachers, neighbors, and any adult could discipline us. There were few problems. After elementary school (Hill Street), we went to Asheland Avenue School across town on Asheland Avenue for grades 7 & 8, then to Stephens-Lee High School where most graduated, matured, married, and reared families. Some went on to higher education, worked, and survived.

50's, 60's, and 70's

There was little or no mass public assistance, no public housing, but we made it.

After streets were paved, more cars, and telephones, came better homes with other modern

(Photos, courtesy Geraldine Hill (above, 1952) and Phyllis Sherrill (below, mid-1940s.)

conveniences. Children still went to segregated schools until the mid 60's when things began to change. Many moved north, others moved out of the neighborhood to other parts of town.

The city began acquiring land from Pearson Drive to Riverside Cemetery, bordered by Gay Street and Jersey Street to build Montford Center with all of the facilities there - tennis courts, playground, ballfield, amphi-theater, etc. Schools were desegregated.

80's and 90's

Only memories afford one a vision of where they once lived. Some areas of Gray Street, Richie Street, Madison and Gay Streets still exist. Courtland and Pearson Drive are almost predominately Black.

The trusted and long standing Welfare Church is still there and active. All of the neighborhood stores are gone. A corner store/drug store now exists on Montford Avenue where the drug store was and adjacent to that is a laundromat and the Community Watch Police location.

Our old Hill Street School on the Hill gone, replaced by a new facility (50's) and now has become another named Isaac Dickson housing grades kindergarten through 5th (integrated from all over Asheville). Montford School (now William Randolph) is integrated housing students from the immediate neighborhood and students bused from north Asheville for grades pre-kindergarten through 3rd. Isaac Dickson was named for the first Black member of the Asheville City Board of Education in the early 1900's.

Very, very few, if any, of the early residents of "Stumptown" remain. The name (I don't know where it really came from) is rarely heard, only on occasions like this where we come together to celebrate our heritage. The memories linger on.

"LONG LIVE THESE MEMORIES."

By: Lettie Wilson Polite

(From booklet prepared for the 3rd Stumptown Community Reunion held in 1997.)

Asheville experienced tremendous physical growth from 1910 to 1930 and the population grew from 18,762 in 1910 to 50,193 in 1930.[12] Prosperity and growth in the white community stimulated development in the black neighborhoods. The roots of this growth for the Stumptown area lay in the development of the village of Montford. While Stumptown was bounded on one side by the hills of Riverside Cemetery rolling down to the French Broad River, the boundary to the east and north was Montford. "Montford's present-day street pattern was established by 1894. The number of dwellings in the neighborhood increased by fifty percent between 1896 and 1900, and then more than doubled by 1910."[13] More sophisticated in architecture than homes being constructed at the same time elsewhere in the city, Montford's homes reflected a "more cosmopolitan population."[14] Residents of these homes occupied by the more affluent of Asheville's population depended upon the availability of laborers in Stumptown for employment as cooks, butlers, yard men, drivers and household help.

> *Pearson Drive went all the way down to Riverside Drive, and that was part of our recreational activity. We would get skates or wagons or bicycles or something and down Pearson Drive we'd have business, down them old curves. And we also had Trash Road. That's now been cut off but it was real curvy, and we'd go down there on skates. We used to do some dangerous stuff and see who could get down there the quickest. It was fun for us but you couldn't pay me to do it now.*
>
> — *Phyllis Sherrill*

Bordering Stumptown on a ridge of land above the French Broad River, Riverside Cemetery was created in August of 1885. Consisting of 55 acres, it was first incorporated as the Asheville Cemetery Company.[15] "The most remarkable landscaping in the [Montford] district can be found in the Riverside Cemetery, a large informal cemetery containing the graves of numerous notable North Carolina

In 1967, most of the physical landscape of Stumptown had not yet been changed by Urban Renewal and other Federal programs. This 1967 photo shows Stumptown children and Dr. Mary Frances Shuford in front of the community center on Madison Street. Dr. Shuford owned the building and converted it to the "Stumptown Neighborhood Center." (Courtesy, Asheville Citizen Times.)

Phyllis Sherrill (1998), former Stumptown resident:

Dr. Shuford, the white lady doctor, she gave penicillin for everything, she was somebody that was well respected in the black community, not only for her assistance when they needed medical attention, but she owned houses there, too. She owned several homes in Stumptown. I rented from her. And if something came up and you had sickness and you didn't have all your rent or anything, she just said, "Give me whatever you got, Honey. Don't worry about it." Or "Just wait till next month." And in the house, if you needed anything, or if you needed a little something to eat, she would say, "Well, here, go get you something to eat." At that time, we used to have an A&P grocery store on Montford Avenue, and we had a drugstore.

would have a big pot of boiling water ready, boil it and scrape it. She'd put apples in its mouth and stuff it with apples and roast it overnight. We had other preachers at supper every Sunday, and they'd eat the possum.

— Phyllis Sherrill

The location of Stumptown was advantageous to both the cemetery and the Montford residential area and was a ten-minute walk for those employed downtown. Stumptown grew in population during the first three decades of the 1900s and became a vibrant community of 250 families former residents speak of as "one big family," where residents looked out for one another in times of need. The residents lived in apartment buildings, other multi-family dwellings and some single-family homes on streets named Madison, Morrow, Richie, Gray, Gay, James and Jane, separated from Pearson Drive by woods. A few of the homes had businesses on the premises.

My grandfather had his little sweet shop over there, Mr. Howard's Snack Shop or Sweet Shop, or something like that, in a room next to his house in Stumptown. 86 Gay Street. He sold all kind of candy, chewing gum, and drinks, stuff like that, chips, and he would get shoe polish and things like that people might need. And at that time we used Royal Crown hair dressing, and stuff we used for our hair. But he didn't do too much — he didn't sell like eggs or anything like that. Had a little table in there where he and his boys would gather when they would talk about the cares of the world. And then he always kept some kind of whiskey. He had a pint of whiskey and a lot of times he had to get him a little toddy. "A toddy for the body." And he'd have just one little nip at night before he went to bed....We had a coal yard right next door to my house — Alonzo and Blondie. They owned it and he sold coal. He was another entrepreneur in the neighborhood. And he would go to the Virginia mines, sometimes kids would get to go along and fill up his coal truck and come back here, break it up and sack it up, take it around and sell it to people. He would get like boulders and he would pay — fellows would get up there and just throw them on the ground. It was fun to us. We'd get one and hit it up against

citizens."[16] Grave sites are arranged alongside "picturesque curvilinear drives that wind through trees and clumps of foliage and along the steep slopes and ravines of the cemetery."[17] Development of the cemetery depended upon the availability of black men and youths in Stumptown for digging graves and landscape maintenance.

We were right there at the cemetery. The cemetery was in our backyard and it was our playground, too. My grandfather would catch possums in the cemetery. He'd put one under an overturned washtub and feed it popcorn to "clean it out." When they were ready to cook it, my grandfather would hit it in the head. My grandmother

another and it would break it loose. And he'd give us two dollars or 50 cents or something.

— Phyllis Sherrill

Prior to the Civil War, there was little formal education for black people in Western North Carolina. In 1880, black people had no public schools they could attend in Asheville but there were several schools founded by churches, missionaries and private individuals.[18] In 1887 the Allen Industrial Training School employed many white teachers and was founded by the Woman's Home Missionary Society of the Methodist Episcopal Church primarily for black girls of elementary school age. The school, located on College Street, later added higher grades, dropping the lower ones, and became an accredited high school. Many black girls from communities in Western North Carolina without high schools for black children came to the Allen High School in Asheville for their education.

The first public school for blacks in Asheville opened on Beaumont Street in 1888 in an abandoned building that had been repaired.

The school began with three black teachers who were paid $25.00 a month and 300 students in grades one through five. The school could not accommodate the 657 school age [black] children in Asheville, so many returned home crying. In 1890, the enrollment reached 1,200 students but it was not until May 4, 1891 that a bond election provided for the purchase of a lot on Catholic Hill where Catholic Hill School was built.[19]

In 1901, Hill Street School opened as an elementary school for blacks and most of the children of Stumptown received their early education there. By 1907 there were five black schools in Asheville—Catholic Hill, Victoria, Academy, Hill Street and Mountain Street.[20] A fire destroyed the Catholic Hill School and it was replaced in 1921 by Stephens-Lee High School, a nineteen-room building constructed on

William Howard beside his home and sweet shop, 86 Gay Street, corner of Gay and Madison, 1954. (Courtesy, Phyllis Sherrill.)

JAN 1962

Hattie "Mutt" Howard stands beside the coal and kindling house on Madison Street in this 1962 photograph. The Welfare Baptist Church, one of the few older structures remaining in Stumptown can be seen in the background. (Courtesy, Phyllis Sherrill.)

Stephens-Lee High School was a center for black activities until the public schools were desegregated in 1965. Seen here are members of the Crown and Scepter Honor Society at Stephens-Lee in the mid 1950s. (Photographer unknown, possibly from the school newspaper "The Skylighter.")

Catholic Avenue.[21] Today the gymnasium of the former high school houses a community center.

The youth of Stumptown attended Stephens-Lee High School from 1921 until it was closed when the school system was integrated in 1965. Stephens-Lee High School was the meeting place for cultural activities for blacks throughout Asheville and Buncombe County.

Many honors were bestowed upon students while attending Stephens-Lee. [Principal] Walter Smith Lee emphasized a curriculum built around Shakespeare, dignity and self-help. There were courses in music, drama, carpentry, radio repair, cosmetology, welding, home economics and English.... Paul Dusenberry and Madison Leonard were the leaders of the famed Stephens-Lee marching band known throughout the southeast for its achievements for over 30 years.[22]

Children living in Stumptown seldom left the area. Teens went to revivals on the other side of town or to teen dances, 10 cents a dance. They had jukeboxes where you put in a quarter for so many songs. I guess that's how they made their money. The kids always walked there and back and had a good time doing it. The YMCA was where the YMI is now. The YWCA was on College Street.... On the Fourth of July my grandfather would roast a pig and it was one of the highlights of the summer. He would go down to the market, right off of River Road, and slaughter a pig. He'd make his own barbecue sauce. He went to his grave with that recipe. But he would roast that pig over coals in the ground and he could sing. He had a beautiful voice and he very seldom sang, but when he did, everybody just listened and would want him to sing. That was one night he sang all night long and slap that hog, and he'd turn it. That's one night they'd let us stay out all night. And there'd be about seven or eight of us and we'd have our blankets and stuff and we would sit there with him and he'd tell us stories. Just so full of wisdom. He would slap that hog and sing. And he sold it. It was a money-maker for the church. Before 12:30 or 1 o'clock, he had no more pork. They were in line. I never will forget.... My birthday was before Halloween but my mama would always give me a party on Halloween because she said if anything

Until the Civil Rights Legislation of the 1960s, black students from Stumptown went to segregated public schools. One of the first schools in Asheville for black girls was the Allen Industrial Training School founded in 1887 by the Methodist Episcopal Church and seen with a different name in this 1914 advertisement in the city directory. (Asheville, North Carolina City Directory, 1914, Vol. XIII, "Special Advertiser's Directory," p. 21.)

*happens or if anything serious goes down,
I'll know where y'all are. You'll be at my
house. And she'd always have hotdogs and
hot chocolate.*

— *Phyllis Sherrill*

Reverend Levonia C. Ray Sr. now pastor of Greater New Zion Baptist Church in Fletcher, North Carolina believes that there was an "overall strength of community, an energy" in Stumptown that he has not observed elsewhere. The children learned through the ways they were taught and by the examples of those in Stumptown. The fruits of these lessons are seen in the lives of their children and grandchildren today. Many grew up to be influential in the politics and services of the greater Asheville community.[23]

*There were more black doctors then,
than now. You didn't run to the doctor for
everything. Most mothers could doctor
quite a bit or they knew of another
woman that would know what to do.
There were also black dentists...more
black-run shops. I think back to things
that were unhygienic, but they didn't
think so at the time: kerosene was sold
from barrels in the stores and big cookies
were sold from containers, two for a nickel;
the men in the stores would handle the
kerosene and then hand out the cookies
which would then have the faint odor of
kerosene on them.... A group of boys
would share a soda and run their grubby
finger into the mouth of the bottle between
swigs thinking they were cleaning the bottle before drinking from it. Overall, they
were healthy.... There were two drug stores
in Montford and although we could go in
to make a purchase, we could not sit in
the booths, so a lot of courting was done
walking in nearby Riverside Cemetery.*

— *Rev. Levonia C. Ray Sr.
(1998), former Stumptown resident*

The upward growth and prosperity Asheville had experienced at the beginning of the 20th century peaked during the early 1920s and took a downward turn a few years later. By November 1930, Central Bank and Trust Company, the largest bank in Western North Carolina, closed its doors.

Geraldine Hill (left) in 1953 with Frank and Shirley Clemmons on Morrow Street. (Courtesy, Geraldine Hill.)

GERALDINE HILL (1999), FORMER STUMPTOWN RESIDENT

I guess I joined [the service] to get away from home. And the Bugg family had a girl that was in the Women's Army Corps. And when she came home in this white uniform–she was in the medic, and I was always fascinated by that uniform. And I wanted to do it.... I wanted to be a nurse and I wanted to go in the same as she and get my medical training. But medical school was all full. And I had three choices: I could go to typing school, cooking school or for clerk-typing and I chose it.... They took me to Charlotte for the test, the examination and all.... I enjoyed being in the service. I guess without that I probably wouldn't have seen the few places that I did see. It was learning to live with people. These girls, all races and everything, and we got along fine. Exchanged clothes, you know, like if you had something I wanted to wear I'd borrow it and I had something–we just exchanged clothes. We did real well.... At Fort Sill, Oklahoma, I worked in the officers' training center printing songbooks, test papers and all this. I had the whole office and the only time I saw my boss was once a month. He would come in and find out what supplies I needed for the month. [1952-1954]

Others followed, taking about $8 million the city and county had on deposit, forcing the city at one point to pay its employees in scrip.[24] "The economic life of Asheville ground to a near halt. A bankrupt Asheville defaulted on its debts; on paper and otherwise, fortunes vanished; [and] families lost homes and livelihoods.... An era had ended in economic paralysis, and a sobered, desperate Asheville faced the long ordeal of depression and war."[25] The previously affluent hired fewer household workers and some of the larger homes in Montford became rooming houses. Businesses that survived operated with as few employees as possible.

Although the 1953 Asheville city directory shows well over 100 heads of household in the area called Stumptown, urban renewal of the 1960s and '70s, or "urban removal" as some of the previous residents refer to it, soon claimed the close-knit community. There had been a steady decline in the condition of the buildings in Stumptown as younger people moved on and the older residents did not have the money to improve the properties. As government funds came into the community to build public housing complexes, landlords did not improve rental properties.

Stumptown families gather for the 1997 Stumptown Reunion, August 26-27. (Photo, Benjamin Porter.)

Certified letters arrived warning residents they had only a few months to find a new home. Bulldozers took house after house in the name of eminent domain. Where formerly there was "deteriorated" housing comprising an intact residential and social fabric, there is now vacant land, a ball field, tennis courts and a community center.

We played horseshoes in "the flats." And we played in "the hollow," which is where the ball field is now. We made sculptures from clay at the bottom of the hollow. We had a place called "the red hill," right behind the center, the street that goes straight out. The hill went up and over, right there where the playground is now. The coal yard was at the top of the hill. And when you came around the corner, and then you'd turn right, you'd go up the hill, and my house was right here — straight was my little street. It's hard to even — when I go over there now — Just to show you what the wonders of machinery could do to a place.

— Phyllis Sherrill

Red Hill, the flats and the hollow, the playgrounds of Stumptown, no longer exist. But the bulldozer's blade lays bare more than earth; it makes perfectly clear the fragile nature of our cultural landscape.

Notes

1. Dr. F. A. Sondley, LL.D, *A History of Buncombe County North Carolina*, Vol. II (Asheville: The Advocate Printing Co., 1930) p. 746.

2. Douglas Swaim, Ed., *Cabins and Castles, The History & Architecture of Buncombe County, North Carolina* (Asheville: Historic Resources Commission of Asheville and Buncombe County, 1981) p. 74.

3. Helen Moseley-Edington, *Angels Unaware: Asheville Women of Color* (Asheville: Home Press, 1996) p. 1.

4. Swaim, p. 41.

5. Swaim, p. 41.

6. Ibid.

7. Frenise A. Logan, *The Negro in North Carolina 1876-1894* (Chapel Hill: The University of North Carolina Press, 1964) pp. 198-199.

8. Swaim, both quotes p. 41.

9. *Asheville City Directory For 1896-1897* (Atlanta: The Franklin Printing and Publishing Co., 1896) pp. 82-84.

10. Logan, p. 87.

11. *Asheville City Directory For 1896-1897* (Atlanta: The Franklin Printing and Publishing Co., 1896) "Classified Business Directory of Asheville," Vol. I.

12. Swaim, p. 42.

13. National Register nomination prepared in 1977 by Sarah Upchurch, consultant, and McKelden Smith, survey specialist, N.C. Division of Archives and History as quoted in Swaim, pp. 83-84.

14. Ibid. p. 84.

15. Buncombe County, North Carolina Register of Deeds, Deed Book 47, p. 583; Deed Book 151, p. 28; Deed Book 151, p. 96; Deed Book 202, p. 85.

16. Swaim, p. 207.

17. Ibid.

18. Moseley-Edington, p.1.

19. Ibid, p. 2.

20. "Dedication Hill Street School," March 29, 1953, brochure, p. 4.

21. Moseley-Edington, pp. 1-2.

22. Ibid., p. 2.

23. Reverend Levonia C. Ray Sr., author interview, 1998, quote and information.

24. Swaim, p. 44.

25. Ibid.

John Wesley Jones Jr. makes a snowball near the corner of Madison and Gay Streets. This site is now a playground adjacent to the basketball courts. (Courtesy, Phyllis Sherrill.)

Mary and Martha Brown pose with their bicycle on Morrow Street, mid-1940s. (Courtesy, Geraldine Hill.)

Residents and visitors often comment on the striking differences in the architecture of the two prominent public buildings at the east end of Pack Square, the Asheville City building and the Buncombe County courthouse. After the two buildings were completed, one resident, Grace Aiken Davis observed that the courthouse looked like the box the city building came in. This study by Dan Vivian examines the architectural history of the courthouse and the reasons the two structures came to be so different. Buncombe County was created in 1792 and has had many structures which were used as courthouses. The courthouse which begins this study was built in 1877, but it had been preceded by several earlier buildings including a log cabin built in 1793 and several brick structures built in the mid-nineteenth century. — R. B.

Public Architecture, Civic Aspirations and the Price of "Progress":

A History of the Buncombe County Courthouse

By Daniel J. Vivian

In the decade after World War I, Asheville confirmed its emerging reputation as the most affluent and cosmopolitan city in the southern Appalachians. Clearly evident in the architecture of the era were signs of the community's escalating prosperity and the increasingly sophisticated, avant-garde tastes of its citizens. Large-scale real estate speculation sparked a wave of urban development that rapidly transformed the face of downtown Asheville. More than 65 significant buildings were erected in the central city: opulent hotels catering to wealthy tourists, high-rise office towers and scores of stylish commercial buildings. In many ways, the 1920s marked downtown Asheville's architectural heyday.1

Of all the buildings erected during the period, few captivated public interest as did the new county courthouse. By the early 1920s, a larger and more modern facility was clearly needed, but construction of a new courthouse was not seriously discussed until the middle of the decade, when it was proposed as part of a larger program for the expansion of municipal facilities in downtown Asheville. From the outset, the prospect of a new courthouse took on a symbolic role in the minds of many citizens—like other large-scale building projects, it afforded a clear measure of civic pride and stood as a portent of future prosperity. But problems beset the project soon after it began, and for a time questions fundamental to its final outcome became subject to open public debate. Long before construction started, it was clear that the courthouse would ultimately stand as one of the most controversial buildings of the era.

An "Imperative and Essential" Need

In the early 1920s, it became apparent that the Buncombe County courthouse, although only two decades old, was no longer able to meet the needs of county government. Beginning in September 1922, court officials called attention on an almost monthly basis to the "congested conditions" that constrained judicial proceedings. The sole courtroom in the building barely accommodated the two terms of court that met monthly, and overcrowding had long been a problem in the county jail. As one superior court judge bluntly remarked in August 1925, "[T]he present building was

Figure 1. The 1877 Buncombe County courthouse as it appeared soon after completion, ca. 1880. Designed by local architect James A. Tennent, the structure was built on a t-plan and featured a bold clock tower. A 400-seat opera hall occupied the third floor. This building served as the seat of county government until its successor was built in 1903. (Courtesy, North Carolina Collection, Pack Memorial Public Library, Asheville, North Carolina.)

a splendid creation when it was erected, but it . . . [has] outlived its usefulness."[2]

Office space was also in short supply. The county treasurer "had to transact his business within the confines of a small office," and the sheriff's department occupied similarly cramped quarters. Diminishing space in the courthouse had forced several agencies to move their operations elsewhere. The county board of education maintained offices in the city hall, the county engineer and draftsman worked in rooms above the county garage, and the county commissioners and auditor rented office space in a nearby private building. Facilities for the storage of public records were virtually nonexistent; documents "were scattered from the basement to the attic," according to one account. Recall-

ing the overall situation some years later, Register of Deeds George A. Digges Jr. recounted that "a new Court House was imperative and essential. . . ."[3]

A quarter-century earlier, similar concerns had led the county to replace the previous courthouse, which dated to 1877 and stood immediately east of the Vance Monument on what later became known as Pack Square. This building, a brick, three-story Second Empire-style structure, was designed by local architect and builder James A. Tennent and erected at a cost of $33,000 (Figures 1, 2). As was common among municipal buildings of the period, it functioned as both the seat of local government and as a community center: offices and courtrooms occupied the first two floors, while the upper story contained a

400-seat opera hall. Although once regarded as "one of the finest edifices of the kind in the State," by the early twentieth century, the *Asheville Daily Gazette* was calling it "a monstrosity . . . unfit for the uses demanded of it, a blot on this progressive city and county. . . ."[4]

In January 1901, the county commissioners eagerly seized the chance to erect a new courthouse when afforded the opportunity by the philanthropy of lumber merchant George W. Pack. Pack, one of Asheville's leading benefactors, offered property on College Street for use as the site of a new courthouse, provided that the county agreed to remove the 1877 courthouse and to make its former site part of the public square. The commissioners considered the proposition for less than a week before accepting it and resolving to build "a modern building that would be abreast of the times."[5]

The new courthouse, designed by Asheville architect Kenneth McDonald, was completed in 1903. At a total cost of $45,000, it was "regarded by most citizens of the county as the utmost in public extravagance."[6] The brick, two-story Classical Revival structure featured an octagonal clock tower and a main facade distinguished by a broad, pedimented portico with six Corinthian columns (Figure 3). Functionally and aesthetically, this stately building seemed capable of serving the needs of county government well into the twentieth century. Unforeseen was the rate of change that would make it wholly inadequate in barely 20 years.

Buncombe County's rapid growth was responsible for the steady pace of government expansion and, in turn, courthouse obsolescence. The principal cause of this growth was the Western North Carolina Railroad, which reached Asheville in 1880 and quickly helped to make the mountain village a popular health and pleasure resort and a center for timbering operations in the mountains.[7] The population of Buncombe County, which numbered 21,909 persons in 1880, grew to 44,288 by 1900 and 64,148 by 1920. Commensurate growth occurred in Asheville, where the population stood at 2,616 in 1880, grew to 18,762 by 1910 and reached 28,504 by 1920.[8] But even these gains would pale in comparison to those that were to be made over the next decade.

Asheville, N.C., Pack Square and City Hall.

COMMUNITY ASPIRATIONS AND THE CIVIC CENTER PLAN

Growth in Asheville and the surrounding area surpassed even the most sanguine expectations in the 1920s. By the end of the decade, the county's population would stand at nearly 100,000; residents of Asheville alone would number more than 50,000.[9] Skyrocketing investments in real estate, a massive building boom and a thriving local economy created an atmosphere of "zealous optimism" within the community. In all, the infusion of wealth and the expectation that it was here to stay engendered lofty civic aspirations.[10]

Increasing interest in the establishment of a civic center figured among the most conspicuous manifestations of such ambitions. The idea was first advocated in a comprehensive plan for urban growth completed by John Nolen, a nationally recognized authority on city planning, in 1922. Such a facility, which would provide sites for public buildings and a large, accessible venue for community activities, was

This circa 1907 color postcard shows an enlarged Pack Square with the 1877 courthouse removed. The 1903 courthouse is hidden behind the city hall. (Private collection.)

Color postcard of the 1903 courthouse published ca. 1908 (Private collection.)

Figure 3. The 1903 Buncombe County courthouse. This Classical Revival structure was designed by Asheville architect Kenneth McDonald and replaced James A. Tennent's 1877 courthouse. Though expected to serve as the seat of county government for at least 50 years, the sharp pace of local growth rendered it obsolete within just two decades. This photograph was taken shortly before its demolition in 1929. Visible in the background are the new courthouse and city building. The marble column in the foreground is the Civil War memorial, which was moved to the north side of the new courthouse in 1928. (Courtesy, North Carolina Collection, Pack Memorial Public Library, Asheville, North Carolina.)

clearly needed, Nolen contended. "Pack Square is at present very crowded and the open space is entirely inadequate to meet the needs of a larger Asheville," he wrote. As part of a larger "program of civic progress" and municipal improvement, Nolen proposed that a civic center be developed as "an extension and development of the eastern end of Pack Square."[11]

But the idea of a civic center remained a mere possibility until "a group of influential and public-spirited citizens" made it their cause in late June 1926.[12] A sense of urgency inspired their activism. Earlier that month, Mayor John H. Cathey had announced the acceptance of Douglas Ellington's plan for a new city hall; construction contracts for the building were

Daniel J. Vivian ■ Public Architecture, Civic Aspirations and the Price of "Progress"

expected to be awarded by early July.[13] At the same time, Edgar M. Lyda, the chairman of the county commissioners, made it clear that the board would soon take steps to build a new courthouse in response to the mounting criticism and obvious inadequacy of the existing building.[14]

Advocates of the civic center, mainly the Asheville Chamber of Commerce and the Western North Carolina Architects' Association, stepped forward "at the eleventh hour" with what the *Asheville Citizen* called "the most far-reaching, progressive move to build a greater Asheville ever undertaken." The group showed conceptual sketches of their proposal to city and county authorities and urged that work on the new city hall be delayed until it could receive full consideration. The fundamental details of the plan called for an eastward extension of Pack Square and "the creation of a handsome and spacious civic center, in the heart of Asheville, to include park spaces, wide boulevards and the convenient and artistic grouping of city and county buildings. . . ." The new city hall and planned county courthouse were to stand along the periphery of the park space; other structures mentioned as possible additions included a county agricultural building and a new auditorium.[15]

The civic center proposal was greeted by enthusiastic public support. Editorially, the *Asheville Times* declared that if carried out, it "would be for all time one of the architectural glories of Asheville."[16] In addition, an informal poll conducted by an *Asheville Citizen* reporter found that of 78 people questioned, 74 favored the plan.[17]

Official endorsement followed immediately. At a July 2 meeting, the city and county commissioners gave tentative approval to the proposal and agreed to cooperate in developing a full-scale plan for its establishment.[18] Only four days later, a joint meeting of city and county officials yielded a decision to erect twin buildings, joined by an arcade and designed by local architect Douglas D. Ellington, at an estimated cost of $1,500,000.[19]

The agreement drew resounding praise. The *Asheville Citizen* called it a "splendid achievement" and predicted, "Buncombe and Asheville will have a well-founded right to pride in magnificent buildings in a parked plaza. . . . Buncombe will have no rival as a leader of counties; Asheville will stand out as a city of repute, a municipality fitted to serve as a model." The creation of a civic center was expected to be "the first step in an entirely new era" for the city.[20]

Of the parties involved, none were more satisfied with the agreement than three members of the board of county commissioners. The *Asheville Citizen* reported that Chairman Lyda was "immensely pleased" with the deal; the two other commissioners, W.E. Johnson and Emory McLean, also stood in agreement.[21] As city officials moved forward with preparations for construction of the city hall, the commissioners expectantly awaited comprehensive drawings and plans for the new courthouse from Ellington.

City Hall, Legal Building, and Pack Memorial Library, on Pack Square, Asheville, N. C.

The dome of the 1903 courthouse (circle) is barely visible behind the city hall (the spire now removed) in this 1920s postcard view of Pack Square. As Asheville's civic needs and public buildings grew, Pack Square expanded to the east. (Private collection.)

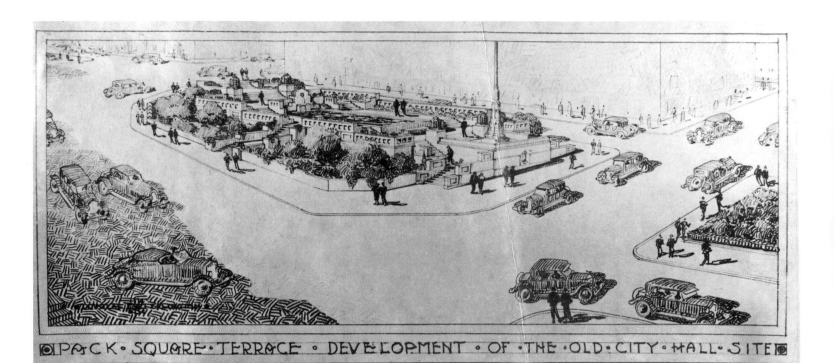

PACK·SQUARE·TERRACE · DEVELOPMENT · OF · THE · OLD · CITY · HALL · SITE

Figure 4. These sketches by Douglas Ellington, probably made sometime in the fall of 1926, depict his plans for the city-county building complex and Pack Square. Above. This view facing the northwest calls for a landscaped terrace situated between the complex and the square to serve as the focal point of the proposed civic center. The stepped terrace Ellington planned, included landscaped walkways. Right. This view looking to the southwest shows art deco motifs on the terrace walls that would have echoed the ornamentation scheme Ellington intended to use for both municipal buildings. The Jackson Building stands in the background. (Private Collection.)

"A Municipal Crisis": Signs of Strain in the Civic Center Plan

If the city and county commissioners had moved quickly in reaching an agreement on the civic center plan—the issue had, after all, progressed from conception to final approval in less than two weeks—it was only a few weeks before tensions arose among those involved in its execution. The August 27, 1926 *Asheville Citizen* reported that a Chamber of Commerce committee formed to monitor the project was claiming that it stood on the verge of "utter ruin" due to the failure of city and county officials to proceed cooperatively. The committee report stated:

> We are reliably informed that the county commissioners have very properly determined to give the plans for the courthouse careful consideration, and have as yet not employed an architect, nor even decided upon the general style of the building. Yet we are also reliably informed that plans for the city building have been drawn and accepted and that [it] is the plan of the city commissioners to proceed [with construction] at once.

The result, the committee predicted, would be a pair of buildings "lacking in harmony of design; and . . . a great waste of public funds." The report recommended that further work be delayed until the city hall and courthouse could be thoroughly planned as a joint project.[22]

Mayor Cathey reacted swiftly and harshly. "I have no intention of quitting the City Hall work which has already been started or of delaying one damned second for anybody," he stated flatly. "The Civic Center isn't in any grave peril," Cathey declared. "I would like to know definitely, once and for all time, what in the hell this so-called Citizen's Committee wants," the mayor exclaimed, clearly annoyed by the intense public scrutiny of his actions. "[N]obody except a few jackasses expected that the two buildings would be absolute twins."[23]

Valid concerns underlaid Cathey's angry comments. The city commissioners

had already awarded most of the construction contracts for the city hall; building materials were en route to the site. "[D]oes this bunch of sore heads and kickers realize that if we dared to stop now the city would have to pay for all the material already ordered?" he asked. "Half of this material," he added, "is on the way." Moreover, Ellington was under contract and would continue to collect fees even if the project were delayed. "The plain truth," Cathey stated, "is that we cannot repudiate these obligations without paying for them in full."[24]

Nor was there any reason that construction of the city hall should not begin as planned, Cathey asserted. In the end, it would be architecturally "well harmonized" with the courthouse and situated amid a beautiful civic center, he stated confidently. Further interference from the Chamber of Commerce, Cathey warned, might prompt him to "kick their Civic Center project into a cocked hat."[25]

So heated was the dispute over the civic center plans that it inspired this political cartoon, which appeared on the editorial page of the Asheville Citizen *at the peak of the controversy. The cartoon shows the city building—Asheville's precious, $800,000 baby—under scrutiny from the Chamber of Commerce. (Political cartoon by Bill Borne,* Asheville Citizen, *August 28, 1926, p. A4.)*

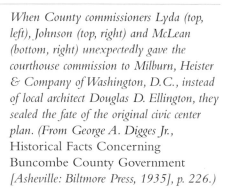

When County commissioners Lyda (top, left), Johnson (top, right) and McLean (bottom, right) unexpectedly gave the courthouse commission to Milburn, Heister & Company of Washington, D.C., instead of local architect Douglas D. Ellington, they sealed the fate of the original civic center plan. (From George A. Digges Jr., Historical Facts Concerning Buncombe County Government *[Asheville: Biltmore Press, 1935], p. 226.)*

The county commissioners agreed with Cathey. According to Chairman Lyda, they had entered into the July 6 agreement with the understanding that construction of the city building would begin as soon as possible. At present, he added, they had no plans for the new courthouse and were unlikely to consider the matter for another several months. Nonetheless, Lyda stated that the two buildings, if not exact twins, would ultimately be architecturally harmonious, contrary to the fears voiced by the Chamber of Commerce.[26]

Such assurances, however, failed to quell concerns about the possible fate of the project, and Cathey's fierce rebuttal to the Chamber of Commerce report did little to garner public favor. Indeed, the commu-

nity's strong response to the dispute demonstrated the importance it placed on the successful completion of the civic center. Local newspaper editorials condemned the mayor for his apparent impetuosity and called attention to the concerns raised by the Chamber of Commerce. "If the City Commissioners persist in their present determination," the *Asheville Times* warned, "they may erect a City Hall that will mutilate the . . . civic center." At worst, the entire undertaking might ultimately "be only an architectural hodge-podge, unnecessarily expensive and offensive to the eye."[27] And with regard to the mayor's behavior, the paper asked "why all this ill-temper and these Fascist tactics?"[28] The *Asheville Citizen* proclaimed the impasse "A Municipal Crisis" and declared, "The glorious project for a Civic Center combining City and County buildings in harmonious design is gravely threatened with wreck. . . ."[29]

Despite the furor it caused, the dispute abated as quickly as it had arisen. As construction of the city hall began on August 28, 1926 the Chamber of Commerce retreated from its position, although its leaders continued to urge that city and county officials work cooperatively on the project; so too did their collaborators, the Western North Carolina Architects' Association.[30] Public concern, however, faded immediately; local residents evidently had greater faith in the mayor's judgment than in the Chamber's claims that a crisis was at hand.

The Chamber of Commerce was correct in contending that city and county officials were exercising almost no cooperative oversight of the project. While perhaps not yet cause for alarm, it soon would be.

"A VERY THOROUGH REPUDIATION OF ME AND MY WORK"

As Christmas 1926 approached, the county commissioners turned their attention to planning the new courthouse. Two members of the board, Chairman Lyda and W.E. Johnson, and several other county officials met with Douglas Ellington on

CITY · COUNTY · BUILDING · GROUP
· ASHEVILLE · N · CAROLINA ·
· DOUGLAS D. ELLINGTON · · ARCHITECT ·

December 22 to review tentative plans and sketches for the building. All in attendance expressed what the young architect understood to be "excited unanimous admiration and satisfaction" with his work. Ellington was further encouraged by the "pervading enthusiasm" that Lyda and Johnson exhibited for the project.[31] Everything seemed on track for a civic center featuring similarly-styled city and county buildings designed by Ellington (Figures 4, 5).

But less than two weeks later, on January 2, 1927, Ellington and other citizens of Asheville were stunned to learn that the commissioners had awarded the architectural contract for the courthouse to Milburn, Heister & Company, a firm with

an "international reputation" and offices in Washington, D.C., and Durham, North Carolina. The new building, the commissioners confidently declared, would "be of the very finest type of architecture obtainable . . . [and would] care for all the needs of the county for many years to come." A conceptual drawing by the architects appeared on the front page of local newspapers, thereby providing local citizens with their first glimpse of the "Accepted Design For New $1,000,000 Court House" (Figure 6). It took no specialized architectural expertise to discern that while the courthouse would be a modern governmental building of monumental scale, it would not bear the slightest resemblance to

Figure 5. Douglas Ellington's proposal for the new courthouse called for a structure styled much like the city building and connected to it by a one-story pedimented arcade. His plan assumed this pair of municipal buildings would anchor the east end of a terraced plaza. (Courtesy, Asheville Art Museum.)

Late in the fall of 1926, the county commissioners received an unsolicited proposal from Greensboro, North Carolina architect C. Gadsden Sayre. Rumors of a possible rift between the commissioners and Douglas Ellington had evidently inspired Sayre to bid for the commission. His drawing proposed a towering structure that drew heavily on New York architect Bertram Goodhue's widely acclaimed Nebraska State Capitol, which was then under construction. The commissioners ignored Sayer's proposal and hired Milburn, Heister & Company as architects for the new courthouse a short time later. (Edgar M. Lyda Papers, Ramsey Library, UNC-Asheville.)

the city building, which by then was well on its way to completion.[32] A civic center of a sort would still be realized, but one substantially different than originally planned.

The commissioners were vague about their reasons for rejecting Ellington's plans, and many questions about the issue remain unanswered. Publicly, they stated that their efforts to ensure adequate office space in the new building left them with no other choice, but this seems to have been more an excuse than a legitimate consideration. During consultations with the commissioners in the preceding months, Ellington had assured them that he could design a courthouse that would be larger than the city building yet still architecturally harmonious.[33] The notion that Art Deco styling and the physical needs of the county government were somehow incompatible seems unlikely.

Architectural historians have uniformly contended that the decision was motivated by stylistic conservatism. Put off by the vibrant colors and daring synthesis of Art Deco ornament and Beaux Arts form that defined the city building, the commissioners opted for a more traditional, classically-inspired design.[34] The aesthetic juxtaposition of the two buildings provides strong support for such a conclusion; issues of personality, however, appear to have been at least as much of a factor. Ellington later admitted that an "atmosphere of misunderstanding" had constrained his relations with the commissioners, and he sensed that they "found me stubborn and impossible to work with. . . ." Clearly disappointed, he understandably regarded the decision as "a very thorough repudiation of me and my work."[35]

Matters of taste and personality must have influenced the commissioners' decision; Ellington's impressive credentials certainly left no doubt about his professional capabilities. He had studied at Philadelphia's Drexel Institute and the University of Pennsylvania, and in 1911 he won the Paris Prize, which allowed him

Figure 6. Milburn and Heister's conceptual drawing of the courthouse envisioned a monumental structure with a broad, rusticated base. The pyramid roof shown in this drawing was not built. This image appeared on the front page of local newspapers on January 2, 1927. (Edgar M. Lyda Papers, Ramsey Library, UNC-Asheville.)

to attend the prestigious Ecole des Beaux Arts in Paris. There, in 1913, Ellington became the first American to earn the Prix de Rougevin, the highest European decorative arts honor. Ellington returned to the United States at the outbreak of World War I and over the next several years taught architecture at the Drexel Institute, Columbia University and the Carnegie Institute of Technology in Pittsburgh. His practical experience, however, was less extensive. Although he had designed a parish house

for St. Paul's Church in Richmond, Virginia, in 1923, the city building was the first major project of his career.[36] There was, however, no mistaking his exceptional talent.

While Ellington was unquestionably capable of designing and overseeing construction of the courthouse, the commissioners nonetheless chose a far more experienced firm for the job. In fact, Milburn, Heister & Company were unrivaled among southern architects of public buildings. Whereas Ellington was clearly an architect on the rise in the mid-1920s, the firm selected by the commissioners had already been at the top for more than two decades.

Frank P. Milburn was the principal force behind the firm's success. Milburn was trained at the University of Arkansas and entered professional practice in the late 1880s. Almost immediately he established himself as an architect of public buildings, designing courthouses and municipal structures throughout the Southeast. In 1895 he became the primary architect for the Southern Railway; ultimately, Milburn designed 19 major depots for the company. By the turn of the century he had won commissions for two high-profile projects: the completion of the South Carolina state house in Columbia and a major renovation of the Florida state capitol in Tallahassee. Milburn, always ambitious, also submitted proposals for a new Kentucky state capitol and an enlargement of the North Carolina state capitol, but neither was accepted.[37]

The peak of Milburn's career spanned the first two decades of the twentieth century. In 1902 he opened an office in Washington, D.C., and soon hired a young draftsman, Michael Heister, who later became his partner. Milburn maintained a particularly strong presence in North Carolina by virtue of a branch office in Durham. Nonetheless, he and Heister undertook their largest projects in the nation's capital, where a lucrative market existed for office and commercial buildings. By the early 1920s, the Department of

Labor, the Interstate Commerce Commission, the Department of Commerce and the American Federation of Labor all occupied buildings designed by Milburn and Heister. Their largest project by far was a building for the Bureau of Engraving and Printing of the Chinese Imperial Government in Peking.[38] Milburn and Heister stood without par among southern architects during the first quarter of the twentieth century.

The firm was in the midst of a transition in leadership when it received the commission for the Buncombe County courthouse. Declining health had forced Milburn into semi-retirement and led him to seek refuge in Asheville, where he died at the age of 56 on September 21, 1926.[39] According to the calculations of one historian, he had designed "at least 250 major structures in the South—in addition to numerous structures of domestic scale" during his career.[40] Succeeding him as president of the firm was his son, Thomas Y. Milburn, who had managed the Durham office for several years. A 1915 graduate of the University of North Carolina, the younger Milburn quickly proved as capable an administrator as his father, and the change of leadership had little effect on the firm's operations.[41]

Thus, while issues of aesthetics and personality surely had some bearing on the county commissioners' decision, Milburn and Heister's proven record was undoubtedly a significant factor. By the mid-1920s, their work in the state of North Carolina alone included at least 12 county courthouses, 13 buildings on the University of North Carolina campus in Chapel Hill and numerous commercial structures.[42] Ellington had considerable promise, but Milburn, Heister & Company had an established reputation and no shortage of satisfied customers to recommend their work.

CONSTRUCTION TO COMPLETION

"This is a great day in the history of Buncombe county," declared County

Commissioner Chairman Edgar M. Lyda as he addressed the nearly 1,000 citizens gathered to observe the laying of the cornerstone for the courthouse on November 7, 1927 (Figure 7). The ceremony's featured speaker, Buncombe County Superior Court Judge Frank Carter, observed, "Men are judged by the houses they build for themselves. . . . Buncombe County judges herself now and submits to be judged by others by erecting the greatest building ever constructed in North Carolina. . . . No county in North Carolina has judged its present and its future heretofore by erecting a building of one half the cost of this one."[43] Carter's speech, though somewhat overstated, captured the civic hopes embodied in the courthouse. In much the same manner, the *Asheville Times* editorially affirmed that "the new courthouse is to stand as a monument for a new and greater era in Buncombe County history."[44]

Construction was well underway by the time the cornerstone ceremony took place. About eight stories of steel framework were already standing, which prompted the *Asheville Times* to report that the courthouse was "rapidly shooting skyward."[45] Initially, the commissioners had hoped to see construction completed by the end of 1927, but such a goal soon proved unrealistic.[46] Thomas Milburn had prepared detailed plans and drawings by late March,

Thomas Y. Milburn (left) became president of Milburn, Heister & Company after his father's death in 1926. Michael Heister (right), a partner in the firm for more than two decades, remained head of the drafting department. These photos appeared in the pamphlet issued for the dedication of the new courthouse. (Dedicating Buncombe County's Courthouse [Asheville: Jarrett's Press, [1927].)

Laying of Corner Stone —
Job No. 11   Photo No.   Date. Nov. 7/27.
Buncombe County Court House
Milburn, Heister & Co., Architects
Washington, D. C.
Angle-Blackford Co., General Contractors

Figure 7. The cornerstone ceremony for the Buncombe County courthouse, November 7, 1927. (Edgar M. Lyda Papers, Ramsey Library, UNC-Asheville.)

Figure 7. The cornerstone ceremony for the Buncombe County courthouse, November 7, 1927. (Edgar M. Lyda Papers, Ramsey Library, UNC-Asheville.)

but the process of awarding building contracts continued well into the summer.[47] The commissioners named a firm based in Greensboro, North Carolina, the Angle-Blackford Company, as the general contractor for the project.[48] Only in the fall did work at the building site begin in earnest, and although construction proceeded at a brisk pace, it was more than a year before the courthouse approached completion.

The community responded to the dedication of the courthouse with an outpouring of civic pride (Figure 8). Local newspapers proudly reported that in terms of size and cost, it outranked "any other public structure in the Carolinas."[49] Crowds numbering in the thousands turned out for the dedication ceremony on December 1, 1928. An *Asheville Times* editorial extolled the "imposing architectural character, dignity, convenience and splendid equipment"

and suggested that the courthouse would usher in a new era in social contentment: "The whole structure and its furnishings are of such character as to inspire in the citizenship a new respect and more devoted patriotism for all things related to the proper administration of the county's great business. . . ."[50]

Citizens of Buncombe County certainly deserved a courthouse that lived up to such claims—they had paid for it. Construction costs had escalated steadily as the project progressed. Initially estimated at $1,000,000, by the time of the dedication ceremony, the final cost was reported at between $1,750,000 and $2,000,000.[51] When all accounts were finally settled, however, nearly $2,500,000 had been expended on the courthouse itself, and the removal of the old courthouse required another $65,000.[52]

Did it matter that the outcome of the

The courthouse under construction, spring 1928. (Courtesy, Ewart M. Ball collection, Ramsey Library, UNC-Asheville.)

Figure 8. The new Buncombe County courthouse immediately after completion, December 1928. Visible at the extreme right is the corner of the old courthouse building and the new city building. (Courtesy, Ewart M. Ball collection, Ramsey Library, UNC-Asheville.)

civic center was much different than originally planned? Evidently not. If any local residents were disappointed with the final result, they kept their opinions to themselves. The fact that Asheville could boast of what the local press generally referred to as "one of the most beautiful civic centers in the United States" was cause enough for celebration.[53] With all of downtown immersed in a virtually continuous wave of construction during the 1920s, civic-minded citizens did not have to look far to find architectural evidence of "progress." Together, the city building and the county courthouse made a significant contribution to the overall picture, even if they lacked a unified design.

A GRAND DESIGN

Upon completion in 1928, the new courthouse, with 15 stories above ground, was the tallest municipal building in North Carolina. Set upon a two-story basement, the steel frame structure progresses in three clearly articulated levels from a broad ashlar

Above. Final product: the courthouse and the city building. This photograph, taken in the early 1940s, shows both structures decorated for an undetermined occasion. Although a far cry from the original civic center plan, the two buildings and the adjoining plaza create an impressive municipal complex. (Courtesy, North Carolina Collection, Pack Memorial Public Library, Asheville, North Carolina.) Below. Postcard view of city and county buildings during World War II. (Private collection.)

base to a nine-story superstructure with Corinthian columns and a double attic. A deep setback on the main facade differentiates the fourth through sixth floors from the first three, and a variety of Beaux Arts forms provide rich ornamentation. The overall effect was monumental and progressive, setting the building squarely within an emerging national idiom for tall office buildings.

A variety of classical motifs give considerable textural complexity to the building's facades. The windows of the fourth through sixth stories, for instance, are separated by Ionic pilasters, and Corinthian half-columns divide those of the 10th through 13th stories (Figure 9). The solid brass doors of the main entrance are framed by a three-story pavilion comprised of a full entablature and centered cartouche that rests on a pair of opposing polished Doric columns (Figure 10).

Milburn and Heister reserved the most impressive decorative features for the interior, particularly the main lobby, which contains a sweeping marble staircase, a cof-fered ceiling with brilliant polychrome plaster work (Figure 11), two brass chandeliers and a mosaic tile floor. No less ornate is the main courtroom. Located on the fifth floor and finished with handsome walnut paneling, it features a richly-detailed octagonal coffered ceiling.[54]

Contemporary observers regarded the placement of the county jail in the uppermost six stories of the building as perhaps the most novel aspect of the overall design. The *Asheville Times*, for example, declared it "a prison of almost undreamed of efficiency."[55] The feature had long been one of Milburn and Heister's trademarks. According to Thomas Milburn, his father had first placed a jail in the upper stories of a court-house in Muskogee, Oklahoma, and then made such designs "general practice."[56]

In the context of Milburn and Heister's public buildings, the Buncombe County courthouse is a significant deviation from the norm (Figure 12). It is in fact more typical of the firm's office and commercial buildings. Most of their court-house designs were characterized by simple

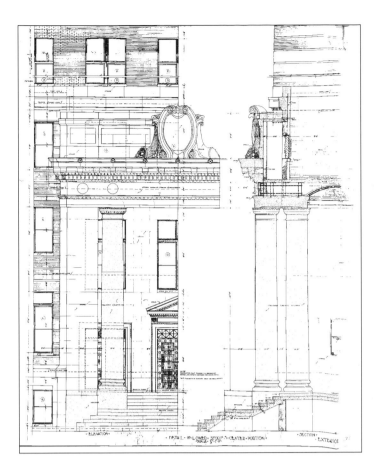

massing and ornamentation, as was common in the early twentieth century. At the time of the dedication ceremony, Thomas Milburn stated that while his firm had undertaken larger projects, he believed the courthouse to be "the best."[57] Evidently, he was entirely sincere: looking back on his career four decades later, in the early 1970s, he again cited the structure as the firm's "best effort. . . ."[58]

In the decades since the completion of the courthouse, observers have been quick to compare it with the city building, which one historian has described as "a colorfeast of Art Deco and stylized local motifs."[59] During construction of the courthouse, the *Asheville Times* predicted almost optimistically that it would ultimately be "[n]ot quite a twin, but at least a first cousin" of the city building.[60] The outcome of the project belied this assertion; the stark contrast between the two structures is immediately apparent. The courthouse is by far the more reserved design; one account aptly characterized its outward appearance as "rather severe. . . ."[61]

IN RETROSPECT: CIVIC FORTUNES AND THE SYMBOLISM OF THE COURTHOUSE

The Great Depression hit especially hard in Asheville, where borrowed money had sustained the bulk of the real estate boom.[62] It moreover irrevocably changed the symbolic role served by the courthouse in public consciousness of Buncombe County. No longer did it stand as a sign of civic progress and the community's escalating wealth; instead, within two years of its completion, the courthouse became a reminder of past prosperity and fleeting fortunes.

Above all, the courthouse demonstrated the costs of poor municipal planning.[63] Given Asheville's thriving economy, no expense seemed too great, and in their efforts to erect a courthouse capable of lasting several decades, the county commissioners saddled the populace with heavy debts. In fact, when construction began, the county was still paying for $50,000 in bonds issued for the 1903 courthouse that were not due to reach maturity until 1932.[64] Construction of the new court-

Figure 10. Main entrance pavilion as seen in the original blueprint and in a contemporary photograph. (Blueprint, courtesy Edgar M. Lyda Papers, Ramsey Library, UNC-Asheville; Photo, Tim Barnwell.)

Main lobby, balcony level. (Photos, Tim Barnwell.)

Detail of fluted walnut pilasters and octagonal coffered ceiling, fifth floor courtroom.

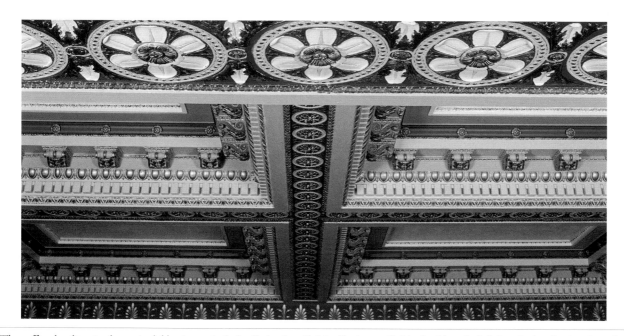

Figure 11. The coffered ceiling in the main lobby is particularly distinctive. Originally, it was finished with a dark beige shade of paint that also contained small specks of yellow, silver, tan and aqua-blue. Only under close examination was the complexity of color evident; the ceiling's general appearance was neutral grey and resembled unpolished granite. Today, the original paint can still be seen on the underside of the main staircase, although it has faded considerably and looks markedly different than it did in 1928.

Between 1990 and 1997, the ceiling was refinished by students in the decorative restoration program at Asheville-Buncombe Technical College. The new paint scheme extracted the several colors contained in the original paint and applied them individually to the various architectural elements of the ceiling. Its overall appearance is Beaux Arts in character.

The gilded band above the doors and windows of the main lobby is similar to the shell and scroll decorative pattern that wraps around the exterior of the building below the 14th floor. (See Figure 9.)

Daniel J. Vivian ■ PUBLIC ARCHITECTURE, CIVIC ASPIRATIONS AND THE PRICE OF "PROGRESS"

Figure 12. The design of the Buncombe County courthouse differs markedly from the vast majority of Milburn and Heister's public buildings. Shown here are two structures representative of their other works. Above. The Mecklenburg County courthouse (ca. 1900; now destroyed) in Charlotte, North Carolina, was typical of the firm's large-scale projects. The basic elements of its design—wings situated on opposing sides of a central block, pedimented porticos, and a monumental tower—immediately identified it as a governmental building. Milburn and Heister cast the hundreds of small municipal buildings they designed in a similar mold. Nearly all were distinguished by balanced exterior features and symmetrical floor plans. Below. One example of this type is the Swain County courthouse (1908) in Bryson City, North Carolina. The design of the Buncombe County courthouse was influenced more by the high-rise commercial buildings of the day than by Milburn and Heister's prior courthouse projects. (Photo of the Mecklenburg County courthouse from Designs from the Work of Frank P. Milburn, Architect, Columbia, S.C. *[Columbia: The State Co., 1903]; photo of the Swain County courthouse from Ewart M. Ball Collection, Ramsey Library, UNC-Asheville.)*

house was financed largely by bonds with lengthy repayment schedules, and unforeseen expenses encountered during the project further strained the county's coffers. These debts weighed heavily on residents of the county for decades.

Seven decades later, the courthouse, largely unaltered and still a strong presence amid the urban landscape of central Asheville, serves symbolically as a subtle reminder of the commercial boom that transformed the city in the 1920s. It proved to be the last and largest municipal project undertaken by, in the words of one historian, "those wildly optimistic city fathers" who could see no end to the prevailing prosperity.[65] As such, it stands as an echo of the heights to which civic ambitions ascended during the heady days of the Jazz Age.

Acknowledgments:

The author wishes to thank the following people for their assistance and contributions to this article: Sallie Middleton, the niece of Douglas Ellington; Scott Fowler; Derick Tickle, director of the Decorative Restoration Program at Asheville Buncombe-Technical Community College; Tim Daniels, special collections assistant at Ramsey Library, UNC-Asheville; and Charlotte Brown, director of the Gallery of Art and Design, North Carolina State University.

Notes

1. Douglas Swaim, "An Architectural History of Asheville & Buncombe County," in Swaim, Ed., *Cabins & Castles: The History & Architecture of Buncombe County, North Carolina* (Raleigh: North Carolina Department of Cultural Resources, 1981), pp. 93-94; Catherine W. Bishir, *North Carolina Architecture* (Chapel Hill: University of North Carolina Press, 1990), p. 412.

2. George A. Digges Jr., *Historical Facts Concerning Buncombe County Government* (Asheville: Biltmore Press, 1935), pp. 228-229 (first quotation on p. 228; second on p. 229). See also *Asheville Times*, June 28, 1926, pp. A1, A15; *Asheville Citizen*, June 29, 1926, p. B12.

3. Digges, Historical Facts, p. 228 (quotations); *Asheville Citizen*, July 18, 1926, p. B6.

4. *Asheville Citizen*, July 18, 1926, p. B6; J.P. Davison, Comp., The *Asheville City Directory and Gazetteer of Buncombe County for 1883-84* (Richmond: Baughman Brothers, 1883), p. 128 (first quotation); *Asheville Daily Gazette* (Asheville, N.C.), January 8, 1901, p. 4 (second quotation). On the limitations of the 1877 courthouse, see *Asheville Citizen*, January 2, 1901, p. 4.

5. *Asheville Citizen*, January 2, 1901, p. 1; January 8, 1901, p. 5 (quotation); *Asheville Daily Gazette*, January 3, 1901, p. 5. On George W. Pack, see William S. Powell, Ed., *Dictionary of North Carolina Biography*, Vol. V (Chapel Hill: University of North Carolina Press, 1994), p. 1.

6. *Asheville Citizen*, July 18, 1926, p. B6; March 18, 1929, p. 6 (quotation).

7. Ronald D. Eller, *Miners, Millhands, and Mountaineers: Industrialization of the Appalachian South, 1880-1930* (Knoxville: University of Tennessee Press, 1982), pp. 101-104.

8. Census Office, *Statistics of the Population of the United States at the Tenth Census (June 1, 1880)* (Washington, D.C.: Government Printing Office, 1883), pp. 73, 278; *Twelfth Census of the United States*, I, *Population* (Washington, D.C.: Government Printing Office, 1901), p. 32; *Thirteenth Census of the United States Taken in the Year 1910*, III, *Population* (Washington, D.C.: Government Printing Office, 1913), p. 272; *Fourteenth Census of the United States Taken in the Year 1920*, II, *Population* (Washington, D.C.: Government Printing Office, 1922), p. 1354.

9. Bureau of the Census, *Fifteenth Census of the United States: 1930*, I, *Population* (Washington, D.C.: Government Printing Office, 1931), p. 785.

10. Swaim, "An Architectural History of Asheville & Buncombe County," p. 79 (quotation). On Asheville's architectural development in the early twentieth century, see Bishir, *North Carolina Architecture*, pp. 412-416. On economic development in the southern Appalachians, see Eller, *Miners, Millhands, and Mountaineers*, pp. 103-110, 121-127.

11. John Nolen, *Asheville City Plan* (N.p.: n.p., [1925]), both quotations on p. 29. On Nolen's work in Asheville, see also Kevan D. Frazier, "Outsiders in the Land of the Sky: City Planning and the Transformation of Asheville, North Carolina, 1921-1929," *Journal of Appalachian Studies* 4, no. 2 (fall 1998), pp. 299-316. Nolan was a leading figure in the City Beautiful movement and early city planning efforts. See especially Thomas W. Hanchett, *Sorting Out the New South City: Race, Class, and Urban Development in Charlotte, 1875-1975* (Chapel Hill: University of North Carolina Press, 1998), pp. 154-156, 165-178, 218-221; William H. Wilson, *The City Beautiful Movement* (Baltimore: Johns Hopkins University Press, 1989).

12. *Asheville Times*, June 27, 1926, p. D1 (quotation).

13. *Asheville Times*, June 6, 1926, p. B1.

14. *Asheville Times*, June 28, 1926, pp. 1, 15.

15. *Asheville Times*, June 27, 1926, pp. D1-2 (first quotation); June 29, 1926, p. 1 (third quotation); *Asheville Citizen*, June 27, 1926, pp. C1-2 (second quotation); June 30, 1926, p. A9.

16. *Asheville Times*, June 27, 1926, p. A4.

17. *Asheville Citizen*, June 30, 1926, p. A9.

18. *Asheville Times*, July 2, 1926, p. A1; *Asheville Citizen*, July 3, 1926, p. A1.

19. *Asheville Times*, July 6, 1926, p. A1; *Asheville Citizen*, July 7, 1926, p. A1; Buncombe County Commissioners' Minutes, November 10, 1926 (Book 14, pp. 305-306), Buncombe County Central Records Archives, Asheville, N.C.

20. *Asheville Citizen*, July 7, 1926, p. A4 (first and second quotations), p. A12 (third quotation).

21. *Asheville Citizen*, June 30, 1926, p. A9; July 3, p. A2; July 7, 1926, p. A12 (quotation).

22. *Asheville Citizen*, August 27, 1926, p. A10; W.H. Lord et al. to the President of the Chamber of Commerce, August 25, 1926, Folder M79.9.1.5, Edgar M. Lyda Papers, Ramsey Library, University of North Carolina-Asheville, Asheville, N.C. (hereafter Lyda Papers).

23. *Asheville Citizen*, August 27, 1926, pp. A1, A10.

24. *Asheville Citizen*, August 27, 1926, p. A10.

25. *Asheville Citizen*, August 27, 1926, p. A10.

26. *Asheville Times*, August 27, 1926, p. 1; *Asheville Citizen*, August 28, 1926, p. A2.

27. Editorial from the *Asheville Times*, quoted in the *Asheville Citizen*, August 27, 1926, p. A10.

28. *Asheville Times*, August 27, 1926, p. 1.

29. *Asheville Citizen*, August 27, 1926, p. A4. For other editorials condemning the mayor's actions, see *Asheville Citizen*, August 28, 1926, p. A4; August 29, 1926, p. A4; *Asheville Times*, August 29, 1926, p. A1.

30. *Asheville Times*, August 28, 1926, p. 1; *Asheville Times*, August 29, 1926, pp. A1-2. Dissatisfied that Ellington had received the commission for the city building, William H. Lord, the key figure in the Western North Carolina Architects' Association, ultimately lodged a protest with the Committee on Practice of the American Institute of Architects. Lord evidently claimed that Ellington was not entitled to the commission because the city and county commissioners had failed to hold an open competition, which would have given other architects an opportunity to submit proposals. The ensuing investigation lasted into the fall of 1927, but it seems that the committee ultimately took no action on the matter. See John H. Cathey to A.H. Albertson, November 5, 1927; and Douglas D. Ellington to A.H. Albertson, November 5, 1927, both in the collections of the Asheville Art Museum, Asheville, N.C.; and also C.G. Sayre to E.M. Lyda, May 9, 1927; and C.G. Sayre to John L. Mauran (copy), n.d. [ca. spring 1927], both in Folder M79.9.1.5., Lyda Papers.

31. Ellington to the Buncombe County Commissioners, January 18, 1927, Folder M79.9.1.5, Lyda Papers.

32. *Asheville Times*, January 2, 1927, p. 1 (quotations); *Asheville Citizen*, January 2, 1927, pp. 1-2.

33. Ellington to the Buncombe County Commissioners, January 18, 1927, Lyda Papers.

34. See, for example, Catherine W. Bishir et al., *Architects and Builders in North Carolina: A History of the Practice of Building* (Chapel Hill: University of North Carolina Press, 1990), p. 298; Bishir, *North Carolina Architecture*, pp. 413-414; Swaim, "An Architectural History of Asheville & Buncombe County," pp. 93-94; Clayton W. Griffith, "Douglas D. Ellington: Art Deco in Asheville, 1925-1931," (M.A. thesis, University of Virginia, 1993), p. 27.

35. Ellington to the Buncombe County Commissioners, January 18, 1927, Lyda Papers.

36. Griffith, "Douglas D. Ellington," pp. 4-5; Ellington to the Buncombe County Commissioners, January 18, 1927, Lyda Papers.

37. Lawrence Wodehouse, "Frank Pierce Milburn (1868-1926), A Major Southern Architect," *North Carolina Historical Review* L, no. 3 (July 1973), pp. 289-294; *The National Cyclopedia of American Biography* (New York: James T. White & Co., 1904), XII, p. 103; Lee H. Warner, *Building Florida's Capitol* (Tallahassee: State of Florida, 1977), pp. 13-15.

38. Wodehouse, "Frank Pierce Milburn," pp. 291, 296, 300-302; Milburn, Heister & Company, *Selections from the Work of Milburn, Heister & Co.* (Washington, D.C.: National Publishing Co., 1922).

39. *Washington Post* (Washington, D.C.), September 22, 1926, p. 8; *Asheville Citizen*, September 22, 1926, p. 1.

40. Wodehouse, "Frank Pierce Milburn," p. 289.

41. See Wodehouse, "Frank Pierce Milburn," p. 290 n. 4, for a synopsis of Thomas Y. Milburn's education and career.

42. Wodehouse, "Frank Pierce Milburn," pp. 301-302. On county courthouses in North Carolina designed by Milburn & Heister, see *100 Courthouses: A Report on North Carolina Judicial Facilities*, vol. 2, *The County Perspective: Facilities Inventory, Needs and Recommendations* (Raleigh: North Carolina State University, 1978), pp. 62, 199, 212, 225, 472, 497, 503, 556, 580, 594, 614.

43. *Asheville Times*, November 7, 1927, pp. 1, 14; *Asheville Citizen*, November 8, 1927, p. B2.

44. *Asheville Times*, November 7, 1927, p. 4.

45. *Asheville Times*, November 7, 1927, pp. 1, 14 (quotation on p. 1).

46. *Asheville Citizen*, January 2, 1927, p. 1.

47. T.Y. Milburn to E.M. Lyda, March 21, 1927, Folder M79.9.1.5, Lyda Papers.

48. *Asheville Times*, November 30, 1928, p. A6.

49. *Asheville Times*, November 30, 1928, p. A6.

50. *Asheville Times*, December 1, 1928, p. 4.

51. See, for example, *Asheville Times*, November 30, 1928, p. 1; December 2, 1928, p. 1; *Asheville Citizen*, November 27, 1928, p. 3; December 2, 1928, p. 1.

52. *Asheville Citizen*, April 14, 1929, pp. 1-2.

53. *Asheville Citizen*, November 7, 1927, p. 2.

54. For thorough descriptions of the building, see *Asheville Times*, November 30, 1928, p. A6; *100 Courthouses*, p. 62.

55. *Asheville Times*, November 30, 1928, p. A6.

56. Wodehouse, "Frank Pierce Milburn," p. 301.

57. *Asheville Times*, December 2, 1928, p. 5.

58. Wodehouse, "Frank Pierce Milburn," p. 301.

59. Swaim, "An Architectural History of Asheville & Buncombe County," p. 93. See also Bishir, *North Carolina Architecture*, pp. 413-414.

60. *Asheville Times*, March 18, 1928, p. C4.

61. *Asheville Times*, November 30, 1928, p. A6.

62. A brief overview of Asheville's fiscal crisis is found in Milton Ready, *Asheville: Land of the Sky* (Northridge, Calif.: Windsor Publications, Inc.), 1986, pp. 85-92.

63. A fruitful area for further study of public buildings in Asheville would be to examine the political party affiliation of city and county commissioners, editors of the major newspapers and other leaders involved in the construction of these buildings.

64. "Tremendous Cost of New County Courthouse is Shown in Report on Structure by Architect East," clipping cited as *Asheville Advocate* (Asheville, N.C.), April 19, 1929, in vertical file 18.4, "Buildings/Courthouses," Pack Memorial Library, Asheville, N.C.

65. Talmage Powell, "Asheville: An Historical Sketch," in *Cabins & Castles*, p. 44.

In the 71 years since the Buncombe County courthouse was constructed, the exterior of the building and surrounding landscape have seen few changes. This February 1998 photograph indicates that aside from the installation of several air conditioning units and minor changes to the grading and landscaping at the site, little has been altered. (Photo, Tim Barnwell.)

Tim Barnwell was born in Franklin, North Carolina in 1955 and has been a professional photographer for the past 20 years. He lived in Madison County where his mother Virginia taught at Walnut School and his father Howard at Marshall High School. The images published here are from a body of work he completed largely in the 1980s, primarily in Madison County, North Carolina. They were shot using a traditional four by five inch view camera. Many of these images have not been published before and in many ways they are the photographer's private collection. For me, their appeal derives in part from the fact that they are without pretense, neither on the part of the subjects, nor on the part of the photographer. —R. B.

Portraits for the Heart:
Images of Western North Carolina

Photography and Interviews by Tim Barnwell

Picking Up Walnuts. *Left to right, Pearl Presnell, wife; Kenny Caldwell, husband; and "Aunt" Pearl Goforth, Big Pine Creek, Madison County, N.C., September, 1982.*

Methodist Church in Snow. *Walnut, Madison County, N.C. Mr. Henderson (1982): "My father used to be church secretary here in Walnut. He kept a record book that told how much the collection was each week. Cash money was hard to come by back then. Out of a congregation of 100 to 150 people, they would average about 40 cents each week. He even wrote down who gave the most. It was usually the doctor. He'd give three or four cents every Sunday. The Methodist Church was the biggest back then. All the funerals were held there, no matter who died." December, 1982.*

James Griffith with Horse. *Burnsville, N.C., June, 1983.*

Elmore Helton and Pup. *Brush Creek, Walnut Community, Madison County, N.C. Helton: "I had a good crop of potatoes this year. I got over 40 bushels out of that piece of bottomland. I used to live down on the French Broad River bank. I had to cross it for 27 years, in all kinds of weather, to get back and forth to the house. I used to build canoes and boats to cross it, or to fish in. I worked in Swannanoa at a lumber mill for almost 17 years. We got a 10-minute break in the morning and 10 in the afternoon, plus our lunch. While everybody else was takin' their break and foolin' around, I'd be out there cuttin' wood to take home so I'd have a fire to cook on and heat with that night. I don't know how these fellows with more than one or two young'uns can make it today. Used to, a big family was the way to go 'cause it meant you had more help around the farm." 1981/1982.*

Roy Mathis and Donald Williams with Mules. *Near Hot Springs, Madison County, N.C., April, 1981.*

McKinley "Doc" Caldwell on Woodpile. *Big Pine Creek, Madison County, N.C. Caldwell: "I can remember the time when I was 12 and my sister, Fanny, and I laid off and planted a field of corn that yielded 300 bushels and my Daddy never set a foot in the field. Fanny was a big girl then, maybe seven or eight years old. Now, that's the way we were raised. I was 19 before my family ever got a horse. I used mules and oxen up to then. My parents started building this place in 1920. I remember they hired an 84-year-old man to build the stone chimney. He used to get up at 4:00 in the morning and start to play his fiddle. The womenfolk would have to get up then, so he got his breakfast early and was up on the scaffolding by 7:00. He put down his tools for lunch at 11:00 and was back laying stone by noon. He would put his tools away for the day at 4:00 and go home. He worked for 35 cents an hour. We lived seven miles from the river at Barnard and you had to cross the creek 14 times to get up to our house. If it came a hard rain while you were out somewhere, you just had to sit down on the bank and wait for the creek to go down again before you could go any further. Back then, if one of us got sick, the doctor would walk miles to come help out. If the creeks were up, he would have to wait on the bank until they went down to cross. Now they tell me to call an ambulance and they'll get to me when they can. The postman got 50 cents a day to deliver the mail up this creek. It cost 25 cents to mail a letter and it took about a month to get anywhere. I'm 83 years old now and I can still chop all my own firewood and do most of the chores that need doing around here." July, 1980.*

Ruby and Mother, Hattie Roberts on Porch. *Rectors Corner Section, Marshall, Madison County, N.C. Right. Ruby Roberts (standing in photograph): "My father was a railroad man. When I was a little girl we lived down the river at Redmond. The railroad run past there and my daddy could see the house when he went by on his runs. I was a sickly child and the people what lived next to us had lost their baby to illness. That happened quite a lot back then. My daddy always worried after me and so he had Momma to put a lamp in the front window so he would know everything was all right. He told Momma to put two lamps in the window if I took sick or died. He told me later how happy he was never to have seen that second light, and how much it comforted him to know things was all well while he was away working."*

"When I was young, I used to love to dance. By the time I was six or seven, I could do the Charleston, but most of what I learned was popular traditional dances. I would travel around to all of the mountain festivals and I won a lot of awards and they would make pictures of me. Now I'm older and can't dance no more. When you get old, there's a lot of things you can't do no more. Momma was 95 last Sunday. She's been sick lately and she can't get around too good, but she still wants to do things. Sometimes she wants to do something so bad, and she can't, that she just sits and cries." August, 1981.

Myrtle and Bertha Marler. *Above, left to right. Bertha with daughter Myrtle. Marshall, N.C. Bertha Marler: "Myrtle's my oldest daughter. She lives with me now. She's an old maid–she's never been married. Her father died when she was 14 and she had to quit school to take care of the younger kids so I could go to work to support us. I'm 88 now, and don't imagine I'll live to see 89. I'm not worried, though. I've lived a clean life, never lied, nor stole, nor cheated, and I haven't associated myself with trash. The Lord will rise in the east and when Gabriel blows his trumpet, it won't scare me a bit. I'm expecting it and I'm ready." August, 1983.*

Tim Barnwell ■ Portraits for the Heart

Reverend Kenneth Parker, River Baptism, Arrington Branch Baptist Church. *Grapevine Section, Madison County, N.C. Reverend Parker: "If the rest of the world saw us now, standing here in this freezing water, they'd probably think we were crazy. I believe that it doesn't matter what time of year it is when a soul is saved—be it July or November. When my grandfather was baptized, it was the dead of winter and they had to break the ice to do it. He was 97 years old then, but it didn't bother him none. He didn't get sick afterwards or anything. You see, if you do something for the Lord, He'll take care of you. None of us knows how long we're on this earth. We may die tomorrow or the Lord may come for us today. There's no time to waste." November, 1982.*

Group of Visitors, Grave Decoration Sunday. *Whiterock Section, Madison County, N.C., July, 1982.*

Aunt Alice Davis in Bed and Niece Peggy Harmon. *Grapevine Section, Madison County, N.C. Peggy Harmon: "Aunt Alice was 89 last April. She never married, but she lives here next to Mama and Daddy and my husband and I, and we keep an eye on her. She started feeling bad a couple of weeks ago. We took her to the doctor and he gave us some medicine to give her. Mama watches her during the day while I'm at work and I stay with her at night. If you have the right medicine, I think you can take good care of someone at home. I know she's happier here than in the hospital. She's in her own bed, all her friends come to visit and she's surrounded by family, not strangers." October, 1983.*

Mrs. Jerome Franklin with Grave Decoration. *Whiterock Section, Madison County, N.C., July, 1982.*

Three Bear Hunters with Dogs. *Left to right, unidentified man, Joe Ferguson and Harold Scott. Bear Hunting Club at Mills Ridge, Madison County, N.C. Dempsey Woody (not pictured):* "A good bear dog will run you around $700. If you find one for two or 300, he won't stay the course. I lost two of the four I had this year. You usually wait 'til a dog's about a year-and-a-half old to start huntin' with them. If you start one when it's too little and it goes up against a bear, it'll get 'buffaloed' and it'll never go up against one again. It should be old enough to run with the rest and learn from them. One of my dogs stayed after a bear for two days and nights. He'd run during the day and walk at night. The bear will walk, too, 'cause he doesn't want to get caught, but he knows how close the dog is at all times." *December 24, 1982.*

Ed Plemmons with Dogs on Porch. *Dry Branch near Marshall, Madison County, N.C. Plemmons:* "When I was growing up you had chores to do every morning, livestock to feed, cows to milk. By the time you got to school, you'd already done a day's work. I think kids today have it a lot easier than we did. Even when they misbehave in school, they get away with it most of the time. It's not like we got punished too much. If you told my principal the truth when he asked you, more than likely he'd let you go with a warning, as long as no harm was done. If you lied to him, though, and he'd always know when you were lying, then he'd really give you the licks!" *June, 1982.*

Bear Hunting Club. *Above, left to right. Eddie Payne, Gary Frisbee, N. Plemmons, Kevin Meadows (boy), Rex Meadows (Kevin's father), Steve Frisbee, Harold Scott and Dwight Meadows. Mill Ridge, Madison County, N.C.*
Rex Meadows: "Kevin's learning to hunt with the rest of our bear club. He did real well this morning. He stayed right with us all the way, and we probably walked five or six miles over these mountains, through pretty rough country. He's learning the safe way to hunt and the proper way to handle a gun–the same type of things my father taught my brother and me."
December 24, 1982.

Car in Creek. *Left. Little Pine Creek, Madison County, N.C., 1981.*

Rector's Corner View. *Madison County, N.C. Ernest Teague, Rector's Corner:*
"I grew up in that old farmhouse right down there on the ridge. When I was a boy we moved
here from Marshall. I remember coming across the mountain in the snow, on the back of a sled
pulled by horses. That was the first time I saw this land and there wasn't a cleared place to be
found. All this pastureland stood in trees. It took a lot of years and plenty of hard work to clear
enough for pasture and farming." January, 1982.

Evia Metcalf in Doorway. *Spillcorn, Shelton Laurel Section, Madison County, N.C.*
Metcalf: "I like livin' here. People have tried to get me to move, but I won't. It gets a
little crazy sometimes with the young folks, though. Last Saturday night, a bunch of
them were down at the house below me, raisin' a commotion. I thought they'd quiet
down after awhile, but at two o'clock in the morning they were still going at it. I
hollered out of my window for them to settle down so I could get some sleep, but they
wouldn't. I laid there awhile longer and then got my gun down and came out to the
door. I told them to quiet down again or I'd shoot. They didn't pay me no mind, so I let
off a couple of shots. I tried to shoot at the treetops, but they all know I can't see a bit
no more, and boy, they cleared out then!" April, 1981.

Tim Barnwell ■ PORTRAITS FOR THE HEART

Cabin, Apple Trees, Snow. *Madison County, N.C., February, 1985.*

Kate Church. *Hot Springs, N.C. Church: "My father served five years during the great Civil War. He told me there was times when he laid his blanket down for the night on top of a foot of snow with a dead man on each side of him within an arm's length. They had to scrounge for any food they could find. He said that sometimes food was so scarce they had to kill rats and eat them. When he died there wasn't even a car around-only trains. What roads there were was meant for wagons, and they were built along old cow trails. Later, when they built roads for cars, every man had to work one week a year on a road crew or pay someone to work in his stead. When I was a girl, we raised sheep to make clothing, cows for milk, chickens for eggs and hogs to slaughter. We kept the milk and eggs in the creek to keep them cold. We grew all our food on the farm. There weren't no stores nearby then, not even a mill to grind the wheat, for a long time. What you didn't grow or raise, you didn't have. We used to take a wooden sled to town about once a year to get coffee and sugar and such, and we traded for that. My mother would spin wool to make yarn for our clothes. Us kids would sit and pull burrs out for her. I did that up until I was growed, and then I learned how to spin. I'm not sure how old I am. Somewheres between 92 and a hundred, I reckon. When I was married in 1910 my husband registered me as being 22, but I think I was older. I raised seven children and most of them were born without any midwife to help. There weren't many of them around then, and we hardly ever saw a doctor in these parts." August, 1980.*

Collie and Zola Payne. *Big Pine Creek, Madison County, N.C. Collie Payne: "We've lived here about 32 years. I built this house during World War II. Cut timber off the land to build it. I built my place up here because I like the mountains, I like to hunt and I like my own privilege. I've hunted all my life and that's one reason I live up here where I do. I've had one pistol for 25 years. I killed nine 'coons my first hunt with it. Now, if I'm out in the fields—and they're about a half mile straight up that mountain, through the woods—and Zola gets sick, or someone comes to the house, all she has to do is come out on the porch and fire it once and I know she needs me. I can tell its 'pop' from any other in this valley."* April, 1981.

Collie Payne and Steer "Berry." *Big Pine Creek, Madison County, N.C. Payne:
"I've raised Berry from a calf and he's 16 now. I trained him to plow and have turned
crops with him for the past 14 years. I've worked mules, too, but the doctor told me to
take it easy, so I use Berry now. He's slower to work than a mule, but he's more sure-
footed." April, 1981.*

Collie Payne and "Berry."
Big Pine Creek, Madison County, N.C., 1981.

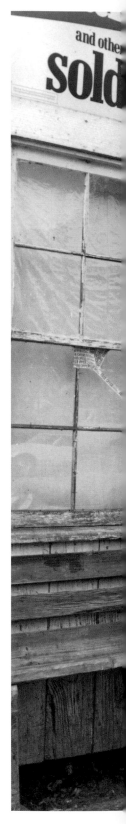

Kelly Ledford and Eleven-Year-Old Son Aldon. *Near Mars Hill, N.C., July, 1985.*

Country Store and Satellite Television. *Left to right, John Freeman, Loyd Fowler and Luther Gosnell. Walnut Section, Madison County, N.C., September, 1984.*

Four Men at Cook's Store. *Left to right, V. "Turk" Franklin, J.B. Roberts, Delmos Cook and Jerry Cook (nephew of Delmos). Belva Section, Madison County, N.C. Delmos Cook: "My uncle moved into this store in 1928, I believe it was. Another fellow and I went in partners for about seven years, then I got out of it for awhile. A little later I moved back in, and now I've got 37, 38 years in this store. That's a lifetime, really. There's not many stores like this left now. Used to be there were several up every creek. There was a fellow named Major Tweed that used to run a store and post office up at Whiterock, near the hospital. Even back then a lot of stores had closed up and he explained it to me the best I've heard it. He told me many a time that 'there's not a merchant around but what's pullin' for better roads, and cuttin' his own throat all the while.' When the better roads came in, people could travel farther and didn't do as much business around where they lived. They didn't need stores as close to home once they could get out more." September, 1981.*

Howard Allen and Jacksie Roberts in Car at Junkyard. *Near Walnut, Madison County, N.C. Allen: "It seems like everything you go to anymore gets spoiled by a bunch of drunks. The car races, the rodeo that comes to Marshall, it always turns out the same. A bunch of drunks turn up and spoil the good times for everybody. I've got no use for people who stay drunk all the time. All they want to do is lay around—or it makes 'em mean and they want to fight. You can get killed just riding by some of these bars at night. One fellow was killed at a bar over on the county line the other night. He heard shooting and went outside to see what was going on and a stray bullet hit him in the head. It's always the innocent ones that end up getting hurt. I never drank a can of beer in my life. That's one thing I can say—I've never been drunk." July, 1983.*

Norman Baker. *Big Pine Creek, Madison County, N.C. Baker: "My farm and two others are the only ones I know of in Madison County that can yield 4,000 pounds of tobacco per acre. I raised 16,000 pounds last year. Anything will grow here, especially weeds! I had a stroke late last year and am still not over it. I still have a lame leg, which makes it hard to work. I can't do things like I used to, but I still try!" October, 1982.*

James "Pop" Story and Linotype. *Downtown Marshall, Madison County, N.C. Story: "My father owned a newspaper in the eastern part of the state and bought the* Marshall News-Record *paper in 1924. He ran both for awhile, but decided it was too much to handle, so he sold the other one and moved us up here to Marshall. I helped him with the paper from the time I was a boy until he got too old to run it, and then I took it over. I never really had much help with it. I'd write the news, sell the ads and lay them out, take the pictures with my Polaroid camera, run the paper over to Waynesville to be printed, wait on it all hours of the morning, and then come back across the mountain to Marshall and put addresses on them, and take them over to the post office and mail them before I could go home. I did that every week 'til I retired in 1970. A fellow came to me then and told me he was going to buy me out. I didn't let on that I wanted to sell, anyway, but I'd spent 35 years meeting deadlines and, to tell you the truth, I was glad to be rid of it." November, 1982.*

Knox Brigman and Dorothy Shupe. *Walnut Rural Post Office and Grocery, Madison County, N.C. Brigman: "The post office here has been in this store about 19 years. My wife operated it 'til she passed away about four years ago. It's not a Class A post office, it's a Class C. That's what they call a rural post office. It's not run by the civil service and all. It's contracted out. You bid on it every so often to keep it. This one here in Walnut is the only one like it still left in Madison County. This post office is to serve the local people. We have about 25 boxes rented and serve about 250 general delivery customers at the window. Rural carriers have taken over from these type operations, though. Back years ago, there were post offices up every creek, and more than one up some. You traveled from one to the next on horseback then, though. It was hard to get back into these parts. It went to horse and buggy when the roads got better and they delivered the mail to each box along the way. Now they use these small four-wheel-drive trucks. Dorothy Shupe has had Box 44 as long as the post office has been here, and I think that was her number when it was in the old store, too. She may have had the same box 40 years now." August, 1982.*

B.W. Payne Family Working Hay. *Left. Little Pine Creek, Madison County, N.C. B.W. Payne: "When I was a boy, I used to slip away every chance I got and go talk to an old fellow who'd tell us kids' stories about the Civil War times and such. He was too young to fight in the war, but his dad wasn't. They had a big family to care for, and, since either army would make you join 'em if they found you, his father hid out in the mountains at the head of Little Pine Creek when they came through. The armies would take your food, horses, and anything else they needed and there wasn't a thing you could do about it. The old man told me he used to have to take food up to his father while he was hiding out, and leather so he could keep working, making shoes and such for the family to wear come winter. …Years ago, there were two schoolhouses along this one creek and a mill right down there in the bottom along the creek. The Presbyterians ran a private school in the big white house across the creek there. Now kids have to take a bus off somewhere to school. There also used to be a lot of mining going on up this creek. My daddy worked in a garnet mine. They would load them out of here with wagons and take them down to the French Broad River to be shipped off. You can still see the mine openings and shafts in these mountains today." 1981.*

B.W. Payne Family Taking a Break. *Top. Little Pine Creek, Madison County, N.C., June, 1981.*

Ramsey Family in Tobacco Field. *Left. Doug Ramsey and wife Sherry with daughters Melinda, 11-years-old and Lela, six-years-old. Madison County, N.C., September, 1985.*

Ben Gahagan and Old Schoolhouse. *Laurel Section, Madison County, N.C., November, 1982.*

Ernest Teague at Swann Farm. *Rector's Corner Section, Madison County, N.C., April, 1984.*

Malcombe Payne with Chain Saw in Tar Paper Shack. *Top, left. Near Mars Hill, Beech Glen, Madison County, N.C. Payne: "I used to cut 'dogwood timber' that was used to make spindles for knitting mills. I would buy contracts to cut the trees on different people's land, and we would cut it and stack it up in piles that would sometimes stand half as big as a house. A man would bring his truck in every week or so and buy up what we had. I cut one dogwood that was 18 inches thick and some 50 feet tall. It was the biggest one cut in this area and the fellow who was helping me couldn't believe it was a dogwood." July, 1980.*

Wade Massey Against Fence. *Top, right. Big Pine Creek, Madison County, N.C. Massey: "I've lived here for 35 years or more. I lived in Detroit, Michigan, for awhile when I found work up there. You couldn't give that place to me now, though. Too much going on even when I was up there and it's probably gotten worse by now. A lot of people from Florida and other places have come up to these mountains each year. None of 'em farm, though. I guess they'd starve if they had to farm for a living. They just stay a few months each year and then go back to where they came from. Back in these mountains, you've got to do it all your life to make a go of it. It's year-round work, and even then it's hard to make it." December, 1982.*

Obray Ramsey Holding Banjo. *Left. Near Marshall, N.C. on Highway 25/70, November, 1981.*

Loyd Fish Holding Split Wood Shingles beside His Dog "Brownie." *Spring Creek, Madison County, N.C. Fish: "My grandfather made wooden shingles (for cabins) and he taught my father the trade. My father picked me out of six boys in our family to learn it. I made them out of chestnut and mountain oak, but almost all of the chestnut is gone now. Even the new trees, once they get big enough to put out chestnuts, they still get the blight. I mostly make the wooden shingles now just to show people how it's done. I tell them that you should cut shingles and nail them on the house or barn on the old moon and they will lay flat. If you make them or nail them on at the new moon, they're more likely to curl." August, 1980.*

"Aunt" Laura Cook by Tree at Gahagan Farm. *Laurel, Madison County, N.C. Cook: "When I was about 14 or 15 years old I came to the Gahagan home to help Lilly Gahagan care for her brother's turkeys. He was known as 'old man Wade Gahagan,' and was going to be gone for a few weeks on business. I've been here ever since. I used to climb up in this tree and shake the limbs to get the turkeys down, because they would roost on them. I'm 91 now and can't climb it no more. That old tree has changed a lot in my lifetime." September, 1981.*

Rita Hayes Quilting. *Big Pine Creek, Madison County, N.C. Hayes: "This quilt is a wedding present for our friends. Everyone in the community made a separate piece for the quilt top. Now we're sewing the pieces to the backing. We have one day to finish it up before they get back home, so we've been working a lot of hours this week to get it ready. We want to surprise them with it." August, 1982.*

Leona Rice Quilting. *Mars Hill, Madison County, N.C. Rice: "My grandfather worked for 25 cents a day cradling wheat. If they didn't have the money to pay him, they would give him a piece of fatback or a small poke of wheat in return. When I was younger, I worked nine-and-a-half hours a day and four-and-a-half on Saturday, and got paid $28 every two weeks. I started piecing quilts when I was 10. My mother and grandmother taught me. I did my first whole quilt when I was 17. It took two to two-and-a-half weeks to make a queen-size quilt, working in our spare time. We'd work in the garden while it was cool, in the morning and afternoon, and would come in when it got too hot to work outside and quilt some. There's different styles of quilts, too. For instance, a log cabin quilt is made of lots of small narrow pieces and takes a longer time to make than the larger patchwork ones. People made them for warmth years ago when they only had a fireplace to heat the whole house with. When oil heat came along, quilts almost disappeared. Back then you'd consider it a good living to get $5.00 for one. Now people use them mainly for decoration and they bring hundreds of dollars." July, 1980.*

Ernest Rector on Bed. *Marshall, N.C. Rector: "When I was growing up, you could count on your friends and neighbors to give you a helping hand if you needed it. I remember once, when Bill Taylor was sick, a bunch of us went over to his place and shucked and put up 700 bushels of corn so his hogs would have something to eat during the winter. We never got a penny for it, and didn't expect it, either. We were glad to help out and knew we could count on others to do the same for us if we needed it. That was an everyday thing a few years back. Today, if you were dying of thirst, you couldn't get a man to give you a drink of water for less than a dollar." November, 1983.*

Amos and Virgie Henderson. *Right. Lonesome Mountain Road, Madison County, N.C. Virgie Henderson: "I've lived all my life on this Lonesome Mountain. Raised eight children, too. Three by my first husband and five more with my second, Amos. My first husband was killed when he fell between the cars of the logging train he was working on. That was 1923 and my youngest was only three months old. I married Amos in 1927. All the children treat him like they didn't know no other father and he treats 'em all like they was his own. I couldn't have done no better than Amos." January, 1981.*

Amos Henderson and Friend. *Below, right. Alvin Chandler. Lonesome Mountain Road, Madison County, N.C., 1981.*

Amos Henderson and Pet One-legged Chicken. *Below. Lonesome Mountain Road, Madison County, N.C. Henderson: "I raised this chicken like a man would a pet. When he was young, he got his foot caught between two pieces of tin. It got pretty messed up and I had to cut it all the way off. I should have killed him then, but I didn't. I kept him. At night he climbs the bank and stays in the little house I built for him. He flies down here the next morning. I have to feed him 'cause he can't scratch for food like the others. I take care of him—just like a man would a cat or dog. I was thinkin' about cuttin' him a wooden leg out of cedar to help him stand up. I think I could do it, too." January, 1982.*

Tim Barnwell ■ Portraits for the Heart

Ola Barnes in Garden with Scarecrow. *Sprinkle's Branch Road, Madison County, N.C. Barnes: "I've strung up these pie pans and done everything in the world to try to keep the crows out of my garden. Nothing seems to work, though. They get used to whatever you do and come on in, anyway. People have passed by here and swore they saw me standing in my garden, but it was only the scarecrow I made. Most people make male scarecrows, but I decided to make mine female. It doesn't seem to make any difference to the crows, though." June, 1982.*

L.D. "Buck" Fender Grinding Sugar Cane for Molasses. *Foster Creek, James Hylton Farm, Laurel Section, Madison County, N.C., October, 1984.*

Ernest Rector on Porch with Photos. *Top, left.*
Marshall, N. C., November, 1983.

Old Barn, Western North Carolina. *Bottom, left.*
Henderson County, N.C., October, 1989.

Dry Branch Freewill Baptist Church and Boy on the Road. *Dry Branch, Madison County, N.C. Ernest Teague: "When I was a boy, my father had a horse he used to deliver the mail. One Sunday morning, we were out washing and currying him, gettin' him all cleaned up, and the preacher came by. He asked if we were coming to church and my father told him that he reckoned not, as we had a lot to do around the house. The preacher looked at him and said, 'Well, I'll tell you what. You just stand there and curry your way right to hell.' Then he turned and rode off. My father thought on that a few minutes and said, 'Son, let's go to the house and get cleaned up. We need to be in church this morning.' And we went, too!" June, 1982.*

Clyde and His Father Homer Reeves. *Spring Creek, Madison County, N.C. Homer Reeves: "I can remember when there wasn't a foot of paved road between here and Asheville. Even with a good team of horses it was a full day's trip from here, and you didn't come back the same day—you stayed in Asheville. I would stay in my wagon at the livery stable. I wasn't the only one, either—there was plenty of fellows that couldn't afford a place for the night and would stay in the livery. There was a lot of liveries in Asheville then. I used to go to Asheville to buy a little fertilizer or to sell a wagonload of tan bark. We would cut down chestnut oaks and then strip the bark and sell it to the tanneries. You would do anything for a dollar then. A dollar was as big as a wagon wheel back then." April, 1981.*

Kella Buckner and Mule. *Big Pine Creek, Madison County, N.C. Buckner: "I haven't been able to do much this year. I've got arthritis bad in my hands and have to go to a specialist in Asheville to take gold treatments. I don't know if I'm goin' to get any better or not. I can't stand to use my hands much anymore so I guess I won't tend tobacco. I've tended it as long as I can remember, but I guess I won't this year–I'll just have to slow down. I'll be 70 soon. I'm slowin' down whether I want to or not. I'll have to cut out a few things. Tobacco may be one of them. I'll just have to see what else I can do." April, 1981.*

Ernie Metcalf and Amy Edgins with Son, James. *Left to right, Ernie, Amy and James (six months old). Laurel Section, Madison County, N.C., October, 1983.*

Oma Hensley and Daughter, Pansy Cutshall. *Madison County, N.C., April, 1981.*

Tim Barnwell ■ PORTRAITS FOR THE HEART

Mr. and Mrs. Rigsby in Garden. *Dorothy and Loyd Rigsby, near Walnut, Madison County, N.C.*

Dorothy: "I must be gettin' feeble. I can't seem to stand up on this hill today."

Loyd: "Yeah, I'm gettin' younger and she's gettin' older. I'll be 82 this Friday and I can still jump a 10-rail fence uphill!"

Dorothy: "Listen to him! Can you believe it? He might could jump the first rail if it was laying flat on the ground."

Loyd: "I was born on May 14, 1900. When I was 19 I nearly died of the flu epidemic. They said I stayed in bed for three weeks, flat on my back, and was unconscious most of that time. Doctors were even afraid of it. Old Doc Moore came to see me once. I didn't get any better after his visit so they sent word for him to come again. He cursed and told them, 'I'm not about to go back up there near that flu!' My two brothers got it, too. Fortunately, my father and stepmother never took it. They spent day and night lookin' after us boys, never knowin' if we'd live or die. Even after I started to get better I couldn't walk 40 feet to the mailbox without having to stop two or three times to rest. It felt like my legs were going to give out from under me. I've heard that more folks died of that flu than they did in the whole of the First World War."
May, 1982.

James and Portia Davis. *Grapevine Section, Madison County, N.C., June, 1983.*

Old Barn, Western North Carolina. *Madison County, N.C., 1981.*

Betsy's Gap. *Madison/Haywood County Line, N.C., 1984.*

Tim Barnwell ■ Portraits for the Heart

Many observers and students of the cultures of Western North Carolina are passionate in their views toward change. Some value continuity and describe changes in cultural traditions as losses. Others value change and celebrate experimentation and innovation. For many, images of an old man playing a fiddle, a man whose family has been in rural Haywood County for five generations, is an archetype for cultural continuity. He will insure that traditions will be preserved and that his music has not been altered by broader influences of the 20th century. Laura Boosinger wants us to understand that in this case, the case of Luke Smathers, his music and the bands he created and shaped, are a monument of innovation and creativity. Luke Smathers, his brothers and other members of his bands, blended traditional fiddle tunes and string band music with the popular music of the 1920-1940s. As you read this study, note when the narrative shifts to the first person, when Laura Boosinger joins the band in 1984. She gives us an opportunity to understand the shifting dynamics of tradition and innovation from the heart of a musician. —R.B.

Luke Smathers, Mountain Swing Musician:
A Biography

By Laura Boosinger

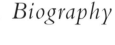

Cultures are often defined by their politics, geography and racial distinctiveness. One of Western North Carolina's prevailing cultural characteristics is its musical traditions. Much of this music dates to early settlers of Scotch-Irish descent. The fiddle tunes and ballads played and sung in Western North Carolina can be traced directly to versions of the same tunes and songs from the British Isles. Much has been made of the purity of the music found in these mountain coves, generations after the settlers' arrival on this continent. Scholars continue to search for strains of unaltered musical tradition.

It may be in the evolution of these musical traditions and among the musicians whose creative insights changed them, however, that some of the true treasures are found. One such musical innovator was Luke Smathers from Haywood County, North Carolina. Steeped in both the traditions of fiddle tunes and string band music, Smathers used these native styles to create a new musical form. He infused this traditional music with the popular music of the 1920s, the swing and early jazz of the 1930s, the big band sound of the 1940s, and music from another hybrid called western swing. From these he created a genre of music he named "mountain swing."

HISTORY OF THE SMATHERS FAMILY

The first generations of Smathers to come to North Carolina were originally called de Smet, and immigrated from Germany in the mid 18th century.[1] Earlier, during the Protestant Reformation, members of the family allied themselves with the Huguenots in the province of Lorraine. In 1572, fleeing for their lives, the Huguenots, including one branch of the de Smet family, sought refuge in nearby Protestant countries, including the Palatinate District of Germany. The family became Lutherans and the spelling of the family name varied with dialects and included Smeter, Smetter and Schmetter.

During the 30 Years War, Smathers ancestors fled to Rotterdam, then to London, and finally to the port of Charleston, South Carolina. In the early 18th century South Carolina was soliciting settlers from the Palatinate region, and by 1750 North Carolina had also attracted a large body of German colonists. They were said to be the "most industrious settlers— willing to endure any amount of toils to secure a permanent home."[2] Wilhelm Schmetter sought such a home in Rowan

County, North Carolina. Family tradition quotes Schmetter as saying "four of our family came to America, Charleston. Three went back while I came to North Carolina."[3] Schmetter may have followed the route of the Moravians from Charleston to the Yadkin River Valley in Rowan County.

The first known record of Wilhelm Schmetter (later records list him as William Schmetter, William Smadder and William Smathers) in Rowan County was an entry made for land in 1778. It is probable that he was a resident of Rowan for a number of years before requesting a title for the land he had been homesteading. Immigrants were asked to pledge their allegiance to England, but many remained unlisted

until they applied for a deed or were enrolled in some civil capacity. Upon listing his property in 1778, Wilhelm Schmetter automatically became a member of the local militia thus renouncing his allegiance to England. Had he defied the local government, his land and property would have been confiscated for the colonies since "An Act To Establish a Militia" was passed in 1777. Under this act, "all effective men in the State from 16 to 50, inclusive, were embraced in the Militia and subject to draft."[4] It seems likely that Wilhelm Schmetter was relieved of active duty as his position in the community as a farmer was deemed more useful and necessary to the survival of the community and to the militia. As a farmer owning and occupying 350

The first Smathers Band included Luke Smathers on fiddle, cousin John Marion Smathers on tenor banjo, and Harold Smathers (left) and George Smathers on guitars. Photo by Echenrod's Studio circa 1930. (Courtesy, George Smathers.)

Smathers Family Musicians In Haywood County:
A Family Tree (Figure 1)

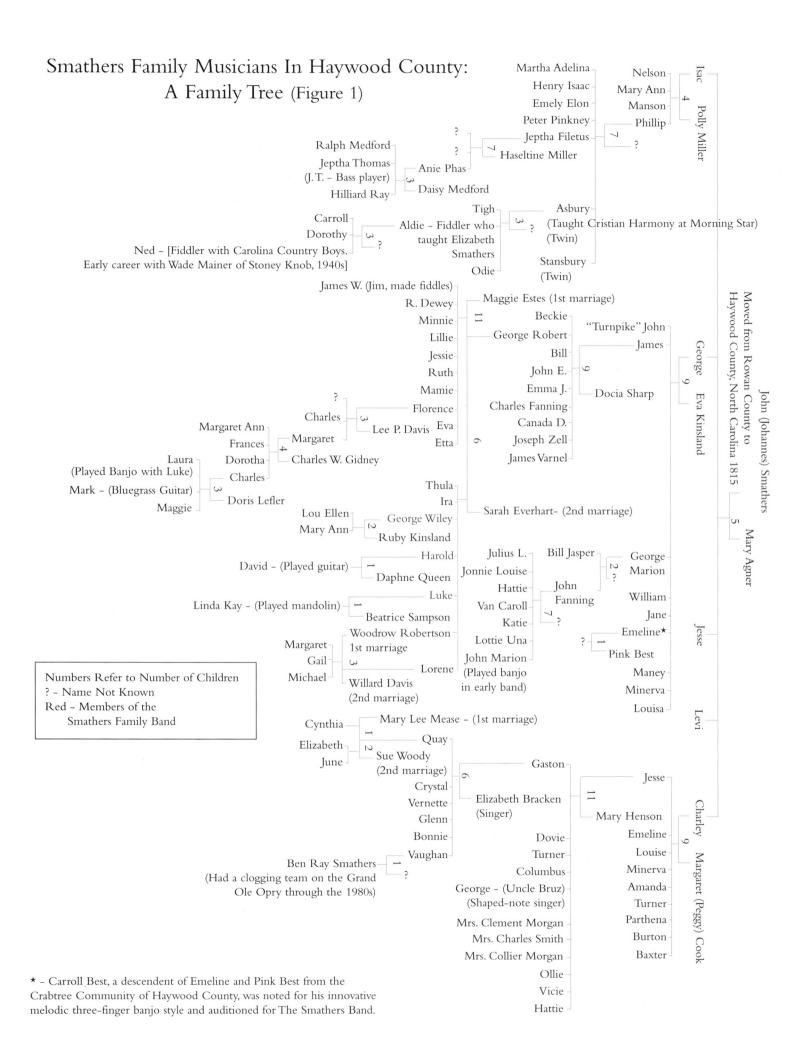

Numbers Refer to Number of Children
? – Name Not Known
Red – Members of the
    Smathers Family Band

★ – Carroll Best, a descendent of Emeline and Pink Best from the
Crabtree Community of Haywood County, was noted for his innovative
melodic three-finger banjo style and auditioned for The Smathers Band.

acres of land, he could be classified as an "industrious yeoman,"[5] whose tillage and furnishing of essential supplies for the people was of sufficient importance to justify his submitting to taxes being assessed against him. The taxes were then used to employ a regular Continental soldier in his stead. In 1784, Wilhelm Schmetter received another grant from the state of North Carolina, and later bought adjoining lands, where he continued to live until his death in 1823.

It is believed that Wilhelm's eldest son, Jacob, was born before or during 1775 and that his father deeded adjoining land to him on February 3, 1796. Jacob's marriage to Katherine Dew was recorded in Rowan County on April 17, 1795. Jacob Smathers is listed in Salisbury in the 1810 census and in tax listings for the Organ section of Rowan County in 1822. After that date no other records are found for Jacob Smathers. Jacob Smathers' brother Henry is listed in the deed records in Rowan County as conveying property in 1797. A third son, listed in county records alternately as John Smether, Johannes Smather and later as John Smathers, was listed for taxes in

Captain Wood's Company of Rowan County in 1809. The first mention of his wife, Mary Agner, occurred in 1810 when land was sold to a John Hartman. In Wilhelm Schmetter's will of 1823, the executor of the estate was named as "my beloved son John Hartman," who was the husband of Molly Smither.[6] At the time the will was executed, John (Johannes) and Henry had relocated to Haywood County, North Carolina.

In 1815 both John (Johannes) and Henry purchased land in Fulbright's Cove in Haywood County. Fulbright's Cove was later renamed Dutch Cove for the great number of Germans who had settled there. John and his wife Mary Agner Smathers, with their German neighbors, were of that "industrious yeoman" stock, and simultaneously built a church and a school house in the settlement. The first Lutheran church west of the Blue Ridge was established in Dutch Cove in 1825; it was named Morning Star. John Smathers died in 1825 before a consecrated burial ground was available at Morning Star. He was buried in Canton in the historic Locust Old Fields, so named by the Cherokee. After her

Figure 2. George Robert Smathers, father of George Wiley, Harold and Luke, poses with seven of his eight brothers and sisters in this undated photograph. Front row, left to right. Charles Fanning, Emma, Canada D. Back row, left to right. George Robert, James Varnel, Bill, John E. and Joseph Zell Smathers. (Courtesy, Linda Smathers.)

"MAC" & "BOB'S"
LESTER McFARLAND   ROBERT GARDNER
WLS
Book of Songs
(Old & New)

Including These Favorites
—
"TWENTY ONE YEARS"
—
"I TOOK IT"
—
"ASLEEP AT THE SWITCH"
—
And Twenty Seven Others

EACH SONG ARRANGED FOR GUITAR

Mac and Bob's Book of Songs was another WLS radio publication which provided popular songs and guitar arrangements for the Smathers brothers. (Courtesy, George Smathers.)

husband's death, Mary Agner Smathers continued to live in Dutch Cove. Around 1850 Mary and John's son Levi purchased the historic Jacob Shook house in Clyde about eight miles northwest of Dutch Cove. Mary Agner Smathers lived in the Shook house until her death in 1868.[7]

John and Mary Agner Smathers had five sons, Isaac, George, Jesse, Levi and Charley. The families descending from these five sons constitute much of the settlement of Dutch Cove (Figure 1). Their second son, George, (1807-1894) was Luke Smathers' great-grandfather, and was the father of James, John, George Marion, Emeline, Minerva, Maney, Jane, Louisa and William. Their second son, John was known as "Turnpike John" because he operated a hotel on the turnpike between Asheville and Waynesville, North Carolina.

He has been called "the finest example of the old-time pioneer."[8] He was a good rock and brick mason, a carpenter, shoemaker, tinsmith, painter, blacksmith and harness and saddle maker. He was at times a master plumber, butcher, fruit grower and bee keeper. All of these talents would have served him well in keeping a store and a hotel. He also contributed to the community as a school master, and as the need arose, a lawyer and a doctor; thus carrying on the traditions of his "industrious yeoman" ancestors.

George's eldest son James, Luke's grandfather, had eight children. James' second son, George Robert, was the father of Luke and 16 other children by two wives, Maggie Estes and Sarah Everhart (Figure 2). The union of George Robert and Sarah produced six children, Thula, Ira, George Wiley, Harold, Luke and Lorene. George Wiley Smathers was born in 1908, Harold David Smathers in 1911 and Luke Smathers in 1914. These three sons all became musicians and later became The Smathers Family Band.

At the marriage of George Robert and Sarah a shivaree was given for the couple. A shivaree consisted of good friends arriving on the wedding night with pots and pans and musical instruments to stir things up for the bride and groom. The revelers would march around the house beating or playing their various instruments. According to his son, George Wiley, George Robert "slipped out the back door with his fife and got in the lineup and was playing along with them."[9]

George Robert made his living as a carpenter, brick mason and a builder, and built several of the buildings at Western Carolina University and many of the buildings in downtown Canton. He was a member of the Masonic Order and was master of the lodge in Canton. When the First United Methodist Church decided to build a new building, Smathers loaned the church over eight hundred dollars. George Wiley recalls attending the Methodist Church on Newfound Street in Canton

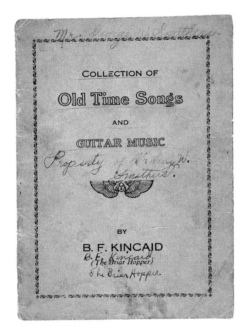

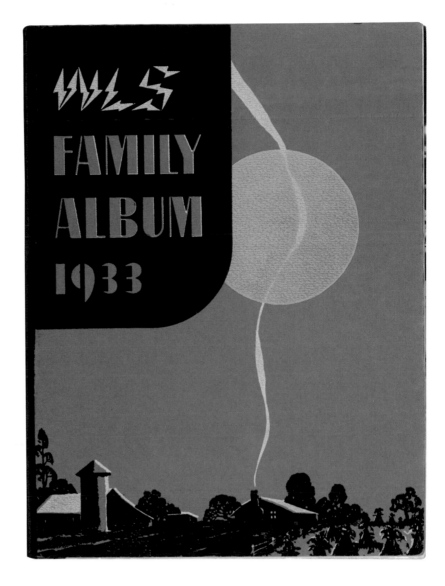

with his father. His father, who played a bit of fiddle and fife, always sang in the choir and at the conclusion of one evening service, he started for home forgetting the little boy who was asleep on the pew. He started down to the depot to watch the 8:00 p.m. train come in as was the custom of the day. As Preacher Matney began to lock up the church, young George Wiley "came to." The preacher carried the little boy home and upon meeting Smathers, the father remembered his son and George Wiley began to cry.[10]

During World War I, George Robert and his eldest son Jim, went to work in the shipyards in Savannah, Georgia. He suffered from high blood pressure and his doctor warned him that going to the coastal, sea-level environs would be dangerous for his health. His doctor feared that George Robert would become acclimatized to sea-

level and his return to the mountain elevation would be hazardous to his fragile health. Whether or not this was medically true, George Robert did return with a case of "the grippe." According to his son George Wiley, "he came home on the 4:18 train and died before 12 midnight. He had a coughing spell and a cerebral hemorrhage and died."[11] It was 1919 and George Robert Smathers was 62 years old. Four of his children, George Wiley, Harold, Luke and Lorene were still under the age of 10.

The Masonic organization in Canton offered to place the children in an orphanage, but Sarah refused. After the death of her husband, Sarah sold some of the family land, raised a garden, canned food and kept pigs to feed the family. Some of the older children went to work to provide financial support for the family. In 1927 George Wiley (henceforth referred to as George)

Figure 3. Bradley Kincaid was a popular singer and entertainer who performed regularly on the radio show The WLS National Barn Dance broadcast from Chicago. The National Barn Dance was sponsored by Sears and Roebuck, the large department store in Chicago. The program influenced many country musicians including the Smathers brothers who listened to it regularly. George Wiley Smathers purchased his first guitar from the Sears and Roebuck catalog, the Bradley Kincaid "Hound Dog" model. Luke Smathers often commented that they learned to play their instruments from the instruction books which came with their Sears and Roebuck instruments. Pictured here (above, right) is the WLS Family Album for 1933 and two Bradley Kincaid instruction books (left, top and bottom). (Courtesy, Linda Smathers.)

Just An Old-Fashioned Locket
and a Curl

It's just an old fashioned locket
and a curl
That brings that old fashioned
tin-type of a girl.
If she were only here today.
That little curl thats tucked
away,
Of golden hair so young and
fair would now be gray.
There's an old-fashioned
likeness in her face,
That makes her picture seem
to be a priceless pearl.
Thru many long and empty
years
I've shed a million lonesome
tears,
On this old fashioned locket
and a curl.

Figure 4. In many rural communities, Saturday nights would find families gathered around the radio listening to programs like The WLS National Barn Dance: the Smathers brothers, instruments in hand were no exception. As they learned melodies and chord structure, their sister Lorene would copy the lyrics, first in shorthand, then in the form pictured here for the band's song book. (Courtesy, Linda Smathers.)

went to work as a clerk at the post office in Canton making 65 cents an hour, a better starting wage than the 35 cents an hour The Champion Fibre Company paid that year.

Even with George's additional income, money at the Smathers household was tight. As a result, before he finished high school, Harold began to work for the biggest employer in Haywood County, The Champion Fibre Company, later known as Champion International Corp. Luke continued his schooling until age 16 when he was stricken with appendicitis. After having his appendix removed, Luke never returned to school. At some point Luke joined his brother at the mill. It was common for many members of a family to work at the mill. As the Depression intensified, George was laid-off from his job with the post office. He hadn't taken a vacation in four years and found this a good time for a little

leisure, but characteristic of his industrious ancestors, the appeal of "time-off" lasted only four or five days before he, too, sought a job at the mill. He started to work on January 9, 1932.

EARLY YEARS OF THE SMATHERS FAMILY BAND, 1928-1938

In December of 1928, just after his 20th birthday, George offered to purchase instruments for his younger brothers from the Sears and Roebuck Catalog. Luke, aged 14, wanted a ukulele; Harold aged 17, asked for a banjo and George selected the highly desirable "Bradley Kincaid Hound Dog Guitar." Bradley Kincaid was a popular entertainer on The WLS National Barn Dance, a radio show broadcast from Chicago, Illinois and sponsored by Sears and Roebuck. Luke always said that the instruments came with instruction books and that they learned to play from those books (Figure 3). They never had a lesson from anyone. After about two weeks, Harold switched to the guitar and Luke, having mastered the ukulele, began to play the banjo.

Not long after this, probably in the spring of 1929, Fred Stokes, who worked in the post office with George, invited Smathers and his brothers over to make a little music. Fred was a fiddler and was looking for some musicians with whom he could start a band. These four started getting together regularly to play fiddle tunes and square dance music. One evening Fred challenged Luke to play a little tune on the fiddle. Without much difficulty, Luke was able to scratch out a little melody on the instrument which marked the beginning of a musical career that was to span eight decades. When the boys returned home that night, Luke asked George to get him some strings and a bow for a three-quarter sized fiddle that their father had earned selling seeds. According to George, in two or three weeks, Luke "could play just about anything you wanted him to play." It became evident that Luke had a natural

QUAY SMATHERS:
TEACHER OF SHAPED-NOTE MUSIC

Because they were close to the same age, both musicians, and both named Smathers, many people confuse Luke and Quay Smathers. They were actually fourth cousins; Quay being the eldest of Gaston and Elizabeth Bracken Smathers' six children. Quay was also a carpenter and built several churches in the area including Morning Star Methodist Church in Dutch Cove in Haywood County, and several buildings on the campus of Warren Wilson College in Swannanoa, North Carolina. He was also an accomplished craftsman and made furniture, quilt racks, stools and candle stands. Quay was known throughout the region as a singing master and the keeper of the shaped-note tradition in Western North Carolina. He sang and led singing schools from *The Christian Harmony*, a mid-19th century seven shaped-note song book.[12]

Quay learned to sing the shaped-notes at the knee of his mother who often sang the old hymns. "Angel Band" was Quay's childhood lullaby. He also attended singing schools at Morning Star Church and learned from Asbury Smathers, father of famed fiddler Aldie Smathers. Uncle George Smathers (known as Uncle Bruz) was another fine singer known for his high tenor voice.

During the 1970s Quay Smathers traveled to festivals and colleges teaching the shaped-note tradition in the old singing school manner. Under Quay's tutelage, students learned the sounds of the characters, the shaped notes on the staff, and then the poetry of the 18th and 19th century hymns sung in four-part unaccompanied harmony. Traditional singing conventions are still held throughout Western North Carolina. One of the oldest, in a tradition over 100 years old, occurs the second Sunday of September on Old Folks Day held at Morning Star Church.

In the 1970s, with his daughters Cynthia, Elizabeth and June, Quay started his own family band, the Dutch Cove String Band. They performed throughout the Southeast for about 10 years and made one recording on June Appal Records. Quay received a North Carolina Folk Heritage Award in the late 1980s. Quay Smathers sang and led the shaped-notes until his death on January 22, 1997.

Photo by Laura Boosinger.

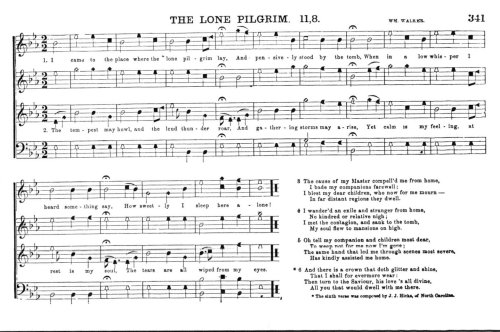

talent and a well-developed ear. He could play almost anything he could hear. He copied songs off of the radio as well as from other musicians, and it wasn't long before Luke needed a better fiddle. Once again, George turned to the Sears and Roebuck catalog and ordered Luke a brand new fiddle at the bargain price of $12. Luke recalled that the new fiddle also came with an instruction book.

Most musicians in the area, including the Smathers, worked a job to support their families, but much of the Smathers boys free time was spent practicing and playing their music. They never planned to make their living playing music. In the region music was considered a worthy pastime, but

Figure 5. Pender Rector was a popular Asheville fiddler in the early 1930s. He often played at events sponsored by WWNC radio and his swing style which reflected popular music heard on the radio was a great influence on Luke Smathers' style of fiddling. (Courtesy, Wayne Erbsen.)

rarely an occupational goal. Times were hard and even the stars of the Grand Ole Opry sometimes had a hard time making ends meet. In fact, the idea of making a living as a musician, especially playing string band or "country music" was generally looked down upon. If you made your living as a musician, you most likely worked at a roadhouse, a place with a low class and generally disreputable clientele with a high instance of fights. Luke's great-nephew Charles Gidney recalls sneaking into a roadhouse as a boy to play with local fiddler Tommy Magness. He recalls it as an exciting time in more ways than one.

As the band became more accomplished, they were invited to play for suppers, local churches and ice cream socials. By 1930 the band was playing regularly for the Thursday night dances at the Champion YMCA. The Smathers Band was the regular band at these community dances until the dances ceased about 1938. For a short time Luke's cousin, John Marion Smathers, played the four-stringed tenor banjo with the band, but due to poor health he gave up his chair to another musical cousin, Quay. Quay Smathers had grown up in Dutch Cove near Luke and Harold, their mother treating him as one of her own. According to Luke, Quay spent more time at their house than at his own home during their youth, and they often played music.

The boys would crowd around the radio, powered by the car battery, so that they could hear the Grand Ole Opry and The National Barn Dance. They had their instruments in hand to pick up the chord progressions and the melodies of the songs. Luckily, sister Lorene was nearby writing down the lyrics using the shorthand that she had learned in high school (Figure 4). Luke said sometimes it would take them months to learn a tune because they might only hear the song once in three weeks on a radio broadcast. Luke always wondered how his mother "stood all of that racket." He often remarked that young people can learn music much more easily today with

THE MOUNTAIN FOLK SONG AND DANCE FESTIVAL

Bascom Lamar Lunsford, known as "The Minstrel of the Appalachians," had searched the mountains of Western North Carolina looking for unusual fiddle tunes, ballad singers and old-time dancers. His discoveries included "Aunt" Samantha Bumgarner, who in 1924 became the first female country performer to record on disc. He also found and promoted "fiddlin'" Bill Hensley, a Native American dance team from Cherokee and Sam Queen of Soco Gap in Haywood County, famous for his innovative square dance team who for many years represented North Carolina at the National Folk Festival. Pender Rector was also a favorite at Lunsford's festival. His festival, became its own event and is still produced annually as the oldest continuing folk festival in the nation. (It is now called The Mountain Dance and Folk Festival.)

Bascom Lamar Lunsford looked at the Rhododendron Festival (see text, next page) as a vulgar misrepresentation of true mountain culture and was pleased to present with pride and respect a true showcase of mountain culture, one that would highlight what he saw as distinct cultural uniqueness found in the mountain region. Other writers describe the climate:

"For all its spectacular success as a promotional scheme, the Rhododendron Festival must at least be seen as a product of the peculiar social and economic pathology of the late 1920s, imported like a gaudy souvenir shawl thrown around a mountain version of Miami madness. Asheville was on the make and speculative subdivisions were springing up almost daily. Fantasies of instant wealth were the dominant preoccupation; pretension was the dominant style."[14]

—David Whisnant

NINTH ANNUAL
Mountain Dance Contest
AND
Mountain Music Festival
ASHEVILLE, NORTH CAROLINA
1936

A 96-YEAR OLD FESTIVAL PARTICIPANT

THREE NIGHTS, JULY 23-24-25, 8 o'Clock
McCORMICK FIELD (BASEBALL PARK)

Twelve Dance Teams and Twelve Mountain Bands compete for Championship Prizes

More than One Hundred Ballad and Folk Singers and Musicians

400 Participants from all Sections of Western North Carolina and Mountain Sections of Adjoining States

A UNIQUE FOLK ENTERTAINMENT, DISTINCTIVE OF THE MOUNTAINS

Under the Auspices of the Asheville Chamber of Commerce

Bascom Lamar Lunsford began the Mountain Folk Song and Dance Festival in 1927 as a showcase for dancers and musicians from the region. This program for the 1936 festival (above) pictures a 96-year-old fiddler. (Courtesy, Linda Smathers.) In 1929 Lunsford published this collection of 30 and 1 Folk Songs from the Southern Mountains. (Published by Carl Fishger, New York. Courtesy, Linda Smathers.)

"The sleepy little mountain village in which he had grown up—for it had hardly been more than that then—was now changed almost beyond recognition. The very streets that he had known so well, and had remembered through the years in their early aspect of early afternoon emptiness and drowsy lethargy, were now foaming with life, crowded with expensive traffic, filled with new faces he had never seen before. Occasionally he saw somebody that he knew, and in the strangeness of it all they seemed to him like lights shining in the darkness of the lonely coast....

The real estate men were everywhere...One could see them on the porches of the houses, unfolding blueprints and prospectuses as they shouted enticements and promises of sudden wealth into the ears of deaf old women. Everyone was fair game to them."[15]

—Thomas Wolfe

the use of tape recorders and records.

It was during these formative years that the band began to take on a musical character which set them apart from their regional counterparts and began to define a unique style for which Luke Smathers became famous. They had heard Asheville fiddler, Pender Rector, who was playing a swing style of music similar to the popular music heard on the radio at the time (Figure 5). Daphne Queen Smathers, Harold's wife of more than 50 years, recalled going to Asheville with George Wiley Smathers where weekly dances were held at Recreation Park, and where Pender Rector was often the resident fiddler. Pender had recorded a few records in 1930 and had returned to Asheville to play at radio station WWNC and for the dances at Recreation Park. Luke loved his style and was inspired by the way Pender played the fiddle.

Luke's band began to play with an emphasis on the beat, not simply keeping time, but with a strict adherence to where the downbeat fell and with more attention to the ensemble sound. Their use of two guitars playing closed sock chords created a thick pad of sound for the fiddle's intricate melody work.[13] Rhythm is emphasized, especially on the downbeat. The banjo was played in a tenor style that emphasized chords and rhythm. With the addition of Harold's strong, clear singing they could no longer be considered merely a dance band. They were true entertainers, a real departure for a string bands of the time whose usual function was to play for dancers.

In the 1920s the Asheville Board of Trade sought to attract visitors and prospective land owners to the Asheville area. By promoting an image of Asheville as a cosmopolitan and modern city complete with symphony performances, opera companies, fine hotels, and the nation's first indoor shopping mall, the Grove Arcade. Produced by the city of Asheville beginning in June of 1928, the Rhododendron Festival was part of this local promotion and included special train fares and the promise of entertainment. It included parades, the crowning of the Rhododendron Queen and her court with participants from a 15-state area, and band concerts to entertain the many seasonal visitors to the mountains. The city of Asheville asked Bascom Lamar Lunsford, founder of The Mountain Folk Song and Dance Festival in 1927, to bring his dancers and musicians to stage a folk festival as part of the Rhododendron Festival's show of "local color."

The Champion YMCA square dancers were invited to participate in Lunsford's festival and The Asheville *Times* listed their band as The Smathers Band. In those days bands appeared with a dance team. The Smathers Band did not play the music they really enjoyed. As George recalled, they only

The Smathers Band was always well received by their audiences, but they often lost points in old-time band competition because they included music from the swing and jazz traditions. This judges' form was used in the Mountain Dance and Folk Festival. (Courtesy, Linda Smathers.)

Laura Boosinger ■ Luke Smathers, Mountain Swing Musician: A Biography

These Musicians Won In WWNC 'Shindig'

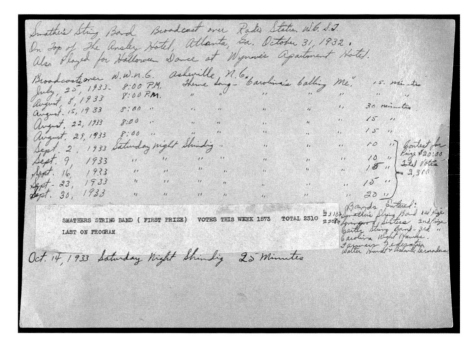

Figure 6. In 1933 local radio giant WWNC sponsored a Saturday night "Shindig." This competition featured six regional bands, and The Smathers Band won first prize based on votes by listeners. This photo (left) of the winning band appeared in the Asheville Citizen *October 14, 1933. The tally sheet (below) indicates they received 2,310 votes and won $20. (Courtesy, Linda Smathers.)*

played fiddle tunes because "that's what they wanted back then." This expectation followed Luke and his brothers throughout their appearances at Lunsford's festival and other competitive festivals in their later years. Their choice of tunes was often too eclectic for the fiddler's conventional format. During the 1970s, '80s and '90s, they performed at festivals like Fiddler's Grove north of Statesville, North Carolina, and even though the band often received the best reception of all the bands, they were often disqualified from the final competition because judges didn't consider their choice of tunes traditional enough.[16]

Luke's music was always innovative for the times. His bowing technique sounded more like a trumpet than a fiddle and he phrased like a trumpet player. Fiddlers more influenced by a Scotch-Irish style played with a light bow. Luke's style was more like the African-American fiddlers of the day, meaning that "he really bore down on it." His style was due in part to playing at those dances with no amplification. Often the "bearing down" was part of the phrasing technique. Jazz trumpet players used this technique to emphasize a note, either by hitting the note hard and backing off, or

hitting the note softly and increasing the volume, thus creating a kind of dynamic blossoming. Luke also made use of the glissando, a rapid slide through a series of tones often in a scale pattern, which he would embellish with improvisation around the notes in that scale. Luke's playing was also characterized by syncopation in which straight quarter notes were replaced by dotted eighths and sixteenth notes.

Noted country music historian Charles Wolfe felt that his style was based more on

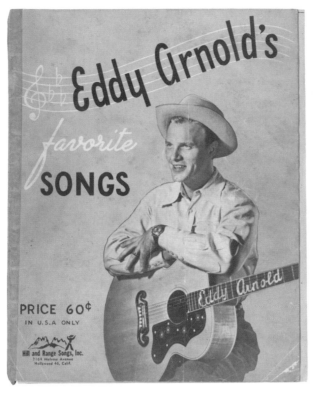

Luke's own inner sense of rhythm than his study of the trumpet:

> He knew how to swing and very few country musicians figured that out. The people in western swing took a long time to figure that out. The early Bob Wills and western swing guys were awful. They had this chunky four/four rhythm. They just didn't get syncopation yet. And Luke had it. I mean, that's something you can hear right off the bat. He knew exactly how to phrase. He understood the kind of swing that people like Benny Goodman and Tommy Dorsey and Duke Ellington and those guys were coming up with. And the key to that is that great swing bands had a great rhythm section.[17]

In the 1970s modern folklorists began to search the archives and recordings of traditional musicians of the 1920s and '30s. They discovered a wealth of string band music that represented a traditional dance band style which came to define the old-time string band style. Charles Wolfe, describes the modern day folklorist idea of string band music being somehow frozen in time between 1925 and 1933.[18] Folklorists tended to look for music that sounded pure and "old-time." They often didn't consider bands that were influenced by other genres of music. Consequently, Luke's band,

because of his interest in expanding his sound and repertoire, was overlooked in the purely traditional string band category. One of the oft-reissued string bands of the 1920s was the Skillet Lickers from northern Georgia. In later years their fiddle player, Clayton McMichen had a band called the Georgia Wildcats whose style was considered slick, with a style very similar to Luke and his brothers. Charles Wolfe describes this style as "...southeastern swing as opposed to western swing. There were other bands in the southeast that were sort of doing that (southeastern swing), none of them as well as Luke."[19] The advent of the Depression put a halt to record companies forays into the South in search of traditional musicians. Had these recording sessions continued, there might have been another period of string band development that would be viewed as traditional music today.

In 1933 the band was asked to compete on the "Shindig" sponsored by local radio giant WWNC. This station, with its strong signal, was well known in Western North Carolina as a showcase for regional and national talent. In the 1920s, '30s and '40s all of the major touring bluegrass and old-time acoustic acts came through Asheville to make an appearance on the station. You could hear national stars Wade and J.E. Mainer who were local boys from Stony Knob just north of Asheville; or the Morris Brothers, Zeke and Wiley, from Old Fort known for their composition "Salty Dog Blues." Other national performers including Bill and Charlie Monroe from Kentucky and Jim and Jesse McReynolds from Coeburn, Virginia were heard on WWNC.

From September 2 through 30, 1933 WWNC sponsored a Saturday night "Shindig"— a live presentation of regional entertainers.

Callers were provided to manage the square dances for those attending, and several specialities are scheduled each week for the entertainment of both the radio audience and the attendants of the "shindig." Much talent in the form of string bands, fiddle bands, yodelers and dance teams is available throughout this section of

PROGRAM

◆

PREMIER
CONCERT

◆

Champion Band

◆

CANTON, N. C.

Figure 7. In the 1930s The Champion Fibre Company hired a band director and organized a brass band. The four members of The Smathers Band at that time all joined the Champion Band (below) and received their first formal musical instruction; Luke on the trumpet, George on the clarinet, Harold on the trombone, and Quay on the tuba. Many of the tunes played by the Champion Band became part of the string band repertoire. Left. Program for the Champion Band. (Courtesy, Daphne Smathers.)

THE RIDGE RUNNERS

● This aggregation of mountaineers we call the Cumberland Ridge Runners, because they all hail from Kentucky and Tennessee, and all grew up somewhere in the vicinity of the Cumberland Mountains; that is, all except Hugh Cross, who came from a little farther up the creek in the Smoky Mountains. They have cheered you up many a time, and their good humor and kindly philosophy seems never to wear out.

So that you can know each one by name in the above picture, reading from left to right in the back row they are: Carl Davis, "Red" Foley, John Lair, Hartford Connecticut Taylor, and in the front row, "Slim" Miller with the fiddle, Linda Parker with the dulcimer, and Hugh Cross with the banjo. They are probably at their best when they cut loose with an old-fashioned "hoedown" — or maybe you learned to call it a "breakdown." Called by any name, it sets the feet a-tapping and the hands clapping in time with the music.

Figure 8. The Cumberland Ridgerunners featuring fiddler Slim Miller were a great favorite of the Smathers and are shown here in a WLS program. When The Smathers Band went to Chicago to play on The National Barn Dance, even though they were not allowed to play because they were not union members, they did meet Slim Miller. This meeting was the first and one of the few personal contacts The Smathers Band had with other musicians performing their style of music. (Courtesy, Daphne Smathers.)

the country, and many of the old mountain ballads find their way to the outside world through the radio. These "shindigs" and air programs have been highly successful, for in addition to the thousands who have attended the Saturday night programs nearly 7,000 mail votes were received during the four weeks of the contest.[20]

The winners were announced on October 14, 1933. Most nights The Smathers Band played 10 to 15 minutes, but this night they played a full 25 minutes. Winners were chosen through a write-in campaign. Luke always said it was a popularity contest "and we were the most popular!" The competition was held on the roof of the Arcade building in downtown Asheville, in front of a "large audience." According to the vote tally, The Smathers Band received 2,310 votes (Figure 6). Second place went to the Lovingood Sisters from Enka, North Carolina who received 2,228 votes. Other competitors were the Carter String Band from Beaverdam in north Asheville who won third place, The Carolina Nighthawks and the Farmer's Federation Band, featuring fiddler Johnny Rhymer. When recalling this event, Luke always said that their favorite fiddler, Pender Rector, was featured with a band in the competition, and that The Smathers Band was proud to win first place ahead of their musical mentor.

Throughout the 1930s the band's musical tastes expanded. They started picking up more and more tunes off the radio and adapting them to the instrumentation of the standard string band. As young men their love of the radio and the musical doors it opened for them became evident at the Thursday night dances at the Champion YMCA. They played square dance standards like "*Under the Double Eagle,*" "*Cindy*" and "*Asheville,*" but soon their repertoire grew to include such pop tunes as "*Darktown Strutters Ball*" and "*Five Foot Two.*" Songs that they heard on The WLS National Barn Dance like Slim Miller and the Cumberland Ridgerunner's "*Miller Blues,*" and Red Foley's "*Methodist Pie*" were added to their repertoire.

Unlike many southeastern string bands of the day, The Smathers Band admired clean, almost orchestrated playing, and good singing. It's not surprising that Harold emulated Eddy Arnold and Vernon Dalhart's vocal styles. The band was truly interested in putting on a good show. An evening of dancing could very well include a number of square dance tunes, a waltz, a fox-trot and a novelty dance number like "*Meet Me by the Ice House Lizzy*" from the Hoosier Hot Shots, complete with slide whistle.

Each instrument in Luke's band was encouraged to take a "break" when each member of the band was featured with solo instrumentation, but this was a rarity in traditional string bands. Luke encouraged breaks as he had heard the great jazz bands take breaks, and his use of this style predated this familiar feature heard in many bluegrass bands. Breaks for individual musicians was not considered old-time.

In the 1930s, The Champion Fibre Company organized a brass band and hired a director to teach music to interested employees. Luke, Harold, George and Quay all joined and learned an instrument. Luke took up the trumpet, George the clarinet, Harold the trombone and Quay the tuba (Figure 7). They learned their band tunes from sheet music and soon those tunes, like "*Dinah,*" started creeping into their string band performances. The brass band's assistant director, Jack Shaefer, was so interested in The Smathers Band's sound, that he would often sit in with them at those Thursday night dances playing the piano and sometimes the clarinet. Someone with Shaefer's training undoubtedly inspired Luke to higher levels. Luke recalled that because of the number of square dancers on the floor they would often play one set dance for 25 minutes. They used no amplification so their playing had to be hard and vigorous to be heard above all of those

dancing feet. Luke claimed that they threw in tunes like "*Sweet Georgia Brown*" so they could rest. "That was rest compared to playing for square dances," he observed.

The band's unique sound fueled by the fiddle and clarinet trading riffs and the 40 or so couples dancing around the hall must have seemed to be a moment stopped in time; a picture of the '20s and that era's gaiety still moving in stride, in spite of a nationwide depression. In Canton, North Carolina life was still pleasurable, partly because of The Smathers Band. The Smathers boys, even in their later years, presented a picture of the Asheville of Thomas Wolfe, an era of frivolous pleasure set in motion by dancing feet and music that was often considered daring and sensual in its sound.[21] Harold's wife, Daphne Queen Smathers, recalls those dances and her father's displeasure at her attendance, because a community event that included dancing, even if sponsored by the religiously affiliated YMCA, bordered on something sinful.

Daphne Queen Smathers and George Smathers' wife, Ruby, another fine dancer, were regulars on Thursday nights. They also became part of the famed square dance team that was sponsored by the Champion

Figure 9. Popular Songs, *a monthly magazine during the '30s of popular music was the source for many songs The Smathers Band most enjoyed performing. (Courtesy, George Smathers.)*

YMCA, and funded by The Champion Fibre Company. On more than one occasion, mill owner Ruben Robertson, showed off these local gems to visiting dignitaries, often at Camp Hope owned by the mill, or at his Flat Rock vacation home. He once invited a gospel quartet, made up of four mill workers, including George Smathers, to sing for noted folk music collector and poet, Flat Rock resident Carl Sandburg.

In 1935, the Champion YMCA superintendent, Grover Suttles, learned that the annual National Folk Festival was to be held in Chattanooga, Tennessee. At the first National Folk Festival in 1934, Bascom Lamar Lunsford had showcased some of the dancers and musicians from his festival held

in Asheville. This year it was to be the dance team and the band from Canton who were invited to perform at Sarah Gertrude Knott's National Folk Festival. The YMCA dancers are probably the single reason that the Smathers' boys played outside of Western North Carolina in the early days of the band. The group traveled by bus to Chattanooga and George recalls staying at a fancy hotel. As they passed through mine ravaged Copper Hill, Tennessee, Quay Smathers, always the jokester, remarked that he felt "so sorry for these little rabbits down here. I'm going to sit up and make them saddlebags so they'll have something to carry their lunch in. There's not anything here for them to eat."[22] The hills were red, the land was bare and the lack of vegetation was startling to these boys from the lush green coves of Haywood County, North Carolina.

In 1937 the band and dancers were once again asked to represent North Carolina at the National Folk Festival, this time in Chicago. While in Chicago, the group from Canton was asked to perform on The National Barn Dance. All of the dancers and musicians were thrilled at the thought of being able to be a part of the radio program that they had tuned in to so

Luke Smathers purchased this bass fiddle in the 1930s to complete his swing band sound. Their string band was one of the first in Western North Carolina to include a bass. This instrument was used by Quay Smathers, Bea Smathers and currently by Amanda Luther of The Lonesome Mountain Serenaders. (Courtesy, Amanda Luther; photo, Robin Mask.)

Laura Boosinger ▪ LUKE SMATHERS, MOUNTAIN SWING MUSICIAN: A BIOGRAPHY

many Saturday nights. To perform and be among the musicians that they revered was a great and exciting honor. Unfortunately, the performance was not to be. Upon arriving at the station, they learned that only card carrying union musicians were allowed to play on the nationally broadcast show. The boys were highly disappointed, but Luke did meet one of his musical heroes, Slim Miller who played with The Cumberland Ridgerunners (Figure 8). Luke and Harold always claimed that their distrust and vehement refusal to vote for unionization of the mill in Canton came from this experience.

The band continued to learn songs off the radio, but it wasn't beyond Luke to gather sheet music of the popular songs of the day from the local music store. *Popular Songs*, a weekly music magazine contained sheet music of popular songs which became part of the band's repertoire (Figure 9). "*When My Blue Moon Turns To Gold Again*," "*Dream a Little Dream*," the western swing favorite "*San Antonio Rose*" and their theme song "*Drifting and Dreaming*" all came from popular magazines. The band played their theme song to close out every show, "*Drifting and dreaming while shadows fall softly...*"

1938-1968, THE INTERIM YEARS

George's participation with the band began to lessen around 1938, no doubt to concentrate on raising his family. Around this time, the weekly dances at the YMCA stopped, leaving the band without a regular gig. When George left the band, the fellows acquired a string bass and Quay stepped up to play it. This was a real musical innovation for string bands of the time. Charles Gidney, one of Luke's great-nephews, recalls the band as being the only one "in this country that had a bass fiddle."[23]

If you put the bass right on the front part of the beat, let the guitars come in right behind it, you get that wonderful swing style that you hear in all the great bandstands. And he was simply adapting it to a string band style. On the radio, for a long

From roughly 1938 to 1968 The Smathers Band was inactive. George (Wiley) and Harold were drafted in World War II but Luke's job at Champion was considered defense related. Bea and Luke are seen here in 1942 with their daughter Linda. (Courtesy, Linda Smathers.)

time, they wouldn't let the bands use a bass because they didn't know how to mic it. It would just blow a mic— you know, totally out. On the Opry for example, they weren't using string basses commonly until about the time that Luke started using them in the late '30s. They did have a few bands with a string bass. I've got pictures of them, but they were bowing it. And the bowing gives it a completely different sound, an old-fashioned, kind of tuba sound.[24]

Luke's sound was anything but old-fashioned: he was going for that big-band sound.

World War II had a visible effect on local music. In 1942 The Asheville *Times* reported that during The Mountain Dance and Folk Festival the Enka square dancers, under the direction of Ralph Case, ended their routine by forming a victory "V" in support of the war effort. Ralph Case was working with the USO in Arlington, Virginia at this time organizing and calling square dances in the Washington, D.C. area. He brought his "best team of dancers

Luke Smathers String Band

In Full Swing

Figure 10. In the late 1970s The Smathers Band issued two LP recordings on the June Appal label. Both albums feature the eclectic style for which The Smathers Band became known, a mix of traditional tunes, western swing and big band standards. (Author's collection.)

composed of girls employed in Washington, but all southern born" to participate in the festival in Asheville. One local team called Beaucatcher, "had lost nearly all of its young men to the Army and Navy." Some of the girls "donned slacks" and the team danced in exhibition ending their routine by holding placards that said "Buy Bonds War Bonds."[25] During one wartime festival, favorite singer Red Raper, from Macon County, North Carolina, made an appearance in miltary uniform to sing "*Johnson's Old Grey Mule*," always a crowd pleaser.

Both George and Harold were drafted in the summer of 1942. Luke's job at the Champion paper mill was considered a defense job and he was not drafted. George and Harold's enlistment was for three years, and when they returned from the war, the band stopped playing together as The Smathers Band. Luke continued to play occasionally, and even assisted his great-nephew, Charles Gidney, with the junior-senior prom in 1943. Luke on fiddle, Charles on the bass, local entertainer Jimmie Haynie on guitar and vocals, and steel guitar player Paul Hawkins provided the dance music for the senior class that year. It must have been a hot band, with Luke's innovative fiddle, Haynie's great singing and the novel steel playing of Hawkins.

In 1946 a tragedy occurred at the mill which by all accounts should have ended Luke's fiddle playing. Luke's job required managing a lot of dangerous machinery and two of his fingers were caught in a grinding machine and "mashed." The ring and little fingers of his right hand were rendered useless and were in Luke's way. In order to have more use of his right hand, he had those two fingers amputated. It is virtually impossible to hold a fiddle bow without these two fingers as they are the balance point for the frog of the bow. Luke put his fiddle down, and like his brothers, he concentrated on raising his family. His only child, Linda Kay, was born in 1942, and Harold's only child, David, was born in 1948. Luke continued working at the mill, and even built a house, from the ground up, for his family. Being as industrious as he was, there were few skills Luke could not learn. After his retirement from the mill in 1977, he took a course in locksmithing, "picking locks" he liked to call it. He was certified, but never took up the vocation because he didn't want "people calling me at all hours of the day and night." Luke, like his older brother Jim, began to make fiddles. He made three in all, and at his death in 1997, there was a fiddle in the basement under construction.

In the early '60s, 1962 or 1963, Harold's son, David, then in high school, became interested in playing music. He came knocking on his Uncle Luke's door for a few lessons on the guitar. By this time Luke had started to play a little bit at home. He had devised a way to hold the bow without the use of his two fingers. He wrapped the end of the bow with double-backed carpet tape which allowed him to balance the bow and hold it so that he could play again. David's interest in music gave Luke another reason to play the fiddle. David also encouraged his dad Harold to pick up the guitar again. Luke's daughter Linda Kay recalls taking some accordion lessons as a child, and in later years learning a bit of the mandolin under her father's tutelage. David's musical interest grew and before long he had a band made up of a few high school friends. Once again the old bass was getting some use with a new generation of Smathers' musicians.

1968-1998, THE LUKE SMATHERS BAND

In 1968, as a result of Luke's renewed interest in playing the fiddle, his great-nephew Charles Gidney, local musician Bill Hardin and relative J.T. Smathers started to come to the house and make music in the kitchen. Quay Smathers had started his girls, Cynthia, Elizabeth and June on instruments and they started to stop by to pick up tunes from their cousin. Elizabeth was a particularly talented musician and learned a lot from both Luke and her other fiddling relative Aldie Smathers. The girls were teenagers in the early '70s and the folk festival/fiddle contest style weekend was appealing to them. Just like their forefathers, the itch to go out and make music was there. During the '70s and early '80s The Dutch Cove String Band, made up of Quay, his daughters and Elizabeth's husband, fiddler Lynn Shaw, was also a mainstay at festivals throughout the region.

It was common-place to see another Smathers band on the bill or in the competition, for Luke had practiced his band and was back playing some of those pop standards from his youth. Their sound was as fresh and innovative as it was in 1933 and soon caught the attention of folklorist and banjo player David Holt. Holt had moved to Western North Carolina and searched out local musicians in hopes of learning traditional music straight from the source.

Luke and Harold Smathers began attending folk festivals again in the 1970s. Here they are seen in 1978 at Fiddler's Grove, one of the oldest fiddle competitions in North Carolina. (Photo, David Holt.)

Luke invited Holt to join the band on banjo. Holt's clear, clean clawhammer style suited Luke's crisp, precise sound.[26] Holt began to learn the tenor style, chording on a five string banjo and playing clawhammer style on dance tunes. The band now was made up of Luke on fiddle, Harold on rhythm guitar and vocals, Charles Gidney playing lead guitar, J.T. Smathers on bass and David Holt on banjo. On occasion Holt would play drum brushes on the head of his banjo in place of a snare drum. And Luke, still a fan of those novelty dance numbers, would pull a slide whistle or a bulb horn out of a brown paper sack and play those for added texture.

With the addition of Holt, the band started to travel. The Smithsonian Folklife Festival, Berea College and folk societies along the east coast were thrilled to hear the Smathers' mountain swing. Their new

---

...LUKE WAS THE ONLY FIDDLER STILL PLAYING SLIM MILLER'S TUNE.

---

popularity led to the release of two albums on June Appal records; a label from Whitesburg, Kentucky specializing in preserving the work of masters of traditional music, most of whom were older and in their last years of playing and performing (Figure 10). Once again Luke and Harold were featured at Lunsford's Mountain Dance and Folk Festival. They also performed at the Lunsford Festival at Mars Hill College and the Fiddler's Grove Old-Time Fiddler's Convention north of Statesville, North Carolina. In 1976 the state of North Carolina celebrated the nation's bicentennial with a folk life festival in Durham, North Carolina at the Eno River Park. It was to become an annual event. The first year featured artists on three stages, a mountain stage, a piedmont stage and the coastal stage. Luke and Harold participated, finally receiving their well-earned accolades as purveyors of a style of string band music forgotten by the collectors.

The Eno Festival featured Madison

County ballad singers, fiddler Byard Ray, master guitarist Doc Watson, piedmont blues guitarist and composer of "*Freight Train*" Elizabeth Cotton, and former state representative LulaBelle Wiseman from Spruce Pine, North Carolina. Finally Luke and Harold were sharing the stage with a former star (LulaBelle Wiseman) of The WLS Barn Dance, and no union card was required. These festivals in the 1970s and '80s, sponsored by arts councils and folk societies, gave many older musicians and keepers of the traditions deserved attention and brought legions of new fans to their doors. Luke's influence on the younger musicians, this time musicians from outside the family and the region, became apparent as their signature tunes started appearing on set lists and recordings of bands around the country.

The innovative clogging team, The Green Grass Cloggers, had several banjo and guitar playing members. In the 1980s, when the team made Asheville their home, there would often be one or two of their members in Luke's kitchen on Sunday nights. The Sunday night sessions in the kitchen became well known, and it was on these nights that young people would drop in to play with and learn from the older musicians. Harold's wife, Daphne, his sister Lorene and other family members would be there just like the 1930s in their mother's kitchen. When Luke's daughter Linda Kay would come home for a visit with her daughter Kaylyn, friends and family alike would fill the kitchen: the music was lively and the requests were many. Daphne always wanted to hear "*The Miller Blues*," maybe because of fond memories and maybe because Luke was the only fiddler still playing Slim Miller's tune. Sometimes fans of the band, made in their new-found celebrity, would call when visiting Western North Carolina and Luke always invited them to the kitchen. Once, an entire family band from South Florida came calling. These folks had gotten hold of the two June Appal recordings and were anxious to meet Luke and his band. The

Figure 11. The Luke Smathers String Band in 1982 at the World's Fair in Knoxville, Tennessee. Left to right. David Holt, Luke Smathers, Bea Smathers, Harold Smathers, Charles Gidney. (Courtesy, Linda Smathers; photograph by World Photo.)

family had learned many of the Smathers' tunes and were thrilled to play them with their musical heroes.

In the the late 1970s, Luke's wife, Bea, began to play the string bass with the band. She used the very bass that the boys had purchased in the 1930s. Bea played a steady rhythm and was a natural for the instrument. She must have been a fast learner having lived with the sounds of mountain swing for more than 40 years. Luke and Bea had eloped when Bea was only 16 years old. According to the family tale, Luke and Bea, and Quay and his sweetheart, Mary Lee, hired a taxi and drove to Greenville, South Carolina where both couples were married by a justice of the peace on July 11, 1936. This must have been a common practice of the day, because Daphne tells a similar story of her wedding with Harold. They drove to York, South Carolina and were married on Christmas day, 1936. Upon returning to Canton, the newlyweds each went home to their families and didn't tell their tale until February. Daphne recalls:

We weren't really ready to get

married...to go to housekeeping and everything. We didn't have everything that we needed to do it and I was just waiting till we got it.... The way Harold and I have always done and always did, we paid for our stuff. And so we just weren't able to do that at that time, so we just didn't tell anybody.[27]

It was a thrill to see the diminutive Bea play the bass with the family band. She and Luke always smiled at each other on stage as if they were sharing some secret joke. In fact Bea had a keen sense of humor. Luke always asked his band members to dress in blue. Bea, however, often favored canary yellow with a little touch of blue maybe on her belt or shoes. Joe Bly, long-time master of ceremonies of The Mountain Dance and Folk Festival, often told a tale on Bea that happened at the festival. One year in his introduction of the band, he went into a glowing tale of his affection for Bea. He claimed, "This next band has the only bass player I have ever been in love with." Bea heard all of this from the backstage wings and handed her bass to "a big old ugly bearded man" to carry it on for her.

Every year on Saturday night at the festival, Luke and the band would play "*The Cacklin' Hen*." At one point in the song the fiddle and banjo make the sound of a hen cackling. One summer, a week or so before the festival, Luke and Bea found a basket of plastic eggs in a novelty shop and Luke purchased two dozen. That year at the Saturday night show, as the band began to cackle, eggs began to roll across the back of the stage and the audience went wild. Then Bea would lay down her bass fiddle, step back and do a little buck dance. In 1986 the crowd gave the band a standing ovation, something rarely seen at this festival. That year the band was given the Most Outstanding Performers Award. After that,

Luke claimed the Saturday night audience looked for the eggs. To stretch the stunt a little further, one of their fans brought them a huge ostrich egg. And the next year that large oval came rolling across the stage. Luke understood the importance of keeping your audience entertained and including them in on the joke.

During the 1980s the cable television network, The Nashville Network, produced a live program of bluegrass and traditional music in Maggie Valley, North Carolina called "Fire on the Mountain." David Holt was the host and naturally wanted to feature The Luke Smathers Band on this nationally syndicated show. The television crew came right to Bea's kitchen in Canton to bring the world a picture of this small town string band. As a result they were

Figure 12. The Smathers Band in 1992. Back, left to right. Charles Gidney, Hilary Dirlam, Laura Boosinger. Front. Luke Smathers, Harold Smathers. (Courtesy, Linda Smathers.)

Laura Boosinger ■ LUKE SMATHERS, MOUNTAIN SWING MUSICIAN: A BIOGRAPHY

featured in the promotional brochure sent out by the station to elicit business from local cable distributors. When the show's producers started their next venture, a syndicated radio show called "The Liberty Flyer," they once again came knocking on the kitchen door. This time segments of the program were to be taped in the kitchen with the band and famed banjo player and songwriter, John Hartford. Since it was radio, sound effects were important. The crew bought a pound of bacon, set up a microphone over the stove and asked Bea to fry the bacon so that they could record the sound of the grease popping. The band found this amusing because they all knew that Bea never cooked on that stove. It was as clean as a brand new electric range. The story goes that when Luke retired from the mill, he made two promises. The first was to never get up at 5:30 a.m. again, which he kept by taking his alarm clock out on the stone wall and smashing it with a hammer. The second promise was that Bea would never have to cook again. And, from his retirement onward they often ate their meals in restaurants. Bea continued to play with the band until her death in May, 1987. When her life-threatening cancer was diagnosed, Bea made it clear to Luke that he was to continue his music with the band.

In 1982 The Smathers Band was invited to spend a week at the World's Fair in Knoxville, Tennessee (Figure 11). There they became close friends with another legendary string band from North Carolina, Whitey and Hogan, The Briarhoppers of WBT radio in Charlotte. They were contemporaries in age and even though their musical styles were different, both bands knew the value of a good show. In 1986 The Luke Smathers Band was honored, along with The Briarhoppers and Snuffy Jenkins, Pappy Sherrill and The Hired Hands, for their lasting contributions to early country music at the first Carolina Legends Festival in Lancaster, South Carolina.

As David Holt's career expanded, his travels often took him far from the kitchen on Sunday nights. I had always been a fan of Luke's music, and during the early 1980s had seen Holt perform with them on numerous occasions. I always went searching for their dressing room at The Mountain Dance and Folk Festival in hopes of playing a tune or two with them on my banjo. In June of 1984 I called Luke and asked him if I could sit in one Sunday evening with the band. He invited me for the very next Sunday. By the Fourth of July the band had a gig at a fire department fundraiser and I was asked to go along. I had never felt such trepidation about playing music in public before, or since. The

---

THE BAND'S TUNES WERE DIFFICULT, FULL OF CHORDS I HAD NEVER PLAYED IN THE CLAWHAMMER BANJO STYLE.

---

band's tunes were difficult, full of chords I had never played in the clawhammer banjo style. I remember Luke describing the chord progressions of these tunes as "F, C, Bb and various other chords." And, for 13 years I kept those "various other chords" in the right order and began to sing early pop tunes like "*Whispering*," and 1940s classics like "*Harbor Lights*." Every Sunday night Harold asked for the Patsy Montana number (she had been a star of The National Barn Dance) "*I Want To Be A Cowboy's Sweetheart*."

I was in my mid-20s when I began to play with the band, and there were times when I am sure that my youth kept the fellows energized during our Sunday night sessions (Figure 12). They always perked up and played better when visitors came to the kitchen. They still played to their audience. After that first Fourth of July fire department fundraiser, I assumed that the evening would end about 10:00 p.m. and I would go home. After leaving the gig, Luke turned around to me and said, "Do you want to go out to eat?" For Luke and Bea their musical evenings were a full evening of fun and socializing. That night, as would be the case for years to come, I arrived home about two in the morning full of Luke's music and Shoney's strawberry pie.

After Bea's death, we played for awhile without a bass player. One or two folks auditioned in the kitchen and it was Hilary Dirlam who joined the band around 1988 and added a new dimension to the band's playing. Luke was always interested in having the band's sound expand. Hilary's playing was intricate and her use of lead breaks on songs such as "*Alabama Jubilee*" delighted Luke. In 1988 the band recorded once again. It was Luke's desire to make a recording in memory of Bea, to be called "*Sounds From Bea's Kitchen*." This recording

---

LUKE KEPT HIS PROMISE TO BEA AND EVERY SUNDAY NIGHT YOU COULD STILL HEAR A STRING BAND IN THE KITCHEN.

---

featured a diverse cross-section of the band's repertoire, classics such as "*The Limehouse Blues*" and Grandpa Jones' "*Old Rattler*" as well as Glenn Miller's "*In the Mood*." Luke kept his promise to Bea and every Sunday night you could still hear a string band in the kitchen.

Every year the Folklife section of the North Carolina Arts Council presents honors and recognition to folk artists throughout the state who have made an important and lasting contribution to the Folklife of North Carolina. In 1993, Luke and Harold were awarded the distinguished Folk Heritage Award. They and their families were invited to a celebration in Raleigh, the state capital, for an evening of accolades. The program for the awards ceremony included a passage from noted folklorist and creator of the Smithsonian Institution's Festival of American Folklife, Ralph Rinzler. He wrote:

> Over the years, my study of folk cultural traditions has always reminded me that the people ...at the center for those of us who seek to understand ...are important teachers because they are really the only carriers of the wisdom of their forebeares. While they may be ostensibly self

effacing, at heart they are confident about their uniqueness.

Luke always knew that his music was different and special and in Raleigh that night, he and Harold and their band played to a thrilled audience as the eggs rolled across the stage once more.

The last years of the band were difficult. Harold's emphysema had worsened and he rarely sang on Sunday nights as he lacked the breath to do so. It was hard for the band members to watch him struggle, and when he talked of quitting, as he did frequently, the group would rally around him and spur him on. One of the last performances with Luke and Harold in the band was in Charlotte, North Carolina for the Charlotte Folk Society. The Smathers Band played to a full house, to more than one encore, and even though he was failing, Harold's humor and strong rhythm guitar playing were there in full force that night. Harold Smathers passed away in October, 1995.

For the next two years, on Sunday nights, Harold's chair sat empty in the kitchen. People still dropped in to visit, the band still played at The Mountain Dance and Folk Festival and new tunes were still being learned. Luke had begun to lose strength in his bowing arm and hoping to improve his muscle tone, went regularly to a health club to work out on weight resistance machines. Luke continued to work as a member of the Folk Heritage Committee of The Mountain Dance and Folk Festival, and was at every Shindig on the Green in Asheville during the summer months. Another group of young musicians from Madison County had fallen in love with Luke's style, and in those last years they would come to the kitchen for a little instruction from the master. Their band, The Lonesome Mountain Serenaders of which Hilary Dirlam was a part, began to play at the same festivals where Luke and his brothers had once performed, and they began to win the same kind of accolades as those Smathers boys had. Luke had to see a

Laura Boosinger ■ LUKE SMATHERS, MOUNTAIN SWING MUSICIAN: A BIOGRAPHY

little of himself in young Josh Goforth, a boy of 15, who could play anything with strings on it.

In the summer of 1997, Luke's health was failing. The band played in June at the old-time music week at Mars Hill College, which was to be their last performance. Luke died of heart failure in an Asheville hospital on July 17. His daughter, Linda Kay, wanted her father's funeral to be a real testament to his musical legacy. A string band played music while the mourners filed in and his pallbearers were fellow members of the Folk Heritage Committee. Linda asked that "*Sweet Georgia Brown*" be part of the service, and asked that Harold's son David sing it. The band was composed of the three teenagers from Madison County who had learned Luke's style, a fitting tribute for a man whose music influenced so many. Linda gave the old bass fiddle to the 16-year-old girl playing bass, the same bass her father had purchased in the 1930s, that her cousin Charles Gidney had played in the 1950s, her cousin David had used in the 1960s and that her mother had played throughout the 1970s and '80s. The old bass went with a fourth generation of musicians influenced by the sounds from Bea's kitchen.

Notes

1. Sadie Smathers Patton, *Smathers, From Yadkin Valley to Pigeon River* (Hendersonville, North Carolina: 1954), p. 17.
2. Ibid, p. 10. Quote and information taken from Bernheim, *The German Settlements and the Lutheran Church in North and South Carolina*, 1872.
3. Ibid, p. 19
4. Ibid.
5. Ibid, p. 23
6. Ibid, p .25
7. For more information on the Jacob Shook house see Robert S. Brunk, Ed., *May We All Remember Well Volume I: A Journal on the History and Cultures of Western North Carolina* (Asheville: Robert S. Brunk Auction Services, Inc., 1997), p. 171.
8. Patton, p. 54.
9. Interview with George Wiley Smathers, Canton, North Carolina, October 14, 1997.
10. Ibid.
11. Ibid.
12. William Walker, *The Christian Harmony* (Christian Harmony Publishing Company, revised, 1958).
13. When using sock chords, the guitarist covers all the strings on the neck of the guitar with his fingers. This style gives the chord a rhythmic sound as opposed to a melodic sound. The guitarist then strums across the dampened strings making a "sock" sound.
14. David E. Whisnant, *All That Is Native & Fine* (Chapel Hill: University of North Carolina Press, 1983).
15. From *You Can't Go Home Again* by Thomas Wolfe as quoted in Loyal Jones, *Minstrel of the Appalachians* (Boone, North Carolina: Appalachian Consortium Press, 1984).
16. Interview with Charles Gidney and Daphne Smathers, Canton, North Carolina, October 15, 1997.
17. Interview with Charles Wolfe, Murfreesboro, Tennessee, October 18, 1997.
18. Ibid.
19. Ibid.
20. *The Asheville Times*, October 14, 1933.
21. Wolfe interview, 1997.
22. George Wiley Smathers interview, 1997.
23. Gidney, Smathers interview, 1997.
24. Wolfe interview, 1997.
25. The Asheville *Times*, August 9, 1942.
26. Playing the banjo clawhammer style makes use of the index finger of the right hand as a kind of plectrum. The melody notes are struck with the index finger and a drone note is hit with the thumb. The notes echo the rhythmic pattern of the fiddle, one-two-and, one-two-and.
27. Gidney, Smathers interview, 1997.

One of three fiddles made by Luke Smathers in the late 1970s. Luke performed with this fiddle for many years. (Courtesy, Linda Smathers; photo, Robin Mask.)

Arthur Hanley Gibbs' Dancing Figures

By Robert S. Brunk

Right. Figures are carved of mixed woods, with slot and tab joints at knees, hips, elbows and shoulders with nails used as pivot pins. Figures have ink details including smiling faces, ears shaped like question marks, fingers and clothing details. Shoes are carved with well-defined heels. Figures have fragments of paint, crepe paper and leather decoration. The female figure has large bows on the back and collar. Figures are mounted on a string which passes through holes in the chests and is tied to the pine frame. The stretcher base is whittled and boat shaped. Figures 16 in. tall, frame 17-1/2 x 18-1/2 x 10 in. (Photos Tim Barnwell; courtesy, Bob and Diane Ruggiero.)

Detail (right). Ink signature on side of base, "A.H. Gibbs, Whittier, NC." (Photos Tim Barnwell; courtesy, Bob and Diane Ruggiero.)

Arthur Hanley Gibbs with his wife Kate and their nephew Cecil Ray Childers. Photo probably 1942. (Courtesy, Penny J. Blount.)

A pair of carved and decorated dancing figures were found in a barn in 1996 on the former Gibbs property in Whittier, North Carolina. Penny Blount, owner of the property states that the Gibbs family moved to Whittier from McDowell County, North Carolina, and that Arthur Hanley Gibbs, born in 1879, was the maker of the dancing dolls. Hanley, as he was known, also played the fiddle and he and his wife, Kate would go to local schools and put on shows with the dancing dolls. Kate would make the dolls dance by manipulating the string on which they were hung while Hanley played the fiddle.[1]

---

1. Information on the Gibbs family from interviews with Penny J. Blount, 1997. For a discussion of similar dancing dolls see Julia S. Ardery, *The Temptation* (Chapel Hill: The University of North Carolina Press, 1998), pp.63-66.

Eleanor Vance and Charlotte Yale were two of many women who moved to the Southern Appalachian Highlands in the late 19th and early 20th century. They came as teachers, missionaries and social workers; many related to the Presbyterian, Episcopal and Methodist churches. Frances Goodrich founded Allanstand Industries, Lucy Morgan helped found the Penland School, Florence Petit began Pine Mountain Settlement School, Olive Dame Campbell established the John C. Campbell Folk School. The work of these and many other women often involved encouraging the production of crafts. There is currently an active and instructive debate among scholars and historians as to whether these women, many from New England, encouraged existing craft traditions, or introduced skills and design elements which were not indigenous to the region, thereby creating "traditional crafts" based on their own aesthetics and values.

This study by Bruce Johnson adds helpful information to the discussion. Eleanor Vance and Charlotte Yale, who met at Moody Bible Institute in Chicago, were missionaries first and craftspeople second. Even further removed was their desire to be business women. Their ideals were shaped by their desire to ennoble hand labor and improve the lot of the people they served. While Yale and Vance's work is broadly considered to be part of the American Arts & Crafts movement, the forms and decoration they taught reflects much of the late Victorian aesthetic movement in England and the revival of the Gothic taste seen throughout the decorative arts in the third quarter of the 19th century. The forms and surface decoration Eleanor Vance initiated in carving classes in Biltmore Village became the prototypes for a generation of similar objects made first at Biltmore Estate Industries, then after 1917 at Biltmore Industries, and later at Tryon Toy-Makers and Wood-Carvers, and The Artisans Shop. —R.B.

"To serve unnoticed and to work unseen":[1]
Eleanor Vance, Charlotte Yale and the Origins of Biltmore Estate Industries

By Bruce E. Johnson

Western North Carolina has long been known for its handcrafted furniture, pottery, baskets and textiles. In the early 20th century notable artisans and cottage industries including the Omar Khayyam Pottery, the Crossnore School, the Spinning Wheel, the Brasstown Carvers, the Penland Weavers and Potters, Allanstand Cottage Industries, and the Southern Highland Handicraft Guild left their mark on the region. Few, however, surpassed the Biltmore Estate Industries (1905-1917) and Biltmore Industries, as it was known after 1917, in the number of people it trained and employed in the fields of woodworking, woodcarving and the weaving of homespun cloth. The company was formed and sustained through the efforts and dedication of Eleanor Vance and Charlotte Yale, and the financial and public support of Edith and George W. Vanderbilt. Each played a pivotal role in the inspiration and organization of the Industries, setting it on a course which would continue in Asheville for nearly 70 years.

In 1917, Biltmore Estate Industries was sold to Fred L. Seely, general manager of the Grove Park Inn and became known as Biltmore Industries. Seely's press releases distorted many facts, especially his descriptions of the origins of the Biltmore Estate Industries. Subsequent histories of Asheville and the handicraft tradition begun at Biltmore Estate Industries were often based on these inaccurate materials. As a result, the two women responsible for the formation of the Industries and the daily training of scores of Asheville's young men and

women has been overshadowed by the credit awarded Edith and George Vanderbilt. Even those historians who recognized Vance and Yale as the inspiration for Biltmore Estate Industries and as the teachers who worked for more than 15 years with the boys and girls living on or near Biltmore Estate have mistakenly assumed that Vance and Yale were summoned to Asheville by Edith Vanderbilt. Vance and Yale came to Asheville in 1901 on their own accord, quite possibly as missionaries hoping to serve the people living in the Blue Ridge Mountains.[2]

Eleanor Park Vance (1869-1954), the daughter of John Park Vance and Ella Robinson Vance, grew up in Mansfield, Ohio. In 1890, at age 21, Vance enrolled at the Cincinnati Arts School, where she was introduced to the ideology of the English Arts & Crafts movement by her woodcarving instructor, William Fry. Fry's father had been a noted woodcarver in England, and had taught his son to work in the Gothic

style, which Vance learned from Fry.[3]

Vance, however, envisioned a future for herself which encompassed more than woodcarving. She and her mother moved to Chicago where Eleanor enrolled in the Moody Bible Institute, presumably in preparation for missionary work.[4] While a student there, Eleanor met Charlotte Yale and the two became life-long partners.

While less is known about her childhood, Charlotte Louise Yale (1870-1958), a direct descendent of the Connecticut family that founded the Yale Lock Company, had demonstrated her considerable artistic talents at the New York School of Ceramics, where she studied weaving, music and ceramics. She, too, was drawn to missionary work and enrolled in the Moody Bible Institute from August 1898 to October 1899,[5] during which time she met Eleanor Vance.

Prior to their graduation from Moody, Vance and Yale traveled to England, where, with the encouragement of William Fry,

Bruce E. Johnson ■ ELEANOR VANCE, CHARLOTTE YALE AND THE ORIGINS OF BILTMORE ESTATE INDUSTRIES

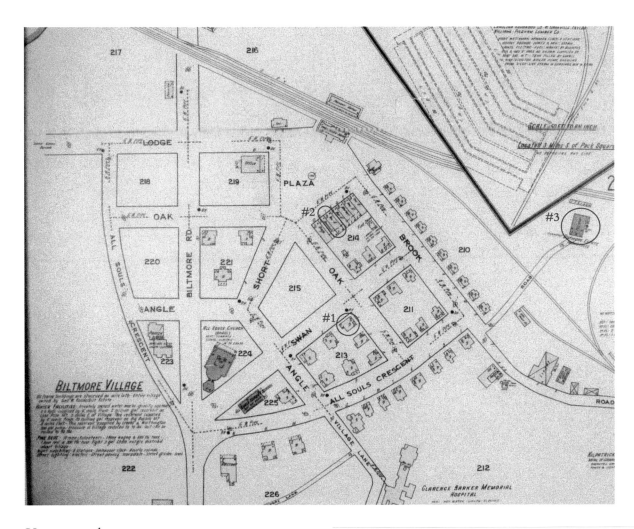

Vance sought out:

> ...Thomas Kendall, the greatest wood-carver of his time, who lived in Warwick, the home of English wood-carving. It was a known fact that he took no pupils, but, nevertheless, with determined will, Eleanor Vance wrote him saying "You have something to give me that I can pass on."

> Through elegant surroundings he led her to a bare loft where he set before her a branch of ivy, a block of linden wood, and an assortment of tools.

> "Show me," he said, "whether it will be worth my while to teach you."

> During the entire morning he watched her as she carved. The result was that she was given lessons and at the end of the summer received the following note:

> I am exceedingly sorry you have been unable to afford the time for a more prolonged course of study. As I can see readily, you have not only the enthusiastic desire but the ability to become, I may say, the best amateur wood-carver of either sex it has been

As part of the development of his estate, George Vanderbilt planned and had constructed a model village known as Biltmore Village. This 1918 map indicates how the train station and All Souls Church stood at either end of a central axis. Vance and Yale first lived at 5 Oak Street when they moved to Asheville in 1901 (red circle #1). Biltmore Estate Industries used the buildings at numbers 7 and 8 Plaza for classes and woodworking (red circle #2). In 1910 George Vanderbilt had constructed a new woodworking shop (red circle #3) which was used until 1917 when the business moved across from the Grove Park Inn. (Courtesy, The Biltmore Village Historic Museum.)

In 1897 George Vanderbilt selected the Reverend Rodney R. Swope (left) to be the rector of the newly constructed All Souls Church in Biltmore Village. Swope actively supported the work being done by Vance and Yale, and soon after they moved to Biltmore Village hired them to be parish workers. Charlotte Yale was the Superintendent of the Sunday School at All Souls and Eleanor Vance was one of the teachers. (Courtesy, North Carolina Collection, Pack Memorial Public Library, Asheville, North Carolina.)

No. A 1   No. A 2   No. A 3

No. A 1—Nut Bowl, Flat, Grape Design, Walnut
No. A 2—Nut Bowl, Flat, Dogwood Design, Walnut
No. A 3—Nut Bowl, Flat, Oak Leaf Design, Walnut

No. A 4   No. A 5   No. A 6

No. A 6—Nut Bowl, Regular, Grape Design, Walnut
No. A 4—Nut Brown, Regular, Dogwood Design, Walnut
No. A 5—Nut Bowl, Regular, Oak Leaf Design, Walnut
Wax Finish

6   *Biltmore Estate Industries*

No. A 7

No. A 7—Nut Bowl, Oak Leaf Design and Squirrels Walnut
No. A 8—Nut Bowl, Oak Leaf Design Without Squirrels Walnut
No. A 9—Nut Bowl, Grape or Dogwood Design Without Squirrels
Walnut

No. X 100

No. X 102   No. X 104   No. X 103

Bowls were some of the Biltmore Estate Industries products that best displayed the carving skills of the workers. The carved walnut bowl with squirrel handles and oak leaf designs is No. A 7 on page six of the 1915 catalogue. 5-1/4 x 16-3/8 x 10-5/8 in., unmarked. The pedestal base walnut bowl with grape designs is similar to No. A 1 on page five of the same catalogue. 3-3/4 x 9 in., marked "FORWARD / BILTMORE, N.C." The grape decorated bowl also has a faint square mark possibly with the initials of a carver; see detail (center). (Private collection; photography, Tim Barnwell and Robin Mask.)

my lot to meet during my long career.[6]

Upon the completion of their training at Moody Bible Institute, Vance and Yale and Vance's mother, who was in poor health, moved to St. Augustine, Florida, "where they enjoyed life until a doctor prescribed a change in climate for Eleanor who had not been well."[7] The three moved to Asheville in April of 1901.[8]

Vance and Yale's religious training in Chicago undoubtedly introduced Vance and Yale to missionary work being done by other women in the Appalachian region in the late 1800s.

The missionary spirit in northern Protestant churches found many outlets for its zeal [and] the South was an

obvious field for mission work.... By the late 1880s, some of the focus of these efforts had shifted from southern blacks to mountain whites.[9]

One such individual was Frances Goodrich, who, after graduation from the Yale School of Fine Arts, studied in New York, and became involved in church and social service organizations. In 1890 Goodrich traveled to Asheville as an unpaid volunteer missionary. Her fund-raising efforts for her newly-formed Allanstand Cottage Industries took her back north, where Vance and Yale may well have heard her speak or read of her work in several periodicals.[10] In the spring of 1900 Goodrich organized the first display of Allanstand crafts at a widely-publicized show in Asheville.

While Goodrich's work in handicrafts focused on weaving, she reported that "there was in this country no general interest in such handicraft and little demand for handwoven fabrics."[11] She also observed that:

> ...the mountaineer, like the Yankee, has a bent for whittling and is never more happy than with knife in hand.... One of our workers in wood made boxes carved out of solid wood, ...decorated them with cut-in designs, using at first his pocket knife and later fashioning himself knife blades to suit his need.[12]

In 1931 Goodrich interviewed Charlotte Yale who described their arrival in Asheville in 1901:

> I cannot think of much to say about our beginnings. It all came about so naturally by doing the next thing. We went to Biltmore in 1901 and rented one of the little cottages. Since Miss Vance had always carved, she used the kitchen table as a work bench, carving for her own pleasure. Two or three small boys became interested visitors, so Miss Vance organized a Boys' Club with four members and taught them wood-carving, little realizing she was making history, for she was the first to bring wood-carving to the section.
>
> Later, Dr. Swope, the rector of All Soul's Church in Biltmore, asked us to be his Parish Visitors, and finally Mrs. George W. Vanderbilt became interested, and out of the little club and the church work grew the Biltmore Estate Industries.[13]

"We came as tourists," Charlotte Yale modestly recalled a few years before her death.[14]

Vance and Yale emphasized that:

> ...religious teaching was always mingled with handicraft instruction. From the beginning the two women, encouraged by what they read in the Bible, took the workers back to verses from the book of Exodus (35:30,31,35) to show the importance of hand work and to give dignity to what was being taught.[15]

Virginia Terrell reported in the *Asheville Citizen* that:

> ...two ladies came South, seeking a

pleasant place in which to live. They were settlement workers from Chicago, but before answering the call to settlement work, Miss Vance had studied wood carving and design and Miss Yale had studied music. They settled in Biltmore, the little English village built by George Vanderbilt near his estate, and might have become, very quietly, a part of the population. But things were moving rapidly in Biltmore.[16]

As an integral part of the development of his estate, Mr. Vanderbilt planned a model village, harmonious in design and construction, consisting of a church as a central feature, a school, a railroad station, office, stores and houses. The site chosen for the village was the area south of the Swannanoa River at the point then

This photo of Bob Stevens carving a picture frame appeared in the first Biltmore Estate Industries brochure, probably published around 1907. (Courtesy, The Biltmore Village Historic Museum.)

Book Trough, Dogwood Design, 7-1/4 x 16 x 9 in. Walnut, "FORWARD" mark. (Private collection; photo Tim Barnwell.)

Squirrel Stamp Box, 3-7/8 x 5-1/2 x 1-7/8 in. Marked "HAND CARVED / BILTMORE INDUSTRIES / ASHEVILLE, N.C." (Courtesy, Pat Fitzpatrick; photo Tim Barnwell.)

Folding book ends, walnut with carved walnut decoration, 6-1/2 x 21 x 6-1/4 in., "FORWARD" mark. (Private collection; photo Robin Mask.)

Two walnut boxes; glove box 3 x 15-1/2 x 5-1/4 in., card box 2-1/8 x 4-7/8 x 3-3/4 in.; both with "FORWARD" mark. (Private collection; photo Robin Mask.)

Pair candlesticks, 18-1/2 in. (Courtesy, the author; photo, The Biltmore Village Historic Museum.)

known as Asheville Junction or Best [about three miles south of the center of Asheville].[17]

After touring Asheville, Vance and Yale "decided that no place would suit them but the beautiful suburb of Biltmore, which was like a bit of old England."[18]

The two young women settled into their rental cottage at 5 Oak Street, where Eleanor Vance resumed her woodcarving at their kitchen table. Miss Yale recalled that:

> ...some mountain boys came by to sell some lettuces. They saw Miss Vance doing some woodworking and inquired. The two women explained, invited them to try their hand, guided their efforts, and let them come back and bring their friends.[19]

Word of the informal meetings spread quickly through the small village and soon Vance and Yale found their little kitchen crowded with boys, carving tools and wood shavings. They also met the Reverend Rodney R. Swope, D.D., rector of All Soul's

Church in Biltmore Village. The Rev.
Swope had been personally selected by
George Vanderbilt in 1897 to serve as rector
for the newly constructed All Soul's Church
in Biltmore Village. According to historian
Mary Hyde, "The Reverend Swope was an
activist in the community, forming several
groups and clubs in the parish, all funded by
Vanderbilt."[20]

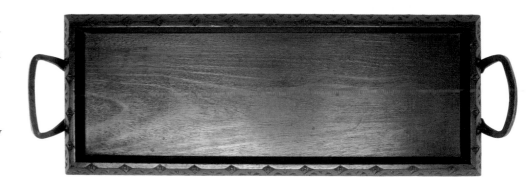

The Rev. Swope immediately recognized the importance and the potential
opportunity which had presented itself to
his parish in the form of Vance and Yale. He
quickly convinced them to form, under his
guidance, a parish club for the boys, and
went to work finding a space for them to
meet so they could expand beyond the limitations presented by their small cottage. In
addition, Swope hired Vance and Yale as
"parish workers." Parish records indicate
that in 1901 Charlotte Yale was serving as
superintendent of the new Sunday School
and Eleanor Vance was one of the
teachers.[21]

Carved tray with handworked copper handles, 1-1/2 x 19 x 6-1/2 in., "FORWARD / BILTMORE, N.C." mark.

Detail of handle. (Courtesy, Helen McCurry; photos Robin Mask.)

One of the boys who had crowded
around Miss Vance's kitchen table was thirteen-year-old George Arthur, whose father
worked for George Vanderbilt. The Arthur
family attended services at All Soul's
Church, where Arthur sang in the choir.
Arthur later recorded his memories of those
early days:

Scroll Sawed Book Ends, 5-1/2 x 5-3/4 x 4 in. Mahogany, "FORWARD / BILTMORE, N.C." mark. (Courtesy, Biltmore Historic Museum; photo Robin Mask.)

Hinged double frame, walnut, 11-1/4 x 17-3/4 in., Biltmore Industries mark. (Private collection; photo, Tim Barnwell.)

> We started as a Boys' Club of All
> Soul's Church [in] Biltmore. Miss
> Vance and Miss Yale organized this
> club in 1901 and limited it to twelve
> of us mountain boys. Then, after the
> club was organized, the next question
> was what should the club do. It was
> Miss Vance who suggested wood
> carving. In the beginning we boys
> just made crude wooden toys for
> church bazaars. For a year we did it
> for the fun of it, and then after we
> had learned to do real work, we were
> paid so much an hour. It was thus I
> began my life work, and I have been
> too busy and too interested to think
> of anything else.[22]

The *All Souls Parish Report* for 1901
documents the formation of the Boys' Club
on September 28, the date of the club's first
official meeting. By that time Swope, Vance

and Yale had determined that it would be restricted to boys between the ages of twelve and sixteen living in the parish:

> The boys decided to take up wood carving, therefore the membership had to be limited to twelve for lack of room.... Wood carving has a disciplinary value which has been very noticeable with the boys, for it requires not only development and training of the muscles of hand and arm but mental effort as well since every touch of the chisel must be guided by thought and intelligence. Some very creditable work has been done and several orders received, so that the boys are hopeful of having the club self-supporting in time.[23]

A Junior Boys' Club for boys ages ten to twelve was formed later in the fall of 1901. As it became apparent that the Boys' Club would quickly outgrow the confines of Miss Vance's kitchen, Rev. Swope "saw to it that the two ladies got a room on Biltmore Plaza so that their house wouldn't be entirely overrun by eager handicrafters."[24]

The earliest surviving financial records appear in 1904 with the following revenues recorded:

June	$2.25
July	none
August	$24.75
September	$7.00
October	$7.65 [25]

By 1903, George Arthur recalled, "Miss Yale and Miss Vance soon realized the boys were receiving all the attention and the girls were being neglected, so the idea of weaving presented itself."[26] With the Rev. Swope's encouragement, Vance and Yale formed the Girls' Club. In 1904 the members of the Girls' Club:

> ...asked permission to take up wood-carving during the summer, and, as the boys had more orders than they could fill, it seemed wise to give the girls the opportunity of trying the work. Some of the members showed ability from the beginning and all through the summer, fall and early winter much faithful work was done. At the beginning of 1905 the club work of both boys and girls was united, forming a small industry

After teaching woodcarving for five years to the Boys' and Girls' Club of the All Souls Parish in Biltmore Village, Eleanor Vance and Charlotte Yale, with financial assistance from George Vanderbilt and public support from Edith Vanderbilt, formed Biltmore Estate Industries in 1905. In this 1908 photo, Vance and Yale pose in front of the Biltmore Estate Industries facility at 7 and 8 Plaza in Biltmore Village with seven of the woodcarvers. Left to Right: Charlie Hayes, Nell Lipe, Miss Charlotte Yale, Randolph Ball, Miss Eleanor Vance, Alice McKain ("Stone"), Ethel Lipe, Nannie Clement, Fonile Ball. The building was torn down in 1940 for the construction of a restaurant and bowling alley. (Courtesy, The Biltmore Village Historic Museum.)

which it is hoped may prove a means of support to many.[27]

As the Boys' and Girls' Club grew, Vance, Yale and the Rev. Swope realized that they would need additional financial support from George and Edith Vanderbilt. The three began working to gain Edith Vanderbilt's attention, introducing her to the activities of the club. Their goal was to form a cottage industry separate from the parish clubs that might provide a career and income for some of the more advanced woodcarvers, some of whom would soon reach the age when their parents would expect them to begin helping to support their families. With financial support from George Vanderbilt, public support from Edith Vanderbilt, and the daily direction from Swope, Vance and Yale, the Biltmore Estate Industries was formed in 1905.

> Here the two young women began the fulfillment of their dream of using their talents in helping young people find a place of usefulness in the world. This gave those under their care a continuing interest and pleasure as well as a means of livelihood for later years.[28]

Edith and George Vanderbilt were busy with travel and social schedules, and their daughter, Cornelia, was born in 1900, but Edith Vanderbilt:

> ...had been deeply interested in the industries, and when, as a bride, she came to Biltmore house, she had spent much of her time visiting among the mountain people with Miss Yale and Miss Vance, as they gradually evolved into a mountain settlement [with] the industries [at] the center.[29]

As Eleanor Yale related to a writer in 1957, "it wasn't long until the public-spirited Mrs. Vanderbilt discovered the quiet beginnings [we] had made in encouraging handiwork among the mountain people."[30]

The Rev. Swope and Edith Vanderbilt convinced George Vanderbilt to provide the financial support necessary to sustain the Biltmore Estate Industries. His name rarely appears in any financial ledgers, and he did not seek public recognition for his philanthropy, but Vanderbilt arranged for payments to be made under Swope's name for any shortfalls the Industries might occur.[31]

Meanwhile, Vance and Yale set about organizing the Biltmore Estate Industry, something neither of them had ever done previously, while continuing to hold meetings for the now-combined Boys' and Girls' Club. As the *All Souls Parish Report* explained:

> The first of January the clubs were reorganized on the plan of a regular industry, both boys and girls working on orders as soon as the required standard was reached. A regular woodworking shop was added to the equipment, with turning lathe, circular saw, etc., run by electricity. An

---

"...IT WASN'T LONG UNTIL THE PUBLIC-SPIRITED MRS. VANDERBILT DISCOVERED THE QUIET BEGINNINGS [WE] HAD MADE IN ENCOURAGING HANDIWORK AMONG THE MOUNTAIN PEOPLE."

> expert cabinet maker gives instructions to the boys who intend to follow the trade, so that all the articles carved are now made in our own shop.[32]

The mention of the cabinetmaker, while brief, may explain how these teenage boys and girls made the leap from carving bookends to producing a variety of household items. In the Industries' financial ledger for 1905, a "Mr. Fellar" was paid $41 in June and $70 in July, compared to $10 for George Arthur, the highest paid of the Industry members. Mr. Fellar's name only appears for those two months, which may mean he was hired to teach cabinetmaking at Biltmore Estate Industries, but his services may have cost more than the fledgling business could justify.[33]

George Arthur provided additional information on the Industries organization in a 1915 interview. As the reporter noted:

> In those days, like all other applicants, he [George Arthur] was received on probation for three months. While the younger workers are still of school age, they are set to work for a certain number of hours each week in a school kept for their

These two pieces, carved by Nancy Rebecca Clement, do not appear in any known catalogues, and were undoubtedly special projects.

Hope chest, carved by Nannie Clement for her sister Lillian Exum Clement, 21-1/2 x 37 x 13 in., oak, three front panels with carved dogwoods, top with three carved initials, "LEC." (Stool and chest, courtesy Stafford Anders; Hope chest photo, The Biltmore Village Historic Museum.)

Spinning stool, 33 x 11-1/2 x 14-1/2 in., carved oak stained black. Detail at base of back with date 1908. (Photo, Robin Mask.)

benefit by the Industries. After a year, they can be guaranteed a regular weekly wage; and thereafter their advancement depends entirely on their own industry and originality. In this connection it is well worth noting, perhaps, that those who have done best in the Industries are the country boys and girls; almost without exception, they have outdistanced those from the larger cities and towns.[34]

The combined Boys' and Girls' Club continued to meet even after the formation of Biltmore Estate Industries.

The Club meets every day but Saturday from 2 until 5 o'clock at No. 9 Plaza, where classes are held for designing and wood-carving. Much enthusiasm is shown among the members and many hope to work up to the standard required for becoming members of the Industry. The boys and girls in the Club design and carve small articles for their own homes, themselves and their friends, and often through this study, real ability has been discovered and then every possible advantage is given for improvement."[35]

Vance and Yale soon included basket weaving and needlework in the Industries' activities (see appendix). In June of 1905 the Industries began paying Sallie Guy and M. J. Fletcher for baskets they had woven. That same month Rev. Swope loaned the Industries $21 to start a needlework program.[36] The *Parish Report* for 1905 confirmed that:

> ...household decorative needlework and basketry were also added to the work of the club, and several busy along these lines live in cottages far out on the Estate and bring the work, which they do at home, to the club room to sell. The decorative needlework has been most successful, some of the girls showing a decided ability in original design.[37]

Biltmore Estate Industries lost money in 1905 and as agreed, George Vanderbilt, through Rev. Swope, made up the shortfall. In the interim, Yale loaned the business $13.00 and Vance $12.50. Both were repaid a few days later.[38]

An early visitor to the workshops and showroom noted that all the woods, except mahogany, that are used by the Industries come from the large forests nearby. They include walnut, cherry, oak, dogwood, ash, and many others; in fact, a most interesting little object made by the Industries is a foot-rule neatly spaced off into twelve partitions of as many different kinds of woods. These rules, made at first for a curiosity, are now a staple offering; and they may be of practical value to any one who is puzzled to decide what kind of wood will best serve a particular need.[39]

At the end of 1905 the founders were encouraged by the response their efforts had created.

> The [Industries] is greatly indebted to the friends in Asheville and Biltmore, as well as to the tourists for the many helpful orders received. Orders were given for chairs, tables, tabourets, large candlesticks, linen chests, book-racks, hat-racks and many small articles, besides a fine quartered oak side table to complete an old dining room set, all of which gave the young workers experience and financial help.[40]

With the woodcarving and woodworking departments at Biltmore Estate Industries established and making rapid

progress with such notable young men and women as George Arthur, Nan Clement and Joe Gatlin, the idea was raised of expanding the Industries to include the weaving of homespun cloth. Credit for the idea has generally been given to Edith Vanderbilt, but it should not be forgotten that one of Charlotte Yale's first interests before coming to North Carolina was weaving. Undoubtedly, everyone associated with Biltmore Estate Industries in 1906 would have been well-aware of the work being done by Frances Louisa Goodrich and other weavers in the Asheville area.[41] Goodrich described the purchase of well-worn equipment for weaving by the Biltmore Homespun Shop from the nearby Reems Creek Woolen Mill which closed in 1914 in her book *Mountain Homespun*.[42]

The first recorded sale of homespun by Biltmore Estate Industries appears in

Some of the most popular carved items created at Biltmore Estate Industries were picture frames. At least seven different designs were available in the 1915 catalogue, pages 38 and 39. Shown here is the "Regular Florentine Design" in walnut with finely carved spandrels. 10-7/8 x 8-3/8 x 1-5/16 in. (Private collection; photo Tim Barnwell.)

One of the brushes made at Biltmore Estate Industries was the "Golliwog" brush based on a caricature of a black man made popular by the author Florence Upton. The worker in the photo is gluing bristles to a brush. (Brush, private collection; photo Tim Barnwell. Shop photo, The Biltmore Village Historic Museum.)

December of 1906. It is interesting to note that the financial records for 1906 reflect that while the highest monthly salary paid to any woodworker that year was $15, George Arthur was paid as much as $35 per month. At the same time, the names of Vance and Yale are noticeably absent from the 1906 financial ledger.[43] These entrees offer the possibility that 1906 may have been the year which Edith and George Vanderbilt sent Vance and Yale abroad to research the weaving of homespun. During their absence, George Arthur would have assumed greater responsibilities in the shops, as reflected in his increased salary.

The *Parish Report* for 1906 confirms the addition of weaving to the Industries line.

> The weaving of all-wool dress goods is a new feature of the Industry the past year. Old looms have been brought out of their hiding places and many have been set to work to recall the old days when the mothers did all the weaving for the family. Some do the carding [cleaning of the raw wool], some the spinning, others the dyeing with the vegetable dyes, while others still do the weaving, so that work is furnished to a large number of people living in the isolated parts of the Estate. It is hoped that the homespun will improve from year to year as the workers grow in experience.[44]

In a letter written in 1950, Charlotte Yale recalled that:

> ...we developed the all-wool homespun at Biltmore, but that work was done by the women and not children. The women had [previously] woven the homespun with a cotton warp which had no market value for suits.[45]

Vance and Yale had returned from their journey to England and Scotland with a great deal of information, samples and a prototype loom, which George Arthur and the woodworkers began duplicating. Their earliest homespun proved disappointing, for it failed to be as soft as the samples carried back from England. The problem was that the sheep at Biltmore had been allowed to roam freely on the estate, where their wool

Bruce E. Johnson ■ Eleanor Vance, Charlotte Yale and the Origins of Biltmore Estate Industries

picked up thorns so small they could not all be removed in the carding process. Once the sheep were restricted to cleared pastures, the quality of the Biltmore homespun improved.

An undated catalog, which appears to have been the first of Biltmore Estate Industries, was issued in 1907 or shortly thereafter. The approximate date is based on the mention of the sale of homespun, which was introduced by Biltmore Estate Industries in December of 1906. The small (3.25 in. w. x 5.75 in. h.) brochure pictured Bob Stevens, one of the youngest woodcarvers, standing at a workbench carving a picture frame. The address listed on the cover was "Number Eight Plaza, Biltmore North Carolina."[46]

The text of the brochure reads:

The Biltmore Estate Industries represents the work done by residents upon the Biltmore Estate in Western North Carolina. The Industries originated in simple forms of handiwork taught as part of the educational system established upon the Estate. A number of the boys and girls soon showed a marked capacity for woodworking and carving, and they now design and produce not only such articles as book-racks, glove boxes, trays, and candlesticks, but all kinds of furniture as well.

Mrs. Vanderbilt, whose active interest and personal direction have brought these industrial matters to their present completeness, has also revived among the natives the manufacture of homespun. Natural dyes, used for coloring the wool, are derived from roots, barks, flowers, etc. The weaving is done by the women in their homes upon the crude looms that were once found in every country cabin. The product of the loom is a distinctively local cloth, durable and attractive in appearance.[47]

Many of the items which were introduced during the early years of Biltmore Estate Industries remained unchanged for more than 30 years. Undoubtedly, many of these were designed by Eleanor Vance, although she never sought credit for them. Woodcarvers at the Industries were not

IDENTIFYING MARKS

Marks on carved wooden objects made at Biltmore Estate Industries, Biltmore Industries, and later at Tryon Toy-Makers and Wood-Carvers, and The Artisans Shop help identify the origins of similar pieces.

1. Biltmore Boys' Club 1901-1905. Although no examples have been found, the letters B.B.C. (Biltmore Boys' Club) may have been burned into some of these pieces.

2. The first known mark of Biltmore Estate Industries appeared in 1905 and was a brand burned into the wood. It was shaped, as a ribbon with an arrow and the word "FORWARD". This reportedly was suggested by Edith Vanderbilt. A later variation added the words "BILTMORE, N. C." beneath the ribbon.

3. In 1917 Biltmore Estate Industries became Biltmore Industries. A new mark was introduced in 1928. The mark used the word Asheville instead of Biltmore and read "HAND-MADE AND HAND-CARVED / BILTMORE INDUSTRIES / ASHEVILLE, N.C."

4. Mark for the Tryon Toy-Makers and Wood-Carvers founded by Eleanor Vance and Charlotte Yale after they left Biltmore Estate Industries in 1915.

5. Mark for The Artisans Shop, founded by George Arthur in 1928.

No. F 11

Plain Paneled Chest. Size 36 in. long, 16 in. high, 16 in. wide in Oak,
Walnut or Mahogany

Woodworkers at Biltmore Estate Industries work on a "Plain Paneled Chest" similar to No. F 11, on page 16 of the 1915 catalogue. (Courtesy, The Biltmore Village Historic Museum.)

taught simply to imitate her designs, however, for as the *All Souls Parish Report* for 1906 documents:

> The boys and girls who are most interested in designing, and who show some ability, have been given an unusual opportunity in the way of a course of lessons from Mr. J. Brys of New York, but recently from Brussels, who is a well-known designer and modeler.[48]

As the earliest members, such as George Arthur and Joe Gatlin, progressed, the evolution from carving bookends and bowls to producing their own furniture must have followed a natural course. As more than one writer of the period noted, "the Biltmore woodwork is notable not only for the high quality of the workmanship, but for the purity of the designs. These are taken, for the most part, directly from old pieces—Sheraton, Heppelwhite, Chippendale—in the collection of Mrs. Vanderbilt; and also from the large library at

the Industries of models produced by these and other masters."[49]

A detailed inventory taken on October 31, 1909 makes a clear distinction between items of the Biltmore Estate Industries and those of the Boys' and Girls' Club. Included in the inventory for the Club were the following books:

Grammar of Ornament
Handbook of Ornament
Style of Ornament
Gothic Architecture
Examples of Old Furniture
Styles of Louis 16th
Patterns of Designs
Woodcarving
Lettering
Lettering in Ornament
Eclesiciastical Woodwork
Handbook of Smithing
Handbook of Embroidery
Needlework

Furniture Draughting
Gothic Designs
Studies of Ornamental Plants
Designs and Draughting
Book on Dyes[50]

The same inventory lists some of the finishes used by the workers. Under "Oils, Stains and Varnishes," are listed Flemish Black, Dark Weathered Oak, Golden Oak, and Mahogany stains, both orange and white shellac, pumice and rottenstone for rubbing out the final coat of finish, plus turpentine as a thinner and "First Coat Varnish," which would have been a sealer brushed onto the raw wood.[51]

Harford Powel, who visited the Industries in 1915, observed that:

> ...everyone connected with the Biltmore Estate Industries, from apprentice to superintendent, is given good models to start with, and is constantly trained to develop his own originality. He may find his model

An October 1909 inventory lists the woodworking machinery used at Biltmore Estate Industries. In addition to the standard assortment of hand tools, power machinery was listed including a wood turning lathe, scroll saw, band saw, circular saw, and glue press. This 1908 photo includes some of the machinery and workers. Left to right. Joe Gatlin, Doke Cooke, Lucius Miller, Wayne Creasman, Lonnie Johnson, and George G. Arthur. George Arthur was the shop foreman from 1910 to 1917. (Courtesy, The Biltmore Village Historic Museum.)

anywhere; for instance, on the terrace of Biltmore House are two great marble lions. A young member of the Industries came up the other day, modeled the lions in clay, and has just finished two little copies in walnut, duly weighted, for use as book blocks. Here was work for his pencil, his modeling tools, and his chisel - it is typical of the variety of the arts mastered by these young boys and girls. They are, of course, extraordinarily fortunate in having Biltmore House so close at hand. From its grinning Gothic gargoyles - which have evidently exercised a strong appeal over the imaginations of the workers - all the way to its many sets of rarest period furniture, Biltmore House is a treasury of admirable models that have been freely offered by Mrs. Vanderbilt to the craftsmen of the Industries.[52]

When searching for design influences on the woodworkers and carvers at Biltmore Estate Industries, it is interesting to note that the Arts & Crafts movement's preference for plain, uncarved oak did not manifest itself among the young woodworkers. The Reverend Swope donated to the Club an annual subscription to *The Craftsman* magazine, published by Gustav Stickley,[53] but we find only minimal evidence in the items produced by the Industries. As one observer noted:

The furniture has none of the earmarks of the Arts and Crafts, so generally affected by such enterprises; it is all in excellent taste, following approved period styles, Flemish, Jacobean and Colonial, and unless we knew better we would suppose it all the work of master cabinetmakers.[54]

While part of this may be due to the fact that oak, which Stickley favored, is more difficult to carve than is the mahogany and walnut favored by the Industries, it also relates to Eleanor Vance's training under English woodcarvers Fry and Kendall and their use of Gothic design elements.

During 1906 and 1907, woodwork continued to provide the most revenue for the Industries, but at the end of each year it still showed a loss. In March of 1907 Edith Vanderbilt, who had been a regular customer, made a $100 donation and purchased several yards of homespun. Buoyed, perhaps, by her purchases, the following month the Industries placed their first newspaper ad for homespun. Financial records also document an increased amount of money being paid to local people for wool and for finished homespun. The young needlepoint department received the great sum of $30 from Edith Vanderbilt in February of 1907 for a bedspread the girls hand-stitched, then received an order for a second one in September from Mrs.

Workers stand beside the new Biltmore Estate Industries woodworking shop built in 1910. Left to right. Tom Johnson, Mark Creasman, George G. Arthur, Wayne Creasman, Doke Cooke, Lucius Miller, Lonnie Johnson, Joe Gatlin, Charlie Hayes. (Photo, The Biltmore Village Historic Museum.)

Bruce E. Johnson ■ ELEANOR VANCE, CHARLOTTE YALE AND THE ORIGINS OF BILTMORE ESTATE INDUSTRIES

Frederick Vanderbilt, again for $30.[55]

By the end of 1907, the Industries had increased its number of workers, but revenues fluctuated widely. The vast majority of pieces which they sold were small items, such as picture frames, boxes, bowls and trays, but very little furniture. Homespun sales increased, but most of the money went to area people who did the work, leaving the Industries with shortfalls each month.

At this time, Vance and Yale were each being paid $970.83 per year as teachers in the parish, although their primary responsibility was the Industries and the Boys' and Girls' Club. The Reverend Swope apparently submitted to George Vanderbilt a breakdown of the expenses incurred by All Souls Parish for each month, then Vanderbilt provided one check to Swope, from which he paid such expenses as salaries for woodworkers and teachers. In 1907, Vanderbilt subsidized the Biltmore Estate Industries with approximately $362 each month, for a total that year of $4354. The following year did not mark any drastic turn-around for the Industries. Once again, George Vanderbilt subsidized their losses, which, including salaries for Vance and Yale, amounted to more than four thousand dollars (Figure 1).[56]

The losses, however, did not deter the Vanderbilts from their goal. To the contrary, in 1909 George Vanderbilt financed a new cabinet shop for the Biltmore Estate Industries between Biltmore Village and the Swannanoa River. Construction of the new shop started in November of that year, and the crew moved their tools and equipment into it in the summer of 1910. Revenues for that year climbed to $7871 (including a new bed for Mr. Vanderbilt for which he paid $46), but were countered by increased expenses, including the new shop, which cost $16,592. In 1911 revenues increased again, this time to $8703, while expenses dropped back to $12,075. In 1912, revenues took an even larger leap to $12,419, against expenses of $16,545. The salaries of Vance and Yale that year were each raised from $80 to $100 per month.[57]

1908	Revenues	Expenditures	Profit	Loss
Woodwork	3162	5023		1861
Needlework	449	499	50	
Homespun	1050	1223		173
Baskets	202	210		8
Administrative Overhead				2242
Loss for Year				$4234

Figure 1. Source: Untitled ledger, Biltmore Estate Industries, private collection.

The opening of the new woodworking shop in 1910 marked the beginning of a new era for the Biltmore Estate Industries. While Vance and Yale remained at #7 and #8 Plaza, supervising the Boys' and Girls' Club, the sales room, and the weaving of homespun, twenty-two-year-old George Arthur became the shop foreman. Under his supervision, the young men and women continued to turn out carved bowls, frames, and trays of exceptional quality, but they also expanded their operation to include custom-made furniture. Seeking to expand their market, George Arthur convinced Vance, Yale and Rev. Swope to exhibit their woodworking at the 1913 National Conservation Exposition in Knoxville, Tennessee, where they were awarded a gold medal. Two years later, Arthur exhibited their work at the widely-heralded Panama-Pacific International Exposition in San Francisco where they received yet another gold medal.

After an interview with George Arthur in 1915, one writer came away with this impression:

> Speaking of the versatility of the workers, a shining example comes to mind in the person of Mr. George G. Arthur, the superintendent. Still in his early twenties, Mr. Arthur has advanced all the way from apprentice. He is a skilled wood-carver, an excellent worker in clay, a practical weaver, and a good man at the blacksmith's forge when there is need of a special hinge or metal bracket. He keeps the books, orders the raw materials, and has instituted a remarkable system of accounting for them and for the manufacturing cost of each article. He supervises all the other workers, a task which calls for motor-cycling

THE 1915 CATALOGUE

In contrast to the earlier brochure published by Biltmore Estate Industries, this forty-page booklet was printed on a high-quality glossy paper and featured many photographs of pieces being produced. The introduction is very similar to the earlier version but the photographs and descriptions provide much more detail about the pieces offered. No prices are listed, but a loose sheet was provided and could be changed as prices were amended. The price list shown here is dated 1916 and probably represents the height of production and variety for Biltmore Estate Industries.

from house to house; and in his odd moments, he is ready to show the Industries to visitors.[58]

The same visitor went on to report:

The various woods are carved, turned and joined with the same patient care that characterizes the work of the best old-time cabinet-makers... If one has... inherited an old chair ...one has but to send it to Biltmore; the Industries will not only make as many duplicates as are desired, but will carry the work still further and create a table, or a side-board, to match... The prices are moderate, since the object of the Industries is to provide useful employment and a good living for their members, and not to make profits for an individual proprietor.

...The work of the Industries is now pretty evenly divided between wood-carving and weaving.... In one corner of the sales rooms, a plain Windsor chair may be seen, and close beside it, a faithful copy of a beautiful little inlaid Sheraton original; in another is, perhaps, a great carved mahogany four-poster with pineapple tops; in still another, a group of gargoyles in miniature that have been adapted to use on stamp boxes, whisk-brooms, and other small necessities. There are picture frames in great variety, tea-trays and coasters, candlesticks, book blocks, and cake stands.[59]

Despite the advancements made by George Arthur after 1910, a series of setbacks rocked the Biltmore Estate Industries in three successive years. On the afternoon of March 6, 1914, George Vanderbilt, while recovering from an appendicitis operation ten days earlier, died suddenly at his home in Washington, D.C. from an apparent blood clot.[60] His death threatened the future of Biltmore Estate Industries.

Despite outward appearances, George Vanderbilt's financial state had never recovered from the outpouring of nearly all of his five million dollars in liquid assets into Biltmore. One biographer reported:

In truth, George Vanderbilt never had been as rich as people thought. The rich often have a way of living luxuriously even after they have spent their last dime. Such was the case

Bruce E. Johnson ■ ELEANOR VANCE, CHARLOTTE YALE AND THE ORIGINS OF BILTMORE ESTATE INDUSTRIES

with George Vanderbilt, whose last dime was still in trust. In fact, aside from his trust, George's assets totaled only a little over a million dollars in 1914 dollars. Biltmore had cost him all his railroad stock. His securities portfolio was worth eleven thousand dollars on the day he died.[61]

During the previous years, George Vanderbilt had been providing the Industries through the Reverend Swope approximately $4354 per year to cover their losses. With no checks forthcoming during March, April and May of 1914, the Industries had to take out a loan, which was repaid by the Estate in June. In January of 1915, as she began to organize and plan her financial future, Edith Vanderbilt sent the Industries a check for $2500 to start the year.[62]

The death of George Vanderbilt forced everyone associated with Biltmore Estate Industries to re-evaluate his or her position. While Edith Vanderbilt's commitment to the people of Western North Carolina may not have changed, everyone realized how over-whelmed she would be with the management of the estate and the raising of her fourteen-year-old daughter. Vance and Yale undoubtedly spend many hours discussing their future. While it is unclear how much they depended on their salary from George Vanderbilt for their personal needs, they, more than anyone else, knew that the

Industries had never shown a profit since its conception in 1905.

In 1915 the two women who had founded and guided the Biltmore Estate Industries announced to their staff and pupils that they were leaving. Their reasons were never made clear, but it may be that they recognized that George Arthur could now assume their roles, and reducing the administrative payroll might make it easier for the Industries to survive. They might also have felt that their role as missionaries to the people living around Asheville had been fulfilled. They may have been looking for another challenge in keeping with their personal commitments even deeper in the mountains and found it in Tryon, North Carolina, 40 miles south of Asheville.

"[I] always wanted to be a missionary," Charlotte Yale told a reporter in 1957. "I never had any business sense at all." And as the reporter noted:

> The Tryon people evinced a strong understanding of what they were trying to accomplish - which was essentially to help their workers, not to build a big business.[63]

Despite the unsteady financial standing and the departure of Vance and Yale, George Arthur had no intention of leaving the workshop and business which he had helped design and build over the past 10 years. In 1915, the year which Vance and

The flood of July 16, 1916 left Biltmore Village with up to 10 feet of water. Biltmore Estate Industries which had moved to new facilities near the Swannanoa River in 1910 was badly flooded. This postcard photo looks south on South Main Street (now Biltmore Avenue): the bridge over the Swannanoa River lies just behind the floating church. Biltmore Estate Industries would have been to the upper left of this photo. (Private collection.)

FOUR CRAFT ORGANIZATIONS WITH SIMILAR PRODUCTION

Many of the objects produced by Biltmore Estate Industries were very similar to objects created by later craft organizations. These similarities relate to the fact that the same people were involved in several concerns. Eleanor Vance and Charlotte Yale left Biltmore Estate Industries in 1915 when they moved to Tryon, North Carolina and founded Tryon Toy-Makers and Wood-Carvers. In 1917 Biltmore Estate Industries became Biltmore Industries when the business was purchased by Fred Seely. George Arthur left Biltmore Industries in 1917 after being with the business for 12 years, and in 1926 founded The Artisans Shop in Biltmore Forest, North Carolina.

The Gothic Bench or Stool appears in several Biltmore Industries catalogues. They were copies of a European stool in Biltmore House. This example was carved by Eleanor Vance and presented in 1937 to Sally Cathey, owner of the Blue Ridge Weavers in Tryon. It is similar to the bench illustrated on page 9 of the 1915 Biltmore Estate Industries catalogue. (Private collection; photo, Robin Mask.)

This detail of The Artisans Shop frame made after 1929 is identical to No. N 2 in the 1915 Biltmore Estate Industries catalogue pages 38-39. (Private collection; photo, Robin Mask.)

Bellows and Hearth Brushes were popular items for the Biltmore Estate Industries. These two examples are identical to those illustrated in the 1915 catalogue, but bear marks for Biltmore Industries which indicates they were made after 1917. Bellows, No. D 3 in catalogue, walnut 19-1/4 x 8-1/2 in.; Hearth Brush, No. D 40, walnut, 22 x 7-1/2 in.; pages 12-13 in catalogue. (Private collection; photos, Tim Barnwell.)

Yale left for Tryon, the Biltmore Estate Industries issued a new catalog proclaiming on the cover:

Biltmore Estate Industries
Hand-Carved and Hand-Finished
Woodwork
Hand-Woven Biltmore Tweeds
Biltmore, North Carolina

That same year George Arthur traveled to San Francisco, where he arranged an exhibit of Biltmore Estate Industries amongst the most well-known furniture manufacturers from across the country. A writer from *Upholsterer Magazine* reviewed their exhibit, noting that:

> ...their display of furniture, which was awarded a Gold Medal, was a surprise and delight. Members of the Jury were amazed at the excellence of the work shown in the Biltmore section. Small pieces showing exceptional skill in wood carving were displayed and large pieces, bedsteads, chairs, chests and settees were shown, of the highest character - Italian Renaissance, Charles II, Flemish, Old Colonial - and all constructed with technical skill and carved in the best taste.[64]

Another writer described the exhibit:

> There is one exhibition that is a distinct surprise, not only because it is the work of an unknown community but because it is distinctively good. The Biltmore Estate Industries represent work done by residents upon the Biltmore Estate in western North Carolina. The Industries originated in simple forms of handiwork taught as part of the educational system established upon the Vanderbilt property. A number of boys and girls soon showed a marked capacity for woodworking and carving, and they now design and produce such articles as bookracks, glove boxes, trays, and candlesticks, but all kinds of furniture as well. Mrs. Vanderbilt, whose active interest and personal direction have brought these industrial matters to their present completeness, has accomplished wonders.
>
> The furniture has none of the earmarks of the Arts and Crafts, so generally affected by such enterprises; it is all in excellent taste, following approved period styles....The small pieces are fashioned with the cleverness of the Japanese and carved as cleverly as by Swiss and I understand that the head of this guild of workers which numbers now about thirty people, is a young fellow, a mere boy of twenty-four years.[65]

Despite the death of George Vanderbilt, and the departure of Vance and Yale, Biltmore Estate Industries continued production. The third setback was the great flood of 1916. On July 8, 1916, the people of Asheville awoke to a rain which did not quit for more than a week. George Arthur and his crew kept an eye on the rising Swannanoa River just yards behind their cabinet shop. On Sunday morning, July 16, the Swannanoa River swelled over her banks and spread across the low-lying Biltmore Village, filling homes and businesses with water and mud. At places in Biltmore water stood up to 10 feet deep. Bridges, power lines and railroad tracks were washed away. Three people lost their lives in Biltmore Village and two people drowned near Depot Street.

As the waters subsided, George Arthur surveyed the damage to the cabinet shop and the salesrooms. A few days later, on July 22, 1916, he wrote to C. Mattison Machine Works, from whom they had purchased a lathe on October 19, 1915 for $725:

> We realize that our last payment

Biltmore N.C.
Aug 20th 1917

Mr F.L. Seely
Grove Park Inn
Asheville N.C.

Dear Sir :-

Owing to the disagreeable relationship between you and myself relative to the Biltmore Industries, I tender my resignation to take effect September 5th 1917.

Very truly yours,
Geo. G. Arthur.

When Fred Seely purchased Biltmore Estate Industries from Edith Vanderbilt in 1917, he began construction of new facilities for the Industries on property adjacent to the Grove Park Inn while George Arthur supervised the workers in Biltmore Village. The relationship between Seely and Arthur was short-lived. George Arthur resigned on August 20, 1917 referring to the "...disagreeable relationship between you and myself relative to the Biltmore Industries." (Private collection.)

This view of Biltmore Estate Industries' carvers was taken at the workroom at #8 Plaza in Biltmore Village. The plaster molds on the wall were purchased by Edith Vanderbilt in Europe to provide examples of relief decoration. Left to right. Nell Lipe, Ethel Lipe, Charlie Hayes, Alice McKain, Edith Arthur, Nannie Clement, George G. Arthur. (Courtesy, The Biltmore Village Historic Museum.)

on the machine bought from you is due but we have had an awful flood, suppose you have seen it in the papers, and every thing we have was under water for several days. As soon as we can get a little dry and the records in condition to use we will send amount and trust you understand and that it will be satisfactory to you.[66]

The final payment of 50 dollars was sent two months later, on September 18, 1916.[67]

Despite the lost revenues and the cost of repairing the cabinet shop and the sales room, Edith Vanderbilt did not close Biltmore Estate Industries. She did, however, begin negotiations for the sale of Biltmore Estate Industries to Fred L. Seely, manager of the Grove Park Inn and son-in-law of Edwin W. Grove, the owner.

Born in New Jersey, Fred L. Seely had married the only daughter of pharmaceutical millionaire Edwin Wiley Grove and moved to Asheville in 1912 to supervise the construction of the Grove Park Inn which opened the following summer. Seely remained in Asheville and, in 1914, leased

the 150-room hotel from his father-in-law. Relations between the two men were strained, however, and Seely, ever-mindful of his tenuous hold on the Inn, may well have been looking for a business which he could develop without interference from E.W. Grove.

In 1916 negotiations between Edith Vanderbilt and Seely were completed and Seely prepared to assume ownership of the Industries in 1917. A newspaper article based on an interview with Fred Seely appeared shortly thereafter and makes clear Seely's plans for what he had already renamed Biltmore Industries. It is also the first of many descriptions of the Biltmore Estate Industries which misinterprets the roles of Edith Vanderbilt, Vance and Yale, and includes other inaccuracies about the work they promoted.

The famous Biltmore Industries, founded by Mrs. Edith S. Vanderbilt over thirteen years ago, have been sold by Mrs. Vanderbilt to Fred L. Seely, proprietor of the Grove Park Inn. The Industries, which produce some of the finest homespun and wood carving in the world, will be located in a model village close to the Inn, and will be enlarged as fast as competent artists can be secured to increase the output.

The Biltmore Industries were Mrs. Vanderbilt's idea, founded to give industrial training to the boys and girls of Biltmore village, the model village built by the late George W. Vanderbilt. Mrs. Vanderbilt started the Industries by securing the services of two able teachers from the north and supplied the buildings, money and machinery that made them possible. The Industries were started as a purely philanthropic enterprise, and many things were taught the boys and girls who attended the school. Time, however, proved that the weaving of homespun and the finer wood carving were the two most useful and practical industries that could be taught to the children, and all other industries were gradually dropped.

The first boy who entered the school was George Arthur, and today Mr. Arthur is general manager and superintendent of the enterprises. He will continue in charge when the Industries are moved to the model village to be built by Mr. Seely near Grove Park Inn....

Mr. Seely has wanted the industries for some time, but only recently has been able to induce Mrs. Vanderbilt to listen to a proposition to part with this child of her own raising, but Mr. Seely explained that he intended to keep the name "Biltmore" associated with the Industries, and only wished to make them bigger and better, and to add the presence of the village, with its quaint hand looms and wonderful carvers, to the Grove Park Inn colony as an added attraction, and finally succeeded in buying the Industries.[68]

During the spring and early summer of 1917, Seely supervised the construction of a series of buildings he had designed to house the weaving and woodworking departments of Biltmore Industries. He had secured from Grove a 99-year lease on several acres of land adjacent to the Grove Park Inn. Meanwhile, George Arthur continued to supervise the woodworkers and weavers at Biltmore Village, and to report to Seely.

On July 23, 1917, Seely wrote to Arthur:

I have been watching the time sheets you are sending over each day, and have been noticing also the way you keep their time.

You have about twenty employees on the average and nearly every day there is one or two who put in from fifteen minutes to half their time short. For instance, I see from Friday's sheet that C. Miller put in four and three quarters hours and C. Cochran eight and a half instead of eight and three quarters.

I have tried to make arrangements that would give all of the employees at the Industries solid time, as most men need that to live. I notice that Mr. Cochran, for instance, is a little short every day. You cannot have any discipline and you will never build up an efficient organization in that way. If Mr. Cochran cannot put in the regulation number of hours, I wish you would secure some one else in his place. There is no reason why the other employees should be asked to be regular and he come late and go early.

I notice, furthermore, that you ask each employee in the evening the time he has put in for that day. It seems to me that it is up to you to know how much time each employee has put in and not have to ask.

I wish that each day after this where any employee does not put in his full time you would explain the reason on the sheet – whether it is sickness or just what is the matter.[69]

On August 20, 1917, George Arthur wrote to Seely: "Owing to the disagreeable relationship between you and myself relative to the Biltmore Industries, I tender my resignation to take effect September 5th, 1917."[70]

Later that year, Biltmore Industries moved to its new location next to the Grove Park Inn. Eleanor Vance and Charlotte Yale moved to Tryon, where they established the Tryon Toy-Makers and Wood-Carvers. George Arthur taught woodworking at Asheville School for nine years before establishing his own cabinet shop, The Artisans Shop.

BILTMORE ESTATE INDUSTRIES WORKERS*

Woodworkers and Carvers (ca. 1905–1908)

George Arthur
Edith Arthur
Frank Arthur
James Arthur
F. Ball
Randolph Ball
Julia Brookshire
Jamie Carr
Nancy Clement
Paul Cochrane
Doke Cook
Mark Creasman
Hardy Fletcher
Joe Gatlin
Charles Hayes
Peate Jarrett
Lon Johnson
Tom Johnson
Ed Lipe
Ethel Lipe
Nellie Lipe
Wallace Lipe
Alice McKain
Lucius Miller
Julia Penniman
Homer Pitilla
Agnes Steele

Needleworkers (ca. 1905–1908)

Ada Knighten
Fanny Knighten
Sue Smith
Amy Taylor
Berta Taylor
Florence Taylor

Homespun Workers (ca. 1905–1908)

Mrs. Butler
Mrs. Carland
M. Case
Emiline Creasman
Mrs. Creasman
Mrs. Green
Mrs. Jackson
Melissa Johnson
Mrs. Johnson
E.S. Jones
Mrs. Hillie Jones
Aunt Polly Lance
Mary Lance
Mrs. Pink Lance
Mrs. S. Lance
Mrs. Parris
M. Stroup
Mrs. Thompson
Cindi Warren

Baskets

Augusta Bradley
M.J. Fletcher

* Other individuals may have worked briefly at the Biltmore Estate Industries; numerous boys and girls learned the art of carving while members of the Boys' and Girls' Club, but did not go on to work at the Biltmore Estate Industries. Some individuals stayed beyond the years mentioned; others left and returned later, or worked part time.

Woodworkers (ca. 1913–1914)

George Arthur
Edith Arthur
Frank Arthur
John Baird
Frances Ballew
Will Ballew
Julia Brookshire
Carl Cochrane
Arthur Creasman
Ethel Creasman
Mark Creasman
F. Eller
Joe Gatlin
Nellie Lipe
Rena Lipe
Clarence Miller
Herman Miller
Lucius Miller
Luther Oates
Robert Stevens

Notes

1. Jane Dusenbury, "Charlotte Yale Pioneered Revival Of Woodcarving," *Asheville Citizen*, October 3, 1957.

2. Ibid. Also, handwritten notes of Betty Barbour after an interview with Vance and Yale, ca. 1951-54, collection of Polk County Historical Museum, Tryon, North Carolina.

3. Mary Grace Knorr, "The Carving of the Mountains – Miss Vance and Miss Yale: A Southern Arts & Crafts Tradition," a lecture delivered and recorded at the All Souls Episcopal Parish Hall, sponsored by Biltmore Village Historical Museum, November 12, 1994.

4. Betty Barbour, "Two Women with an Idea," unpublished manuscript based on interviews with Vance and Yale, Polk County Historical Museum, Tryon, North Carolina, ca. 1955, p. 2.

5. Mary Hyde, interview, November, 2000.

6. Barbour, pp.6-7.

7. Ibid., p. 3.

8. Ibid., p. 4.

9. "Southern Arts and Crafts: An Introduction," *Southern Arts and Crafts: 1890-1940* (Charlotte, N.C.: Mint Museum of Art, 1996), p. 16.

10. Articles on Frances Goodrich were published in the *Presbyterian Home Mission Monthly*, the *Pratt Institute Monthly* and in *House Beautiful*, December, 1898.

11. Frances Louisa Goodrich, *Mountain Homespun* (Knoxville: University of Tennessee Press, 1931, 1989), p. 22.

12. Ibid., p. 29.

13. Ibid., p. 30.

14. Dusenbury.

15. Barbour, "Two Women with an Idea," pp. 4-5.

16. Virginia Terrell, "All the Time Is Toy Time in Tryon," *Asheville Citizen*, December 4, 1927.

17. Marie Louise Boyer, *Early Days of All Souls Church and Biltmore Village* (Biltmore, North Carolina: Gallifox Press, 1933), p. 3.

18. Barbour, "Two Women with an Idea," p. 4.

19. Dusenbury.

20. Mary Hyde, interview, August 17, 1999.

21. *Report for All Souls Parish*, 1901, pp. 50-51.

22. Asheville *Citizen*, April 7, 1929, newspaper clipping.

23. *Report for All Souls Parish*, 1901.

24. Dusenbury.

25. Untitled ledger, Biltmore Estate Industries, private collection.

These photos (this and previous page) in the collection of The Biltmore Village Historic Museum are of objects made at Biltmore Estate Industries, but not found in any known catalogues. They may represent some of the many custom projects completed by the workers. Dimensions and materials unknown. (Courtesy, The Biltmore Village Historic Museum.)

26. Asheville *Citizen*, April 7, 1929, newspaper clipping.
27. *Report for All Souls Parish*, 1904.
28. Barbour, "Two Women with an Idea," p.4.
29. Atlanta *Constitution*, November 28, 1920, newspaper clipping.
30. Dusenbury.
31. Untitled ledgers, Biltmore Estate Industries, private collection.
32. *All Souls Parish Report*, 1905.
33. Untitled ledger, Biltmore Estate Industries, private collection.
34. Harford Powel, Jr., "Turning Industry Backward In Its Flight," February 1915, loose clipping, magazine unknown.
35. *All Souls Parish Report*, 1906.
36. Untitled ledger, Biltmore Estate Industries, private collection.
37. *All Souls Parish Report*, 1905.
38. Untitled ledger, Biltmore Estate Industries, private collection.
39. Powel.
40. *All Souls Parish Report*, 1905.
41. See Goodrich, *Mountain Homespun* for a detailed account of weaving in Western North Carolina.
42. Frances Louisa Goodrich quoted in Blanche R. Robertson, "The Waterpowered Mills of Reems Creek," *May We All Remember Well, Vol.I*, (Asheville, North Carolina: Robert S. Brunk Auction Services Inc., 1997), p. 88.
43. Untitled ledgers, Biltmore Estate Industries, private collection.
44. *All Souls Parish Report*, 1906, pp. 35-36.
45. Charlotte Yale, letter to Betty Barbour, October 9, 1950, Polk County Historical Museum collection, Tryon, North Carolina.
46. Biltmore Estate Industries brochure, undated, private collection.
47. Ibid.
48. *All Souls Parish Report*, 1906, p. 36.
49. Powel.

50. Untitled ledger, Biltmore Estate Industries, private collection. Publisher and author of each book title was unrecorded.
51. Ibid.
52. Powel.
53. *All Souls Parish Report*, 1905.
54. "The Biltmore Estate Industries," *Upholsterer Magazine*, May 15, 1915, loose clipping.
55. Untitled ledger, Biltmore Estate Industries, private collection.
56. Ibid.
57. Ibid.
58. Powel.
59. Ibid.
60. "G.W. Vanderbilt Dead," Washington *Post*, March 7, 1914, newspaper clipping.
61. John Foreman and Robbe Pierce Stimson, *The Vanderbilts and the Gilded Age: Architectural Aspirations, 1879-1901* (New York: St. Martin's Press, 1991), p. 296-297.
62. Untitled ledger, Biltmore Estate Industries, private collection.
63. Dusenbury.
64. "The Biltmore Estate Industries," *Upholsterer Magazine*, May 15, 1915, loose clipping.
65. Untitled review, *Upholsterer Magazine*, May 15, 1915.
66. George Arthur letter to C. Mattison Machine Works, July 22, 1916, private collection.
67. Untitled ledger, Biltmore Estate Industries, private collection.
68. C. H. Hites, untitled article, publication date and newspaper unknown, loose clipping.
69. Fred L. Seely letter to George Arthur, July 23, 1917, private collection.
70. George Arthur, letter to Fred L. Seely, August 20, 1917, private collection.

Artists and writers have come to Western North Carolina to live and work for many years. Most have found that an agrarian life style in an isolated place was conducive to their inventiveness. Many are attracted to the cultural and physical uniqueness of the region and incorporate elements of what they find into their work. Only the naive though, have believed that life closer to the earth is simpler than urban life. Understanding the intricacies of social interaction, finding linkages between the Southern Appalachian subculture and the larger industrial culture, and the requirements of mooring oneself to a place over time are complex tasks that differ from the requirements of urban life only in kind, not in their intricacy. Olive Tilford Dargan first came to the region in 1906 and struggled with these and other themes in both her life and her writings until her death in 1968. This essay by Rob Neufeld, himself a writer, interprets the events and shifting ground of Dargan's life against his own sentiments. He, like Dargan, allows what he finds to inform his work. —R. B.

Olive Tilford Dargan: Writer and Social Critic 1869-1968

By Rob Neufeld

In the first quarter of this century, she was one of the most highly acclaimed playwrights and poets in America. Her collection of short stories, *Highland Annals* (1925), republished as *From My Highest Hill* in 1941, portrayed Swain County, North Carolina farm families with a degree of candor and wit that endeared her to a wide range of regional readers.

Who was she? Olive Tilford Dargan. She lived in a historic cabin she called Bluebonnet Lodge in West Asheville the last 40 years of her life. She produced 13 books. Yet now, despite her former critical status and despite the reissuance of her acclaimed first novel, *Call Home the Heart*, by Feminist Press, few people remember her greatness.

There are several possible explanations as to why Dargan is a largely forgotten literary figure. It may be that she did not follow the call of the market; or that she could not spare the time to pursue fame, or that she lacked a good agent. The most persuasive explanation is that the political views she reflected, based on her sympathies with struggling mountain people, caused critics to label her work in ways that overshadowed its literary quality.

In 1930, Dargan cloaked herself with a pseudonym, Fielding Burke, and embarked on her first novel, *Call Home the Heart*, published two years later. It was in part, a vindication of oppressed workers. The first half of the novel takes place in fictionalized Swain County, but Dargan then followed her protagonists to North Carolina's lowland mills, to a city based on Gastonia,

Olive Tilford was born in Kentucky in 1869 and lived in Missouri as a child. She taught in her father's academy in Warm Springs, Arkansas in 1883 and is seen here about the time she enrolled in Peabody College in Nashville, Tennessee in 1886. (Courtesy, Charlotte Young Collection, Ramsey Library, University of North Carolina at Asheville.)

Beebread, two miles below us, was our nearest village and Post Office. From vantage points on the farm we could look down upon it and follow the lap of the valley as it narrowed along the Little Tennessee, passed High Lonesome and began to climb the Nantahalas. There was pleasure, too, in looking up to Horizon Farm from Beebread. Fields reached to the skyline where the farm boundary followed what my documents of title called the meanders of the ridge. There was satisfaction in possessions viewed from untroubling distance. Particularly so when the look upward gave them the charm of two elements, green earth and blue air.

"Coretta and Autum" in From My Highest Hill, *page 27.*

where the workers were organizing.

Dargan was very sensitive about her reputation. She was at heart a lyric poet without the nerves for public confrontation. She lived in fear of reactions to her politics. The negative climate did exist, and had been directed at her at times; but she felt it was virulent. Opinion about her ranged from the very highest praise to condemnation by friends.

Alice Stone Blackwell, the leader of the woman's suffrage movement early in this century, referred to Mrs. Dargan as "a charming woman, an exquisite soul—a saint as well as a genius."[1] One eminent critic said her poetry "marks the high tide in blank verse since Shakespeare";[2] and another called her first novel, "the best novel yet written about the industrial conflict in contemporary America."[3]

Charlotte Young, a poet and Dargan's friend from Hominy Valley, west of Asheville, called Dargan one of the best poets in the country in her time, but snapped that she was someone who hobnobbed with Communists and who would "fall for anything that came along if it was sold to her with a glib tongue."[4]

Who was Olive Dargan? It seems that, from the beginning of her life, she was a precocious child finely attuned to other people's hurts. In a family of idealists, some of whom were survivors and others, tragic heroes, she was a survivor.

CHILDHOOD, EDUCATION, AND EARLY WORK

Dargan's maternal grandfather, Mordecai Day, had been an abolitionist preacher.[5] Both her grandmothers had been Kentucky pioneer women, and had filled Olive with stories of their struggles. Dargan's parents, Elisha and Rebecca Day Tilford, were progressive teachers. From their farm in Tilford Springs, Kentucky, where Olive had been born in 1869, they moved to Doniphan, Missouri and then Warm Springs, Arkansas, establishing schools that expressed their ideals. Dargan once described her father as someone "who was always suspecting that Eldorado lay over the next border."[6]

The scanty record of Olive Dargan's youth affords a few glimpses of her experiences growing up. At age seven, she outraced her father to the daily Louisville *Courier Journal* and pestered him with questions about current events.[7] "I remember...I watched eagerly for it," Dargan recalled, thinking of the paper, "so I could talk 'politics' with my father...[He] seemed to enjoy our discussions."[8]

At age nine, Olive saw with dismay a black woman's frostbitten feet amputated for lack of home heating.[9] At age 12, she lobbied her father to help improve the conditions of prisoners. When her mother died, just after the move to Arkansas, Dargan, age 14, went to work, teaching 40 children in a one-room school in the Ozarks.[10]

Her mother's death fueled her mission. In 1907, after losing a child in infancy, Dargan wrote a friend:

I thought that this child might be in reality what its parents had been only in dream and desire, just as I used to think that perhaps I might take up my mother's unbroken, unfinished life—but failures are not rewarded in that way.[11]

Compounding Dargan's sense of thwarted promise, was her older brother Tilden's fate. He had had a novel published by a major publisher (Appleton) when he was 20, and Dargan considered him the literary genius of the family. Then, when family responsibilities and poverty buried his youthful dreams, he committed suicide.

In 1886, Dargan entered and won a competition for a scholarship from Peabody College for Teachers in Nashville, Tennessee, ushering her away from her father's academy and her family home. After graduating, she moved on to San Antonio, Texas, where she had procured a teaching job, and then gained admission to Radcliffe College in Boston, Massachusetts. It was at Radcliffe that she met her future husband, Pegram Dargan, a Harvard student; and it was there that she switched from studying teaching to political science, and then to literature.

The American philosopher, George Santayana, taught her political science at Radcliffe. Santayana thought that human beings were primarily filters for experience, and that idealism was irrelevant. Dargan could not be so scientific. She turned to literature to "shatter the sorry scheme of things entire and remold it nearer heart's desire."[12] Idealism was central to human existence, she felt; and the denial of it was deadening.

In 1894, after a year at Radcliffe, Dargan took a teaching job in Nova Scotia, and then, setting aside her mission to assist disadvantaged children, moved to Boston to work as the secretary to the president of a big rubber company. That didn't last long. One day, after dictating two letters—the first ordering the closing of a factory and the second complaining about the quality of upholstery on the president's yacht[13]— she cracked and hardened against capitalism. She needed a break.

Dargan's health broke. In 1897, she traveled to Blue Ridge, Georgia to recuperate. She wrote a play (which has been lost) about Saint Joan, the woman Pope.[14] She received visits from Pegram Dargan, who camped on her doorstep. The two had reconnected in a Boston curiosity shop, as she told a reporter years later. She'd been searching for a bust of Keats, and he for a statue of Venus.[15]

Olive Tilford and Pegram Dargan

Olive Dargan as a young writer. Date unknown. (Courtesy, Charlotte Young Collection, Ramsey Library, University of North Carolina at Asheville.)

were married in Blue Ridge, March, 1898. Evidently, Olive had some doubts, and Pegram's parents intervened. Dargan's friend, Sylvia Arrowood Latshaw, later revealed, "the family told Mrs. Dargan that if she would marry him, they would see that she'd never suffer any, and that she would be provided for."[16] Pegram was "crazily in love" with Olive. She, Latshaw believed, "was more interested in ideas...than she was in men."[17]

The newlyweds moved to New York City to write and, in 1904, Olive Dargan published her first work, *Semiramis, and Other Plays*, written in verse. She enrolled in

Ishma came slowly up from the branch on the opposite side of the house.... Reflections from the western sky colored the slow curves of the Little Tennessee as it flowed errantly and golden from its source in the Nantahalas, whose distant peaks were a panting radiance above their dark, blue bodies. When Ishma came up the steps at the end of the porch she turned again and stood looking down on the long stretch of valley, and on out to the horizon where the rolling transparency of the mountains was inundating earth with dream. Her whole body seemed caught in an intent gaze.

Call Home the Heart, *page 18.*

Olive Dargan sold the stage rights for her play titled The Shepherd *in 1906 and with this money made a down payment on 1,000 acres of barely accessible land, a ridge called Round Top, near Almond, North Carolina. She lived at various sites for varying periods of time in the Almond area for the next 38 years. Seen here is the Dargan house on Turkey Creek near Almond to which she retreated after the publication of her first novel in 1932. (Courtesy, J.C. Freeman.)*

Right. The site of Dargan's riverside house in 1998, showing the surviving chimney and the surrounding woods. (Photo, the author.)

a writing course and completed several more plays, including, in 1906, *The Shepherd*, a portrayal of a sensitive poet racked by conscience and protected by a priest in pre-revolutionary Russia. The stage rights to *The Shepherd* were purchased by Henry Sothern, and Dargan used the check to make a down payment on a barely accessible thousand-acre ridge called Round Top in Almond, North Carolina.[18]

THE EARLY ROUND TOP MOUNTAIN YEARS

Olive and Pegram Dargan moved to Round Top in 1906. There was no road going up to the home site, and wouldn't be until 1916.[19] Two houses existed on top—log cabins built in 1860 by a couple of brothers named Stillwell—but the Dargans couldn't inhabit either of them. Olive wrote to her friend Alice Blackwell that she and Pegram were working 12 hours a day, "half camping in a tiny room by the riverside."[20] They had bought a few other tracts of property in Almond, including a camp near town that served as a refuge.

Over the next year, the Dargans

completed their own structure, but their home life was soon shattered by grief. In 1907, Olive's only child, a daughter named Rosemary, died after a premature birth while Dargan was spending time with her friend, Ruth Stokes, in Connecticut. Pegram was in Oregon.[21] From Stokes, Dargan learned about socialism. She then returned to Round Top's tasks, which were made intolerable by Pegram's incapacitation. A horse had fallen on him and had made him something of an invalid.[22]

Immersed in farm work, Olive Dargan had no time for writing. Her third book, *The Mortal Gods and Other Plays*, would not be published until 1912. Feeding the people who worked for her occupied half her time, prompting her to write an editor at Scribner's, "When literature seems to be on the other side of the world, as it always does now, I am at least permitted to feel that I'm good for something on this side."[23]

The frustration of slow progress and little comfort combined with personal dissatisfactions to make the homesteading years seem desperate. Olive Dargan began to spend less time on the farm. She visited Alice Blackwell in Boston, and, on Blackwell's referral, lived for two years with the sculptor Anne Whitney in Shelburne, Massachusetts, making fast friends and writing new plays. In 1911, Whitney funded Dargan's three-year excursion to England and Europe, largely to get her away from Pegram.[24]

Dargan's mental condition was fragile. Blackwell wrote Whitney that:

... [Dargan's] nerves were for years under a severe strain—all the time that she was with her husband....I have no means of knowing whether she was so originally, for I did not become acquainted with her till after her health was all broken up owing to the terrible and prolonged strain that she had been under with that half-insane man....It has been worth everything to her that your affection made it possible for her to put the ocean between herself and that man.[25]

Pegram was indeed unstable. When his parents had persuaded Olive to marry him,

Granpap's toleration of me passed into liking very slowly. His stolidity often brought my imagination down as if it had struck a wall; and while I gathered up the pieces, the wall would become human and wonder why I had given such an invidious thrust. Naturally the essence of comradeship eluded us for some time. But finally he understood that my assaults were harmless; that he merely happened to be on the horizon when my enthusiasm was spraying the skies; and I began to see that he was too much a part of Nature to become consciously her note-book. He wore externality as a tree wears its bark, receiving all winds with passionless impartiality; but those winds of change were his breath of life.

One day I asked him if he did not sometimes feel that he would like to live in the city.

"No," he said, "I have to stay whar thar's somethin 'happenin'."

Not an eyelash of me betrayed my glee. The least sign of emotion, and the gates of confidence would be snapped and sealed.

Highland Annals, *pages 6-7.*

they had reasons to worry about their son's suitability. His relationship with his brother, Robert, would develop into a double suicide pact made in response to the bankruptcy of a publicly held company Robert managed. According to various versions of the incident, Robert had gone through with the suicide and Pegram hadn't. Pegram was accused and acquitted of murder charges. (Investigators even exhumed Robert's body.) The coroner's inquest confirmed that Robert died of an overdose of carbolic acid.[26]

Olive Tilford married Pegram Dargan in Blue Ridge, Georgia in 1898. The two young writers then moved to New York City. Pegram Dargan died in 1915 on a boat trip to Cuba. (Courtesy, North Carolina Collection, Pack Memorial Public Library, Asheville, North Carolina.)

DARGAN'S LIFELONG LOVE OF CHILDREN

In a life filled with tragedies and betrayals, Dargan looked to the young people who lived near her in Almond, North Carolina for renewal of hope. She especially cared about those held back by circumstance.

"I am blessed with the power to love all children—any child—as dearly as many mothers love their own," Dargan wrote after the death of her child, "and if I ever have a home in which little ones can be happy I can easily fill it."[1]

After Dargan had published her first novel, *Call Home the Heart*, she returned to the home she had established with her husband, Pegram Dargan, nearly two decades earlier, seeking a haven from a society that she felt had grown intolerant of her views. Almond embraced her, and she it, for the people accepted her on a personal level, uninfluenced by her urban critics.

Children surrounded Dargan when she was out and about, and respected her privacy when she was writing. In the 1930s, the children represented by Bayard Wootten's photos for Dargan's stories in *From My Highest Hill*, knew her as an eccentric, bag-carrying kind of Santa Claus.

J.C. Freeman remembers the fudge she always carried "in a big old bag."[2] Ray Simonds and Ralph Stanberry remember gifts of oranges, knives, candy and a hatchet. Ralph would spot her walking along the road in Almond, hefting bagfuls of paraphernalia, talking to herself. He wouldn't disturb her then, but later might catch up with her to be given some chore. [3]

When Dargan took a special interest in a child, she'd offer to pay for his or her education. She sent Edna Edwards, the oldest daughter of a tenant family, to nurses' school; and Vestal Franklin, the most serious child in a large, struggling family, to barber school.[4]

Sylvia Arrowood Latshaw, a teacher and a lifelong friend of Dargan, related how Dargan had saved money for years to create "a home for girls who came in from the neighboring country around Asheville—working girls who came in there. Until they found themselves and…could live nicely, she'd take care of them so they wouldn't be helpless and just so lonely."[5]

Notes

1. Dargan to Alice Stone Blackwell, July 30, 1907, Olive Tilford Dargan Papers, Houghton Library, Harvard University.
2. J.C. Freeman, author interview, December 23, 1998.
3. Ralph Stanberry and Ray Simonds, author interview at Simond's house in Bryson City, February 5, 1998.
4. Ibid.
5. Sylvia Arrowood Latshaw and her sister, Mrs. Mason, interview by Ellen Neal and Carol DeWallis, November 24, 1976, Southern Historical Collection, University of North Carolina at Chapel Hill.

Sylvia Latshaw provides a glimpse of the Dargans' marital life in Almond:

> …[Dargan] and her husband had a tiff about something or another and she went out in a…field and sat out along a big boulder there and was trying to compose herself—and she composed a poem! She sent it to the *Atlantic Monthly*, and it was published.[27]

It was her first published poem.

Was Pegram writing about this "tiff" or one of many others in his poem titled, "The Quarrel"? In it, he complains about "truth ruined, wrecked," and how he'll never forgive the unnamed woman. Still, when night comes, he writes, he's ready to "end it now in bed!" As a moral, he comments, "A woman gives a woman's deeds the lie."[28]

Olive Dargan often sought sanctuary in the woods surrounding her home. A friend's grand-niece, who had access to Mrs. Dargan, made note of the many benches situated in inspirational locations throughout her woods.[29] Likewise, Ishma Waycaster, the mountain heroine of Dargan's first novel, *Call Home the Heart*, ritually followed long, toilsome days with escape and reverie, sitting on a bench atop Lame Goat Ridge.[30]

J.C. Freeman tells how his father-in-law, when he'd been a boy, had climbed onto the roof of the Dargan house with another fellow and peered in through an opening into the attic which Mrs. Dargan had turned into a studio. There, on her desk, rested a pistol.[31] Freeman also reports that Pegram was known to have a mean streak. Once, Pegram "got mad at the [mule] team and tied them to a tree to whip them. She [Mrs. Dargan] came out with a pistol. 'Why don't you shoot them?' she said to him," and offered him the weapon as a recrimination.[32]

In September, 1915, Pegram drowned, having fallen from a boat on a trip to Cuba, taken while Olive was caring for his mother.[33] His death was the last in an awful series of tragedies beginning in 1913 with Olive Dargan's brother's suicide. Olive's sister Leona, mother of two girls, was writing from Texas, informing Olive about her destitution.[34] Olive's friend Anne Whitney struggled with a malignant illness; and Pegram's father had also died.

Dargan, unable to stay in the house she'd shared with her husband, took up residence elsewhere in Almond. Jessie Anderson Johnson, granddaughter of Ida Conley, who managed the lodging house in Almond in which Dargan rented a room, clearly remembers Dargan living there in 1915 and 1916. The men working on the road to Dargan's house were also guests at that time. In 1917, a fire that started in Dargan's room destroyed the building, taking with it the doll that seven-year old Jessie had gotten for Christmas.[35]

At times, Dargan stayed overnight on Round Top, but not in her own house. She wrote Blackwell in 1916 that she was staying in a tenant cabin with a family of nine.[36] She was probably referring to one of the two Stillwell cabins located not far from her house, each accessible only by the mountain road. She completed *The Cycle's Rim*, a sequence of sonnets that strove to distill her husband's pure, idealistic spirit and cast him as a tragic hero. He fit a pattern she knew well: the genius warped by society. Now, she wrote, she must "chant these mortal staves/ And lay my leaf of laurel on the waves."

RENEWAL AND A RETURN TO THE FARM

Eventually, Dargan returned to Round Top, burying herself in work on her farm and devoting herself to its community. Surviving letters document the intensity of her involvement. In April, 1916, she wrote Blackwell that she was "mending fences, digging ditches, carrying rock, cutting poles, and other incredible things."[37] In June, she described to William Crary Brownell at Scribner's how she was "inoculating" bushels of peas and building a pig-proof fence down the hillside, "besides mulling early and late over schemes to keep my tenants from starving while I am away."[38]

Needing to meet expenses, Dargan put aside her own resolve not to write about her tenants and neighbors,[39] and composed her first short story, "Evvie: Somewhat Married," published in *Atlantic Monthly* in 1917. This was the first of eight sketches published in 1925 as *Highland Annals*. Dargan's work combines rural realism with the subtle portrayals of the highland farmers' intelligence, superstition, civility and pride. The author's appearance as a landlady, helper, and bungling meddler adds to the honesty and

"They been called Unaykas since my gransir's day," said Uncle Jess, his eyes levelling their rods of brown fire on Sam from a face as Greek as Socrates'. When he said a thing was thus or so, so it was. In this instance I was glad to believe him. My newly adopted region was still unchristened, and I was casting about for a name. "Snowbird" was too cold for the warm, green slopes, and "Unikers" could never be revamped into Unicoi. The watered valleys and heights lying within the crescent bounded north and west by the curve of the Unakas and the Smokies should be Unaka land. With this decided, my inheritance was easily lifted from prose to poetry. The hundred circling hills became tipped with song. Bloom called to bloom from Three Pine Point to Sunrise Spur, and Blackcap answered from his hemlock shroud with a melodious shake that did no harm to his hidden acres of anemone and trillium.

"About Granpap and Trees" in From My Highest Hill, *page 14.*

drama of the stories, but never distracts attention from the main characters.

In "Serena Takes a Boarder," Dargan's alter ego, Mis' Dolly, persuades Serena—"Reenie"—to change her natural ways and apply herself to productive work. She does, becoming a workhorse and making her family, who had depended upon her for joy and love, miserable.

Reenie's husband, Len, unburdens himself to Mis' Dolly:

> I knowed I could work hard enough fer both of us, an' ef I wanted to do it I wuz my own fool an' nobody else's. But here's Reenie goin' against her own sef, seems like, an' so different I'm about to fergit where I live. I want you to go an' talk to her, Mis' Dolly. That's what I've come fer. She'll listen to what you say....

> He knew, of course, the part I had played in the change that afflicted Serena, but in his eyes, pleading so humbly for her restoration, there was no reproachful sign.[40]

The reader gets glimpses of Dargan's roles as writer and landlady. Called away one summer, the author returned in autumn to find that her manager, Sam, had neglected the farm. He and his wife, Coretta, were planning to work in the mills in Georgia. The author set to harvesting beans, and, she noted, "my typewriter was moved into the kitchen, where odd moments might go into the making of a masterpiece."[41]

THE MOVE TO WEST ASHEVILLE

By the time *Highland Annals* was published in 1925, Dargan had found a new home. In 1923, her Round Top cabin was destroyed by fire, and she was once again displaced. It wasn't until 1925 that she felt impelled to resettle. Traveling through Asheville with a friend, she discovered a log cabin that reminded her of what she had lost.[42]

The house, located in woods at the end of Balsam Avenue in West Asheville, was more than 100 years old then.[43] It had belonged to Rutherford Platt Hayes, son of United States president Rutherford B. Hayes. R. P. Hayes had bought it in 1897, a few years after his father had died, and had added rooms for his sister. He became an important force in the area, establishing an experimental farm as well as the city's first water system, Buckeye Water Company, drawing from the Deaver View Mountain watershed.

Hayes called his estate Falconhurst. The subdivision fashioned from a part of it in the 1920s still bears that name. Dargan changed the name of her home to Bluebonnet Lodge. She planted an acre of bluebonnets, the Texas state flower, but they didn't take.[44] Sylvia Latshaw once noted that Dargan "seemed to think she was a Texan in some ways."[45]

Latshaw also noted Dargan's attempts to increase her privacy. By 1925, West

Asheville had doubled its population within five years. Dargan encircled her house with rhododendrons.

At the end of Balsam Avenue, flagstones led from the street to the house, "virtually hidden by massive trees and shrubs."[46] A visitor in 1936 met Dargan on the stone path as she "turned back from an intended visit next door."[47] A spacious lawn set back the house from the close neighborhood. "Climbing roses, clematis and trumpet vine run riot over those ancient logs," the visitor noted, "and boxwood and evergreens peculiar to the mountains add their beauty to a house that bespeaks the primitive, sturdy mountaineer."[48]

The house no longer exists. It was demolished to make way for a commercial development that backs onto Balsam Avenue. Yet, for many years, it served as the place where Dargan wrote most of her works, including all of her novels.

Dargan liked an outdoor office. Maxine Wright, a Swain County native, recalls that many times Dargan:

> ...would borrow a horse from Dad and off she would ride to the top of some quiet mountain with her typewriter strapped on in front of her. Most of the time the women would pack her lunch in a lard bucket and not see her until the next day. My sisters and I thought it great fun to sit quietly beside her and watch her fingers fly on the keys.[49]

An Asheville *Citizen* reporter, visiting in May, 1932, noted that Dargan, having just returned from a two month stay in New York City, had "moved her small portable typewriter outside beneath the tall, stately pine trees to write." Dargan had also created an indoor-outdoor space. The reporter told how she'd followed Dargan to a small outbuilding enclosed in screen wire. "This is my study," Dargan said, "when the weather's nice."[50]

Dargan was conscious of the impression she was making in her new community, one much more connected to national affairs than Almond. She was

already somewhat famous, and was about to embark upon controversy over her new book, *Call Home the Heart*. Yet, no matter how outspoken she became in her writing, she remained by temperament a recluse, a romantic who honed her lyricism with unaffected realism.

Dargan retreated to nature to write, but she often mused about social injustice and the human soul. "I am more interested in humanity than in literature," she told Anthony Buttita in an interview for the Raleigh *News & Observer* in 1935. "My interest in literature is probably in my effort to put humanity into it."[51] She took pains to defend the literary merit of workers' struggles. They lie closer to real experience, she said:

> ...than the "flutter of an eyelid," which has occupied bourgeois writers for years and is considered by standpat

Bluebonnet Lodge was demolished for commercial development that now backs onto Balsam Avenue in West Asheville. This is the site as it appeared in 1998—graded, paved, with no trace of Dargan's home. A sign recognizing Dargan's West Asheville home as a North Carolina historic landmark was erected by the Department of Transportation on Haywood Road in 1994. (Photo, the author.)

Ishma Waycaster goes to town to solicit food from farmers for striking workers.

> *Gradually she became possessed of a secret. Every sordid and ugly life had its hidden war in the service of a dream; it's struggle behind drab matter-of-fact; its timidity and pride, fearing to be found out. That was the mystery she had so often seen in chilled, coffined faces. Dead lips drawn over life-long, unconfessed defeat; curved with the triumph of concealment; the dream safe from life's insolences and surprises. But suppose it could be released into life?*

Call Home the Heart, *page 332.*

"An' Emmie, I don't know her now.
She works an' sews, as busy as me
In the field rows.
Of mornin's before I go
She gets the breakfast an' milks the cow,
Then hurries to sweep an' make the bed
So she can sit an' sew.
Her hair is tight around her head,
Like crinkled ropes, 'cause her mother grinned,
An' hinted an' sniffed till she had it pinned,
An' I wish she never had come about;
For Emmie's hair when she let it fly
Made me think of the yellow rye
When a July storm comes quick an' the wind
Blows it backward up the hill.
It's queer to see it smooth and still,
Though it's shiny yet as a sleepy trout.
She says it's got to be out of the way,
With much to do an' more ahead,
An' a lookin' glass won't earn our bread.

"Far Bugles" in The Spotted Hawk *pages 26-27.*

critics as art. Still, these same critics will call the struggle of workers to free themselves "propaganda."[52]

Dargan worked hard to avoid writing propaganda. In an interview with Carol Bird for "Writers' Markets & Methods," she stressed that an aspiring writer must enjoy solitude, transport him or herself into other people's skins, and "shy from writers who seem magnetized by the dump-heap and its hopeless pathology."[53]

To the end of her life, Dargan continued to express conflicting feelings about being a poet and being socially responsible. "The thing that most frequently stymies me," she wrote a friend, "is a suffocating sense of guilt. In the world we breathe in to-day every moment calls one to its own job, and it isn't 'poetry.'"[54]

TURNING TO NOVELS

Dargan's acquaintances were constantly advising her to turn her talent to popular romances. In her story, "Serena and the Wild Strawberries," a Chicago woman visiting the author at her mountain farm dispenses such wisdom.

The woman tells the author:

I think, my dear, that if you wish to memorialize a passing folk, you will find material more worthy of your pen in the twilight of the bourgeoisie....These mountain people will not have even a fossilized survival. They live in a cul de sac, a pocket of society, and will never fit into its limits.[55]

In West Asheville, Dargan began work on *Call Home the Heart*, a novel that made the transition from the heartache of a mountain woman's life to the horror of the industrial promised land. Not completely sure about her new path, Dargan depended upon the man who was to become her most important friend, Grant Knight, University of Kentucky professor and author of *The Novel in English*. Knight filled a vacuum in her life, and Dargan sought him out as a mentor.

On Bluebonnet Lodge stationery dated November 6, 1929, Dargan told Knight about her feeling of isolation in her new home. "When I said 'there are no people here,' I did not mean artists and writers," she explained. "We do have them with us. But 'real people' to me are only those who understand that a new society is a-borning. That is why I fell so quickly for you and Mrs. Knight." In a postscript, she added, "The book is coming on—a not too warm red—and not, I hope, 'doctrinaire.'"[56]

By 1932, when *Call Home the Heart* was completed, Dargan knew that her novel would lose her friends. She even hesitated to publish it, as her friend Virginia Terrell Lathrop related, "until a friend from Kentucky [Grant Knight]—a critic and author—persuaded her to let him take it to a publisher, under the pseudonym of Fielding Burke."[57]

Originally, Dargan had chosen the pseudonym, Tradd Burke—a sword-like and Charlestonian name, she thought—to throw off political opponents.[58] Later, she changed it to Fielding Burke, affected by the tragic death of Fielding Truett, a friend's 16-year old relative.[59] On February 12, 1932, Dargan wrote Grant Knight, "you mustn't do anything that would connect Fielding Burke with Olive Dargan. The publishers are taking every precaution to guard my pseudonym."[60]

On February 27, Dargan wrote Mr. Chase, her publisher at Longmans, Green and Company, that she feared that Helen Stallings, wife of the reviewer Laurence Stallings, would blab. Helen had gushed to another friend, Joy Kime Benton, "Of course it [the novel] is red, but who with intelligence isn't nowadays?" If her friends revealed "what they must know I have taken great pains to conceal," Dargan flared, "I shall embarrass them with a public denial. I shall lie like Jehovah, and foreswear friendship forever."[61]

One week after the book was out, Laurence Stallings, who called Dargan's novel stunning and great, did blab. Dargan wrote to Knight, "I actually felt as if I wanted to meet him publicly and slap his [Stallings'] face. Slap it hard."[62]

REFUGE IN ALMOND

In the wake of her exposure as the author of *Call Home the Heart* and her feelings of being censured, Dargan retreated to a house she owned in Almond along the Nantahala River. The previous summer, she had already been hustling to fix up the place. In a letter to Grant Knight, in May, 1931, she alluded to having "to surrender and give up" her house in West Asheville and move to what she called a shack with no conveniences and no furniture. "One has to sled things uphill for about three hundred yards, leaving one's car at the foot" of the "camping place."[63] A month later, Dargan wrote Knight that the little camp "will be my address for some time."[64]

One old neighbor, Sylvia Latshaw, reflected that Dargan had been blacklisted, but she didn't mind because in Almond:

> ...nobody knew anything about it and no one cared....We weren't even reading the daily papers. We don't get them out there. And we didn't have

time to read them if we had gotten them. There she [Dargan] stayed until the hue and cry died down.[65]

Ralph Stanberry, a young neighbor at the time, says, "She was just looking for a place that would accept her and let her have her privacy."[66] Commenting on the local code of behavior, Louis Wild, a cultural historian and an Almond family descendant, notes that Almond was one of the last places in the eastern United States that actually had a shoot-out in the street. Yet, according to wisdom he attributes to his uncle, Clyde Bates, "As long as you minded your own business, you never had any trouble with anyone in Almond."[67]

In *Highland Annals*, Dargan wrote about farm managers who confront a deacon who's been stealing the narrator's hogs. Accusations are inferred and a fight boils up, but two factors prevent it from happening. The deacon's retort comes with a smile, for "you could say anything in the mountains if you took care to say it laughing." Finally, the deacon backs away from an admission of dishonesty by

In 1941 Dargan published a second edition of Highland Annals *retitled* From My Highest Hill: Carolina Mountain Folks. *This edition included stories and 50 photographs by North Carolina photographer Bayard Wootten. The original dust jacket pictures local realtor Bergin Edwards posing as a character written about a generation earlier. (Dust jacket,* From My Highest Hill: Carolina Mountain Folks, *[Philadelphia: J. B. Lippincott, 1941]. Cover photograph Bayard Wootten.)*

suggesting an exchange of favors. "Asking a favor was more disarming than laughter," Dargan notes.[68]

Residents of Almond may have minded their own business, but some still had strong political sentiments. Louis Wild quotes his mother, Mildred Bates' observation that "anyone who was not a Democrat was considered a Communist."[69]

Dargan was on the acceptable side in this case. In one of her few forays into active politics, she had worked with Sylvia Latshaw's husband getting out the Democratic vote in Almond. She put a number of men up overnight to make sure they got to the polls the next morning.[70]

LIVING THROUGH THE SCARE

Back in Asheville, it was different. In 1950, when the Red Scare became legitimized in government hearings, Dargan wrote Ruth Knight, "Asheville is rapidly progressing backward, with no one left in the vanguard to be talked to with safety."

Above. Bayard Wootten's photo of the bee-tree that was felled in 1939 and then written into Dargan's revision of "About Granpap and Trees." (Photo by Bayard Wootten; first published in From My Highest Hill; *courtesy, North Carolina Collection, University of North Carolina Library at Chapel Hill.)*

Above. Bayard Wootten photograph, published in From My Highest Hill, *of Joe Simonds' family around the dinner table in their Round Top cabin. Simonds was caretaker of Olive Dargan's property in the '30s and '40s. (Photo by Bayard Wootten; first published in* From My Highest Hill; *courtesy, North Carolina Collection, University of North Carolina Library at Chapel Hill.)*

She related how a local chaplain had been made to resign because he was Secretary of the Peace Fellowship of Presbyterians, "and not a voice has been heard in protest. I myself adopted the discretion of an oyster."[71]

For two decades, Dargan jockeyed back and forth between two homes, living a double life. When inhabiting one place, she used the other to provide friends a refuge. In July, 1932, she invited the Knights to stay at Bluebonnet for "cool, creative hours." She let them know about the spartan accommodations.

> There are four beds counting the one in the study, and there is a cot in the yard, and mattress on the shed-bench, which can be put wherever you want it....The frigidaire has never been out of order since I've had it....Of course you know about de-frosting the snow rods once a week....You will find the little cage for the fuse on the wall....If ants should begin to bother, get a 25 cent box of stuff at Eckerd's that will banish them.[72]

She added the note: "Mrs. Jones—my daughter = friend—will be out to see you and give you any helpful information in the domestic line." Marie Dobbs Jones was a close friend to Dargan in Asheville. During the 1932-33 school year, Jones stayed at Bluebonnet along with her eight-year-old daughter, Bubbles. Sixty-six years later, Bubbles Marlowe recalls how Dargan made several trips to Almond, loading her Buick with supplies and carting them up a hill.[73]

Dargan cared so much about Marie Jones and her daughter, and was so fearful of any harm that might come to them because of her, she arranged to have a fellow whom Bubbles described as "a cowboy" come down from the mountains and walk Bubbles to and from Vance School every day. The cowboy wasn't available the first days of school, so Bubbles stayed home until he arrived.[74]

Later in her life, Bubbles' mother told her that Dargan had received a note threatening kidnapping. This was the year that Charles Lindbergh's son had been kidnapped. In fact, Marie Jones had called the police when, on a walk with Bubbles in the nearby woods, she'd come across a mattress. Everyone across the nation had been looking for clues to the Lindbergh case.[75]

In Almond, Dargan's relocation was not going so well. She was so busy, she missed the Knights completely on their visit. She wrote them, "I've thrown away the whole summer. My shelter on the hill does not protect me from guests—and the woods are full of 'chigoes.' So where can I flee?"[76]

Privacy to write was always a big

Bayard Wootten's photo of Ralph Stanberry (left), a Beebread boy and Dargan's riverside neighbor, posing in the stream by his home. (Photo by Bayard Wootten; first published in From My Highest Hill; *courtesy, North Carolina Collection, University of North Carolina Library at Chapel Hill.)*

Ralph Stanberry (below), nearly 50 years later, posing in the same location as in the Wootten photo. (Photo, the author.)

issue. Ralph Stanberry, who grew up just over the rise from Dargan's home along the Nantahala River, recalls stopping by Dargan's cabin once to ask if he could hunt rabbits in her woods. Dargan had no objection to hunting, but she noted, "I just need quiet. It's okay with me if the dogs don't bark."[77]

DARGAN WRITES AND TRAVELS

During the mid-1930s, Dargan's situation was in chaos, as she told Ruth Knight, excusing her failure to send a letter she had written the year before.[78] She traveled, partly for business reasons; she attended to friends in need; and she worked on *A Stone Came Rolling*, the sequel to *Call Home the Heart*. In that same letter to Ruth Knight, she asked that she "please tell Dr. Knight I've a new book nearly ready to tumble onto the public, and if he finds he can't like it, I hope he can be patient with it and me."[79]

The new novel was more exclusively "proletarian" than the first, and Dargan was fretting over what she had wrought. A few months after the book's publication in 1936, she heard from John Townshend, bookseller and her "dear old sweetheart." He requested a copy of her book and apparently teased her about the time that had passed without any contact.

Dargan responded:

My dear Johnny: Talk about desertions! It was you who left me lone. I thought you had thrown me over because of my political heresies so I said "That's that" —and tried to forget.

As he'd asked, she'd try to find a copy of *A Stone Came Rolling* for him, but, she commented:

I can't keep one unless I hide it. Isn't that fine? But I warn you that you are not going to like the book. I shall get out another volume of poetry, just to make you forgive me for the novel.[80]

By the end of the 1930s, Dargan was already 70 years old. She did not turn to writing poetry just then. A far more inter-esting opportunity came up—to work with the famous Chapel Hill photographer, Bayard Wootten, to produce images for a revised edition of *Highland Annals*. It would be retitled, *From My Highest Hill: Carolina Mountain Folks*, with the addition of two new stories by Dargan, and published in 1941.

It must have been a sweet time for Dargan—a return to the spirit of her earlier work and to a simpler time. The neighborhood kids who had gotten to know her posed as if they were the previous generation of kids—characters in stories written in the teens and early 1920s. The juxtaposition created some ironies.

For the front cover of the book, the publisher used Wootten's photo of Bergin Edwards sitting on a rail fence looking out over the mountains from the highway. Edwards was the man who, years later, completed the deforestation of Round Top. Wootten also had fourteen-year-old Ralph Stanberry pose on a rock in the creek that ran past his house to the river. A few years later, Ralph's home was razed by the Tennessee Valley Authority and the foundation covered by Lake Fontana.

In the Wootten photos, Dargan assigns the figure of James Simonds the character name, Len, the tireless farmer married to light-hearted Serena. James Simonds, in actuality, was the overseer of Dargan's farm just before she sold it. To help her, he arranged to have another resident, Isaac Wiggins, log Dargan's property for the lumber while he retained the cord and pulpwood for her.[81]

James Simonds' son, Ray, about 15 years old at the time, remembers how Wiggins "would get through logging in the evening, and he would let me ride the steers back to the barn."[82] The steers pulled the felled trees to the "landing," where they were loaded onto a truck. One evening, the truck overturned on the steep road, and Wootten was there to photograph it.

Ray Simonds also remembers cradling wheat in the fields with his father and brother when Wootten came by. In the book, the reference is to Len's crop of wheat, rye, and produce. At the time of the photo shoot, Ray recalls Dargan coming out to them with the exotic present of bananas.[83]

James and Ray are also pictured in a Wootten photo of a bee-tree being felled for the benefit of its wood and honey, evoking a traditional mountain practice and an important episode in *From My Highest Hill*. The earlier edition of the story—in *Highland Annals*—had barely mentioned bee-trees. Granpap, searching with the narrator for a board tree, allows himself to be distracted from the author's favorite specimen with talk of bees, and Grandpap recites:

> A swarm in May,
> Count a dollar a day;
> A swarm in June,
> A silver spoon;
> A swam in July,
> Not worth a house-fly.[84]

But, the revised edition adds one-and-a-half pages to Granpap's bee-tree reverie. He remarks that the huge yellow poplar that the narrator had once hated losing would have rotted with the "holler" working on it. Instead, they all got 5,645 feet of good saw timber. "Better you let it put money in yer pocket," Granpap says, "than turn it over to dry rot an' the bees."[85]

The revision allowed Dargan to connect the story to the bee-tree cutting that took place in 1939; and to have Wootten's photos correspond exactly to the action. The WWII generation could truly believe that they were represented in the book written shortly after WWI—because they <u>were</u> represented there, once the book had been revised.[86]

Folks in Almond remember Ed Bates, the champion bee tracker. His son, Clyde, confirms that his family had been share-croppers on Round Top, and his dad had been the one who had located the tree shown in the Wootten photo. Ed had located many others as well, despite the fact that he'd been allergic to bees![87]

Clyde's nephew, Louis Wild, who col-

The village of Almond was flooded by the TVA in 1943 to form Fontana Lake. This 1939 photo by Bayard Wootten of the valley prior to the flooding shows the cluster of buildings Dargan called "Beebread" in her fiction. (Photo by Bayard Wootten; first published in From My Highest Hill; *courtesy, North Carolina Collection, University of North Carolina Library at Chapel Hill.)*

View of same site, 1998. (Photo, the author.)

lects Almond history, recalls, "Back in the old days, one of the skills was locating bee trees. He [Ed Bates] would set up a board, put sugar on it, mix water with it. He would get a beeline and mark the tree...with his brand." Those who harvested the honey had to ask him for permission.[88]

When in the story, Granpap finds and cuts down the beautiful, old tree—the one

A visiting black Harvard graduate makes a speech at a Fourth of July celebration.

"Let's suppose a case [says the speaker]. Suppose that some great disaster were to sweep ten million families out to sea and leave 'em on a desert island to starve and rot. That would be what you might call an act of God, maybe. But suppose a manner of government that humans have set up and directed, drives ten million families into the pit of poverty and starvation? That's no act of God. That's our fool selves actin' like lunatics. What humans have set up they can take down....Whoever says we've got to have a capitalist government when we want a workers' government, is givin' the lie to the great founders of these United States...."

A Stone Came Rolling, *page 161.*

that Dargan's narrator most revered—it symbolized what was to happen in reality on Round Top.

"If tree-worship was ever the religion of any tribe," Dargan had commented in "About Granpap and Trees," "I know that I am ancestrally bound to that folk."[89]

Yet, finances led Dargan to sell her property to Bergin Edwards in 1944 for $3,500.[90] Edwards held it for a few years for the timber,[91] and then sold it to a realtor[92] who sold it to DeWitt Tree Farms for a white pine nursery.[93] The DeWitts then sold a piece to Tom Thrash, owner of a pulp mill outside of Waynesville. Now, no tree on Round Top survives as a Dargan landmark.

THE FLOOD

Not long after Dargan finished working on *Highland Annals* with Bayard Wootten, the Tennessee Valley Authority began buying up lots in Almond in order to create Lake Fontana and a hydroelectric plant. In March, 1943, Dargan reported to Grant Knight in a postscript:

I have lived over here for the most part since last July. The TVA is tearing up the country, and I am impatiently waiting to know what they will do with my "forty acres" and buildings.[94]

Two months later, reviewing Grant Knights' sonnets for him, Dargan noted that she herself had been half-drowned in a "flood of practicalities." She meant to dedi-

cate the summer to "that long hoped-for book," but the TVA, whose principles she endorsed but not its methods, snatched that plan out of the picture.[95]

I needn't repeat to you how I feel in this era of transition, she wrote. I sympathize most deeply with the sensitive nature that abhors it....But I...submit to the terrific moral drive within, keeping the future before me like a present and actual reward. You say the struggle isn't worth it even if we attain our dream, but it is all that keeps me alive. The dream, when attained, may drop into the void that you expect, but we'll have had a great run for our money.[96]

In the prophetic, closing pages of *Highland Annals*, the author gazes at the new highway, which was so "monstrously magical, so rapidly obliterating" the region which she dubbed Unakasia—"the Unakasia of my intimate care and delight. Within a few years, the ways and customs of Atlantis would not be more dim in time."[97]

DARGAN'S LAST DECADE

In 1956, when she was 87 years old, and still writing (two more books, including the award-winning poetry collection, *The Spotted Hawk* were still to come), Dargan sold her home in West Asheville to a couple who agreed to let her live upstairs. Dargan had "always dreaded the thought of going into a nursing home"[98] so "she hunted up a couple," Sylvia Latshaw, Dargan's friend, recalled. "She actually sold them her house with the understanding that she would live in it as long as she lived, and they would look after her. She turned over the first floor to them...."[99] The house was only a story and a half. Dargan's space was reached by stairs. There was "a makeshift arrangement with her water and toilet," said Latshaw.

Nancy Brown, who owned Book Mart, an antiquarian bookstore in Biltmore, from 1947 until she closed it in 1990, has keen memories of her visit to Bluebonnet Lodge, Christmastime, January, 1958. She

THE CABIN THAT SURVIVED THE FLOOD

Right. James and Nola Simonds' cabin and yard with stacks of posts. (Courtesy, North Carolina Collection, Pack Memorial Public Library, Asheville, North Carolina.)

One of the buildings with which Dargan had been associated has survived the flood created by the damming of Lake Fontana in 1943: the 1860 Stillwell cabin. James Simonds, Dargan's farm manager, and his family had been the last tenants, occupying it from December, 1937 to December, 1945.

A half century later, Bob Robinson, Clyde Bates' brother-in-law, looking for an ideal cabin, found the disused Simonds house, and entered into an agreement with Dennis DeWitt, owner of DeWitt Tree Farms, by which he moved it to a site a few miles away on New Fontana Road in Bryson City.[1] The find ended Robinson's long quest to emulate the 1821 Brannon cabin in Wilkinson County, Georgia, which he had come to love through a photograph in a book.[2]

A close look at Robinson's cabin reveals how it had been constructed with the timber that had been close at hand in Dargan's old woods. The ten big logs that make up what is now the front side (but had been the back) are, from top to bottom: poplar-chestnut-chestnut-chestnut-poplar-chestnut-poplar-pine-oak-pine.

Notes

1. Bob Robinson, author interview, January 30, 1998.
2. Alex W. Bealer and John O. Ellis, *The Log Cabin: Homes of the North American Wilderness* (Barre, Massachusetts, 1978).

The Simonds cabin after being moved and renovated by Swain County resident, Bob Robinson. (Photo, the author.)

The Round Top cabin occupied by Dargan's caretaker, James Simonds, and his family. James and Nola Simonds stand in front. The photograph is dated between 1937 and 1945. (Courtesy, Ray Simonds.)

and her partner stopped by to obtain copies of *From My Highest Hill*, already rare.

Nearly 90, Dargan climbed the rickety stairs to her room. "The stairway went up the wall," Brown observed. "One side had a rail you could hold to. She could have fallen and broken her neck."[100] After a half hour of searching, Dargan asked Brown to come help her. "I've never seen as much stuff in one room," said Brown. "The table, the floor, the bed, under the bed." Brown fetched the books from under the bed and took them downstairs to the dining table.

"Of course, I wanted her to sign them," Brown related. "We pulled up a chair to the table with two or three big books on it." Dargan sat aloft. "She was a very small person. Like a little doll."[101]

Brown confirms the existence of a large mass of papers and manuscripts in the West Asheville house at a late date, and she explains the disarray:

> I think she had things arranged better but the people she had sold the house to wanted more and more room, and they just piled her stuff up any which way, and when she moved from there out to the nursing home, none of us had any idea what happened to her papers and her manuscripts. I'm afraid they just hauled them out and burned them.[102]

Dargan's will, dated February 28, 1961, bequeathed her papers and manuscripts to the University of Kentucky at Lexington, but her papers are not there. According to a telephone interview that Kathy Ackerman, a doctoral candidate, had with Peter Oliver, Dargan's great-grand nephew, Dargan's heirs had been instructed to burn her controversial letters after her death.[103] Yet in 1960, at the time that Dargan had been approached by University of Kentucky librarian, Lawrence Thompson, about her archives, Dargan had written her friend Ruth Grant:

> I am beginning to horrify myself with a creeping fear that instead of getting things finished and in place, I may drop off suddenly leaving everything in disorder, with a bonfire as the only result.[104]

Dargan had reason to fear the loss of her papers since much of her work had already been consumed by fire. In 1917, the boarding house in Almond, which Dargan had used as an office away from her cabin on Round Top, had burned. The fire had started in Dargan's room and had left its contents in ashes.[105] The destruction of her mountain cabin by fire in 1923 had been the event that had impelled her purchase of the house in West Asheville. In that fire, she lost what she considered to be her best play, "The Baron of Verulam," about Francis Bacon.[106] In the 1950s, a large mass of papers she had stored in a friend's barn were lost to a fire, at a time when Dargan had been seeking to avoid persecution during the McCarthy hearings.

In her West Asheville years, Dargan did not "drop off suddenly." She lived for 25 more years until the age of 99 despite a crippling procession of illnesses and ailments.

In June, 1955, she had written the Knights that she was "fighting for time to complete several literary projects," and adds, "I seem to have lived too long," her old admirers all dead, her "last and best novel wiped from the public slate." Then this uncharacteristic admission:

> ... most of the time I've felt like a paralytic deprived all over of move-

ment except the power to smile. I have built up an inner dignity that makes life bearable, but that is all.[107]

Dargan invited the Knights down for a visit, remarking that the new West Asheville Bridge shortens the distance to downtown Asheville. But no visit came. Grant Knight died nine months later.

Dargan published *The Spotted Hawk*, a perfectly pitched and focused book of poems, in 1958. It won the Thomas Wolfe, Roanoke-Chowan, and Oscar Arnold Young awards; and led to her being honored as one of the nation's great poets by the Poetry Society in New York City.[108] In one poem, "Vain Rescue," she imagines her death. It ends with these words:

> But rising now no inner fires out-flow,
> No gleam around me save a pale moon's haze.
> I know a wood of beech and birch and snow
> That waits my step. And come the June-warm days,
> Where two brooks wed I'll find a lulling seat,
> And stir white pebbles with my slow, bare feet.[109]

Reading the good reviews for *The Spotted Hawk*, Dargan in 1960 wrote Sylvia and Harry Latshaw that the comments have given her the "courage to go on writing." She also gained new friends and found satisfaction in "the small circle of the life we know." Summing up, she recalled "an old motto, or guide-post, that I found (I think in the Bible) that gave me serenity and strength....'I tarry in peace, and am clad with power.'"[110] In 1962, at the age of 93, Olive Dargan published her last work, *Innocent Bigamy and Other Stories*.

About one year before her death in 1968, Olive Dargan was moved to a nursing home—a modest one by Nancy Brown's description. The facility was in Biltmore, just south of Asheville, and Brown, who visited at least once a week, did not remember encountering other visitors.

But there had been at least one other visitor—the acclaimed novelist and chronicler, Wilma Dykeman. In her 1968 book of essays, *Look to This Day*, Dykeman describes coming upon Dargan in her small square room, "strapped into a rocking chair so that she would not, in her feebleness, fall."[111] She wrote:

> I told her about all the books she had written in the past and she struggled to remember, seemed overwhelmed that I should have remembered. I saw her spirit fluttering feebly in a cage, caught between a yesterday that had been quick with creativity and accomplishment and a tomorrow that was bleak with inertia.
>
> It took some effort to break her grip on my hand as I made ready to depart.
>
> Don't leave me. Her eyes were wide and round, desperate in their emptiness, Don't leave me.[112]

In 1994, the new residents of Dargan's old West Asheville neighborhood, Falconhurst, persuaded the State Department of Transportation to erect a sign on Haywood Road designating the site of Dargan's home a landmark. They also used the Dargan legacy to influence Buncombe County's commissioners to allow the seven acres of woods the county owned in Falconhurst to be preserved as a woods. In October, 2000, Olive Tilford Dargan's contributions as a writer were recognized with her induction into the North Carolina Literary Hall of Fame.

Olive Tilford Dargan's grave marker, Green Hills Cemetery in West Asheville. (Photo, the author.)

Notes

1. Alice Stone Blackwell to Juan B. Delgado, September 1918, *Letters and Papers of Alice Stone Blackwell*, Records of the National Woman Suffrage Association, Library of Congress.
2. John Henry Chadwick, speaking of Dargan's first book of plays, *Semiramis and Other Plays,* as quoted in the *Charlotte Observer*, July 24, 1932.
3. Jonathan Daniels about *Call Home the Heart* in *The Saturday Review of Literature*, February 20, 1932.
4. Charlotte Young interview by Louis D. Silveri, August 26, 1975, Southern Highlands Research Center, University of North Carolina, Asheville.
5. Virginia Terrell Lathrop, "Olive Tilford Dargan," typed manuscript, August 25, 1959, from Southern Historical Collection, University of North Carolina, Chapel Hill.
6. Dorcas Carland, "The News Personality of the Week" interview with Dargan, reported in *West Asheville News*, December 11, 1942.
7. Letter to John Townshend, November 1, 1958, *Olive Tilford Dargan Papers*, Special Collections and Archives, University of Kentucky at Lexington.
8. Ibid.
9. Sylvia Arrowood Latshaw and her sister Mrs. Mason, interview by Ellen Neal and Carol DeWallis, November 24, 1976, Southern Historical Collection, University of North Carolina, Chapel Hill.
10. "Mrs. Dargan Dies at 99," January 23, 1968, *Asheville Times*.
11. Dargan to Alice Stone Blackwell, July 30, 1907, *Olive Tilford Dargan Papers*, Houghton Library, Harvard University.
12. Carland.
13. Kathy Cantley Ackerman, "Olive Tilford Dargan: Recovering a Proletarian Romantic," (Ph.D. thesis), University of South Carolina, 1991.
14. Lathrop.
15. Carland.
16. Latshaw, interview.
17. Ibid.
18. Ackerman.
19. Dargan to Alice Stone Blackwell, April 7, 1916, Records of the National Woman's Suffrage Association, Library of Congress.
20. Dargan to Alice Stone Blackwell, n.d., May 1906, *Olive Tilford Dargan Papers*, Houghton Library, Harvard University.

21. Dargan to Alice Stone Blackwell, July 30, 1907, *Olive Tilford Dargan Papers*, Houghton Library, Harvard University.
22. Dargan to Alice Stone Blackwell, April 28, 1908, *Olive Tilford Dargan Papers*, Houghton Library, Harvard University.
23. Dargan to William Crary Brownell, January 7, 1909, *William Crary Brownell Papers*, Amherst College Library.
24. Elizabeth Rogers Payne, "Anne Whitney: Nineteenth Century Sculptor and Liberal" (Masters thesis), Wellesley College, Margaret Clapp Library Archives.
25. Alice Stone Blackwell to Anne Whitney, April 13, 1913, quoted in Payne, op. cit.
26. Horace Rudisill, phone interview. A Darlington County historian, he bases his information on his grandmother's stories and on a large file of documents in the Historical Commission's office.
27. Latshaw, interview.
28. Pegram Dargan, "The Quarrel," *Carolina Ditties* (New York: The Literary Collector Press, 1904), pp. 11-12.
29. Fern McHan, "Mrs. Olive Tilford Dargan," high school term paper, Almond High School, ca. 1933.
30. Olive Tilford Dargan, *Call Home the Heart* (New York: Longmans, Green and Company, 1932), p. 1.
31. J.C. Freeman, author interview, December 23, 1997.
32. Ibid.
33. Lathrop.
34. Dargan to Alice Stone Blackwell, May 12, 1913, Library of Congress.
35. Jessie Anderson Johnson, author interview, March 11, 1998.
36. Dargan to Alice Stone Blackwell, April 7, 1916, Library of Congress.
37. Ibid.
38. Dargan to William Crary Brownell, June 12, 1916, *William Crary Brownell Papers*, Amherst College Library.
39. Carland.
40. Olive Tilford Dargan, *Highland Annals* (New York: Charles Scribner's Sons, 1925), p. 204.
41. Olive Tilford Dargan, "Coretta and Autumn" in *From My Highest Hill: Carolina Mountain Folks* (Philadelphia: J.P. Lippincott Co., 1941), p. 38-39. This volume is a revised edition of *Highland Annals*.
42. Lathrop.
43. Ibid.
44. "Olive Dargan Starts Work on New Novel," *Asheville Citizen*, May 24, 1932.
45. Latshaw, interview.
46. *Asheville Times*, May 26, 1932.
47. "A Western North Carolina Club Woman Interviews the Author of *A Stone Came Rolling*," *The North Carolina Clubwoman*, January, 1936.
48. Ibid.
49. *The Smoky Mountain Times*, March 26, 1998.
50. "Olive Dargan Starts Work on New Novel," op cit, both quotes.
51. Rachel Dyas, "Noted Poet Lives in Log Cabin Gathering Her Inspiration from Blue Hills Around Her Home," *Asheville Times*, n.d., in clippings file, Sondley North Carolina Collection, Pack Memorial Public Library, Asheville, North Carolina.
52. Anthony Buttitta, "Rebellion in the South," Raleigh *News & Observer*, September 29, 1935.
53. Carol Reed, "Write for the Future: Advice on Writing with Social Purpose—An Interview with Fielding Burke," *Writers' Markets & Methods*, February, 1950.
54. Dargan to Ruth Knight, September 19, 1950, Grant Knight Papers, Special Collections, University of Kentucky at Lexington.
55. Dargan, *From My Highest Hill*, p. 59.
56. Dargan to Grant Knight, November 6, 1929, Special Collections, University of Kentucky at Lexington.
57. Lathrop.
58. Dargan to Grant Knight, written in Almond, N.C., July 12, 1931, Special Collections, University of Kentucky, Lexington.
59. Annie Mae Truett, author interview, Bryson City, November, 1997.

You hear the bees hum skyward in the poplars,

Making the sweetest honey of the year,

And watch a cloud that like a tinted mop blurs

A neighbor mountain's bold and green half-sphere

With freakish push and start, and with a drop leers

In at the cabin doors, or dares to take

A roll in gardens, like a playing lake.

And there's a sound so near it seems to bubble

Out of your heart and tingle through your skin.

You creep around the lin that rises double

And where a clump of forest lilies thin

Themselves to three that rise with little trouble

To a graceful score of feet before they droop

Their spotted heads, you catch your breath and stoop;

For you have found it; found the mossy parting

Where a mountain rillet breaks into the light;

An infant on its seaward way outstarting.

"Sall's Gap" in Lute and Furrow, *pages 42-43.*

60. Dargan to Grant Knight, February 12, 1932, *Grant Knight Papers*, Special Collections, University of Kentucky at Lexington.
61. Dargan to Mr. Chase, February 27, 1932, *Grant Knight Papers*, Special Collections, University of Kentucky at Lexington.
62. Dargan to Grant Knight, April 1, 1932, *Grant Knight Papers*, Special Collections, University of Kentucky at Lexington.
63. Dargan to Grant Knight, May 18, 1931, *Grant Knight Papers*, Special Collections, University of Kentucky at Lexington.
64. Dargan to Grant Knight, June 22, 1931, *Grant Knight Papers*, Special Collections, University of Kentucky at Lexington.
65. Latshaw, interview.
66. Ralph Stanberry and Ray Simonds, author interview at Simonds' house in Bryson City, February 5, 1998.
67. Louis Wild, author interview, April 1, 1998.
68. Dargan, *Highland Annals*, p. 151.
69. Louis Wild, author interview, January 24, 1998.
70. Latshaw, interview.
71. Dargan to Ruth Knight, September 19, 1950, *Grant Knight Papers*, Special Collections, University of Kentucky at Lexington.
72. Dargan to Grant Knight, Almond, N.C., July 27, 1932, *Grant Knight Papers*, Special Collections, University of Kentucky at Lexington.
73. Bubbles Marlowe, author interview, March 11, 1998.
74. Ibid.
75. Ibid.
76. Dargan to Ruth and Grant Knight, n.d. [1932], *Grant Knight Papers*, Special Collections, University of Kentucky at Lexington.
77. Ralph Stanberry, author's walking interview, February 5, 1998.
78. Dargan to Ruth Knight, September 24, 1935, *Grant Knight Papers*, Special Collections, University of Kentucky at Lexington.
79. Ibid.
80. Dargan to John Townshend, May 30, 1936, *Olive Tilford Dargan Papers*, Special Collections and Archives, University of Kentucky at Lexington, both quotes.
81. Simonds and Stanberry, interview.
82. Ibid.
83. Ibid.
84. Dargan, *Highland Annals*, p. 18.
85. Dargan, *From My Highest Hill*, p. 21
86. Dargan, *From My Highest Hill*. For more information on photographer Bayard Wootten see Jerry W. Cotten, *Light and Air: The Photography of Bayard Wootten* (Chapel Hill, N.C.: The University of North Carolina Press, 1998).
87. Clyde Bates, author interview, January 24, 1998.
88. Louis Wild, phone interview with the author, January 24, 1998.
89. Dargan, *Highland Annals*, p.16.
90. Simonds and Stanberry, interview, February 5, 1998.
91. Ray Simonds, phone interview with the author, March 29, 1998.
92. Swain County Register of Deeds.
93. Simonds interview, March 29, 1998.
94. Dargan to Grant Knight, March 18, 1943, *Grant Knight Papers*, Special Collections, University of Kentucky at Lexington.
95. Dargan to Grant Knight, May 24, 1943, *Grant Knight Papers*, Special Collections, University of Kentucky at Lexington. Both quotes.
96. Ibid.
97. Dargan, *Highland Annals*, p. 285.
98. Latshaw, interview.
99. Ibid.
100. Nancy Brown, author interview, November 17, 1997.
101. Ibid.
102. Ibid.
103. Ackerman, p. 64.
104. Dargan to Ruth Knight, December 27, 1960, *Grant Knight Papers*, Special Collections, University of Kentucky at Lexington.
105. Jessie Anderson Johnson, granddaughter of Ida Conley, the Almond boarding house owner, author interview, March 11, 1998.
106. Lathrop.
107. Dargan to Ruth and Grant Knight, June 10, 1955, *Grant Knight Papers*, Special Collections, University of Kentucky at Lexington, all four quotes.
108. Dargan obituary, *Asheville Times*, January 23, 1968.
109. Olive Tilford Dargan, *The Spotted Hawk* (Winston-Salem: John F. Blair, Publisher, 1958), p.60.
110. Dargan to Sylvia and Harry Latshaw, January 16, 1960, *Sylvia Louise Arrowood Latshaw Papers*, Southern Historical Collection, University of North Carolina at Chapel Hill.
111. Wilma Dykeman, *Look to This Day* (New York: Holt, Rinehart & Winston, 1968), p. 106.
112. Ibid.

Literary Works of Olive Tilford Dargan

Semiramis, and Other Plays, (New York: Brentano's, 1904). Drama in verse. 255 pages.

Lords and Lovers and Other Dramas, (New York: Charles Scribner's Sons, 1906). Drama in verse. Stage rights for one of these plays "The Shepherd" was purchased by Henry Sothern, allowing Dargan to buy the property in Almond, North Carolina. 315 pages.

The Mortal Gods and Other Plays, (New York: Charles Scribner's Sons, 1912). A collection of plays. 383 pages.

The Welsh Pony, (England, 1913). Privately printed. A collection of short stories.

Path Flower and Other Verses, (London: J.M. Dent & Sons Ltd. and New York: Charles Scribner's Sons, 1914). Dargan's first published book of poetry. 120 pages.

The Cycle's Rim, (New York: Charles Scribner's Sons, 1916). A collection of 53 sonnets, dedicated to the memory of Dargan's late husband, Pegram. 73 pages.

The Flutter of the Gold Leaf and Other Plays, (New York: Charles Scribner's Sons, 1922). A collection of plays co-written with Frederick Peterson. 114 pages.

Lute and Furrow, (New York: Charles Scribner's Sons, 1922). Poetry. 140 pages.

Highland Annals, (New York: Charles Scribner's Sons, 1925). 8 sketches based on Dargan's experiences with her Almond, North Carolina neighbors. 286 pages.

Call Home the Heart, (New York: Longmans, Green and Company, 1932). Written under the pseudonym Fielding Burke. Proletarian novel depicting the role of mountain folks in the Gastonia, North Carolina mill strike. 432 pages.

A Stone Came Rolling, (New York: Longmans, Green and Company, 1935). Also, written under the pseudonym Fielding Burke. Sequel to *Call Home the Heart*. 412 pages.

From My Highest Hill: Carolina Mountain Folks, (Philadelphia: J. B. Lippincott, 1941). A revised version of *Highland Annals* with two additional sketches and 50 photographs by North Carolina photographer Bayard Wootten. 221 pages.

Sons of the Stranger: A Novel of Men, Women and Mining, (New York: Longmans, Green and Company, 1947). Historical, proletarian novel written under the pseudonym Fielding Burke set during a coal miners' strike in Colorado at the turn of the century. 405 pages.

The Spotted Hawk, (Winston-Salem: John F. Blair, 1958). Dargan's last published book of poetry. Winner of several book awards. 128 pages.

Innocent Bigamy and Other Stories, (Winston-Salem: John F. Blair, 1962). Dargan's last published book. A collection of 11 short stories. 261 pages.

This study is the result of two men trying to record and understand the building of Interstate 26 through Madison County, North Carolina. Construction moves like a fast glacier leveling and evening all in its path. Perhaps what is most mourned when the terrain is changed so radically, is the loss of mystery: it is now a known and defined place.

Our family often traveled the slow, winding road north to Johnson City, Tennessee, creating a repeating memory of the familiar landmarks. For many years we passed a sign which read "Locust post for sale." When, on one trip, the sign was gone, someone in the car commented that the man had finally sold his post, and on all later journeys when we passed the curve where the sign once stood, we would repeat the comment and laugh together. Now, not only the sign is gone, but the road and its curve rest under hundreds of feet of soil and crushed rock. Will there be similar signs on the new road to mark our journeys? Will we say "It used to take an hour and now it takes 15 minutes?" Perhaps the new road, and the system of which it is a part, will become a source of mythic visions, of new mysteries, songs and poetry, much as the railroad was in the 19th century. Songs and poetry have been written about memorable roads and gaps before. Surely there will be words and music about a road as historic as Interstate 26. —R.B.

The Roads of Madison County:

An Interpretative History

Text by Sam Gray,
Photography by Rob Amberg

MAP AND TERRITORY

It is not down on any map. True places never are.

-Herman Melville, *Moby Dick*

When Herman Melville wrote these words in 1851 the southern portion of the Appalachian mountain range abounded in "true places." It was well into the 20th century before the Southern Appalachian mountains began to relinquish their "true places" to survey-based cartography. The earliest maps of eastern North America that depict the southern mountains offer as little threat to the true places as they do real information about physiography, trails or place names. They often strike contemporary readers as graphic curiosities of nomenclature and iconography rather than actual maps. In the 17th and 18th centuries, details and features of the eastern coastal plain gradually appeared on maps, while the mountains to the west remained a wilderness; fanciful, unknown and "not down on any map." Mountains that were depicted seemed to have been drawn indiscriminately, with large areas left blank. They bore designations such as *Cheraque Mountains, Montes Auriferi, Apalchee, Apalty* or *Apalachee Mountains.* The latter word, destined to become the name of the great range, was

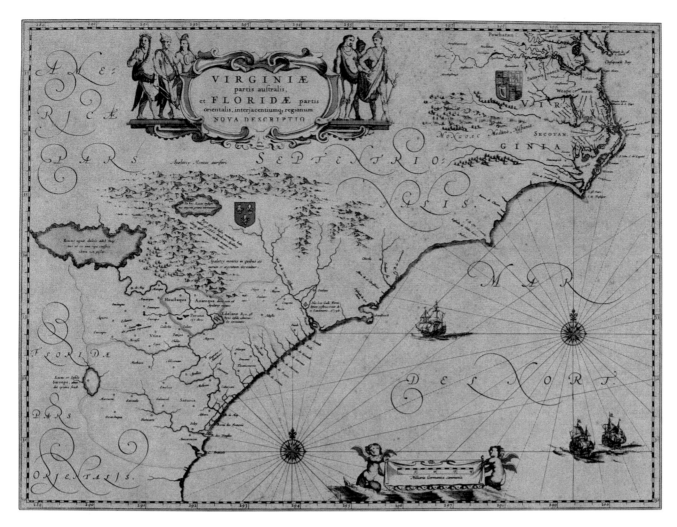

the name of a now extinct Muskhogean Indian tribe that became identified with this unknown region, even though the tribe's native ground lay outside the southernmost boundary of the range.[1]

Gerardus Mercator, the great Dutch cartographer who introduced spherical projection into western cartography, was the first to portray the Appalachians as a single unified mountain range, hundreds of miles long and lying along a southwest to northeast axis (Figure 1). Mercator, in a series of maps issued from 1564 to 1606, incorporated information from Spanish explorers including Hernando De Soto and Juan Pardo, both of whom passed through Western North Carolina. In spite of the customary 16th-century errors and omissions, it is clear on the Mercator maps that the Appalachians as a whole, particularly the portion of the range in the Carolinas, presented a formidable and rugged barrier for European immigrants moving west.

The first English-speaking explorer and cartographer to actually see Western North Carolina and contribute to its cartographic history was John Lederer, a German physician who traveled in the region in the early 1670s and wrote about his adventures in a book that included a map.[2] Unfortunately, Lederer's contributions were largely erroneous. He exaggerated the occasional swampy areas in the vicinity of Piedmont North Carolina into a vast swamp lying at the foot of the Blue Ridge Mountains. He ascribed the term "deserta arenosa" to the sandhills region southeast of the "Marsh." He also compounded the intriguing error made in previous and subsequent maps of placing an inland lake deep within the southern mountains (Figures 2-A, 2-B). Historians have speculated about the origins of this body of water that never was. Some have suggested that it is the misplaced Mississippi River; others implicate misunderstood accounts told by native peoples.[3] The Cherokee, who lived closest to the depicted lake, often told the story of a

Figure 1. Depictions of Western North Carolina on early European maps were not based on surveys or accurate cartographic information. Gerardus Mercator, the Dutch cartographer, produced a series of maps from 1564-1606 which did show the Apalatcy Montes as a range of mountains toward the west of the region, though their placement and other details were not accurate. This 1640 map by Blaeu, based largely on the Mercator-Hondius map of 1606, was the most accurate map then published and included more detailed nomenclature and geographic data than its predecessors. (Willem Blaeu, Virginiæ partis australis, et Floridæ; courtesy, Ingrid Wuerth.)

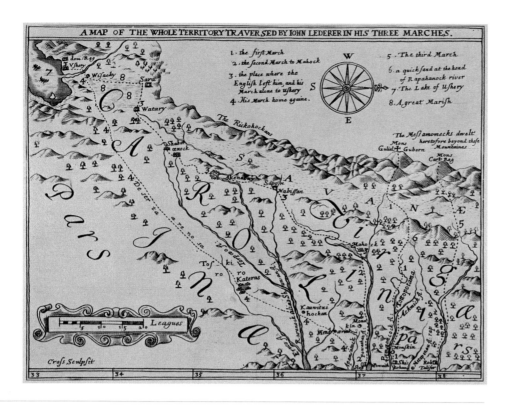

Figure 2-A. *Although John Lederer's map was based on his travels across Virginia and North Carolina in the 1670s, it contributed little to a geographic understanding of the region. The upper left of this drawing shows the "Great Lake of Ushery" which apparently referred to the Catawba Indian town of Ushery near the Catawba River. The "Great Marsh" is roughly in the area of Piedmont North Carolina. The eye strains to organize the information in this map: the Atlantic Ocean lies at the bottom of the image. (John Lederer,* A Map of the Whole Territory Traversed by John Lederer in His Three Marches*., 1672.)*

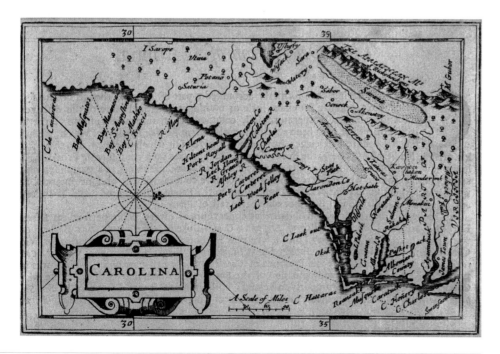

Figure 2-B. *About 1672 John Ogilby issued* The First Lord Proprietor's Map *based on the work of John Lederer with improved information but continued reference to the swamp in the Piedmont, and the great lake to the west. This miniature version (3-1/4 x 4-7/8 in.) titled* Carolina *was published by John Speed after the work of Ogilby in 1675. (Courtesy, Ingrid Wuerth.)*

magical healing lake called *Atagahi*, located somewhere deep within the mountains now called the Smoky Mountains. It could not be seen or reached except through diligent prayer and long fasting and was understood, at least by the Native Americans, to exist only within the domain of mythic narrative.[4] The North American map published by Dr. John Mitchell in 1755 was one of the most significant maps in American history. It was commissioned by an act of Parliament and drawn to facilitate understanding and manipulation of 18th-century geopolitical boundaries between English, French, Spanish and Native American territories[5] (Figure 3). Mitchell's cartographic depiction of the southern Appalachians was an improvement on all previous maps. The direction of flow of the important rivers is generally correct; the Cherokee lower, middle and upper towns are indicated with major towns individually named; and the north and south boundaries of the colony of North Carolina are established by surveyed lines. The western boundary of the state was at this time, the Mississippi River. Since Mitchell's map portrays all of North America, it could now be understood how expansive, significant and unique a feature the southern Appalachians were in the physiography of North America.

European settlement of the Western North Carolina mountains began in the decades following Dr. Mitchell's 1755 map and proceeded without benefit of better maps until long after the Revolutionary War. Veterans of that war were paid for their services in grants of frontier lands, and the Carolina back country was some of the most attractive real estate available.[6] Some of these settlers had newly arrived from the Shenandoah Valley of Virginia and the Watauga Settlement in northeast Tennessee. Others came from the Piedmont of North Carolina, moving generally west from settlements in Guilford, Burke and Rutherford Counties. These settlers were small scale agriculturists and livestock herders of mostly Scotch-Irish and Germanic origins.

Left. North Carolina Department of Transportation geologist, Rick Lockamy looking at survey maps, trying to locate the center line of the I-26 Corridor so core samples can be taken. Buckner Gap, 1994. (Photo, Rob Amberg.)

Figure 3. The 1755 map by the English cartographer, Dr. John Mitchell, portrayed the northern and southern boundaries of North Carolina based on surveyed lines. North Carolina included the current state of Tennessee. The western boundary of the state was the Mississippi River. (John Mitchell, detail of A Map of the British and French Dominions in North America, *1755.)*

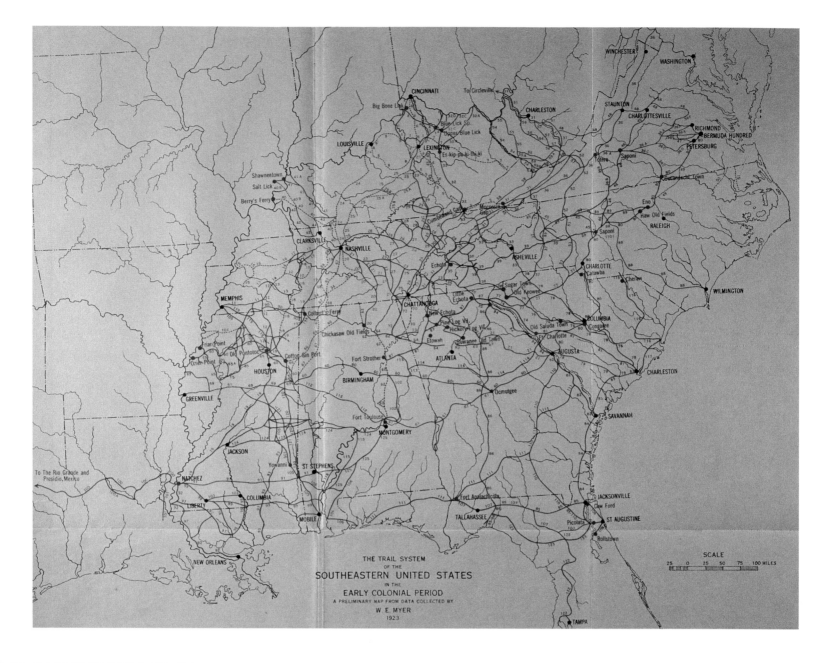

THE TRAIL SYSTEM
OF THE
SOUTHEASTERN UNITED STATES
IN THE
EARLY COLONIAL PERIOD
A PRELIMINARY MAP FROM DATA COLLECTED BY
W. E. MYER
1923

SCALE
25 0 25 50 75 100 MILES

Their farming practices combined Native American crops (squash, corn and beans) with old world herding and field management patterns derived from the Celtic regions of the British Isles and the upper Rhine areas of Germany.[7]

ROADS

One of the salient differences between contemporary and 18th century maps of the southern Appalachians is the relative absence of roads and trails on the latter. Edward Mosely published a map of North Carolina in 1733 which showed a trading path which ran diagonally across the Piedmont of North Carolina from western South Carolina to central Virginia. Mosely labeled this trail, *Indian Trading Road from the Cataubos and Charokee Indians to Virginia.*[8] This trail was one of many connecting pathways that had been created originally by movements of wild herd animals (bison, elk, deer) from salt licks to distant grazing areas. These game paths were incorporated by aboriginal peoples into an extensive trail system which was used for trade and warfare. The most famous of these, the Natchez Trace and the Warriors Trace, ran through hundreds of miles of Southeastern forest and were connected by dozens of tributary foot trails (Figure 4).

One of the earliest paths in what is now Madison County was called the Catawba Trail by European settlers and followed a route similar to what would later become the drovers road. This Indian trail was likely a game trail which had been in existence in some form for many years and probably ran from the area of Augusta, Georgia to near Knoxville, Tennessee.[9] One of the earliest references to a road in Madison County is found in papers submitted by Gov. William Blount to the Council of Tennessee in 1795 concerning opening a wagon road from the Buncombe courthouse to Tennessee. Two wagons arrived in Knoxville "having passed through the mountains by way of Warm Springs."[10]

In the 18th-century, portions of many 'traces' became mountain roads extending into new territories. The more seminal routes later became wagon roads such as the Buncombe Turnpike, completed in 1827, from Greeneville, Tennessee, to Greenville, South Carolina, both towns named for the same Revolutionary War hero, Gen. Nathaniel Greene. The Western Turnpike, much of it along the Rutherford Trace, ran from Salisbury, North Carolina, through Buncombe County to points west. It was well underway by the 1820s and completed by 1850. These two roads, like the Swannanoa and French Broad Rivers that partially shaped them, intersected at Asheville.

The first published map to indicate the existence of the creeks which fed into these two rivers, the small communities which had formed along the creeks, and some of the earliest roads in Western North Carolina, was the 1808 map of North Carolina published by Jon A. Price and John Strother (Figure 5). County survey information, and data from the 1799 commission to establish the North Carolina-Tennessee state line were the basis of this map.[11] Buncombe had been formed from Burke and Rutherford Counties in 1791, and the creation of the state of Tennesee in 1799 set the western boundary of Buncombe County and North Carolina. John Strother was the surveyor for this line and was later a major land owner in Buncombe County.

The Price-Strother map was the first map of the region to be drawn by a sur-

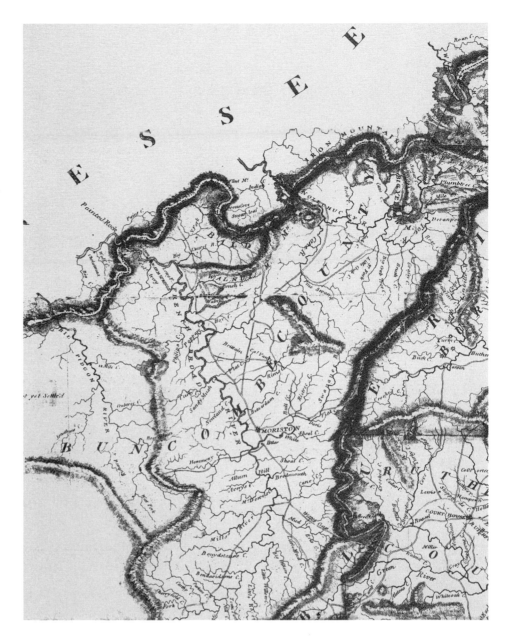

veyor who actually walked the trails and climbed the mountains, and is arguably the earliest published map that could have been used by a traveler to locate and travel a road in the mountains of Western North Carolina. Though not accurate by today's standards, the map clearly shows the stock road near the French Broad River between Warm Springs and Asheville that would in the next 20 years be improved to become the Buncombe Turnpike. An important tributary, the Bald Mountain Road, which veered to the northeast near present-day Weaverville and crossed into Tennessee through the Bald Mountains is also shown. The Bald Mountain Road was mentioned in Buncombe County road juries as early as 1792 and probably existed as a foot trail long before that.

Figure 5. The Price-Strother map published in 1808 was one of the first maps of Western North Carolina to indicate roads. The map shows the stock road from Moristown (Asheville) to Warm Springs, the Bald Mountain Road, and the Western Turnpike which ran from Salisbury (Rowan County), through Asheville and west to Georgia. (W. P. Cumming, North Carolina In Maps, *[Raleigh: State Department of Archives and History, 1966] Plate IX.)*

The creation and maintenance of some of the earliest roads was often a community effort, albeit not always voluntary. Groups of men and women who lived near the proposed route would assemble on specified days and work on the common road.[12] After the formation of Buncombe County in 1791, this work was obligatory in the same way as county taxes and was

---

... BE A JURY TO VIEW MARK AND LAY OFF A ROAD FROM THE BAULD [BALD] MOUNTAIN ROAD, NEAR THE PINE CABIN [WEAVERVILLE], THE NEAREST AND BEST WAY TO CAPTAIN BARNARDS, ON BRUSH CREEK...

---

referred to as 'labor tax.' The process began with the appointment of a road 'jury' by the Buncombe county court.

Ordered by court that John Roberts, Jonathan Blevins, Philip Mason, Jacob Barnard, Richard Blevins, James Boys, Benj. Griggory, William Balyley, James Standfield, John Blevins, John Chambers, John Tinker, Austen Hackworth, Henry Roberts, William Griggory, be a jury to view mark and lay off a road from the Bauld [Bald] mountain road, near the pine cabin [Weaverville], the nearest and best way to Captain Barnards, on Brush Creek, and report to July Sessions 1794.
(April Term, 1794).

Ordered by Court that the Sheriff summon the following Jury to view mark and lay off a road the nearest & best way from Asheville to the head of Beaverdam Creek and from thence through Craven's Gap to the road leading from the head of Catawba to the Warm Springs near to Joseph Holton's.
(January Term, 1799).[13]

Consisting of interested citizens, some of whom might own land along the proposed route, the jury would lay out a 'best' route and report back to the court which would then assign the clearing of the route to a crew of labor tax 'volunteers' working under a court-appointed foreman. No one in this process, neither jury members, workers or foreman was paid. Often, in the

absence of discipline and the presence of strong drink, these workdays resulted in a festival more productive of fun, than miles of road.[14] Western North Carolina counties and townships in the 19th century began to experiment with variations on the labor tax system with combinations of prison labor and, occasionally, contracted labor paid for by bond revenues.

Private entrepreneurs who owned inns and stores along the same road would also hire labor for road improvements near their place of business. This was the case in an unusual instance of cooperation between two competing innkeepers on the drovers road in Buncombe County, Phillip Hoodenpile and Job Barnard, for whom Barnardsville was named. In 1802, they worked together to procure from the North Carolina legislature a franchise for road improvements near their businesses.[15] None of these methods of finance and construction produced good roads; and North Carolina as a whole, and Western North Carolina in particular, was famous among the eastern states for the wretchedness of its roads.[16]

Lacking powered earth moving equipment and dynamite, early 19th-century road builders had little choice but to follow the natural topography of existing trails and paths. Thus, road building consisted of clearing the route of obstructions such as stumps and boulders, raising and leveling the road bed with sand, clay and gravel and establishing side ditches for drainage. Paving, other than an occasional stretch of planks or logs [corduroy], was non-existent. Sometimes, a charge of ordinary gunpowder would be used to help reduce a stump or boulder. Unless they were boulder-strewn or swampy, creek and river flood plains often provided the easier routes, but nearness to rivers and streams also left many roads vulnerable to flooding and washouts.

In the early years of the 19th century, few portions of any roads in Western North Carolina were good stage coach or wagon roads. The roads existed for moving stock to market and were used by traders and settlers

moving to and from the region. During wet weather they were turned into quagmires by the hooves of thousands of cattle, pigs, turkeys and horses. An ox-drawn sled or "stone-boat" could also make the journey, albeit slowly (Figure 6). The few wagons that attempted either passage often ended up badly. Bishop Asbury, an early 19th-century circuit-riding clergyman, described, in his journal, a wagon incident along the French Broad route on November 6, 1800:

> Thursday 6. Crossed Nolachucky at Querton's ferry and came to Major Cragg's, eighteen miles. I next day pursed my journey and arrived at the warm Springs, not however without an ugly accident. After we had passed the Small and Great Paint mountain, and had passed about thirty yards beyond the Paint Rock, my roan horse, led by Mr. O'Haven, reeled and fell over, taking the chaise with him; I was called back, when I beheld the poor beast and the carriage, bottom up, lodged and wedged against a sapling, which alone prevented them both being precipitated into the river.

> After a pretty heavy lift all was righted again, and we were pleased to find there was little damage done. Our feelings were excited more for others than ourselves. Not far off we saw clothing spread out, part of the loading of household furniture of a wagon which had overset and was thrown into the stream, and bed-clothes, bedding, &c. were so wet that the poor people found it necessary to dry them on the spot.[17]

While the French Broad route is known to have sustained steady usage and improvements throughout the 19th century, there is nothing in the historical record that indicates improvements in the upper reaches of the Bald Mountain Road in the years after the Price-Strother map. Usage, however, is not in doubt. There are indications in land deeds of numerous settlers along this road and along the Laurel and Ivy Rivers, the two main tributaries to the French Broad River from the east. The Shelton clan was so prodigious along the middle branch of the Laurel that by 1830,

Figure 6. Sleds, often used to haul rock from fields and usually having runners made from curved sourwood timbers, were a common means of conveyance on early rough roads. The one pictured here belonged to Dellie Norton, Sodom Laurel, Madison County, 1977. (Photo, Rob Amberg.)

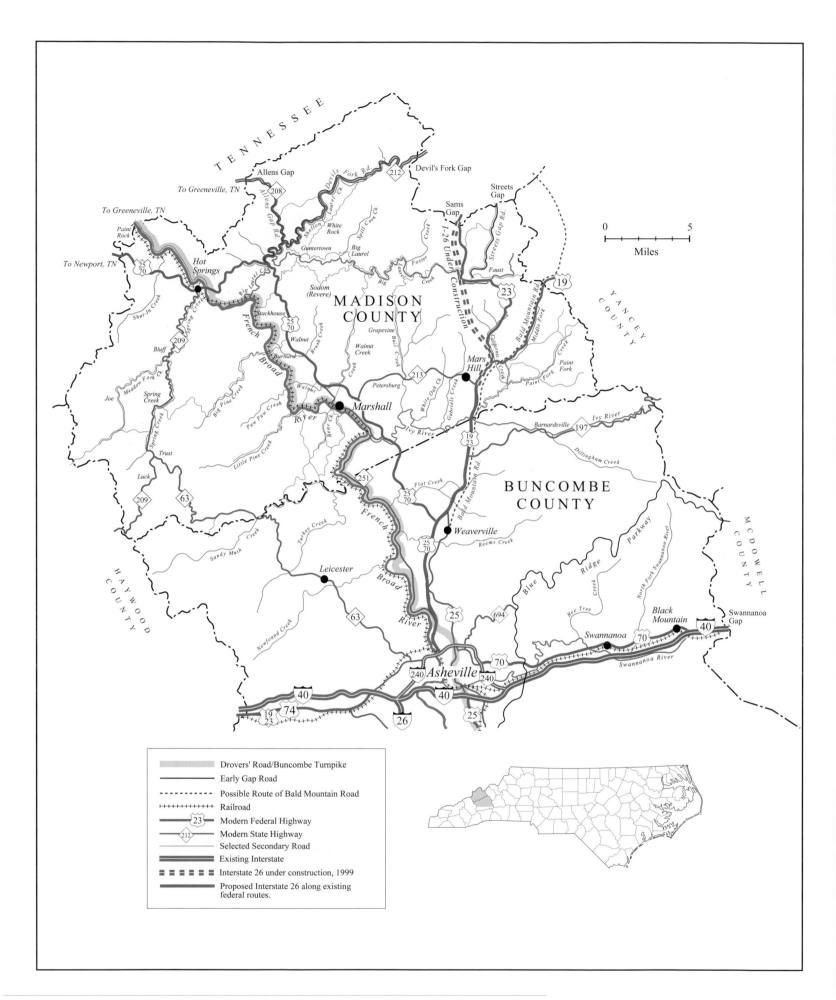

Figure 7. Map of Madison County, Indicating Principal Roads 1820 - 1999. (Map, Michael Southern.)

Sam Gray, Rob Amberg ■ THE ROADS OF MADISON COUNTY

the creek and its valley were already called Shelton Laurel. A road connected these homesteads up the slopes of the Walnut Mountains and eventually made its way to a gap called Devils Fork, then crossed into Tennessee in the direction of Erwin. This road can be traveled today as State Highway 112.

By 1851 when Madison County was formed from Buncombe, there were at least two routes connecting North Carolina and Tennessee through the Walnut and Bald Mountain ranges. The westernmost passage, shaped by the French Broad River flowing north, was the drovers road or Buncombe Turnpike. The second passage, Devils Fork Road, branched off the Turnpike and followed the Laurel River in a northeasterly direction. A third route, the Bald Mountain Road, crossed into Tennessee through the Bald Mountains near the Cane River in Yancey County and may have passed through part of what is now Madison County between Weaverville and the Tennessee line. The exact path of the Bald Mountain Road is not known. An 1849 Road Jury also called for a road from Nemiah [sic] Blackstock's in northern Buncombe County to the Tennessee line through the Walnut Mountains, probably at Sams Gap.[18] By the start of the Civil War, two more primitive gap roads crossed these mountain ranges: Streets Gap Road that branched from the Bald Mountain Road and served the Upper Laurel Creek watershed and Allens Gap Road, 18 miles west of Devils Fork Gap which is currently North Carolina State Road 208[19] (Figure 7).

A gap is a low place in a ridge or mountain range that offers the best route across a mountain or mountain range. Mountain gaps are significant in Southern Appalachian history and folklore. Daniel Boone blazed a trail through the Cumberland Gap making possible westward expansion from southwest Virginia. Songs and stories recalled memorable passages through southern mountain gaps where travelers were frequently subjected to extremes of weather, fatigue and loneliness.

The soil was less productive and the weather more extreme at the ridge line where the gap crossed the mountain. The few families who lived along the gap roads were mostly clustered in the narrow fertile valleys of the lower creeks.

The Buncombe Turnpike followed the valley of the French Broad River and con-

THE IDEA OF A BATH OF ANY KIND WAS NOVEL ENOUGH IN THE 18TH-CENTURY BACK COUNTRY. A WARM ONE, GIVEN UP FREELY FROM THE INNER EARTH, WAS A SURPASSING DELIGHT.

trasted sharply with the gap roads both in cultural and physical terms. When thermal springs were discovered near the river in 1778, it caused a ripple of excitement among the sparse settlers of Western North Carolina and East Tennessee. The idea of a bath of any kind was novel enough in the 18th-century back country. A warm one, given up freely from the inner earth, was a surpassing delight. People immediately began showing up at the springs to camp, bathe in and drink the warm waters, which quickly acquired a reputation as a restorative tonic. By 1790, the first of many successive inns at the springs was built, and the fact that it was located near the northern end of the region's most important drovers route increased its economic significance. At the height of the stock-drive era there were as many as a quarter million animals per year plodding down the road, through Pack Square in Asheville, to lowland markets in South Carolina. The returning drovers had, for a brief time, the only money they would see until the next drive. Numerous stores, inns, taverns and diversions sprang up between Warm Springs and Saluda Gap on the North Carolina / South Carolina line to help relieve them of their burden of cash, much of it in payments against credit extended on the previous drive south. By the mid-19th century the route was an enormous artery of commerce and human activity. The contrasts between the lonely and difficult over-

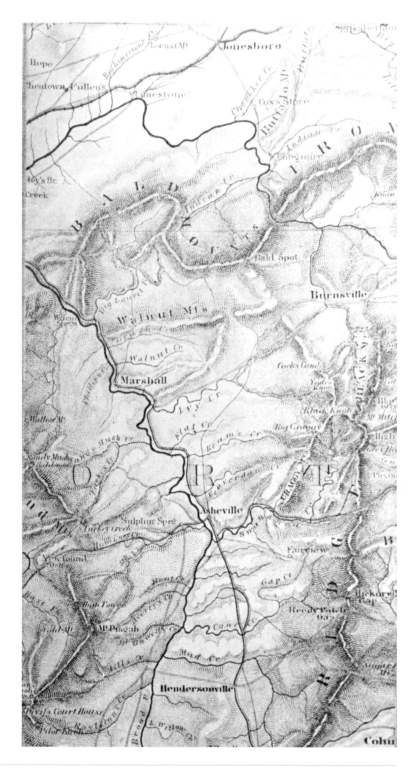

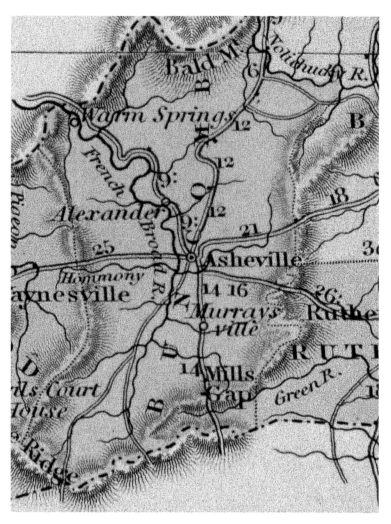

Figure 8-B. This detail from the Tanner atlas indicates how little the Buncombe County roads changed between the publication of this map in 1833 and the later Union Army field map shown at left. (H. S. Tanner, Tanner's Universal Atlas, "A New Map of Nth. Carolina;" private collection.)

Figure 8-A. This Union Army field map was based on the topographical work of Arnold Guyot, a Swiss cartographer. The Buncombe Turnpike linking Tennessee to South Carolina through Warm Springs and Saluda Gap, respectively, was the only developed north-south road in Buncombe County. (Author's collection.)

Figure 9. The word "turnpike" sometimes carries connotations of a well-developed road for fast travel. The Buncombe Turnpike, though an improvement on existing roads, did not present travelers with this kind of experience. In places such as those pictured here, the road and the wagon are on the Buncombe Turnpike in the French Broad River itself, an arrangement called a side ford. (Courtesy, North Carolina Collection, Pack Memorial Public Library, Asheville, North Carolina.)

Sam Gray, Rob Amberg ■ THE ROADS OF MADISON COUNTY

mountain gap routes such as Devils Fork or Bald Mountain, and the social delights of the tavern-studded turnpike along the river, were apparent to anyone who knew both.

Printed maps of the region in the mid 1860s were based on the survey work of Arnold Guyot, a Swiss-born American geographer who worked in Western North Carolina in 1847. Guyot was an expert surveyor and a meticulous cartographer. His work provided relevant geographic information into the 20th century, and his maps were the basis for the military maps used during the Civil War. Guyot's most important contribution was the barometric determination of elevation for the higher peaks in Western North Carolina allowing him to produce the first maps of the region with reasonably accurate topography. To do this, he had to lug a huge atmospheric barometer up and down the mountains he measured. Guyot's cartography was thus less concerned with roads and towns and more with topological features of the principal

ranges. In an 1863 topographical field map based on Guyot's work and belonging once to a Col. Fox of the Union Army, the over-mountain gap roads of Madison County are not all shown, but the Buncombe Turnpike with its narrow defile through the water gap was clearly the route of choice for any invading army from the west (Figures 8-A, B). The Union generals unquestionably considered this strategy. Gen. Grant himself came to Union-controlled East Tennessee in 1863 to assess the possibility of an invasion through Western North Carolina into South Carolina to split the Confederacy. Hoping to take advantage of the strong Union sentiment in the mountains, he reconnoitered the region. He concluded it would invite disaster to try to move an army down the Buncombe Turnpike with a river on one side and steep mountain slopes on the other (Figure 9). Had he known that there were only about 500 rebel troops based in and around Asheville at that time, he doubtless would have marched anyway.

Clinton Norton waiting for the school bus on the first day of school, Sodom Laurel, fall, 1977. (Photo, Rob Amberg.)

150 ton dump truck moving the mountain from one location to another, North Buckner Gap, 1998. (Photo, Rob Amberg.)

THE COMING OF THE RAILROAD

The Civil War left Madison County's roads and most of its infrastructure depleted. Schools, churches, businesses, local politics, even families bore the wounds of the long and violent hostilities. A palliative of sorts came with the construction of a railroad line between Asheville and Warm Springs in 1882, the railroad having reached Asheville in 1880. The drover era ended when it was no longer necessary to drive the herds so far south by road. Cattle, pigs and fowl were still important commodities on Madison County farms, but the frontier agricultural pattern based on large free-range herds was receding. The vast forest of free-range acreage began to be timbered, subdivided and fenced. Timber, tan bark and bright-leaf tobacco were the emerging commodities, all made more feasible by the railroad. The railroad also brought tourism which was based in Asheville but reached to Warm Springs, renamed Hot Springs in 1884, due to the discovery of an additional, warmer spring and the hope that the hotter the water, the better the weary traveler would like it.

The railroad stimulated construction of new roads and the improvement of existing ones in Madison County in two ways. First, the technology required for railroad construction was applicable to road building. The availability of dynamite, steam-powered machinery and steel for bridges allowed road builders to open up sectional routes that had heretofore proved intractable. Second, the existence of the railroad itself posited a model of regional transportation efficiency that called into question the necessity of putting up with an inadequate road system. The ancient east-west political rivalry[20] that made it so difficult for the State legislature to agree upon and fund western road improvements now seemed less a permanent fact of political life. In the spring of 1882, when

anyone with the price of a ticket could get on the train in Warm Springs and ride to Raleigh in two days, the whole idea that there was no solution to the problem of bad roads became questionable.

It was easier to finance a railroad than general road improvements. Those most likely to profit (timber, mining, business) could be drawn into railroad capitalization plans, whereas road money still had to come primarily from public sources – county and state revenues or bonds – all slow methods. To address these and other issues related to mountain road improvements, the first road association in the state, Good Roads Association of Asheville, was formed in 1899.[21] Under the leadership of Dr. C.P. Ambler, an indefatigable booster of tourism in Western North Carolina, the association paved a demonstration macadam road from central Asheville to the Biltmore Estate in 1900. The association held a series of meetings with neighboring counties, including

Madison, to consolidate support for better roads. A North Carolina Good Roads Association was formed in 1907, and a regional Association for the Southern Appalachians was organized in 1909. These associations carried the name and goals of the national good roads movement which for many people was linked to American archetypes of progress, democracy, manifest destiny and the freedom (mobility) of the individual.[22] This movement began just before automobiles entered the Western North Carolina mountains and still lives on in highway advocacy groups such as the I-26 Corridor Association.

THE COMING OF MOTOR CARS

It is not possible to determine when the first automobile ventured on to the dirt roads of Madison County. We may surmise that by late 1914, when Henry Ford was selling over a quarter million Model Ts a

Cleared hillside looking south from Bear Branch, Madison County, 1998.
(Photo, Rob Amberg.)

Mile 0 of the Tennessee portion of I-26 at Sams Gap, North Carolina-Tennessee state line, 1995. (Photo, Rob Amberg.)

year and General Motors not far behind, a few motorized vehicles of some kind would have been seen in the Western North Carolina mountains, particularly in the vicinity of well-known resorts like Hot Springs, Asheville and Hendersonville. It can also be stated with some certainty that the roads they traversed were among the most challenging that any early automobilist could find. Difficult roads in all of the rural south were a fact of life for motorists in the first decades of the automobile.[23] After World War I, manufacturers could supply automobiles to eager consumers faster than local and state governments could improve roads. As motoring became a national enthusiasm and a commercial necessity, state and federal governments recognized that a wholesale transformation of the nation's travel habits was underway and a corresponding transformation of the road system was necessary.

A significant shift in southern political philosophy in regard to roads occurred at this time. Throughout the 19th century, the South had opposed federal aid for building roads, bridges and canals, believing that such aid compromised state sovereignty. Southern spokesmen argued for the states to retain the rights of eminent domain necessary for these improvements.[24] They claimed the constitution authorized only postal road construction by the federal government, all other road building being the domain of county and state governments or private enterprise. The result, throughout the South, was an inadequate network of stagecoach and wagon roads. As automobiles became accessible to more people, the backwardness of the states' rights position in regard to roads became apparent. States' rights were one thing, but the right of the people to move about was clearly being infringed by bad roads. Federal money would help relieve the South's intransigent road problems. The good roads movement in the southern states, particularly in North Carolina, made sure the public understood this.

A Federal Aid Road Act was signed into law by President Wilson in July 1916 with a $75 million allocation to the states

Sam Gray, Rob Amberg ■ THE ROADS OF MADISON COUNTY

THE DIXIE HIGHWAY

OFFICIAL

AUTOMOBILE BLUE BOOK

1922

"Standard Road Guide of America"
Established 1901

VOLUME TWO

Covering the shaded territory indicated on the map below
with extension routes to Chicago, Detroit and Buffalo

The Blue Books cover the entire United States and Southern
Canada in four volumes (See Volume Index Map inside back
cover). They tell you where to go and how to get there, giving
complete maps of every motor road, running directions at every
fork and turn, with mileages, all points of local or historical
interest, state motor laws, hotel and garage accommodations,
ferry and steamship schedules and rates. A veritable motorist's
encyclopedia

SEE TABLE OF CONTENTS, PAGE 5

Copyright 1921 by

The
AUTOMOBILE BLUE BOOKS CORPORATION
259 West 39th Street   910 So. Michigan Ave.
New York   Chicago

Page 539   **Route 640**

Route 640—Asheville, N. C., to Knoxville, Tenn.—136.0 m.
Reverse Route 998.

Via Marshall, Hot Springs and Newport. First 14 miles macadam; 32 miles sand-clay; 15 miles dirt with some clay; 10 miles narrow dirt; last 64 miles stone road.
Thru a hilly and mountainous country to Newport, winding up and down long, easy grades, narrow and with many sharp hidden curves with deep ravine on the side. Extreme caution should be used and horn sounded constantly. From Newport route is thru a hilly farming country. It is reported that this road is to be widened.
Connects at Newport with Note (a) to Greenville, connecting there with route to Bristol. Note (b) gives a connection from Greenville to Tate Springs.

Miles

Detail Map, page 524.
0.0 **ASHEVILLE**, at Pack square.
　　Asheville City Map, page 526.
　　North with trolley on Broadway.
0.3 Fork; left.
0.7 Fork; left from trolley.
0.8 Fork; right.
3.6 4-cor.; left.
3.8 Fork; right.
8.7 **Weaverville.** Thru.
12.7 Fork; right.
13.4 Fork; left.
16.0 Fork; right.
16.8 Fork; left.
20.0 **Mars Hill**, left-hand road. Left.
24.0 Fork; right downgrade.
25.7 **Petersburg.** Thru.
31.8 End of road; right.
32.8 **Marshall.*** Thru.
33.0 Fork; right upgrade.
33.2 **Caution**—fork; left upgrade.
39.2 **Walnut.** Thru.
　　　HOTEL: Switzerland.
43.2 Fork; left. Cross French Broad river 52.7.
52.9 **Hot Springs, N. C.*** Keep ahead across RR.
53.0 Right-hand street; right.
53.1 Fork; right upgrade. Cross N. C.-Tenn. line 60.4.
65.4 End of road beyond bridge; left along river.
72.2 Fork; left. Avoid right 73.6.
77.8 End of road; left across bridge and right beyond.
82.3 **Newport, Tenn.**, Church & Peck

Miles

Sts., at bank. Thru on Church St.
　　Right on Peck St. is Note (a) to Greenville.
Thru 4-cor. 82.6. Thru Clavengers Cross Roads 87.0; **Reedtown** 88.2.
88.4 Fork; left. Thru **Trion** 91.4.
91.7 Fork; left across bridge.
94.8 End of road; right. Cross French Broad river 100.0.
100.2 Left-hand road; left upgrade.
100.4 **Dandridge.** Thru. Avoid left 102.4.
106.7 End of road; left. Thru **Piedmont** 108.4.
119.0 End of road; left.
119.4 **Straw Plains.** Thru. Avoid left.
132.3 Fork; left.
133.7 End of road; right.
133.8 Fork; left.
135.1 Right-hand road; right from river.
135.2 Fork; left on McCannon St.
135.4 End of street; left on Swan St. and right on Hill St. across bridge.
　　Knoxville City Map, page 780.
135.9 End of street; right on Gay St.
136.0 **KNOXVILLE,*** at court house.
　　HOTELS: Farragut, Whittle Springs Hotel & Health Resort, ¾ mi. from Dixie Hwy. on Broadway Pike.
　　Route 984-985 to Chattanooga: 989 to Lexington.

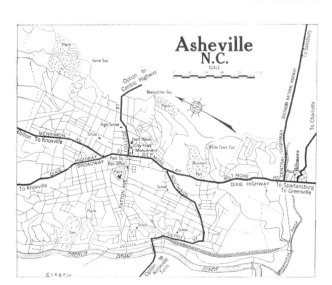

T he *Automobile Blue Book 1922* published this narrative map describing the road from Asheville to Knoxville, Tennessee (above). The old drovers road, which had been the route of the Buncombe Turnpike from 1827 until the 1880s, was now U.S. 25 and part of the famed Dixie Highway which ran from Michigan to Florida. The turnpike, which had entered Asheville from the northwest on what is now Broadway, had been the muddy and dusty path for hundreds of thousands of animals and their drovers in the 19th century. This course, which passed through the center of Asheville at Pack Square, was now the route for similar numbers of motor cars which would use the old path throughout the 20th century. *Automobile Blue Book 1922* (Automobile Blue Books Corporation, Chicago and New York, 1921).

for national road improvements. Although World War I delayed receipt of the money, it was becoming available to southern states by the early '20s. A redistribution of road-making responsibilities and methods quickly followed the money. The state of North Carolina took over maintenance and jurisdiction of all primary roads in 1921. At the same time, the various state road commissions began to work with the Federal Highway Commission to establish national routes that would retain the same identification numbers and names across state lines. This made possible the first road maps for motorists. Prior to standardized highway numbers, automobile travelers relied on prose descriptions of their proposed route over unfamiliar territories.

Madison County now had a national road bearing a number: the old drovers road or Buncombe Turnpike was now U.S. 25 and later became U.S. 70, part of the famed Dixie Highway which ran from Michigan to Florida. Those who motored it agreed that Madison County, North Carolina offered some of its most difficult and picturesque miles. In the 1920s federal money also made possible an over-mountain automobile route through Madison County's northeast sector. The road across Sams Gap was paved and became U.S. 23. This road was the most efficient route between the emerging urban centers of Asheville, North Carolina, and Johnson City, Tennessee, and a connector between the Ohio Valley and the southern Atlantic Coast. It quickly became a heavily traveled road and is currently being transformed into Interstate 26.

A 1922 survey listed 337 automobiles and one school bus in Madison County.[25] The principal means of conveyance for most people was still horse and wagon over the same dirt roads that had, in many cases, been in the same location for a very long time. By 1935 there were 1,200 cars and 395 trucks and trailers registered in the

county,[26] moving over roads that, for the first time in human memory, began to show real improvement. The automobile began to assume its transformative role in the life and culture of Madison County, as in almost every other county across America.

INTERSTATES

In June of 1956 Congress enacted the Interstate Highway Bill and President Eisenhower signed it. Stimulated by reports of Germany's autobahn system, an earlier Congress had approved the idea, in principle, during the last months of World War II. The allied command, particularly Gen. Eisenhower, had been impressed by the German model of a modern, engineered, divided highway system and the military advantages it secured. When Eisenhower became president in 1952, he gave the interstate highway project his full support but insisted there be no general tax

increases to finance it. Congress responded in 1956 with a bill that proposed to build the highway of the future and define its place in American society. It would be financed by a "pay as you go" tax on gas, tires and cars. Its characteristics were: national defense capability (controlled access/egress and ability to withstand heavy military vehicular loads), a high standard of safety and comfort, economic linkage of discrete geographic areas, and something referred to in the text of the legislation as "democratization of mobility." The publicly-owned interstate system was to provide long-distance transportation and economic potential for all regions and classes. This was the vision in 1956 and remains a major article of faith among highway advocates today.[27]

Because of its geographical location between large military bases to the east and the Oak Ridge Nuclear Laboratory west of Knoxville, Tennessee, Western North

Bridge abutments for the I-26 Corridor, Higgins Branch, Madison County, 1998. (Photo, Rob Amberg.)

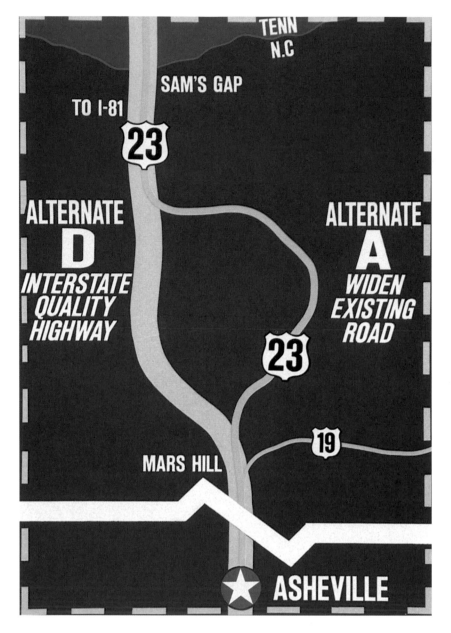

separated two lanes of eastbound from the two lanes of westbound traffic, 15-foot shoulders, rest stop areas and controlled access ramps without toll booths. These were features known only to those Western North Carolinians who had traveled the freeways of Southern California or the urban Northeast.

As I-40 was completed through Asheville, planners began to work on the north-south corridors over the southern mountains. In the North Carolina foothills, Interstate 77 passed through Charlotte, connecting the Yadkin River basin with the Shenandoah Valley of Virginia. Further west, Interstate 26 beginning in Asheville connected Western North Carolina with the South Carolina coastal plain, terminating at Charleston, partially recreating the old Dixie Highway which moved traffic between the Ohio valley and the southern Atlantic seaboard.

I-26 was completed from Charleston to Asheville in the mid-1970s, a time of critique and reassessment in many areas of national policy, including interstate highways and the automobile and trucking culture they served. After a half-century of American social history increasingly shaped by roads, automobiles and the exercise of democratic mobility, cultural observers began to ask questions about the environment built to accommodate the automobile culture. Critics such as Lewis Mumford, Helen Leavitt, Peter Blake and Jane Jacob began to analyze the tarnish on the chromed image of the automobile and its proliferating infrastructure of highways, parking lots, congestion and pollution.[28] Critics felt that the need for individual mobility and speed had too often resulted in degraded environments of formless suburban sprawl, deteriorating air and water quality and dislocations in traditional community structures. When President Nixon signed into law the National Environmental Protection Act of 1971 it was, for many observers, an implicit recognition that the uncritical and optimistic phase of American automobility was over.

Figure 10. The I-26 Corridor Association emphasized the dangers of Alternate A, to widen and improve U.S. 23, rather than build I-26, in a brochure they published. Images of runaway trucks colliding with school buses shifted attention away from social and environmental concerns. (Courtesy, the author.)

Carolina was regarded as an area of high strategic priority by interstate planners. New interstate construction began just a few months after the 1956 legislation when engineers started laying out an east-west route for Interstate 40. This new interstate in some places was laid on the route of the old Western Turnpike which ran west from Salisbury, North Carolina through Asheville. The new road was, however, of an altogether different order than any previous one built in the mountains. The road specifications called for 10-inch thick solid concrete laid on a two-foot bed of crushed stone pressed into a machine-packed surface, gradual curve and hill gradients that required entire mountains to be removed or tunneled through, a spacious median that

Sam Gray, Rob Amberg ■ The Roads of Madison County

It was in the climate of this complex reassessment of highways and automobiles that the I-26 over-mountain link with East Tennessee was studied, planned, debated and revised. The first public expression of the North Carolina Department of Transportation's (DOT) intent to widen and improve U.S. 23 from Mars Hill to the state line at Sams Gap came in an Environmental Impact Statement in the 1978 Transportation Improvement Plan (TIP).[29] The report recommended that, out of seven alternate improvement plans, Alternate A be chosen. This plan, called for widening U.S. 23 into a divided four-lane highway that would modify, but not replace, existing slope and curve gradients and the open access of tributary roads. Alternate A was clearly not to be an interstate, but was, nonetheless, costly enough to be dropped from DOT's 1983 TIP because of funding constraints.

Meanwhile, due largely to political momentum generated by Gov. Ned McWhirter, Tennessee began construction of a new highway that would replace U.S. 23 and meet interstate standards. The North Carolina DOT responded by reinstating the U.S. 23 project in the 1988 TIP, and emphasized that Alternate A was still the plan, principally because, relative to the other plans, it saved money. This emphasis on cost was a function of the sheer size of the state's public road system. By the mid-1980s North Carolina was maintaining over 76,000 miles of streets, highways and interstates - the largest in the nation.[30] The state had, within a century, progressed from among those with the worst roads to one of the best road systems in the nation. Just as had been the case in the 19th century, highway construction and maintenance costs rose faster than revenues to pay for them. In 1988, the existing revenue structure and statewide road building obligations forced the North Carolina DOT to stay with the less expensive Alternate A, no matter what Tennessee did.[31]

Regional political and economic leaders questioned the wisdom of Alternate A and perceived that the North Carolina DOT's commitment to doing anything very soon about U.S. 23 was limited by the lack of money. In 1987 an advocacy group called the I-26 Corridor Association was formed in Asheville. The association stated its position forthrightly:

> The US 23/I-26 CORRIDOR ASSOCIATION is a non-profit, bipartisan grassroots coalition of Western North Carolinians. We believe that it is imperative to:
>
> • Advance the US 23 project to top priority on the North Carolina Transportation Improvement Plan to meet Tennessee's schedule for upgrading US 23.
>
> • Secure an immediate appropriation that will allow the N.C. Department of Transportation to study, design, and survey Corridor "D" as an interstate-quality highway.[32]

Led by Mayor Lou Bissette of Asheville, the Corridor Association assembled a strong coalition of regional leaders and began to have an immediate effect on the North Carolina legislature, the governor's office and the DOT. Assisted by an effective media campaign and public education effort, the association focused on the contrasting plans, Alternate A (widening and improving U.S. 23) vs. Alternate D (interstate linkage with I-26). Legislative appropriations to study Corridor D became available by late 1992. The association's goal of a newly located interstate quality highway that would replace U.S. 23 from Mars Hill to the state line, funded and constructed on a fast-track basis became North Carolina DOT policy by 1994.[33]

Perhaps the most important factor in the association's success was their effectiveness in framing the issue of highway safety in comparisons of the two plans. The disturbing vision of two lanes of fast, southbound interstate traffic crossing the Tennessee-North Carolina state line and feeding into the steep curves of U.S. 23 was evoked in a Corridor Association publication of 1988 (Figure 10):

> Danger looms if we do not meet Tennessee's improvement standards and schedule. Traffic accidents, injuries, and deaths will soar above levels already too high. Motorists now face safety hazards along the 11 miles between Sams Gap and Mars Hill. Steep grades, 14 uncontrolled intersections, 43 curves, and 129 driveways pose inherent safety problems that widening alone will not solve.[34]

In the course of the decade-long public discussion of alternate plans for U.S. 23, no issue, be it fiscal, environmental, economic or social, came close to the safety issue in capturing the public's attention about the road. With an average accident rate of more than 30 per year on the 11 miles between the state line and Mars Hill,[35] it was little wonder that road opponents had difficulty in shifting public awareness to social or environmental concerns.

From an environmentalist perspective there was much to be concerned about. The 11 miles of four-lane highway from the state line to Mars Hill will bury deep moist coves, rich in some of the rarer flora; entomb clear mountain streams, equally rich in aquatic life, inside two miles of 60-inch aluminum pipe; and blast away acres of upland wilderness that includes bear and bobcat habitat near the Appalachian Trail. The estimated 27,000 plus cars and trucks per day that will eventually travel the completed highway will deposit a constant and significant quantity of emission pollution along the entire corridor.[36]

The environmental impact of I-26 is extensive and difficult to access visually or conceptually. More immediate is the effect of the highway on the human ecology of northeastern Madison County. The highway had its most immediate impact on those whose land lay in or near the road's right of way. All of the right of way acquisition negotiations for I-26 were conducted by the negotiations section in the Office of Right of Way Acquisition for North Carolina Department of Transportation

HEADWATERS OF LITTLE CREEK

In the autumn of 1998, I hiked with a small group of botanists/ecologists up Little Creek, crossing and recrossing this last uncleared section of right of way. Our mission was to make a rough inventory of the flora and determine if any rare or endangered species were about to be destroyed by the road. We walked up the watershed and after an hour we left the headwaters of Little Creek and emerged onto the ridge top near Sams Gap. From the crest, we could look west into Tennessee. The completed portion of I-26 on the Tennessee side of the mountain was visible and we could hear the big trucks gear down as they topped the gap and started down the winding, narrow grade of U.S. 23. The Appalachian Trail was only a few yards away. On the return trip, we moved fairly rapidly down slope, following the undulations of a hill that began on the ridge as a dry, southwest face and ended as a rich, moist cove oriented to the southeast. We crossed several soil zones and plant biomes. The species profile changed every few hundred feet. Paul Myers, the most astute botanist of the group and a veteran of many such assessment expeditions, took out his tape recorder to record the Latin names of the species his eyes happened to catch. "*Quercus alba, Cornus florida, Kalmia latifolia, Lilium superbum, Aesculus octandra, Polygonatum biflorum*," his low voice intoned softly as we moved steadily through the leaves. These were the only sounds. The botanical Latin resounded through the cathedral of poplars. It was a brief autumnal requiem for the trees, bushes and herbaceous plants on the Little Creek watershed. —Sam Gray

Blast supervisors from Gilbert Southern Corporation inspecting a recent blast at Buckner Gap, 1998. (Photo, Rob Amberg.)

Division 13 which includes Madison County. Gladys Lance chief of this section described their work as "... the most difficult negotiations we've ever conducted....no one wanted to leave, though not everyone opposed the road itself."[37] A total of 42 family relocations were necessary on the I-26 right of way. There were 160 additional settled land claims that did not require relocation, and there are 42 outstanding claims that will be settled in court. In all these claims the state of North Carolina, operating within the legal framework of *eminent domain*, makes an offer to the landowner based on "fair market value" which is determined by real estate appraisals on comparable properties. The landowner is allowed to make a counteroffer which, if close enough to the DOT figure, can usually be negotiated into a settled claim. When the two evaluations cannot be reconciled, the DOT proceeds with condemnation proceedings through the courts. The property in question is taken by the State, and the court determines the amount paid to the landowner.

One of the "difficult" claims that was settled by the Right of Way Acquisition Office was that of the Kenneth Buckner family who live on the head of Sprinkle Creek up near Buckner Gap, so named because Buckners have lived on this watershed for well over a century. The Buckner farm, one of breathtaking pastoral beauty, is being dramatically altered by I-26 construction. The right of way passes immediately above and behind the Buckners' house and barn and required relocation of a new woodworking shop and other farm buildings. Kenneth Buckner struggles with his feelings about the road and the changes to his way of life:

> Well, it's hard to put in words what I was thinking because it just affected me real deeply to even imagine this place being torn up. It really did and it would be very easy to be

real depressed with it if you allowed yourself to be. There was, for a good while, that I had trouble really facing it, to be honest with you. Because I was just so fond of this place. And it's hard to put in words, hard to explain, even [to] my brothers and sisters who don't have the love for this place that I do....[38]

About a half-mile downstream from the Buckner place and also living almost in the path of the interstate, Harold Wallin, in contrast to the Buckners, has emerged as an enthusiastic booster of the road, in spite of the fact that immediately behind his home is now a huge landfill where once there were wooded hills. The fill forms a steep slope that rises 200 feet above the Wallins' modest and impeccable home. At the top of the landfill will soon be a four-lane highway. Harold loves it. Sixty-seven years old and related to the legendary folk musicians Cas and Doug Wallin, the excitement in his voice is palpable as he describes what is happening: "All they are doing is taking useless mountain land and making a highway. They're not taking good farmland. It'll put us on the map. It's the best thing that could happen here." Harold speaks of how the road will "bring folks in and let folks leave," a process that he acknowledges has already begun to change Madison County.[39] Harold Wallin is not alone in his delight over a new interstate in his backyard. Most of the people of rural Madison County have suffered tortuous and rutted mountain roads enough to understand Harold, if not altogether agree with his vision of the future.

By early 1997 the rights of way had been secured; the timber cut; houses, barns, churches and graveyards were being moved or razed; and the gardens' and orchards' last harvest taken and tasted. Demolitionists and the operators of huge and powerful machinery then began the largest dirt - moving project in North Carolina history,[40]

Pile of field stones collected by three generations of the Harold Wallin family as land was cleared for planting. Sprinkle Creek, 1996. (Photo, Rob Amberg.)

Cemetery vault being exhumed from the Little Ivy Baptist Church Cemetery to clear right of way for I-26 Corridor, Mars Hill, 1996. (Photo, Rob Amberg.)

gnawing away at the massive slopes of Murray Mountain and Buckner Gap. When the highway is finished, 13 million pounds of explosives (ammonium nitrate and diesel fuel) will have been used to blast this corridor through the mountains. An estimated 37.5 million cubic yards of Madison County rock and dirt will be displaced, and over 300 million dollars of federal and state road funds will have been spent.[41] For the next several years, the blasting, dozing, hauling and dumping will continue 24 hours a day, six days a week, reducing the mountains to rubble, filling the valleys and redirecting the streams. This latest and most remarkable of Madison County's roads will change the physical and cultural map of this fabled region for all time. A place scarcely known on any map 200 years ago will have given up its secrets and become part of I-26. It will have become similar to 47,300 other miles of interstate highway in the country.[42]

Notes

1. William P. Cummings, *The Southeast in Early Maps* (Chapel Hill, North Carolina: UNC Press, 1962), p. 10.
2. William P. Cummings, ed., *The Discoveries of John Lederer with Unpublished Letters By and About Lederer to Governor John Winthrop, Jr.* (Charlottesville, 1958).
3. For discussion cf. Cummings, p. 31.
4. James Mooney, *Myths of the Cherokee, Nineteenth Annual Report of the Bureau of American Ethnology* (Washington, D.C.: G. P. O., 1902), p. 47.
5. Cummings, p. 224.
6. Ora Blackmun, *Western North Carolina to 1880* (Boone, N.C.: Appalachian Consortium Press, 1977), p. 277. Ed. Note: North Carolina lands were not granted for service in the Revolutionary War. North Carolina soldiers received land in what is now Kentucky.
7. Tyler Blethen and Curtis Woods, Jr., *From Ulster to Carolina* (Cullowhee: Western Carolina University Mountain Heritage Center, 1983), p.22.
8. Cummings, plate 51.
9. Sadie Smathers Patton, *The Story of Henderson County* (Asheville: Stephens Press, 1947), p. 90.
10. Ibid., p. 90.
11. William P. Cummings, *North Carolina in Maps* (Raleigh: N.C. Division of Archives and History, 1966), p. 23.
12. F. A. Sondley, *A History of Buncombe County North Carolina, Two Volumes in One* (Spartanburg, S.C.: The Reprint Company, 1977), p.483.
13. Ibid, p. 484.
14. Ibid, p. 602.
15. Manly Wade Wellman, *Kingdom of Madison* (Chapel Hill: UNC Press, 1973), p. 30.
16. Blackmun, p. 130.
17. Francis Asbury, *Journal* (New York: N. Bangs and T. Mason, 1852), p. 481.
18. Yancey County, North Carolina, Minute Docket Court of Pleas and Quarter Sessions, Vol. I, Fall Term, 1849, (Film C107.30001).
19. Delia Tipton Brittain, *Upper Laurel and Her People*, (Mars Hill: Mars Hill College Southern Appalachian Center, 1987).
20. Blackmun, p. 125-138.
21. Ina W. and John J. Van Noppen, *Western North Carolina Since the Civil War* (Boone: Appalachian Consortium Press, 1973), p. 324.
22. Howard L. Preston, *Dirt Roads to Dixie: Accessibility and Modernization in the South, 1885- 1935* (Knoxville: University of Tennessee Press, 1991), pp. 38-68.
23. Ibid, p. 40.
24. Ibid, p. 51.
25. Wellman, p. 174.
26. Internal Document 49.711, N.C. Department of Revenue, Motor Vehicle Division, N.C. State Library.
27. Tom Lewis, *Divided Highways* (New York: Viking Press, 1997), p. 119.
28. Christopher Finch, *Highways to Heaven* (New York: Harper Collins, 1992).
29. N.C. Department of Transportation, *Transportation Improvement Plan* (Raleigh: DOT 1978).
30. Richard Stiles, *Unpublished Economic Analysis of I-26 Corridor for Western North Carolina Tomorrow*, Western Carolina University, 1988, p. 2.
31. Ibid, p. 3.
32. I-26 Corridor Association Brochure, (I-26 Corridor Association, 1988).
33. William Smart, District Engineer, N.C.DOT, interview, May 6, 1999.
34. I-26 Corridor Association Brochure, 1988.
35. Stiles, p. 9.
36. *Asheville Citizen-Times*, editorial, August 15, 1998.
37. Gladys Lance, interview, February 8, 1999.
38. Kenneth Buckner, interview, May 17, 1997.
39. Harold Wallin, interview, May 30, 1997.
40. *Asheville Citizen-Times*, August 2, 1998. Ammonium nitrate/diesel fuel is the explosive of choice in contemporary road construction.
41. Ibid. (N.C.DOT estimates.)
42. U.S. Department of Transportation web site.

Sam Gray carrying a piece of chestnut log from the proposed site of the I-26 Corridor, Buckner Gap, 1996. (Photo, Rob Amberg.)

Ben Porter and I have been working on this study for several years, looking at images and trying to understand all the dimensions of Herbert Pelton's work. Ben's interest in Herbert Pelton has a long history including his discovery several years ago that a picture of Ben's father, displayed on Ben's mantle, was actually taken by Pelton many years ago. Ben Porter became a panoramic photographer because of his study of Herbert Pelton, and now about 80% of Ben's work is panoramic. Ben's understanding of Herbert Pelton and panoramic photography is tangible. Like Pelton, his personal history is grounded in Western North Carolina, and like Pelton, he takes panoramic photographs with a Cirkut camera. These images offer detailed documentary and narrative information, and thereby provide us with effective tools for measuring cultural change. The images, particularly the panoramic photographs, also raise several questions. How much information can be contained in one image? With very large subjects, do these two photographers seek control, or is it the accidental and idiosyncratic elements which make the work so alive? Where, if anywhere, do they wish for our eye to linger? —R.B.

Herbert W. Pelton:
"...Expert in Taking Pictures of This Kind."

By Benjamin Porter

People considered him to be an outsider from the North when he arrived in Asheville in 1905 at the age of 26. A skilled draftsman but jobless, he soon found work as a cashier at the Victoria Inn. Within a year he had married and embarked upon a new career in photography.

His name was Herbert Pelton, and when he left Asheville in 1930, he had become one of the best and most prolific commercial photographers in the region. His work consisted of thousands of images: panoramic views, photographs of historic events, portraits, posed groups and hundreds of postcard views of Western North Carolina scenery and structures. Pelton documented school gatherings, business groups, dramatic productions, conventions, and parades. He recorded the city's joy with the victory of the Asheville home team over Ty Cobb and the Detroit Tigers in the first professional baseball game played at McCormick Field (Figure 1). He also photographed the distress and devastation of the Great Flood of 1916.

Herbert Woollard Pelton was born in Illinois on December 6, 1879, the second of six children born to the Rev. Charles Pelton, a Presbyterian minister, and Georgina Woollard Pelton. In 1897 the family moved from Illinois to Cincinnati, Ohio, Georgina's hometown. Herbert Pelton was employed in 1901 as a draftsman at the City and Suburban Telephone & Telegraph Association of Cincinnati, and in 1905, he was listed in the city directory as a "principal" in the E.C. Hogrebe Company.

Pelton may have moved to North

Figure 1. Panoramic photograph of McCormick Field, 1924, Herbert Pelton. This photograph records the first professional baseball game played in Asheville, North Carolina. The Asheville Skylanders defeated the visiting Detroit Tigers winning 18-14. Ty Cobb is seen in center field flanked by Harry Heilman in right field and Heine Manush in left field. (Courtesy, Bob Terrell.)

Figure 2. Panoramic photograph, "Indian School ~ Cherokee, N.C.," 1908-1910, Herbert Pelton. (Reproduced from the Collections of the Library of Congress.)

One of Pelton's most interesting group of photographs depicts road survey work done in Madison and possibly Buncombe Counties. Herbert Pelton's brother, Walter Pelton, may have worked for the Highway Department or worked as a road engineer.

Top, opposite page. This survey photo includes the waterpowered sawmill on Walnut Creek in Madison County. Note the man holding the survey pole on the ridge behind the mill. (Courtesy, North Carolina Collection, Pack Memorial Public Library, Asheville, North Carolina.)

Benjamin Porter ■ HERBERT W. PELTON: "...EXPERT IN TAKING PICTURES OF THIS KIND."

THE CIRKUT CAMERA

The Cirkut camera appears similar to a large antique view camera seated atop a wooden tripod. The camera, a beautifully crafted instrument, was made of prime mahogany covered with high quality leather. The interior wood of the camera was finished in a natural varnish and all exposed metal hardware parts were brightly nickel-plated. A high quality red leather bellows came on the early Cirkut models.

What makes the Cirkut camera unique is its rotation during the picture taking. The photographer must wind up a spring clock-work motor in the camera magazine, and when the camera is activated, the entire camera rotates atop a gear head plate seated on the wooden tripod. As the entire camera rotates in one direction, the motor pulls film in the opposite direction past an exposure slit (about 1/4 inch wide) inside the camera magazine. As the film moves opposite to the camera's rotation, the movement is effectively stopped at the moment of exposure when it passes the slit. The photographer is free to make the panorama as long or as short as needed for the pictorial effect desired. The camera's shutter stays open during the entire exposure, and the effective shutter speed as the slit passes across the subject ranges from 1/2 second to 1/12 second. Depending on the length of the pan and the lighting conditions of the day, the entire exposure may last from five to 30 seconds.

The entire process is one which requires patience and care on the part of the photographer: the camera must be perfectly level, and groups must be arranged in an arc similar to the rotation of the camera so that people will appear in a straight line in the photograph. If not positioned in an arc, a visual "cigar effect" will make those in the middle of the group appear larger than those standing at both the ends.

The Achilles' heel of the Cirkut camera design is "banding," a noticeable vertical blur in the print caused by a change in the camera's rotational speed during exposure. Banding, which can be caused by anything from a gust of wind blowing against the large bellows of the camera to a small piece of grit located in the gear bed, can ruin the photograph. Herbert Pelton's Cirkut photographs were remarkably free of banding.

Benjamin Porter ■ HERBERT W. PELTON: "...EXPERT IN TAKING PICTURES OF THIS KIND."

Carolina in 1905 to follow his sweetheart, Sarah B. Edmonds, who had also been a resident of Cincinnati. On October 17, 1906, Sarah and Herbert Pelton were married at All Souls Episcopal Church in Biltmore: she was 34 and he was 27 years old. Her employment was listed in the Asheville city directory as proprietor of the Sun Shine Inn at 198 Chestnut Street while he worked as a cashier at the Victoria Inn. After their marriage, the Peltons became proprietors of "The Reverie," a boarding house located at 57 North Spruce, across the street from the "Old Kentucky Home," the boarding house run by Julia Wolfe and immortalized as "Dixieland" by son Thomas Wolfe in *Look Homeward, Angel*.

Asheville's population was nearly 16,000 in 1906, and more than 100 boarding houses supported a strong tourist economy, but the Peltons maintained their boarding house business for only one year. By 1909 the Peltons had moved to another boarding house at 17 North Spruce,

Reception of Mr. Herbert B. Race And Mr. J.E. Mc Cants By Asheville Motor Club At Finish of Record Breaking Run – Jacksonville, Fla. To Asheville, N.C. In Ford Car. Sept. 26, 1910 – Time 2½ Days – Car Indicated At X.

Figures 4 A-D. Pack Square offered Herbert Pelton many opportunities for interesting images. These panoramic views are of the north (Figure 4-A, above), and the south (Figure 4-B, below) sides of Pack Square and are both dated 1910. (Courtesy, North Carolina Collection, Pack Memorial Public Library, Asheville, North Carolina.)

Figure 4-C. Left. Pelton used many of his panoramic views in his production of postcards. This color postcard of Pack Square uses portions of his panoramic views. Postcards were often altered, and this view of the Langren Hotel is an interesting example. In the black and white panoramic view, dated 1910, the Langren Hotel (circled, opposite page, top) is seen as an uncompleted skeletal structure. In the color postcard,(circled, left) the identical image, the Langren Hotel is a completed structure. The Langren Hotel opened on July 4, 1912. (Private collection.)

Benjamin Porter ■ Herbert W. Pelton: "...Expert in Taking Pictures of This Kind."

Figure 4-D. Right. This 1913 postcard view of Pack Square by Herbert Pelton looks west toward Patton Avenue and was probably taken from the City Hall. It shows a busy square, crowded with street cars, with the Battery Park Hotel in the distance in the upper right. (Private collection.)

and Herbert Pelton is listed in the city directory as an optician.[1] Another resident at 17 North Spruce was Luther Higgason, a photographer. The contact with Higgason may have influenced Pelton to turn his attention to photography, for the two later formed a business partnership. In 1910 Herbert Pelton opened his first photography studio in the Reed Building overlooking Pack Square in downtown Asheville.

Although this was his first commercial photography address, he had been credited for published photographs as early as 1907. In the April 14, 1907 *Asheville Citizen*, Pelton photographs accompany the article "Asheville's Fifth Annual Horse Show." The five images show prize-winning contestants mounted on horses.

In 1908, Pelton began using a specialized panoramic camera, the Cirkut camera, which would become a trademark of his photography. Among the earliest Pelton panoramas are forestry students of the newly formed Biltmore Forest School flanking their teacher and school founder, Carl Schenck; a school group from the Cherokee Indian Reservation (Figure 2); and a reunion of Confederate veterans at Camp Ray, located near Haw Creek. Evidently, Pelton was the only Asheville photographer using a Cirkut camera in the

Figures 5 A-C. Herbert Pelton's numbering system indicates that he probably made well over 1,500 panoramic views in the years between 1905 and 1930 when he lived and worked in Asheville. He was highly skilled in the use of the panoramic camera which was ideally suited for photographing large groups of people. Figure 5-A. Top. The "Southern Appalachian Good Roads Convention," poses in front of the old Asheville Auditorium in October of 1909. Figure 5-B. Center. In this photograph, the Asheville Presbytery gathered along the west side of Church Street in 1916. Figure 5-C. Bottom. The Asheville Board of Trade met in Hot Springs in July of 1915. From 1914 to 1917 Pelton worked with Luther Higgason and their photographs, including this one, were signed "Pelton & Higgason." Pelton is seen here kneeling at the extreme right holding his bow tie. (Three panoramic photographs, courtesy, North Carolina Collection, Pack Memorial Public Library, Asheville, North Carolina.)

In 1922, E.W. Grove, who had built the Grove Park Inn in 1913, purchased the Battery Park Hotel. He built the new Battery Park Hotel, seen here, but also demolished the old Battery Park Hotel and leveled the high hill upon which the old Battery Park Hotel stood. The fill generated was used to level the ravine just south of Patton Avenue and create what is now Coxe Avenue. This Pelton photograph shows the area after the hill was removed just before the Grove Arcade was built. About 70 feet of dirt was removed at the highest point. Visible on the right is the Basilica of St. Lawrence. On the left is O. Henry Avenue and the top of the Margo Terrace Hotel. (Courtesy, North Carolina Collection, Pack Memorial Public Library, Asheville, North Carolina.)

early 1900s. The number of professional photographers working in Asheville from 1910-1930 ranged from eight to 12, but no panoramic images created with the Cirkut camera by any of Pelton's competitors have been found.

The Cirkut camera, manufactured between 1904 and 1940, represented photography's state of the art technique for making long panoramic images. During Pelton's time, this camera was the workhorse of commercial photographers wishing to photograph large groups and capture sweeping panoramic views.[2]

The Cirkut camera was produced in five different sizes as model numbers 5, 6, 8, 10 and 16. The No. 8 and 10 models could be used as a standard view camera in addition to their panoramic capability. Pelton owned a No. 6 Cirkut Outfit which used film 6-1/2 inches wide by 6 feet long. The photographer created an image panning to a degree of his choice—even up to a complete 360 degree view. Pelton's model could also be used as a standard view cam-

era with a 5 x 7 inch format. Later, in the 1920s, he evidently obtained a No. 10 Cirkut camera which used film 10 inches wide and up to 12 feet long.

Use of a Cirkut camera does not necessarily mean success in creating interesting images.[3] As with any new technology, there are those practitioners seduced by the technique alone. There are others, in the case of photography, usually a select few, who use the new technology to reach new dimensions in their work. Pelton falls into this second group; his use of the Cirkut camera brought attention and praise to his panoramic work from the very beginning of his career. On September 26, 1910, in an article describing the record-setting entry of Herbert Race's motor car into downtown Asheville arriving from Jacksonville, Florida, in two and a half days, the *Asheville Citizen* referred to Pelton as an "expert in taking pictures of this kind" (Figure 3).

Successful use of the panoramic camera requires several skills. Initially, the photographer must master the technical workings of the camera and it's unique process. The challenge of using the Cirkut deters trigger-happy, snap-shooters from even considering dancing with the big and slow Cirkut. Camera banding will drive a photographer to tears and organizing a large group (anywhere from 30 to 1,000 people) will also discourage the faint of heart.

Pelton's mastery of the camera is apparent in his sharp, clear and well-printed images. His prints reflect a photographer who has mastered the Cirkut and takes pride in his craftsmanship. His works seem inspired beyond monetary demands. The monetary compensation for selling group panoramas is proportional to people's ability to see themselves clearly in the final print. Usually, the Cirkut photographer would work free, speculating to sell moderately priced prints to a large number of people.

Both in his landscape and group panoramas, Pelton had the ability to see as a panoramic camera sees. This is the paradox of using a truly panoramic camera.[4] The uninitiated can experience this visual stretch simply by turning the head in a 180 degree arc looking for the best panoramic view. The visual information on one side of your view tends to disappear by the time you have completed scanning to the other side of the 180 degree arc. Pelton had the ability to locate the best position to place

his camera and his subjects to capture the essential elements and make the panorama interesting from edge to edge. There is no excess or wasted space in his panoramas, and this skill elevates his images above many panoramas produced–both in the past and today. The observant viewer is invited to take a slow visual journey through a Pelton panoramic print. The strength of his panoramic compositions make them as compelling today as when he created them 80 years ago.

Contemporary designers and historians, among others, appreciate these qualities in Pelton's work. The 1910 Pelton panorama of "Pack Square Looking South," enlarged to mural size, is currently exhibited in two locations flanking Pack Square (Figures 4 A-D). The larger of these two murals serves as a diorama in the historical exhibit at the entrance to Pack Place Education, Arts, and Science Center. A better reproduction of this same panorama is located in the lobby of the Biltmore Estate corporate offices on the north side of Pack Square.[5]

Another distinguishing facet in Pelton's panoramic work was his skill in photographing diverse subjects (Figures 5 A-C). Pelton's panoramas reflect an interest and awareness of his subjects, a unique variety of people and views available in Western North Carolina, both then and now. In

View of Sunburst, North Carolina, 1912, Herbert Pelton. (Reproduced from the Collections of the Library of Congress.)

Benjamin Porter ■ Herbert W. Pelton: "...Expert in Taking Pictures of This Kind."

325

Figure 6-A. Above. When the Great Flood of July 16, 1916, struck Western North Carolina, Pelton recorded scenes of the devastation in Asheville with his panoramic camera. Pelton used the Cirkut camera like a photojournalist. First, he recorded the entire, sweeping view showing the French Broad River swollen over its banks from both sides of the river. Then he moved closer and set his camera atop a railroad boxcar to capture the details of lumber strewn like matchsticks, buildings submerged and crowds of people watching wreckage float down the river. This view looks south toward the Southern Railroad Depot from Park Avenue, near the site of the current four lane Riverlink Bridge over the French Broad River. (Courtesy, North Carolina Collection, Pack Memorial Public Library, Asheville, North Carolina.)

Figure 6-B. Center. The Asheville Fire Department, 1922, Herbert Pelton. (Courtesy, North Carolina Collection, Pack Memorial Public Library, Asheville, North Carolina.)

Figure 6-C. Below. About one-third of the Asheville Fire Department, 1994, Benjamin Porter. As part of the Western North Carolina Re-photographic Project, the author re-photographed images created earlier by Herbert Pelton. The work of Asheville photographer George Masa was also featured in this project sponsored and exhibited by the Asheville Art Museum. (Author's collection.)

photographing groups, he exhibited a careful regard for arranging his subjects so that people did not block each other. Often they appear comfortably posed, relaxed and in positions reflecting the group identity. Actors pose as their stage characters in a "Pirates of Penzance" panorama, Camp Greystone campers resemble mythical maidens of the Cherry Blossom Festival, and when the Asheville Board of Trade (the predecessor of the Asheville Area Chamber of Commerce) convened in Hot Springs, North Carolina in 1915, Asheville banners were held proudly, as if the subjects were ready to cheer for their hometown. The men, women and children are comfortably intermingled from the foreground of the panorama to a pinnacle six rows deep. Pelton jumped into this panorama as he was a Board of Trade member. He is on the extreme right of the photograph, squatting on one knee with hand raised to his ever-present bow tie.

Among Pelton's city and landscapes, there is a unique series in which he used his Cirkut camera to document a monumental disaster with immense destruction: the Great Flood of 1916. Following days of

torrential downpour, the French Broad and Swannanoa Rivers overflowed their banks causing great destruction and loss of life. On the day when the flood crested, Herbert Pelton recorded sweeping views of the swollen rivers and drenched cityscape with his panoramic camera (Figure 6-A).

His choice to use the Cirkut for this catastrophe is unusual. For Pelton, it would have been easier to use a smaller, more easily transportable camera to photograph the flood. His decision to photograph with the Cirkut that day may be an indication that the Cirkut had become his personal choice even though it was bulky and difficult to use, and he had little control over the arrangement of his subject. In selecting and using the panoramic camera on July 16, 1916 Pelton created a very special documentation of the flood.[6]

Pelton formed several business partnerships during his years in Asheville. In 1914, he joined with Luther Higgason whom he had known since 1907 when they had both lived at 17 North Spruce, to form the firm of Pelton & Higgason. Their studio provided "Portraits, Commercial, Land of the Sky Views, and Local View Post

Cards."[7] Their first address was 11 West Pack Square. They were later located at 9-1/2 North Pack Square until 1917, when their partnership ended. Pelton kept the studio on the square and Higgason moved to 16-1/2 Patton Ave.

This merger and separation was not unusual for photographers of this period as they sought ways to survive and profit in a small town boasting a dozen photographers. Three other photography studios besides Pelton & Higgasons already operated on Pack Square: Ray's Studio at 2 North Pack Square; Branagan Studio at 6 North Pack Square and Brock's Studio at 18 North Pack Square. Other noteworthy photographers who appeared subsequently in Asheville city directories are William Barnhill in 1916, George Masa in 1921 and Ewart Ball Sr. in 1926.

Pelton formed another business partnership in 1920 with George Masa. Masa, a gifted Japanese photographer, made Asheville his home from 1915 until his death in 1933.[8] Pelton and Masa became partners in the Photo-Craft Shop located at 16 Biltmore Avenue. The extent and workings of their partnership are unclear as both photographers maintained their respective studios during this period. Later, Masa acquired all interest from Pelton in their joint business venture and changed the name to The Plateau Studio. Masa sold The Plateau Studio in 1924 and Ewart Ball Sr. acquired ownership of The Plateau Studio in 1926.[9]

The Pelton-Masa partnership was showcased in the 1994 exhibition, "Coming to Light: the Re-photographic Survey of Western North Carolina" at the Asheville Art Museum. Selected locations of Pelton panoramas and Masa landscapes were re-photographed by contemporary photographers Gil Leebrick and Benjamin Porter. The exhibition included vintage prints by Herbert Pelton and George Masa displayed with the contemporary images made by Leebrick and Porter. Prior to the exhibition, it had not yet come to light that Pelton and Masa were former business part-

ners, and that the site of the exhibit on Pack Square was also the site of the previous business partnership. Both the spirit of their work and their many early images of the region were revived, albeit posthumously (Figures 6 B-C).

Pelton Studios remained on Pack Square until 1926. The stability of his business address was offset by the continual change in his place of residence. After Herbert and Sarah Pelton married in 1906, they moved to a different residence nearly every year until 1917 when they purchased a home in Norwood Park, "a residential park n.e. of the city on the Grace car line."[10] In addition to this nomadic lifestyle, there is another peculiarity in the Peltons' home life: Sarah Pelton is not listed in the Asheville city directory in the years 1909-1912. Did she leave Asheville during this period? As Herbert Pelton resided at three boarding or shared houses during this time, they may have been separated. Sarah B. Pelton reappeared in the 1913 directory and was employed at the Pelton Studio in 1916. She also is listed on two copyright notices at the Library of Congress in 1912 which confirms her collaboration and assistance to her husband.[11]

Herbert and Sarah Pelton's marital life changed in the 1920s. His mother, Georgina, and his older sister, Edith, moved

Many early 20th century photographs of Asheville were staged. They often pictured wagons with produce outside the downtown market which was on the first floor of the City Building at the east end of Pack Square. "Asheville about 1902" was published by Burt Calahan about 1892. Marked lower right "H Pelton…Copy." (Courtesy, North Carolina Collection, Pack Memorial Public Library, Asheville, North Carolina.)

Womanless Wedding Asheville, N.C. Apr. 29, 1921

CC.56

Commercial photographers are often called upon when people gather. Pelton's camera took him to many gatherings: people of many persuasions posing in many ways. Above. This 1925 gathering of the Federated Clubs of Asheville featured a "Womanless Wedding." Right. The Ku Klux Klan rode this truck in a 1925 Asheville parade. Opposite page, bottom. In 1910 Pelton captured the festivities of the Y.W.C.A. Conference Field Day. This gathering is in front of Lawrence Hall at the Asheville Normal and Collegiate Institute, now the site of part of Memorial Mission Hospital. Opposite page, top. The Bingham School Football Team, date unknown. (Courtesy, North Carolina Collection, Pack Memorial Public Library, Asheville, North Carolina.)

FREE PUBLIC SCHOOLS
NON SILBA SED ANTHAR — NOT FOR SELF BUT FOR OTHERS

ASHEVILLE KLAN N° 4½

B·480

to Asheville in 1922. They lived at 121 Annandale in a house owned by Pelton. Georgina is listed as "widowed" in the Asheville city directory. They may have moved to Asheville as the result of Rev. Pelton's death, or perhaps to help the Pelton's repair their failing marriage.

In 1923, Georgina and Edith moved in with the couple at "Spurwood" located on Vernon Hill. "Spurwood" was one of the five country houses built as rental property for George Vanderbilt. Vernon Hill is located in the area now occupied by Asheville-Buncombe Technical Community College. However, in the same city directory, Sarah Pelton was listed as a resident of 146 Virginia Avenue (now Norwood) in Norwood Park.[12]

On April 7, 1924, Herbert and Sarah Pelton were divorced. On September 6, 1924, he married Allie Vivian Moore. Allie Vivian Moore was a divorced, single parent and had been employed at Pelton Studios since 1920. The groom was 44 years old and the bride was nine years his junior. Wendell Moore, Vivian's 12 year-old-son, was one of the witnesses to the marriage ceremony held at 60 Flint Street. Pelton became a father figure to Wendell, and his influence lead Wendell to choose a career

in photography.

The last Asheville city directory listing Herbert Pelton as a photographer is 1928. He signed a two-year lease for a house on Charlotte Street in 1928 and evidence indicates that he may have stayed in Asheville until 1930 when he moved to Washington, D.C.

What prompted Pelton, an active photographer with 20 years in Asheville, to move to the nation's capital? Interviews

Y.W.C.A. Conference Field Day — Asheville, N.C. ~ 1910

Benjamin Porter ■ HERBERT W. PELTON: "...EXPERT IN TAKING PICTURES OF THIS KIND."

331

PELTON'S STYLISH CALLIGRAPHY

One identifying characteristic of nearly all Pelton photographs, both panoramic and standard, is the distinctive, neatly written titles. This stylish calligraphy might have been Pelton's own hand. He had worked as a draftsman and had presumably acquired the care and attention to detail of that profession. If Sarah Pelton was absent from 1909-1912, this lends credence to the belief that Pelton labeled his own negatives and prints.

Pelton was meticulous in the labeling of his imagery. The title or occasion and date was usually centered beneath the group. On the far left side of the print was written a filing number for the negative; panoramic negatives would begin with the letter "c" or "c.c.," ostensibly the former for the No. 6 Cirkut camera and the two "c's" to denote the No. 10 Cirkut camera, followed by a filing number. On the standard format negatives (either 5 x 7 inches or 8 x 10 inches) the code would begin with either an upper case "A," "B" or "O" followed by a sequential number. On the right side of the print, Pelton signed the print, most often as "HW Pelton-Asheville, NC," or with a simple "HP" (Figure 7).

The numbering system for the panoramas began in 1913. The highest numbered panoramic print cataloged to date is "c-1529." As this image was made in 1921 it is safe to assume that Pelton added significantly to this total over the next nine years. His standard format images number in the thousands.

with those who knew Herbert and Vivian Pelton indicate several possibilities, but no clear reasons. Was the move based on the new marriage? Pelton may have moved to Asheville to marry Sarah Edmonds, and now, in the early stage of his second marriage, was he repeating a pattern? Or, did the move relate to a weak demand for Pelton's photography? Mary (Moore) Keller, the former wife of Wendell Moore speculates, "Why did he (Pelton) come to D.C.? I don't know, perhaps it's because of the Depression at that time. I understand he got a job at a high-class studio there as a photographer, and later told Wendell he could get him a job there at another studio, Harris & Ewing. Both of these studios have since gone out of business."[13]

Or was the marriage to Vivian Moore too disruptive? A common description of his second wife was that she had a strong domineering personality compared to his quiet nature. Mary Keller remembered, "Herbert was very kind and a gentle person, the few times I saw him. Occasionally, I would see Herbert at the Cherry Blossoms photographing as a freelance at the Tidal Basin in D.C....Some of the photographs he made of Wendell's mother [Vivian] were beautiful. One day in a fit of anger she tore them up and burned them."[14]

The move to Washington, D.C. did not have a positive effect on their marriage.

I remember well my first experience with a Herbert Pelton panoramic photograph. I had traveled to Morehead City to give a presentation of my own photography as a visiting artist working in the North Carolina Community College system. In a friend's library, while looking through Illustrated North Carolina History *published by H.G. Jones, I saw a reproduction of one of Pelton's views of the Champion Paper Mill in Canton, North Carolina. Little did I know that my initial curiosity would become a long-standing preoccupation with learning more about this unacclaimed Western North Carolina photographer.*

Ben Porter, 1986

They separated shortly after arriving and never lived together again.

Initially, Herbert Pelton found work at C.O. Buckingham Company, Inc., a photography studio located at 1219 M Street N.W. In 1933, Pelton opened his own business, a photography studio called the Vogue Studios at 817 14th Street N.W. The Washington city directory listed his commercial trade as "Portraits, Commercial, Technical, and Passports."[15] He operated Vogue Studios until 1937. The year 1939 was the last year in which Pelton was listed as a photographer, when he was located at 1310 20th Street N.W. in Washington, D.C. He appeared intermittently in the city directory in the 1940s.

Whereas there is a plentiful trail of

Panoramic View, "Overlooking Plant of Champion Fiber Company, Canton N.C. From South Side," 1911, Herbert Pelton. (Reproduced from the Collections of the Library of Congress.)

Benjamin Porter ■ HERBERT W. PELTON: "...EXPERT IN TAKING PICTURES OF THIS KIND."

333

Panoramic View, "Overlooking Whittier, N.C. And the Tuckasegee River," 1913, Herbert Pelton. (Reproduced from the Collections of the Library of Congress.)

Pelton photographs from his time spent in Asheville, nothing has been found documenting his commercial work in Washington, D.C. In Asheville he had been judicious in recording the copyright for his images, but only one Pelton copyright entry exists for his years in Washington. On December 16, 1944, Pelton registered a copyright for an 8 x 10 inches photograph titled, "The Bond Baby." This image has not been found, but presumably relates to fundraising efforts for World War II.

His wife worked as a receptionist for another commercial photographer in Washington, D.C., Joseph Naiman. Although she and Pelton were still legally married (they never divorced), she used her former name, Mrs. Vivian Moore. Her son lived with her and was hired as a photographer at the prominent photography studio of Harris & Ewing. Wendell Moore married Mary (Moore) in 1934 and they lived with his mother in a rooming house on 18th Street. In a letter dated July 30, 1996, Mary (Moore) Keller described her memories of that period:

> "....I was a teenager when I married Wendell, in 1934. Our life was very hard, as after the [D]epression we did not have much money. We lived with his Mother [Vivian] in a rooming house on 18th St. She rented rooms to supplement our existence. When Mrs. Moore [Vivian] would go to his [Pelton's] shop, she

would bring some small items home that Herbert would give her. They never divorced as they neither had the money for a lawyer, so she used the name of Moore, even up to the time she died."

> "One day Herbert was unloading things from his car in downtown and was struck by a car. He was in a hospital for a couple of weeks, that's when Wendell suggested he come stay with us to recuperate. He was awarded a small settlement for that. Then, as I understand, he resumed his second hand business. That's when Mrs. Moore [Vivian] found out he was at our house and was furious. He heard and left and that was the last time I saw him. Wendell never visited his shop that I ever heard about, although he gave Wendell a couple of hundred dollars from his settlement for the accident."[16]

Herbert Pelton's final listings in the Washington D.C. city directory appeared in 1954 and 1956. No longer listed as a photographer (he was 75 years old in 1954), it is apparent that he had fallen on hard times. He is listed with two jobs: as the owner of "The Economy Shop," a used household goods store at 616 Massachusetts Avenue N.W., and also, as an inserter for the *Times-Herald* newspaper. In 1956, he is still listed at The Economy Shop with his residence located in the basement.[17]

What had become of his work as a photographer? Did he still own cameras or

hittier, N.C. And The Tuckaseyee River.

possess negatives and prints from his years in the business? Had he become senile in his old age? Mary Keller never visited The Economy Shop but she proffered this painful possibility, "As for his cameras and negatives, I suppose they were discarded after his eviction for non rent payment at his shop. This is only heresay."[18]

As Herbert Pelton's work and career have come to light in the last 10 years, it seems incomprehensible that his life's work may have been destroyed in this manner, yet the history of photography is filled with such anguish and tragedy. Matthew Brady lived in near-poverty late in life, unable to interest the U.S. government in his Civil War images until Mark Twain managed to help procure a sale, but Brady died before he could enjoy monetary reward for the massive photo project he had funded. Eugene Atget's glass negatives of France were put on the street as garbage following his death, but fortunately were saved by Bernice Abbott. Carlton Watkins life's work and historical collection were destroyed in

the fire following the 1906 San Francisco earthquake, four days before their purchase date. This final calamity broke Watkins mentally and financially; he was committed to an insane asylum for the remainder of his life. Lewis Hine, the great documentarian whose work inspired the passage of the Child Labor Laws, had to go on welfare and died destitute in 1940.

Sadly, Herbert W. Pelton's final years most resemble those of Carlton Watkins or Lewis Hine. On Thanksgiving 1956, Pelton was committed to Saint Elizabeth's Hospital, a mental hospital in the Anacostia area of Washington, D.C. As his patient files are sealed, the details of his commitment and treatment are not known. He spent the last 4-1/2 years of his life at Saint Elizabeth's and died of a heart attack on July 22, 1961. His brother, Walter E. Pelton, signed the death certificate and Herbert Pelton's remains were cremated at Lee's Funeral Home on July 24, 1961. He was 81 years old at the time of his death.[19]

HERBERT PELTON'S POSTCARDS

The first two decades of the 20th century marked the peak of the national craze for postcards. Many commercial photographers took advantage of the fact that millions of cards were mailed, often sent home by people vacationing. Asheville was a popular tourist destination, and Herbert Pelton took advantage of the demand for scenic views, village scenes and virtually any subject he might capture with his camera. For many years, Pelton's display ad in the Asheville city directory referenced his postcard work. As late as 1917, when interest in postcards was declining, his ad still mentioned postcards: "Pelton Studios, Photography, Portraits, Commercial, Land of Sky Views, Local Post Cards, Located next to the Princess Theatre." Pelton published many of his postcards himself, but also used other publishers including, the Southern Post Card Co., Brown Book Co. and S.H. Kress & Co. (Private collection.)

Capitola Cotton Mills, Marshall, N. C.
"In the Land of the Sky."

Balsam Mountains from the top of
Plotts Balsam, near Eagles Nest, North Carolina.
"In the Land of the Sky."

Moores Lake Juanita, (Altitude 2250 feet)
Weaverville, N. C.

Despite the fact that Herbert Pelton produced hundreds if not thousands of postcards, he approached his work as a skillful photographer. Most of his views are well-composed with clear details. Pelton's postcards are marked in many ways including "Copyright By Herbert W. Pelton, Asheville, N.C.," "Photographed By Pelton" and "© H.W. Pelton." Above. Many are marked on the backs in green ink with a circular logo and the conjoined letters HP. (Private collection.)

Blue Ridge Association Grounds from Black Mountain, near Asheville, N. C.

Herbert Pelton traveled throughout Western North Carolina to photograph subjects for his postcards, and by so doing created an interesting vernacular history. These three 1912 cards highlight scenes from (top, clockwise) Black Mountain, Lake Toxaway and Linville. (Private collection.)

Esceola Inn, Linville, N. C.

Scene in front of Toxaway Inn, Lake Toxaway, N. C.

The postcard boom of the first two decades of the 20th century coincided with the development of the automobile and the growth of auto travel. Pelton and many other postcard publishers often photographed roads and emphasized "new auto roads" to encourage travel and tourism and thereby the sale of postcards. (Private collection.)

A Glimpse of Craggy Mountains from New Auto Road, "In the Land of the Sky."

Auto Road along Grandfather Mountain, Elevation 5964 feet, "In the Land of the Sky," near Asheville, N. C.

Benjamin Porter ■ HERBERT W. PELTON: "...EXPERT IN TAKING PICTURES OF THIS KIND."

337

VERANDA VIEW, HIGHLAND HOSPITAL, ASHEVILLE, N. C.

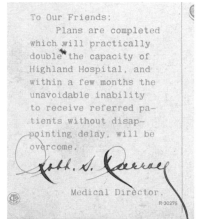

We have been informed by the
local Board of trade that you
desire information regarding
Asheville Hotels.

    If you desire we shall be
glad to send you booklet and
quote you rates.

        BATTERY PARK HOTEL

*Many of Pelton's clients typed or printed
advertisements on the backs of their
cards. The backs of these three have
messages from Highland Hospital (top),
The Battery Park Hotel (center) and the
logo of the Asheville Chamber of
Commerce (bottom). (Private collection.)*

St. Genevieve's College, Asheville, N. C.

Pelton's many postcards create a rich visual archive of Western North Carolina and of Asheville in particular. These three examples (top, clockwise) provide architectural history of three very different but important structures. (Private collection.)

Asheville School for Girls, Asheville, N. C.

KALMIA COTTAGE, ALBEMARLE PARK, ASHEVILLE, N. C.

B695

MOUNTAIN MEADOWS INN, NEAR ASHEVILLE, N. C.

Hotels and inns were an ideal subject for Herbert Pelton's postcard business, and these three cards (bottom, counter clockwise) are typical exterior views Pelton chose. (Private collection.)

The Alba Hotel and Lake Montreat, N. C.

THE GLADSTONE HOTEL, BLACK MOUNTAIN, N. C.

Lake Eden
Black Mountain, North Carolina

Benjamin Porter ■ HERBERT W. PELTON: "...EXPERT IN TAKING PICTURES OF THIS KIND."

3 panoramic views by Ben Porter. Top. "Billy Graham Dedicates Billy Graham Freeway," April 25, 1996. (Author's collection.) Center. "Black Mountain College Reunion," October 28, 1995. (Author's collection.) Bottom. "Stephens Lee Reunion," 1996. (Author's collection.)

Bird's Eye View of Hendersonville, N. C. ALT 2250 FT.

Herbert Pelton postcard view of Hendersonville, North Carolina. (Private Collection).

Acknowledgments

The author wishes to thank Zoe Rhine and Ann Wright of the North Carolina Collection at Pack Memorial Library in Asheville, North Carolina for their help with his research.

Notes

1. In the early days of photography, painters and opticians, among others, had been drawn to this new image-capturing invention. Two of photography's inventors, the Frenchmen Joseph Nicéphore Niépce and Louis Jacques Mande Daguerre met through an optician, M. Vincent Chevalier, who made lenses for their rudimentary cameras. This fortuitous meeting led to a partnership which resulted, some years later, in the daguerreotype process in 1839. Herbert Pelton, in his brief work as an optician, followed a historical path experienced by other early photographers.

2. Bill McBride, "The Evolution of the No.10 Cirkut Camera," "IAPP Newsletter," August 1988, pp. 5-10. In the early days of the camera, a photographer made a circuit around a military camp to take photographs of military units and troop formations. The circuit refers to traveling around the periphery of the tents. Since the Cirkut panoramic camera did a better job of covering the periphery of the tents than the conventional view camera, it was given this name by the inventors. "Circuit" which was already a registered name could not be used, so they used "Cirkut" instead for their panoramic cameras.

3. Eastman Kodak Company, *The Cirkut Method* (Rochester, N.Y.: Century Camera Division, c. 1915), p. 3. The applications of a Cirkut camera are numerous. This early Cirkut sales brochure claimed: "The photographer who owns a Cirkut has an unlimited field in which to exercise his originality in creating new business; the Summer and Winter Hotels want pictures to hang in other hotels; the railroads are always in the market for new and original pictures of some interesting feature of their line; panoramic views of real estate development projects; real views of manufacturing plants that include everything required, without having to take the picture from such a distance that many important details are too small to be of value. There are many other openings, for Cirkut photographs soon enable the owner of a Cirkut to deal with big business people in a dignified and profitable way."

4. By definition, "panorama" is derived from Greek roots and means "seeing all." Debate within the International Association of Panoramic Photographers reveals there is no unanimous agreement of what is and what is not a panoramic photograph. There is a consensus, however, in the I.A.P.P. that the disposable "panoramic" cameras marketed today are simply a panoramic illusion; the manufacturer uses a wide angle lens and crops the 35 mm film to make the picture look panoramic.

5. Herbert Pelton's name and copyright are included on the enlargement at the Biltmore Estate corporate office building, but his identity and signature are not visible in the Pack Place diorama.

6. The region's most thorough archive of Pelton prints and panoramas is located in the North Carolina Collection at Pack Memorial Public Library in Asheville, North Carolina. This author is indebted to their valuable assistance with his Pelton research.

7. *The Asheville, N.C. City and Suburban Directory*, Vol. XIII, 1914. (Asheville: Piedmont Directory Co., 1914) p. 107.

8. For more information on the life of George Masa, see *May We All Remember Well Volume I: A Journal of the History & Cultures of Western North Carolina*, Robert S. Brunk, ed. (Asheville: Robert S. Brunk Auction Services Inc., 1997), pp. 249-275.

9. Obituary of George Masa, *Asheville Citizen*, June 22, 1933. This photographic lineage from Pelton to Masa to Ball may explain why some of Peltons' negatives are found in the Ball Collection at the University of North Carolina at Asheville. In the late 19th and early 20th centuries, it was not uncommon for a photographer liquidating his or her business to sell negatives and prints along with camera equipment and supplies. Pelton's name remains on some of these original negatives in the Ball Collection, but others clearly have had his name removed. This can be cross-referenced by Pelton's numerical cataloging system in which he opaqued his negatives, wrote directly on the negative with opaque ink so it would appear white on the print, and the fact that a number of these same images were taken in the period before Ewart Ball Sr. was a working photographer in Asheville.

10. *Asheville, N.C. City Directory*, Vol. XVI, 1917. (Asheville: Hackney & Moale Co. Printers, 1917) p. 422.

11. Library of Congress, Washington, D.C., copyright to Sarah B. Pelton, JJ136496 "By the River" & J136494 "The Close of Day Near Asheville," ca. 1912. Herbert Pelton protected a number of his photographs by copyright with the Library of Congress. Under copyright law of the time, he sent an original copy of the print with the copyright registration to The Library of Congress. He seemed to follow this practice for several of his panoramas and postcard views. The Library of Congress has approximately 30 of Peltons' panoramas in their collection.

12. *Asheville, North Carolina City Directory*, Vol. XXII, 1923. (Asheville: The Miller Press, 1923) p. 696.

13. Mary Keller, Letter to Benjamin Porter, July 30, 1996.

14. Ibid.

15. *Polk's Washington (District of Columbia) City Directory*, 1936. (Richmond: R. L. Polk.)

16. Keller.

17. *Polk's Washington (District of Columbia) City Directory*, 1954 & 1956. (Richmond: R. L. Polk.)

18. Keller.

19. District of Columbia Department of Public Health, Certificate of Death, July 24, 1961, No. 61 5569.

The author with the Cirkut Camera.

The building of the Biltmore House in the 1890s dramatically changed the skyline of the rolling hills just south of Asheville. Farm land and modest rural homes were replaced by George Vanderbilt's 250 room mansion styled after the French chateaux. The complex architecture of the building and the thousands of objects in Biltmore's collection present the observer with an interesting dilemma: what should one look at in this ocean of interesting details? This study focuses on one of the many artists whose work is part of the texture of the great house. Karl Bitter, a 30-year-old Austrian-born sculptor, designed and/or executed a variety of sculptural works in stone, wood and steel in both the interior and exterior of the house. This study enables us to understand the collaborative process by which the architects Richard Morris Hunt and Richard Howland Hunt, and George Vanderbilt conceived the architectural decorations, and how the work of Karl Bitter gave their ideas definition and life of their own. — R.B.

Karl Bitter was one of this country's most accomplished Beaux-Arts sculptors. He was both prolific and versatile (Figure 1). By 1910, five years before his untimely death, he had executed well over 100 sculptural projects in a wide range of styles and media including individual relief panels and free standing sculpture. In the last five years of his life he was awarded numerous important commissions for monumental sculptural works. Some of the most distinguished of his later projects include the Thomas Jefferson Memorial in St. Louis, the Thomas Lowry Monument in Minneapolis, the Fountain of Abundance on the Plaza in New York City and the sculptural program for the Wisconsin State Capitol in Madison.

Bitter is remembered primarily for his

Karl Bitter's Sculptural Work at Biltmore

By Kate Plowden

monumental works and especially so for the Carl Schurz Memorial which overlooks Morningside Park in New York City. This monument, completed in 1913, features a nine foot bronze portrait statue of the German-American reform politician Carl Schurz and three distinctive granite relief

Karl Bitter in his studio with plaster cast of Venus andiron and a throne chair relief panel, ca. 1897. (Published in John Nilsen Laurvik, "Karl Bitter - A Master of Decorative Sculpture," Booklover's Magazine 3 (May 1904), p. 604.)

Figure 2. Among his large outdoor commissions which reflect a modernist taste, Karl Bitter is best known for the Carl Schurz Memorial in Morningside Park, New York. Although the statue of Schurz is traditional, the stylized and austere design of Bitter's granite relief panels represent some of the earliest American forays into sculptural abstraction and modernism. (Courtesy, James M. Dennis.)

panels. The unusual and austere design of these panels, composed of stylized, flat-surfaced male and female allegorical figures, is a synthesis of archaic Greek and Egyptian prototypes in combination with Bitter's own sculptural innovations (Figure 2). These designs are some of the first attempts toward abstracted and simplified sculptural forms in American sculpture and were, therefore, precursors of the 20th century's artistic concern with modernism.

In addition to his sculptural expertise, Bitter gained much recognition and respect for his administrative skills. He directed the sculptural programs for three of America's World's Fairs: the Buffalo Pan-American Exposition in 1901, the St. Louis World's Fair in 1904, and the San Francisco Panama-Pacific Exposition in 1915, which was taken over by Stirling Calder due to

Bitter's death in that year. He was also active in numerous sculptural and artistic organizations, including the City Beautiful Movement, and served as president of the National Sculpture Society for two terms.[1]

This study concerns Bitter's largest and most ambitious residential commission undertaken during an earlier and lesser known period of his career in America, from approximately 1895 to 1898. These sculptural projects were executed for Biltmore Estate, a baronial manor designed by Richard Morris Hunt and built for George Washington Vanderbilt, an intellectual, connoisseur and patron of the arts. The elaborate 255-room mansion was inspired by the chateaux of the Loire Valley and is situated in the rolling hills adjacent to the French Broad River near Asheville, North Carolina. It is one of the most ambitious architectural examples in a period of American architectural history, from about 1875 to 1914, when a small but wealthy leisure class drew upon the arts in an attempt to identify themselves with the venerable history and traditions of European aristocracy.

Karl Bitter was born in 1867 in Vienna and immigrated to the United States in 1889. During the 1890s, he worked almost exclusively as an architectural and decorative sculptor for some of America's best known architects, including George B. Post, Frank Furness, James Brown Lord and, most importantly, Richard Morris Hunt and his son Richard Howland Hunt. Bitter was trained in Vienna at the Imperial Academy of Fine

Arts and worked on several Crown sponsored structures built along Vienna's Ringstrasse, a majestic boulevard area developed under the auspices of Emperor Franz Joseph I. Bitter immigrated to New York just before his 22nd birthday and just after having deserted his post in the Imperial Austrian Army. Although unable to speak English, his impressive talent enabled him to immediately obtain a job with Ellin, Kitson & Co., a New York firm of architectural decorators often used by Richard Morris Hunt for his lavish residential projects.[2] Within Bitter's first few months in New York, Hunt "discovered" him and encouraged him to establish his own studio. From 1890 until the turn of the century, Bitter executed sculptural embellishments for most of the Hunt firm's architectural projects. Bitter collaborated with the Hunts on all of the Vanderbilt residences the Hunts either built or renovated during the last decade of the 19th century—five new residences and two renovations (Figure 3).

Bitter's sculpture from this period, usually classically inspired and often allegorical in nature, included figural groupings, relief panels and friezes, caryatids, keystones, portrait medallions, and mantel and ceiling decorations. His commissions for Collis P. Huntington's Fifth Avenue mansion, completed in 1894 (now demolished), provide a typical example of his early work. Bitter sculpted twelve marble *Months* panels for the main hall, nine oak *Muse* panels for the first floor corridor, two stone figures representing lyric and epic poetry for the library mantel and three small classical heads for the dining room mantel. The architect George B. Post paid Bitter $23,310 for this work. This sum equates to over $200,000 by today's standards and indicates that Bitter, though only about 25 years old and still relatively unknown, was generously compensated for his early domestic commissions.[3]

To appreciate Bitter's work at Biltmore it is important to understand the level of autonomy he enjoyed in relation to Hunt's firm. It is sometimes assumed that the role

of the often anonymous architectural and decorative sculptor was to essentially copy, in three-dimensional form, designs provided by the architectural firm. This was likely not the case with Hunt and Bitter, for although there is no direct proof that Bitter designed much of his own work for the Hunt firm, there are compelling reasons to believe that he did.

Though Hunt had a strong interest in Beaux-Arts sculpture, prior to his collaborations with Bitter, his projects employing architectural sculpture were much smaller in scale and scope.[4] Hunt's three sculpturally ambitious designs for public buildings, the New York Stock Exchange, the Union League Club and the New York Historical Society, were unsuccessful competition entries and never constructed. His

Figure 3. Karl Bitter collaborated with Richard Morris Hunt and Richard Howland Hunt on all the Vanderbilt residences built or renovated in the last decade of the 19th century by the Hunt firm. Bitter is seen here with a clay model of Diana for W. K. Vanderbilt's Long Island home, ca. 1893. (Courtesy, James M. Dennis.)

New York Lenox Library was completed in 1877 but was almost devoid of sculpture except for pediment busts of Apollo and Minerva. As for his residential architecture, only the W.K. Vanderbilt Fifth Avenue mansion, completed in 1882, was significantly ornamented with sculpture. Much of this was standard stock from patterns and could be executed by ordinary stonemasons, while the more elaborate works were imported from France.

Further, the Hunt firm had far too much to do to concern themselves with the detailed designing of a vast number of sculptural projects. For example, for the Administration Building of the 1893 World's Columbian Exposition, Bitter executed 28 complex allegorical sculptural groups.[5] That he also designed them is almost certain. Bitter had received excellent training and experience in Vienna and was well versed in a variety of historical styles, allegorical motifs, and mythological, medieval and ecclesiastical subject matter. Most telling, however, is a statement by

Ferdinand Schevill concerning the Administration Building. He wrote that Hunt:

> ...immediately consulted with Bitter, accepted from his hands a decorative program on a scale very unusual in America, and in the next few years the two men worked out a monument destined to make their linked names heard far and wide.[6]

Finally, despite his stylistic diversity, Bitter's early sculpture tended to be distinctively his own. Much of it, regardless of the original notions of the architectural firm, displayed quick modeling, swirling movement and a sense of contrast tempered with restraint. Bitter's preferred style was essentially an amalgamation of High Renaissance, Mannerist and naturalistic Baroque elements. Some examples of his pre-1900 work include caryatids for the Metropolitan Museum of Art and for the Havemeyer Building, pediments and panels for Philadelphia's Broad Street Railroad Station, figures of Mercury and Abundantia for New York's Chamber of Commerce building, and a pulpit and choir rail for

New York's All Angels Church.

The most conclusive evidence for Bitter's artistic autonomy, however, lies in the comparison of the architectural drawings with the finished product. The main entranceway, for example, to New York's Trinity Church, a Hunt/Bitter collaboration that was planned and executed between 1891 and 1894, was a project in which Bitter was operating under some significant artistic constraints.[7] Hunt's firm had provided a very detailed pen and blue wash architectural drawing.[8] The six relief panels, though rough and sketchy, were derived directly from Ghiberti's *Gates of Paradise* at the Baptistry in Florence, Italy. A church committee, however, selected several scriptural passages to be depicted by Bitter. No architectural drawings have been found which attempt to portray these passages, a matter almost certainly left up to Bitter. It is the tympanum figures of Christ in glory with attending angels that best represent Bitter's sense of artistic individualism in this work. The drawing from Hunt's firm depicts a very stylized Gothic tympanum with Christ in mandorla, whereas Bitter's figures contain no hint of Gothicism (Figure 4). The finished work exhibits a naturalistic Renaissance Christ attended by della Robbia-like angels. Although Bitter was required to work within existing architectural parameters and, in this case, was provided with the subject matter to be depicted, there is no reason to believe that the finished design was not his own conception. There is no evidence to indicate that this was not essentially the case with Bitter's work at Biltmore.

Karl Bitter's sculpture for the Biltmore estate was by far the most extensive and ambitious of his residential collaborations with Hunt. It may also have been his most diverse work, and, in some cases, his most unique. His seven projects at Biltmore range in style from medieval to late 19th century popular whimsy and are variously executed in stone, wood, bronze and polished steel. An eighth project was ecclesiastical in nature and executed for All Souls Episcopal

Church in nearby Biltmore Village.[9]

Two popular misconceptions have arisen regarding Bitter's work at Biltmore. The first is that the sculpture was executed by Bitter on site. The projects were actually completed in either his Manhattan or Weehawken, New Jersey studios, and were

Figure 4. Karl Bitter won the competition to sculpt the bronze doors and portal for the main entrance to New York's Trinity Church in March of 1891. He accomplished this just 16 months after his arrival in America and at only 23 years of age. (Courtesy, The Parish of Trinity Church in the City of New York.)

This pen and wash sketch (below) done by the Hunt firm was a preparatory study for the doors and was based on Ghiberti's Gates of Paradise, executed in Florence in 1435. Bitter designed his own panels for the bronze doors after a church committee provided a list of the Biblical passages the church wished to have represented. Bitter's tympanum figures of Christ with attending angels bear no resemblance to the medieval Christ in mandorla seen in the drawing. (Courtesy, The Prints and Drawings Collection, The Octagon Museum, The American Architectural Foundation, Washington, D.C.)

Bitter designed and executed his commissions for Biltmore in his studios in Manhattan, New York, and Weehawken, New Jersey. The stone works were completed first by Bitter in plaster, then shipped to Biltmore where stone cutters carved them in stone on site with the aid of a sculptural measuring instrument known as a pointing machine. Seen here is one of the three original plaster models for the Return from the Hunt *frieze above the fireplace in the Banquet Hall (top), and the completed version in stone (bottom). (Used with permission from Biltmore Estate, Asheville, North Carolina; photo, Tim Barnwell.)*

then shipped to Biltmore. In the case of his stone sculpture, Bitter made full-size plaster casts of the works and shipped them south to Biltmore, where a stone cutter translated them into the finished product on site. The plaster statues of St. Louis and Joan of Arc are displayed at Biltmore in the Banquet Hall and the *Return from the Hunt* (also known as *Return from the Chase*) is on display on the fourth floor next to the observatory.[10] The only evidence that Bitter was ever at Biltmore comes from George Vanderbilt's guest book.[11] Bitter signed it only twice, once on October 14th, 1896, and again on December 12th the same year. Both visits were made with Richard Howland Hunt, undoubtedly to check on the already installed sculpture and to discuss evolving designs with George Vanderbilt.

The second misconception is that Bitter's sculpture was complete and in place by Christmas of 1895, when George Vanderbilt formally opened the house. Only two of Bitter's works had been placed at that time. Four others were installed in 1896 and 1897, and his last project did not arrive at the estate until 1898. Mr. Vanderbilt occupied a palace in progress for several years, as portions of Biltmore's interior, including much of the architectural sculpture, remained unfinished for some time.

The study of Karl Bitter's Biltmore projects, their development and significance, is variously surprising, fascinating, and problematic. Although sculpture was intended to be an integral part of the residence from its inception, some of the sculptural designs,

and particularly the later ones, underwent numerous and significant stylistic and thematic changes. No documentation has been found concerning the rationale for any of the chosen subject matter; however, Bitter's first three projects, the statues of St. Louis and Joan of Arc, the *Boy Stealing Geese* fountain, and the walnut library statues, are straightforward examples of the type of domestic decorative art enjoyed by the Gilded Age elite. The subject matter for these projects was likely chosen by Richard Morris Hunt and came from his fairly standard decorative vocabulary influenced by the popular tastes of his wealthy and rather ostentatious clients.

On the other hand, three of Bitter's four later sculptural projects, the *Return from the Hunt*, the *Contest of the Minstrels*,

and *Alfred the Great and His Teachers*, are more unique in their symbolism and unlike any of his other domestic commissions, which were usually classical in origin. These works were designed and executed after the elder Hunt's death in late July of 1895. It seems likely, therefore, that some type of collaborative effort by Vanderbilt, Bitter and Richard Howland Hunt was responsible for the fact that this sculpture is much more tailored to Vanderbilt's home and interests than are the earlier works. Each of the seven projects will be examined chronologically, based upon when they were positioned at the estate.

The first sculptural project consisted of larger than life-sized plaster casts of St. Louis and Joan of Arc in full battle dress. They were shipped to Biltmore in late July of 1895, carved in limestone by a stonemason, and placed in late Gothic style canopies on the exterior staircase of the mansion (Figure 5).[12] Stylistically, the figures are a restrained version of Bitter's favored Renaissance and naturalistic Baroque tastes. Employing a common Baroque device, Bitter placed one or both of their feet well over the edge of their pedestals, thereby projecting the statues into their surrounding space and creating the visual effect of jeopardizing their balance. These two highly revered French historical figures set off the exterior ornamentation of the stair tower at Biltmore, a lavish example of historically derived French architecture.

Bitter's second Biltmore project was a bronze fountain figural group for the Winter Garden entitled *Boy Stealing Geese* (Figure 6). The sculpture arrived at Biltmore in mid-December of 1895, just in time to be placed before Vanderbilt opened his home for the holidays.[13] Whimsical garden statuary of this style first became popular in the United States at the 1893 World's Columbian Exposition. This genre was a modernized, Beaux-Arts version of earlier Baroque examples. Works of this nature became popular additions to a number of late 19th and early 20th century large country estates.[14] Bitter's Biltmore

fountain was the first of three of this type he executed during his career. In 1899, he sculpted one for Jacob Schiff's home in Seabright, New Jersey and, in 1914, he completed another for John D. Rockefeller's Pocantico Hills estate in New York.

The third of Bitter's Biltmore commissions was a pair of carved walnut statues for the overmantel of the library (Figure 7). No information has been found regarding the arrival of these statues at Biltmore, but other information suggests that the statues were most likely placed sometime between March and June of 1896. The French walnut shipped from William Baumgarten & Co. for the paneling in the library and in George Vanderbilt's bedroom arrived in November of 1895, but was too green to be usable. The woodwork in both rooms was delayed and it was "impossible to complete either of these two before Christmas."[15] This meant that the library paneling was not put up until the first few months of 1896 and, since the statues were to be bolted onto the paneling, neither were they. Bitter did, however, exhibit models of the figures at the Architectural League of New York in 1896, so they were almost certainly in place at Biltmore by mid-1896.[16]

Although Bitter only described them as "heroic figures," these statues were apparently intended to represent two Greek mythological subjects. James M. Dennis, Bitter's biographer, concluded that the left figure is Hestia, goddess of the hearth, and the right figure is Demeter, goddess of the earth. This theory is both alluring and has some basis in fact. The goddess Hestia has rarely been depicted in art; furthermore, her domain encompassed not only the hearth but the family, the city and even the earth. Hence, a goddess holding an orb could logically be construed to represent Hestia through her analogous affiliation with the earth. Factor in her location above a hearth and Hestia becomes a rather compelling choice. Demeter, who is generally depicted with ears of corn, has been portrayed here

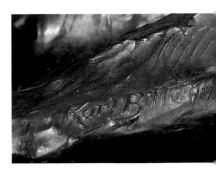

Figure 6. Left. This bronze figural fountain of a boy stealing geese is the centerpiece of the Winter Garden at Biltmore. 57 x 38 x 31 in., excluding marble base. This genre of garden statuary, characterized by quickly modeled, naturalistic children and animals at play, became a popular form in the late 19th and early 20th centuries. The fountain was cast by A. T. Lorme of New York and arrived by rail at Biltmore on December 10, 1895, just in time for George Vanderbilt's first Christmas in his new home. Bitter liked the design and had another cast made for himself and placed it in his garden in Weehawken, New Jersey. (Used with permission from Biltmore Estate, Asheville, North Carolina; photos, Tim Barnwell.)

Top. Detail of Karl Bitter's signature.

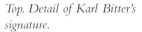

Bitter designed several versions of this fountain including one for the Jacob Schiff home in Seabright, New Jersey in 1899 (left), and one for the John D. Rockefeller estate in Pocantico Hills, New York in 1914 (right). Another version of the fountain was exhibited at the Art Institute of Chicago in 1904. (Courtesy, James M. Dennis.)

with a dish and snake, as in the Demeter relief from the Pergamon altar in Berlin.[17]

The library figures have been accepted as Hestia and Demeter for some thirty-odd years. A reexamination by the author and Biltmore's associate curator now raises doubt about these attributions. Research indicates that Hygeia, the goddess of health, has repeatedly been depicted with a snake feeding from a dish held in her hand, making her a more promising choice than Demeter for Bitter's statue. Similarly, in Greco/Roman mythology, the orb is the attribute of Urania, the muse of astrology. Numerous depictions of Urania with her orb can be found.[18] An ancient Roman statue of Urania in the Vatican Museum, strikingly similar to the Biltmore figure heretofore regarded as Hestia, could even have been Bitter's prototype since he is known to have visited Rome in 1895-96.[19]

Bitter's failure to disclose the identity of the library hearth statues remains a mystery. When listing his works, he generally designated his subject matter unless the sculpted figures of any given project were meant to be solely decorative. For example, he described two stone mantel figures for C.P. Huntington's library as "representing lyric and epic poetry," and figures for the library mantel of Louis Stern's residence as "Art and Science." Colossal statues "in marble representing Mercury and Abundantia" for New York's Chamber of Commerce building were specified as such by Bitter.

In the absence of primary documents that identify the Biltmore mantel figures, any conclusions as to whom or what they represent is preliminary. It was common practice in the Gilded Age to appropriate the iconographical attributes of a specific god or goddess in order to fashion a personification of a more abstract and symbolic concept. Figures represented with Mercury's caduceus came to symbolize medicine. A female figure holding Urania's orb, such as Bela Pratt's statue at the entrance to the Boston Public Library, was meant to represent science. In keeping with the Gilded Age's rather generalized borrowing of the symbols of the classical past, Bitter's carved library figures may represent Science and Health. Perhaps these figures were not identified simply because George Vanderbilt wished it to be something of a mystery for his guests.

Bitter's fourth project for Biltmore was a 25-foot-long stone frieze depicting the *Return from the Hunt* for the mantel of the huge triple fireplace in the Banquet Hall (Figure 8). The plaster version of the frieze was shipped by rail in several crates to Biltmore in August of 1896.[20] One of Bitter's assistants arrived to carve the work on August 29th, so it was probably completed by late September.[21] The subject matter is a medieval procession of hunters, game and beasts of burden returning from a successful hunt, but Bitter's stylistic and spatial approach was based upon Renaissance and Baroque ideas. He enlivened the scene with movement and rhythm through the use of naturalistic diagonal curves and relief contrasts. To add compositional order and balance, Bitter utilized horses to divide the frieze into three almost equal areas, an essentially Renaissance construct.

Of the approximately 10 known architectural drawings of the fireplace and frieze, none depicts a hunting scene.[22] The most popular design depicts kneeling angels flanking an escutcheon embellished with a V with attending figures. Another design depicts Christopher Columbus and his crew on their voyage to the New World, a subject popularized by the World's Columbian Exposition of 1893 when most of these drawings were executed.

By 1895 or 1896, new subject matter had been chosen. The hunt was an appealing subject for several reasons. It was intended as an artistic play on words to pay homage to Richard Morris Hunt. It was also an activity which provided a source of food; thus, it was suitable for a medieval style banquet hall. The hunt has likewise symbolized the union of man and nature.[23] This is appropriate to Biltmore, an architectural masterpiece nestled among thousands of acres of natural terrain. Further, medieval

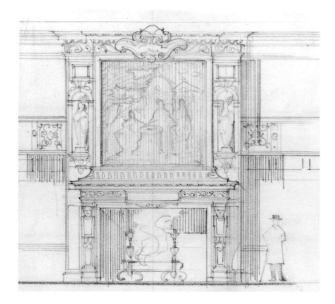

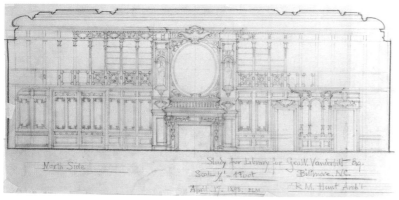

North Side

Study for Library for Geo.W. Vanderbilt Esq.
Scale ¼" = 1 Foot   Biltmore, N.C.
April 17, 1893. FLM   R.M. Hunt Arch't

Figure 7. Top, right. The pair of carved walnut statues located on the overmantel of the fireplace in the library at Biltmore and the pair of andirons in the fireplace below are both products of Bitter's workshop. The library was not finished when George Vanderbilt formally opened Biltmore House in December of 1895, and was probably completed in the summer of 1896. (Used with permission from Biltmore Estate, Asheville, North Carolina; photos, Tim Barnwell.)

Top, left. These two drawings by Hunt's firm of the North Wall of the library and the fireplace indicate how Bitter's work related to the general architectural plan for the room. (Both drawings, courtesy, The Prints and Drawings Collection, The Octagon Museum, The American Architectural Foundation, Washington, D.C.)

Left. The carved walnut figure now thought to represent Urania, the muse of astrology, was mounted on the left side. The figure on the right with dish and snake probably represented Hygeia, the goddess of health. Models of these figures were exhibited at the Architectural League of New York in 1896. Although Bitter identified them only as "heroic figures," based on their attributes it seems probable that the pair represent personifications of Science and Health. Each figure 93 x 27 x 19 in.

hunting and chivalry equated with noble and even royal status.[24] This likely appealed to George Vanderbilt, an upper class gentleman who identified easily with aristocratic European traditions. Finally, the young man leading the procession toward a distant castle on the far right of the frieze may be intended to represent Tannhauser on his journey to Wartburg, the scene preceding the "Contest of the Minstrels" in the *Tannhauser* opera which Bitter depicted at the other end of the Banquet Hall.[25]

The *Contest of the Minstrels*, Bitter's fifth Biltmore sculptural commission, is a five-panel frieze carved in English oak and located on the balustrade of the organ gallery. The panels arrived at Biltmore in late July of 1897, and were put in place by Bitter's chief assistant, Gustave Gerlach, during the first week of August (Figure 9).[26] The five relief panels represent the "Singing Tournament" episode from *Tannhauser*, a popular opera composed by Richard Wagner in 1843 and inspired by three medieval German legends.[27] Bitter's 61 roughly carved figures look somewhat like cutouts attached to their flat gilded background. This treatment serves to enhance

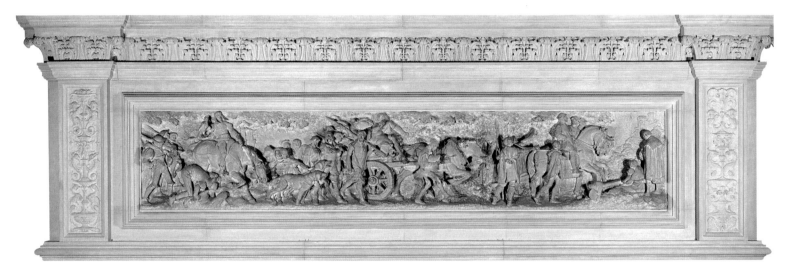

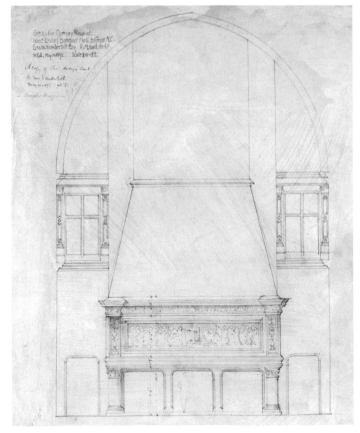

Figure 8. Above. The stone frieze for the Banquet Hall fireplace was one of Bitter's largest works at Biltmore. 3 ft. 10 in. x 20 ft. 2 in. The Return from the Hunt *depicts a medieval hunt scene with figures returning from a hunt carrying game. The subject was a subtle means of honoring Biltmore's architect, Richard Morris Hunt, and of associating George Vanderbilt, a gentleman of leisure, with hunting and chivalry. The procession may also have been intended to portray a scene from* Tannhauser, *the opera depicted in the carvings at the opposite end of the Banquet Hall. The plaster model for the Banquet Hall fireplace frieze was shipped to Biltmore in three crates in late August of 1896. (Used with permission from Biltmore Estate, Asheville, North Carolina; photos, Tim Barnwell.)*

Left. This drawing of the Banquet Hall triple fireplace is one of at least 10 known. The design seen here with kneeling angels flanking an embellished V crest is the most common version of the proposed frieze. This drawing, though accepted by Vanderbilt in May of 1895, was never used. None of the proposals depicted a hunting scene and the final design for all the Banquet Hall sculpture was likely the result of a collaborative effort by Vanderbilt, Bitter and Richard Howland Hunt. (Courtesy, The Prints and Drawing Collection, The Octagon Museum, The American Architectural Foundation.)

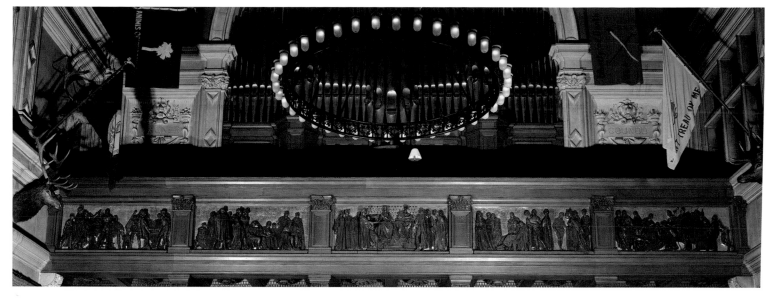

Figure 9. Bitter's five carved-wood relief panels, located on the balustrade of the Banquet Hall organ gallery, represent the "Singing Tournament" episode known as the "Contest of the Minstrels" from Tannhauser, an opera composed by Richard Wagner in 1843. The five panel oak frieze arrived by rail at Biltmore on July 26, 1897, and was put in place by Gustave Gerlach, Bitter's chief assistant. Frieze, 4 ft. 2 in. x 41 ft. 10 in. (Used with permission from Biltmore Estate, Asheville, North Carolina; photos, Tim Barnwell.)

The medieval character of Bitter's panels, with roughly carved figures mounted to a flat gilded background, was inspired by the German medieval subject matter of Wagner's Tannhauser. The panels were gilded in situ at Biltmore and without the contrast of the carvings and the gilding, the panels would be difficult to recognize from their position 9-1/2 feet above the floor. (Used with permission from Biltmore Estate, Asheville, North Carolina; photo, Tim Barnwell.)

Bitter is seen here posing with his carved oak Tannhauser panels. The photo was taken in Bitter's Weehawken, New Jersey studio just before the panels were shipped to Biltmore in the summer of 1897. (Courtesy, James M. Dennis.)

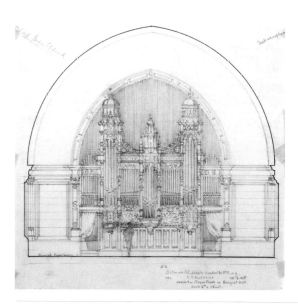

This drawing (above), dated April 19, 1895, was one of several suggested designs for the Biltmore organ front at the west end of the Banquet Hall. It was drawn by W.G. Lawrence, the Hunt firm's head draftsman. None of the known drawings bear any resemblance to the completed project, whose design evolved from George Vanderbilt's and Karl Bitter's shared love of opera. (Courtesy, The Prints and Drawing Collection, The Octagon Museum, The American Architectural Foundation.)

the medieval character of the reliefs as does the staging of the figures on oak platforms, much like an opera stage.

Two of the architectural drawings of the organ front are dated April 19th, 1895.[28] Both are fussy, theatrical and extremely ornate, and neither resemble the finished product, either in style or subject matter. A new design and subject matter were selected at a later date, apparently with much input from George Vanderbilt himself. The *Contest of the Minstrels* may be Bitter's most interesting sculptural work at Biltmore and perhaps one of the most unique ever conceived for a Gilded Age mansion. The subject matter is comparable to the artworks commissioned in the 1870s and early 1880s by the eccentric King Ludwig II of Bavaria, a man who so loved Wagner and his operas that he decorated two of his magnificent castles, Neuschwanstein and Linderhof, with art inspired by *Lohengrin*, *Tannhauser* and *Parsifal*.[29]

There are several reasons for the appearance of one and likely two Wagnerian opera scenes at Biltmore. Both George Vanderbilt and Karl Bitter were devoted opera buffs and both loved Wagnerian operas which were very popular at the time.[30] In 1895, when Consuelo Vanderbilt married the Duke of Marlborough, Wagnerian music was played for the wedding marches.[31] The Vanderbilt family was also intimately associated with New York's Metropolitan Opera, having contributed much of the capital needed to get it up and running.[32] *Tannhauser* opened the Met's second season on November 17th, 1884, ushering in seven seasons of opera performed exclusively in German.[33] The medieval *Tannhauser* setting matched that of the Banquet Hall, and the scene, a musical event, was fitting for an organ gallery. The names Wagner and Gounod are carved into the walls above the organ gallery balustrade, further evidence of operatic themes. Gounod was a 19th century French composer whose best known opera, *Faust*, opened the Met's first season on October 22nd, 1883.[34] The basic theme of *Faust* is similar to that of *Tannhauser* and also to that of the five Venus and Vulcan tapestries which hang in the Banquet Hall. All deal with a love triangle and a conflict between man's spiritual and sensual nature. The depiction of scenes from *Tannhauser* were thus linked to the Vanderbilt's interest in the Metropolitan Opera House, to one of Vanderbilt's favorite operas and to his Flemish tapestries.

Karl Bitter's set of six bas-relief "stall" panels, *Alfred the Great and his Teachers* located on the backs of the two Banquet Hall throne chairs, were delivered to Biltmore by rail on January 31, 1898. Oddly, the panels were left in their shipping crates for eight months, likely due to a prolonged absence by Mr. Vanderbilt. Following some confusion as to their proper placement, the panels were finally positioned in early October of 1898. (Figure 10).[35] The pair of chairs, which were designed by Hunt's firm separately from the six panels, were probably in location in the Banquet

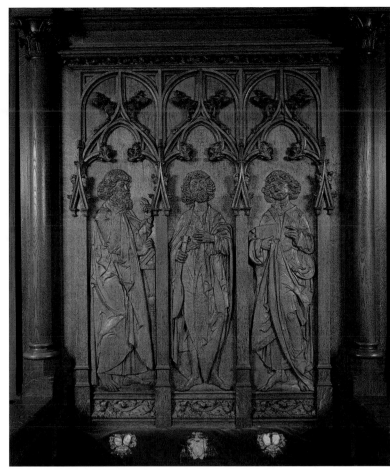

Figure 10. The Banquet Hall at Biltmore was the site for a pair of throne chairs designed by the Hunt firm (below, left). Karl Bitter, however, designed and carved the oak "stall" panels which make up the back of each throne. The dimensions of the Banquet Hall were determined from its inception by the five 16ᵗʰ century Flemish Venus and Vulcan tapestries mounted on the north and south walls of the great room. The pair of thrones are placed at each end of one of the North wall tapestries. Each measures 14 ft. 3 in. x 6 ft. 10 in. x 3 ft. (Used with permission from Biltmore Estate, Asheville, North Carolina; all photos, Tim Barnwell.)

Top, left. The left throne depicts Alfred the Great surrounded by two of his five teachers. King Alfred was one of the most revered Anglo-Saxon monarchs, known as the father of English prose and education. In the 19ᵗʰ century many biographies and literary works were published to commemorate the millenary of his reign. As an intellectual and patron of the arts, George Vanderbilt no doubt found King Alfred an appealing subject.

Top, right. The three panels of the right throne depict three of Alfred's teachers holding respectively a lectern, mandolin and book, all symbols of knowledge and enlightenment. The carved oak panels were not placed at Biltmore until October of 1898.

Above. Detail of figure holding oak leaf with acorns, a motif also found in the Vanderbilt family crest created by Alva Vanderbilt.

Hall by Christmas of 1895, but they remained backless for almost three years. A photograph of Bitter in his studio published in 1904 shows Bitter with his completed cast for the Biltmore Venus andiron and one of the relief panels for the throne chairs.[36] The panel appears to be a work in progress rather than a leftover studio model. Furthermore, the andirons were not cast until 1898 and, because Bitter was often operating behind schedule, both projects must have been in progress at about the same time in 1897.

Each of the throne chair backs is composed of three narrow relief panels and each panel portrays a medieval style figure carved in bas-relief underneath a Gothic cloverleaf arch. The central figure on the left throne chair depicts King Alfred and the remaining five figures are his teachers. These linear, stylized reliefs have a sense of spirituality and quietude not found in any of Bitter's other Biltmore sculpture, and demonstrate his ability to produce stylistically diverse works. The carving is of the highest quality.

The images and symbolism depicted in the panels are intriguing. Alfred the Great was the most revered of all Anglo-Saxon kings and is known as the father of English prose and education because of his efforts to restore learning, religion and cultural standards in early medieval England.[37] His five teachers are depicted with the following attributes: a candle, oak leaves with acorns, a mandolin, a lectern and a book. The candle is a symbol of enlightenment, wisdom and the light of knowledge. The oak leaves with acorns are symbolic of knowledge, wisdom and the universe. They also relate to the Vanderbilt family, as they are found on the Alva Vanderbilt devised family crest. The mandolin symbolizes culture and the arts. As a standard teacher's tool, the podium refers to the transfer and dissemination of knowledge. Finally, the book, as a source of knowledge, symbolizes the wisdom and enlightenment gained from it.[38]

In the latter half of the 19th century, there was renewed interest in Alfred the Great occasioned by the millenary of his reign.[39] As a scholar and an intellectual, George Vanderbilt was surely familiar with the Victorian literary works which dealt with Alfred the Great. England's beloved medieval king inspired the publication of poetry, prose, and theatrical works.[40] Vanderbilt's and King Alfred's shared interest in intellectual and scholarly concerns are thus reflected in Bitter's panel designs.

The library fireplace is the setting for a pair of Venus and Vulcan andirons, Bitter's final sculptural project at Biltmore House. They are of iron and polished steel and were cast by the Henry-Bonnard Bronze Company of New York in 1898. Henry-Bonnard was the largest and most prestigious bronze foundry in America during the last decade of the 19th century (Figure 11).[41]

The andirons feature standing figures of Venus and Vulcan, each placed above a base composed of a variety of allegorical elements. The Vanderbilt escutcheon, a pair of dolphins, a shell motif surrounded by suspended clusters of fruit and a pair of cornucopias are found on both bases. The Vulcan andiron includes two nude males seated on the dolphins' heads, a pair of satyrs flanking the Vanderbilt crest and a small relief of a boy from mythology at the top of the andiron base. Corresponding details on the Venus andiron include nude females astride the dolphins, mermaids rather than satyrs, and a small relief of a girl. The andirons derive from 16th century Italian late Renaissance and early Baroque prototypes, such as the *Andiron with Figure of Mars* located at the National Gallery of Art in Washington, D.C. and attributed to the circle of Tiziano Aspetti. Only the Vanderbilt crest on the two bases distinguish these works as having been designed and executed for a Vanderbilt, though the figures of Venus and Vulcan may have been selected to repeat the subject matter of the Flemish tapestries in the Banquet Hall.

After the turn of the century, Karl Bitter's work became largely monumental, and his career as a decorative and residen-

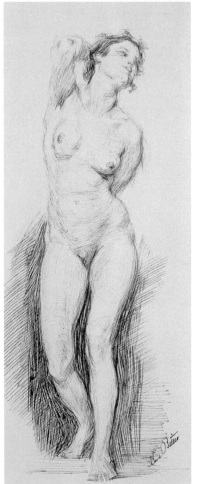

Figure 11. Karl Bitter's last work at Biltmore was the pair of iron and polished steel andirons for the library fireplace. They were cast by the Henry-Bonnard Bronze Company, New York, and placed at Biltmore in 1898. The andirons feature finials with figures of Venus, the goddess of love (top, right), and Vulcan, the god of the forge (top, left). The bases incorporate nude male and female figures astride dolphins below crests of the Vanderbilt family. Each 66 x 32 x 57 in. (Used with permission from Biltmore Estate, Asheville, North Carolina; photos, Tim Barnwell.)

Center, left and right. The andirons were based on late Renaissance prototypes such as those after Girolamo Campagna (Andiron with Figure of Venus), and Tiziano Aspetti (Andiron with Figure of Mars). (Courtesy, Samuel H. Kress Collection; photographs © Board of Trustees, National Gallery of Art, Washington, D.C.)

Left. Though not identical, this drawing by Bitter is remarkably similar to Bitter's Venus and was undoubtedly used as a preparatory sketch for the sculpture. A bronze version of the Venus was donated by Bitter to the National Academy of Design in New York as his Diploma Work when he became an Academy academician in 1903. Drawing, 13 x 20 in. (Author's collection; photos, Tim Barnwell.)

Pediment for the Cleveland Trust Company completed by Karl Bitter in 1907 for architect, George B. Post. The seven figures make reference to land and water (sources of wealth) and reflect Bitter's modernist tendencies. (Courtesy, James M. Dennis.)

tial sculptor was essentially over. He became an important and well-respected artist and was sought after for commissions of a monumental and public nature. In 1915, at age 47, he had firmly established himself as a leader in the field of monumental sculpture. That year his life ended tragically when he was killed in an automobile accident. At the time of his death Bitter was still remembered for his early decorative sculpture and especially for his work at Biltmore. More than half of his obituary notices included information about his Biltmore projects, claiming that much of his finest decorative sculpture was to be found in George Vanderbilt's North Carolina residence.[42]

Notes

1. Unless otherwise cited, sources for background information on Bitter are James M. Dennis, *Karl Bitter - Architectural Sculptor 1867 - 1915* (Madison: University of Wisconsin Press, 1967); Ferdinand Schevill, *Karl Bitter, a Biography* (Chicago: University of Chicago Press, 1917); and "Karl Bitter Papers," Archives of American Art, Washington, D.C., microfilm.

2. See Dennis Steadman Francis, *Architects in Practice: New York City 1840 - 1900* (New York: Committee for the Preservation of Architectural Records, 1979), p. 29; and exhibition entries for Karl Bitter, Sculptor, 1890 - 1915, The Architectural League of New York, New York, p. 1. The listed address for Ellin & Kitson, 519 W. 21st St., is the same as that documented on Bitter's first exhibition entry.

3. Bitter contracts and certificates of payment for Fifth Avenue and 57th Street, *Collis P. Huntington Papers*, George Arents Research Library, Syracuse University, Syracuse, New York.

4. For information regarding Hunt's architectural projects, see Paul R. Baker, *Richard Morris Hunt* (Cambridge: The MIT Press, 1980); Montgomery Schuyler, "The Works of the Late Richard M. Hunt," *Architectural Record* 5 (October - December 1895), pp. 97 - 180; and Susan R. Stein, ed., *The Architecture of Richard Morris Hunt* (Chicago: University of Chicago Press, 1986).

5. James W. Shepp and Daniel B. Shepp, *Shepp's World's Fair Photographed* (Chicago: Globe Bible Publishing Co., 1893), p. 238.

6. Schevill, p. 22.

7. Schevill, p. 24. Here, Schevill noted that Bitter "regretted that most of the subjects, which, being assigned to him by a supervising committee of the church, were not of his choosing, hardly admitted of a simple solution."

8. This drawing, one of several of the doors housed in the Prints and Drawings Collection of the American Institute of Architects Foundation in Washington, D.C., most closely resembles Bitter's actual work.

9. Although not discussed in this article, the work is a baptismal font cover carved from English oak. It is pyramid shaped and depicts the symbols of the four Evangelists.

10. The *Return from the Hunt* (also named *Return from the Chase*) plaster frieze (in three separate pieces) is on display on the fourth floor of Biltmore House in a room next to the observatory. Each piece was professionally conserved in 1993, and special display cases were custom made in which to house them.

11. Guest Book, Biltmore Estate Archives, Asheville, N.C., p. 4.

12. Edward J. Harding to Richard Morris Hunt, July 25, 1895, Vol. 13, *Biltmore Letter Books*, Biltmore Estate Archives, Asheville, N.C. The idea for the canopied statues derived from the Chateau de Blois, as did the staircase itself.

13. Charles McNamee to Richard Howland Hunt, December 16, 1895, Vol. 5, *Biltmore Memoranda Books*, Biltmore Estate Archives, Asheville, N.C. Foundry marks on the base of the sculpture indicate that it was cast by A.T. Lorme of New York in 1895.

14. Katherine Solender, *The American Way in Sculpture 1890 - 1930* (Bloomington: Indiana University Press, 1986), p. 5.

15. Charles McNamee to H. Kaufmann, superintendent, Asheville Woodworking Co., November 16, 1895, Vol. 14, *Biltmore Letter Books*, Biltmore Estate Archives, Asheville, N.C.

16. Architectural League of New York, p. 2.

17. Felix Guirand, *Greek Mythology* (London: Paul Hamlyn, 1963), pp. 104-05. It is likely that Bitter saw or was aware of this relief when it was on exhibition at Berlin's Old Museum in the 1880s.

18. For descriptions and/or illustrations of Hygeia and Urania, see, for instance, Joseph Fattorusso, *Wonders of Italy* (Florence: The Medici Art Series, 1952); Felix Guirand, *Greek Mythology* (London: Paul Hamlyn, 1963); Oskar Seyffert, *The Dictionary of Classical Mythology, Religion, Literature and Art* (New York: Gramercy Books, 1995); and A.R.A. van

Aken, *The Encyclopedia of Classical Mythology* (Englewood Cliffs, N.J.: Prentice-Hall, Inc., 1965).

19. Bitter was in Italy from early December, 1895 to mid-January of 1896, visiting museums and sketching. It is possible that he was influenced by a classical Roman statue of Urania located in the Salle delle Muse of the Vatican Museum in Rome. Her pose and characteristics are remarkably similar to the Biltmore library figure. Furthermore, a Venus statue, also in the Vatican Museum, is almost identical to Bitter's andiron figure. Darren Poupore, Biltmore's Associate Collections Curator, is currently researching possible direct linkages to Vatican prototypes for Bitter's classical figures at Biltmore.

20. Charles McNamee to Richard Howland Hunt, August 18, 1896, Vol. 17, *Biltmore Letter Books*, Biltmore Estate Archives, Asheville, N.C.

21. Charles McNamee to Richard Howland Hunt, August 29, 1896, Vol. 17, *Biltmore Letter Books*, Biltmore Estate Archives, Asheville, N.C.; and Richard Howland Hunt to Charles McNamee, September 1, 1896, Biltmore Estate Archives, Asheville, N.C.

22. Richard Morris Hunt Collection, Prints and Drawings Collection, American Institute of Architects Foundation, Washington, D.C.

23. Kenneth Clark, *Animals and Men* (New York: William Morrow and Company, Inc., 1977), p. 211.

24. See, for instance, D.H. Madden, *A Chapter of Medieval History* (London: John Murray, 1924).

25. John M. Bryan, *Biltmore Estate: The Most Distinguished Private Place* (New York: Rizzoli, 1994), p. 133; and Kate B. Plowden, "Karl Bitter's Sculpture at Biltmore House: A Study of His Most Ambitious Collaboration with Richard Morris Hunt," M.A. Thesis, University of South Carolina, Columbia, 1993.

26. Edward J. Harding to Karl Bitter, July 27, 1897, Vol. 20, *Biltmore Letter Books*, Biltmore Estate Archives, Asheville, N.C.; and Edward J. Harding to Karl Bitter, August 2, 1897, Vol. 20, *Biltmore Letter Books*, Biltmore Estate Archives, Asheville, N.C.

27. J.W. Thomas, *Tannhauser: Poet and Legend* (Chapel Hill: University of North Carolina Press, 1974), pp. 81-82.

28. Hunt Collection.

29. Wilfrid Blunt, *The Dream King, Ludwig II of Bavaria* (New York: The Viking Press, 1970), pp. 138 & 151.

30. John Foreman and Robbe Pierce Stimson, *The Vanderbilts and the Gilded Age: Architectural Aspirations 1879 - 1901* (New York: St. Martin's Press, 1991), p. 275; and Dennis, p. 13.

31. "She is Duchess of Marlborough," *Asheville Citizen*, November 8, 1895.

32. Irving Kolodin, *The Metropolitan Opera, 1883 - 1966* (New York: Alfred A. Knopf, 1968), pp. 4-5.

33. Ibid., pp. 87-88.

34. Ibid., p. 83.

35. Richard Howland Hunt to Charles McNamee, September 21, 1898, Biltmore Estate Archives, Asheville, N.C.; Charles McNamee to Richard Howland Hunt, September, 23, 1898, vol. 23, *Biltmore Letter Books*, Biltmore Estate Archives, Asheville, N.C.; and Karl Bitter to Richard Howland Hunt, September 28, 1898, Biltmore Estate Archives, Asheville, N.C. McNamee wrote to Hunt that, "An examination of these panels by Mr. Lipe shows that they are in several pieces, with no indication as to how they shall be grouped in the back of each chair." Bitter responded to Hunt, stating "the backs of Banquet Hall Stalls were sent to Biltmore...each back in one complete solid piece. As there are only two stalls there are only two backs to them. I believe that upon further examination the 'several pieces' will dwindle to two only, and it is perfectly immaterial to which of the two stalls one of the two backs is fastened."

36. The photograph was published in John Nilsen Laurvik, "Karl Bitter - A Master of Decorative Sculpture," *Booklover's Magazine* 3 (May 1904), p. 604.

37. James Campbell, ed., *The Anglo-Saxons* (London: Penguin Books, 1982), p. 156.

38. Some of this information comes from Arnold Whittick, *Symbols, Signs and Their Meanings* (London: Leonard Hill Limited, 1960). Also, Foreman and Stimson, p. 253. The acorn motif was a spurious device appropriated by the Vanderbilts to symbolize their family.

39. Douglas Woodruff, *The Life and Times of Alfred the Great* (London: Weidenfeld and Nicolson, 1974), p. 207.

40. Histories of King Alfred included those by J.A. Giles, Reinhold Pauli, Jacob Abbott and Thomas Hughes. Two of the best known poetical works about King Alfred were penned by Joseph Cottle and G.L.N. Collingwood. Thematically, the most intriguing of the plays in relation to the Banquet Hall is Robert and William Brough's *Alfred the Great; or the Minstrel King*.

41. Michael Edward Shapiro, *Bronze Casting and American Sculpture 1850 -1900* (Newark: University of Delaware Press, 1985), p. 72. A bronze version of the Venus figure is located at the National Academy of Design. It served as Bitter's Diploma Work when he became an academician in 1903, and was cast by Bureau Bros. of Philadelphia.

42. Karl Bitter newspaper clippings, *Karl Bitter Papers*, Archives of American Art, Washington, D.C., microfilm.

Biltmore as seen from the Lagoon. (Used with permission from Biltmore Estate, Asheville, North Carolina.)

Rob Amberg lives on a farm in Madison County, North Carolina with his wife and their two children. He was the recipient of a John Simon Guggenheim Memorial Fellowship in 1990 for his work in rural communities. He currently has a book of his early photographs and writing from Madison County in production at the Center for Documentary Studies at Duke University. He is also documenting the construction of the I-26 Corridor as it cuts through Madison County. This work was the recipient of the Dorthea Lange/Paul Taylor Prize from Duke University.

Peter Austin is a native of Asheville with a BA in history from Warren Wilson College. He lives in Greensboro and works as a college librarian in Winston-Salem, North Carolina. He contributed a study on architect Rafael Guastavino for *May We All Remember Well, Volume I.*

Tim Barnwell, born in the Bryson City area, is a commercial photographer based in Asheville, North Carolina. His photographs have appeared in dozens of regional and national magazines, including *Time, Newsweek, House Beautiful, Southern Accents, Astronomy* and *American Style.* His work is included in the High Museum of Art, the New Orleans Museum of Art and the Metropolitan Museum of Art. The photographs selected for use in this article were chosen from a group of over 140 images which began as a project for *Mountain Living* magazine in 1979.

Laura Boosinger earned her degree in Appalachian music from Warren Wilson College. She was a member of The Luke Smathers Band for 13 years and continues her work as a performer, recording artist and educator throughout the Southeast.

Robert S. Brunk is President of Robert S. Brunk Auction Services and publisher of *May We All Remember Well, Volume I and Volume II*

Pat Fitzpatrick is an antiques dealer and collector of folk art. She has resided in Western North Carolina for the past 23 years. She contributed an article on the Harriet Elizabeth Alexander sampler for *May We All Remember Well, Volume I.*

Sam Gray is a native of Western North Carolina and is currently director of the Mountain Gateway Museum in Old Fort, North Carolina. For the past 25 years, he has conducted research, written articles and curated exhibitions on numerous topics of regional history and culture. He resides with his family in southern McDowell County, North Carolina.

Clay Griffith is a Preservation Specialist with the North Carolina State Historic Preservation Office. He serves the Western Region of the state and lives in Asheville.

William A. Hart Jr, a native of Weaverville, North Carolina maintains an active interest in the history and lore of the Western North Carolina region.

Bruce E. Johnson is the author of several books on the Arts and Crafts movement and directs the annual Grove Park Inn Arts and Crafts Conference. He is currently working on a biography of William Waldo Dodge, silversmith.

Phyllis Martin Lang is Associate Professor of Mass Communication at the University of North Carolina at Asheville. She co-produced a documentary video entitled "Thomas Walton Patton: Asheville's Citizen and Soldier" and is editing Patton's Civil War letters for publication.

Rodney H. Leftwich is a full-time potter in Asheville, North Carolina who bases his work on Appalachian themes and traditions. A collector and researcher of Western North Carolina folk and art pottery, he is currently preparing for publication a book on the pottery of Walter B. Stephen.

Rob Neufeld is a writer for the *Asheville Citizen-Times* and is an administrator at Pack Memorial Public Library. He wrote the scripts for "A Walking Tour of Historic Downtown Asheville" and "The Urban Trail: A Walk into History," released December, 2000. He has written and produced historical dramas for the Thomas Wolfe Festival and the Biltmore Estate. He is currently working on a comprehensive, narrative history of Buncombe County.

Jacqueline Burgin Painter, local historian and preservationist, has written three histories of her native Madison County, North Carolina: *The Season of Dorland-Bell, History of an Appalachian Mission School; The German Invasion of Western North Carolina, A Pictorial History;* and, *Appalachian Medley, Hot Springs and the Gentry Family*. She resides in Sylva, North Carolina, and is a partner in her husband's construction business.

Kate Plowden holds a master's degree in Art History from the University of South Carolina and is a dean at Piedmont Technical College in Greenwood, S.C. She teaches Art History courses both at Piedmont and at U.S.C.-Union. Currently, she is researching the works of the Italian-American sculptor Giuseppe Moretti.

Benjamin Porter, Asheville, North Carolina photographer and educator, directs the photography program at McDowell Technical Community College. He is presently using a Cirkut camera to complete a re-photographic survey of Herbert Pelton's historical panoramas.

Daniel J. Vivian holds an M.A. in Applied History from the University of South Carolina and has published articles in Historic Preservation Forum and the South Carolina Historical Magazine. A former resident of Asheville, North Carolina, he currently manages the architectural and historic resources program of the South Carolina Department of Archives and History.